Blank Canvas
My So=Called Artist's Journey

1

STORY &
ART

**Akiko
Higashimura**

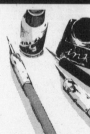

Blank Canvas

My So-Called Artist's Journey

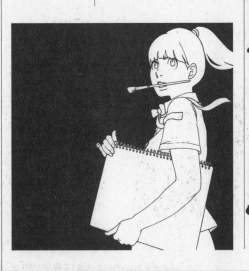

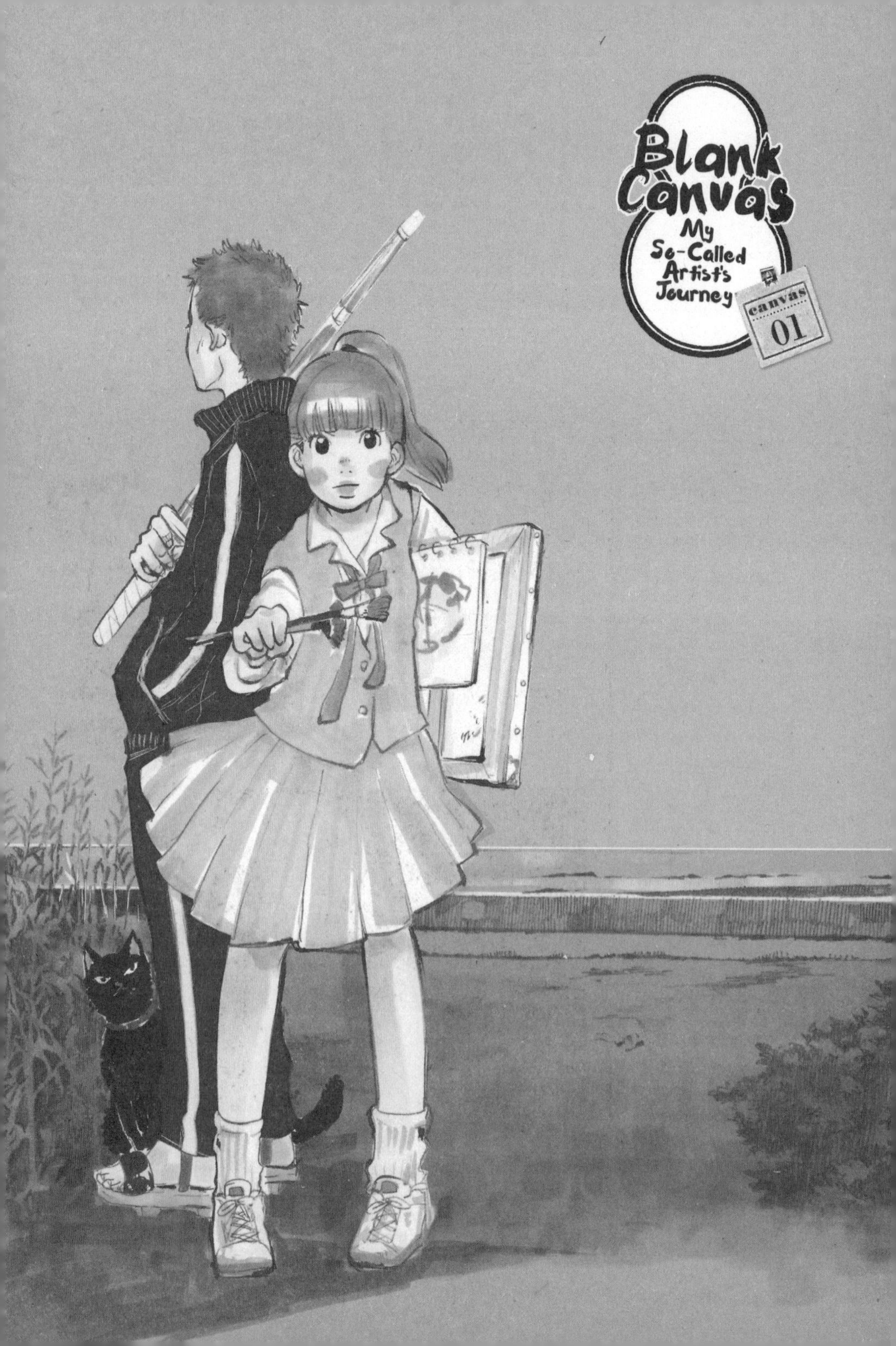
Blank Canvas
My So-Called Artist's Journey
canvas
01

Blank Canvas
My So-Called Artist's Journey

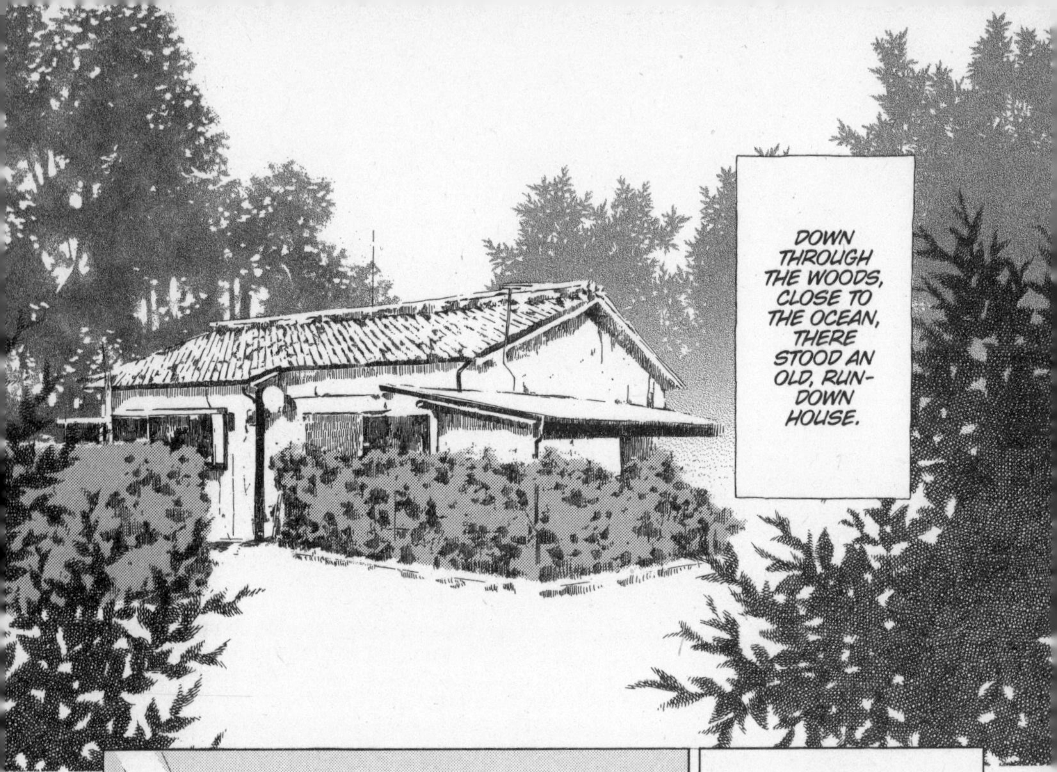
DOWN THROUGH THE WOODS, CLOSE TO THE OCEAN, THERE STOOD AN OLD, RUN-DOWN HOUSE.
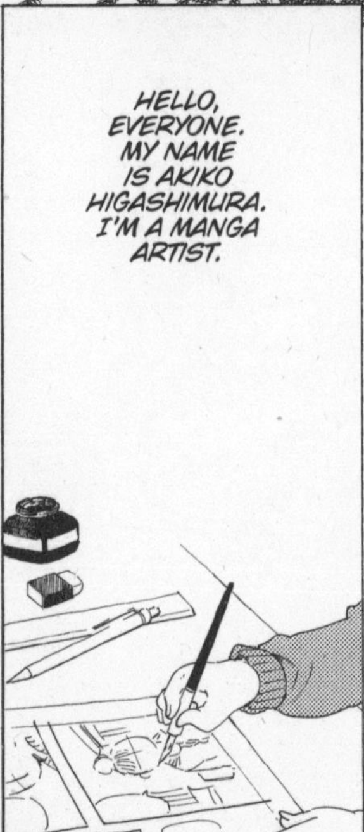
HELLO, EVERYONE. MY NAME IS AKIKO HIGASHIMURA. I'M A MANGA ARTIST.
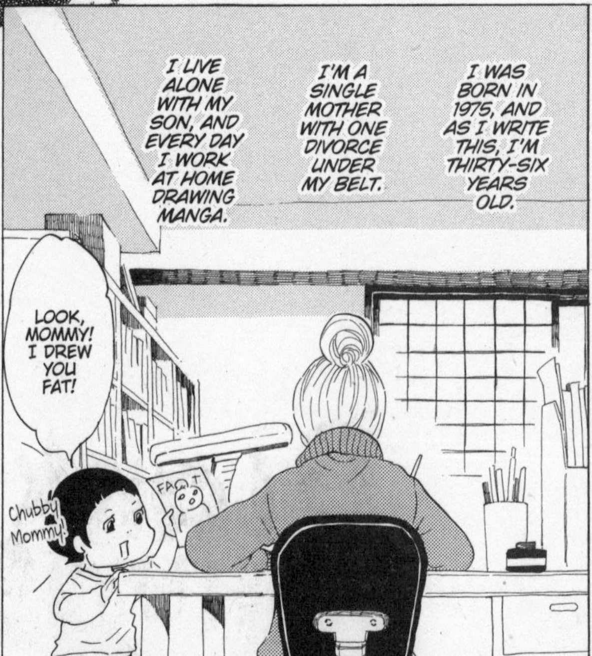
I WAS BORN IN 1975, AND AS I WRITE THIS, I'M THIRTY-SIX YEARS OLD.
I'M A SINGLE MOTHER WITH ONE DIVORCE UNDER MY BELT.
I LIVE ALONE WITH MY SON, AND EVERY DAY I WORK AT HOME DRAWING MANGA.
LOOK, MOMMY! I DREW YOU FAT!
Chubby Mommy!

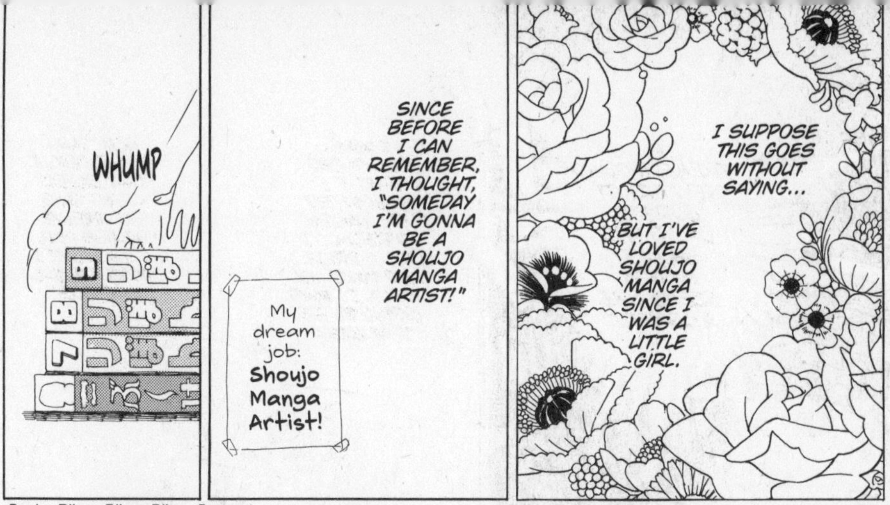
I SUPPOSE THIS GOES WITHOUT SAYING…
BUT I'VE LOVED SHOUJO MANGA SINCE I WAS A LITTLE GIRL.
SINCE BEFORE I CAN REMEMBER, I THOUGHT, "SOMEDAY I'M GONNA BE A SHOUJO MANGA ARTIST!"
My dream job: Shoujo Manga Artist!
WHUMP

Books: Ribon, Ribon, Ribon, Bouquet.

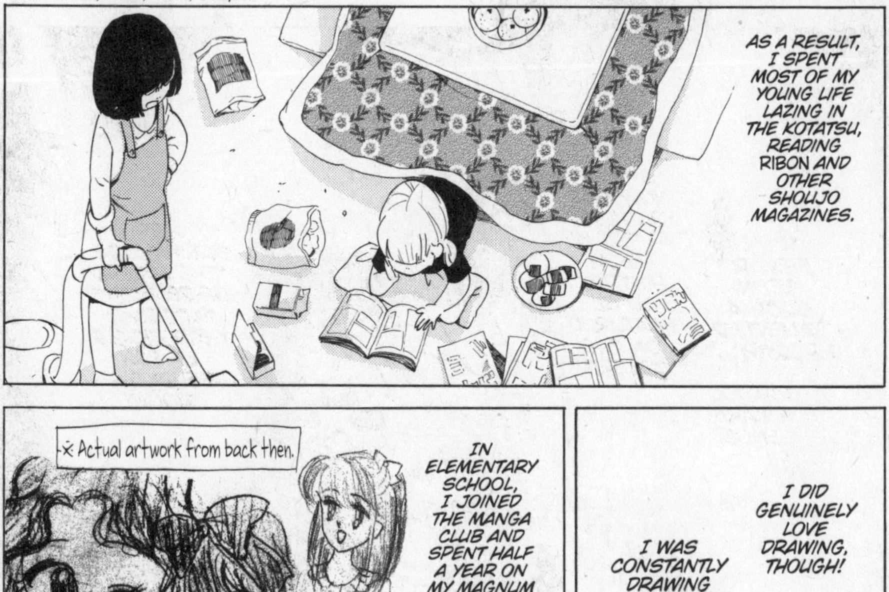
AS A RESULT, I SPENT MOST OF MY YOUNG LIFE LAZING IN THE KOTATSU, READING RIBON AND OTHER SHOUJO MAGAZINES.

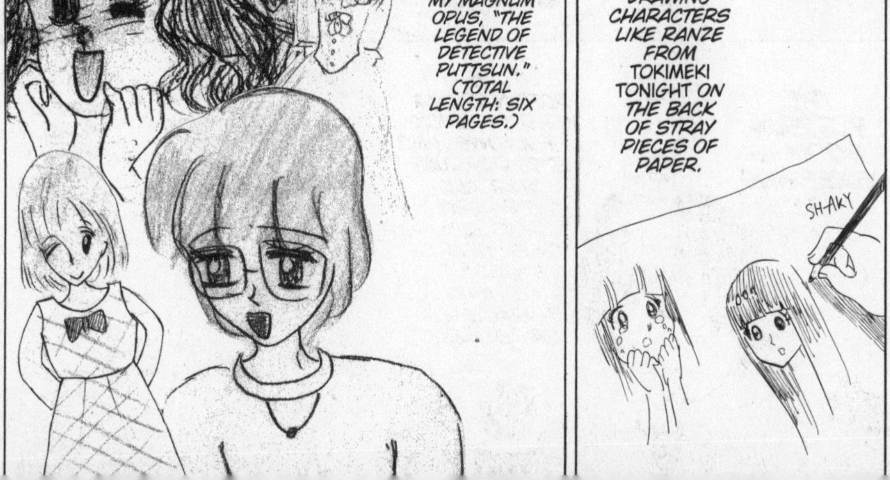
I DID GENUINELY LOVE DRAWING, THOUGH!
I WAS CONSTANTLY DRAWING CHARACTERS LIKE RANZE FROM TOKIMEKI TONIGHT ON THE BACK OF STRAY PIECES OF PAPER.
SH-AKY
IN ELEMENTARY SCHOOL, I JOINED THE MANGA CLUB AND SPENT HALF A YEAR ON MY MAGNUM OPUS, "THE LEGEND OF DETECTIVE PUTTSUN." (TOTAL LENGTH: SIX PAGES.)
※ Actual artwork from back then.

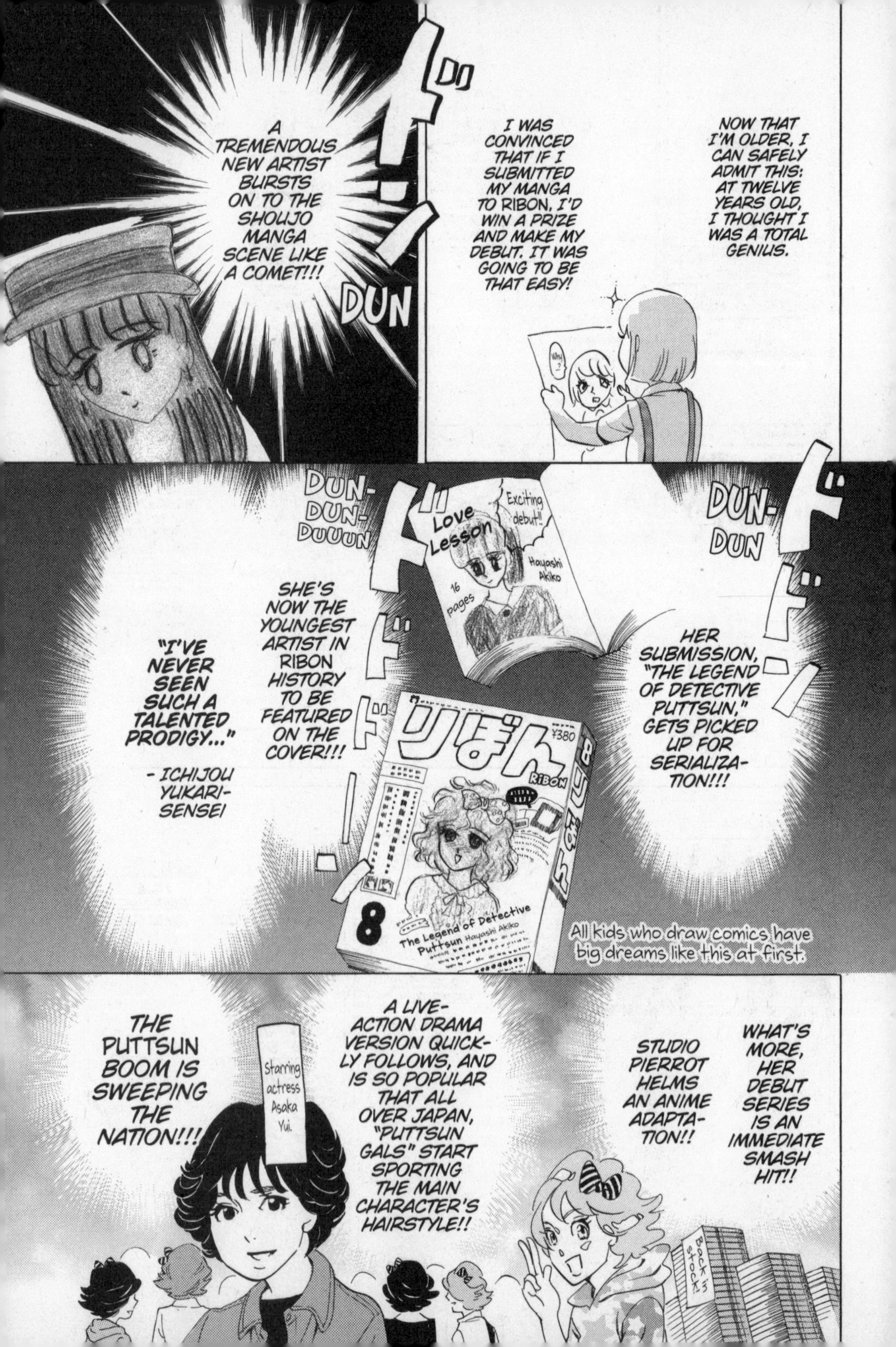

NOW THAT I'M OLDER, I CAN SAFELY ADMIT THIS: AT TWELVE YEARS OLD, I THOUGHT I WAS A TOTAL GENIUS.
I WAS CONVINCED THAT IF I SUBMITTED MY MANGA TO RIBON, I'D WIN A PRIZE AND MAKE MY DEBUT. IT WAS GOING TO BE THAT EASY!
DO
A TREMENDOUS NEW ARTIST BURSTS ON TO THE SHOUJO MANGA SCENE LIKE A COMET!!!
DUN
DUN-DUN
HER SUBMISSION, "THE LEGEND OF DETECTIVE PUTTSUN," GETS PICKED UP FOR SERIALIZATION!!!
Exciting debut!!
Love Lesson
Hayashi Akiko
16 pages
DUN-DUN-DUUUN
SHE'S NOW THE YOUNGEST ARTIST IN RIBON HISTORY TO BE FEATURED ON THE COVER!!!
"I'VE NEVER SEEN SUCH A TALENTED PRODIGY..." - ICHIJOU YUKARI-SENSEI
りぼん
¥380
RIBON
8
The Legend of Detective Puttsun Hayashi Akiko
All kids who draw comics have big dreams like this at first.
WHAT'S MORE, HER DEBUT SERIES IS AN IMMEDIATE SMASH HIT!!
STUDIO PIERROT HELMS AN ANIME ADAPTATION!!
Back in stock!
A LIVE-ACTION DRAMA VERSION QUICKLY FOLLOWS, AND IS SO POPULAR THAT ALL OVER JAPAN, "PUTTSUN GALS" START SPORTING THE MAIN CHARACTER'S HAIRSTYLE!!
Starring actress Asaka Yui.
THE PUTTSUN BOOM IS SWEEPING THE NATION!!!

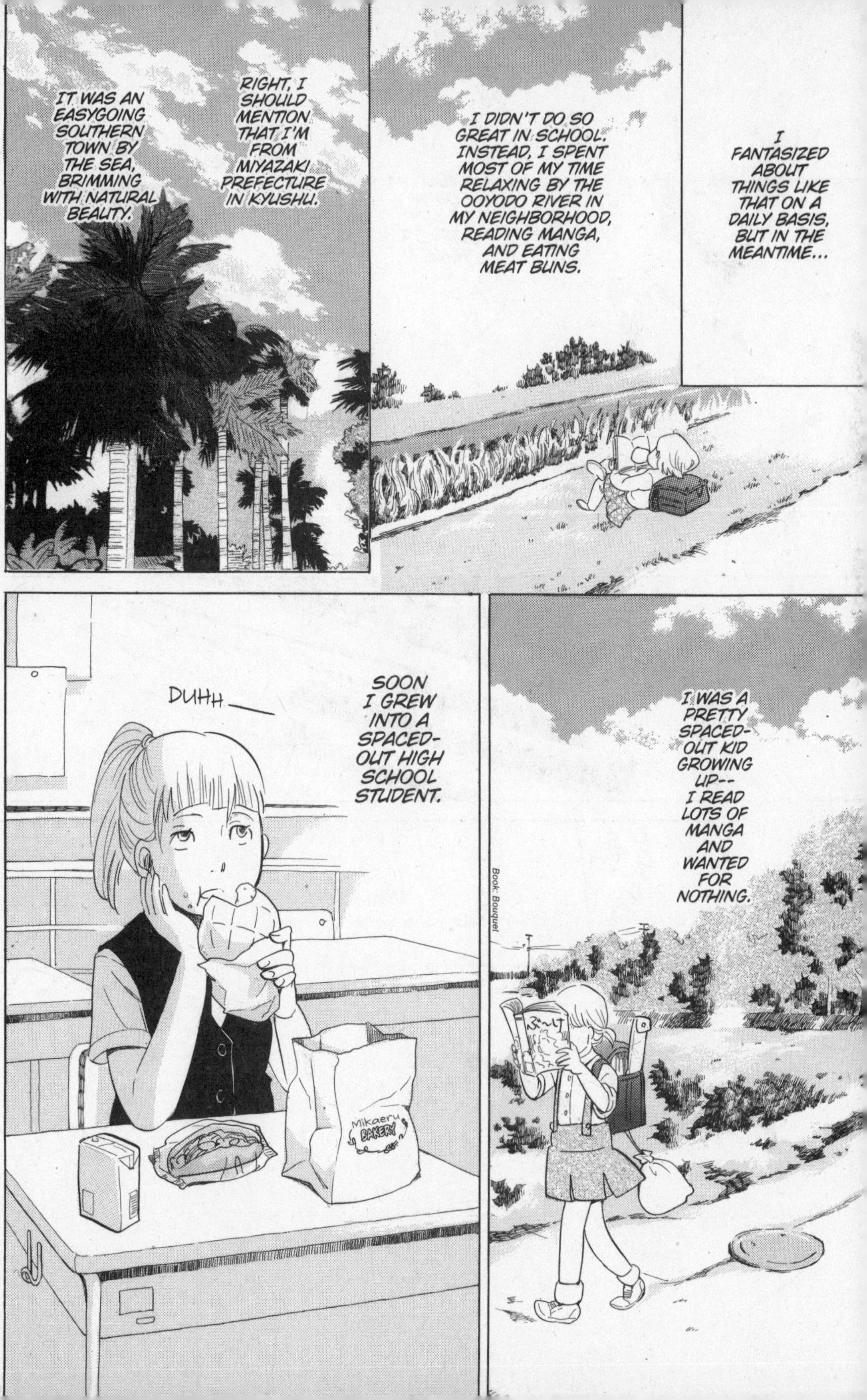
I FANTASIZED ABOUT THINGS LIKE THAT ON A DAILY BASIS, BUT IN THE MEANTIME...
I DIDN'T DO SO GREAT IN SCHOOL. INSTEAD, I SPENT MOST OF MY TIME RELAXING BY THE OOYODO RIVER IN MY NEIGHBORHOOD, READING MANGA, AND EATING MEAT BUNS.
RIGHT, I SHOULD MENTION THAT I'M FROM MIYAZAKI PREFECTURE IN KYUSHU.
IT WAS AN EASYGOING SOUTHERN TOWN BY THE SEA, BRIMMING WITH NATURAL BEAUTY.
I WAS A PRETTY SPACED-OUT KID GROWING UP-- I READ LOTS OF MANGA AND WANTED FOR NOTHING.
Book: Bouquet
SOON I GREW INTO A SPACED-OUT HIGH SCHOOL STUDENT.
DUHH
Mikaeru BAKERY

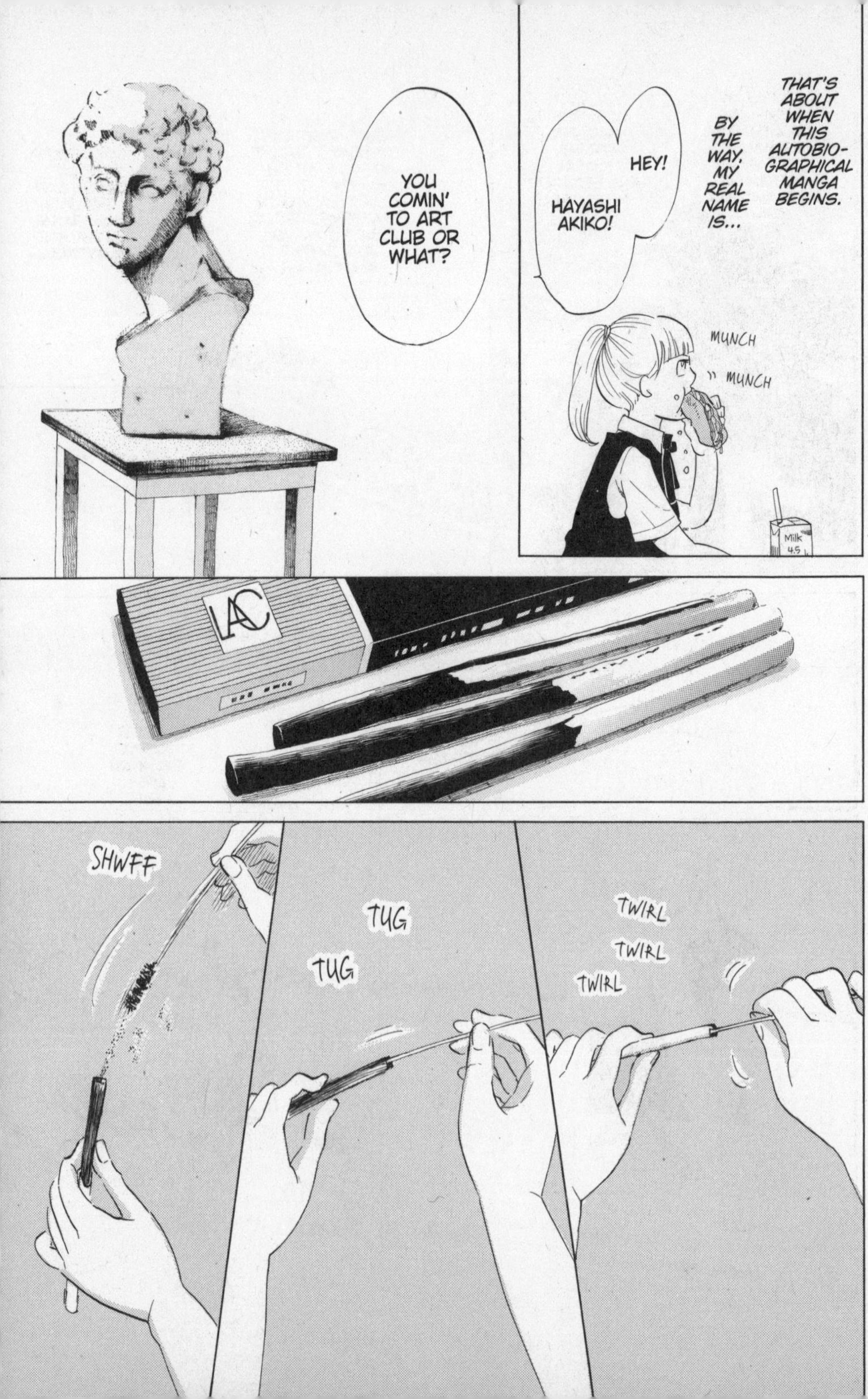
THAT'S ABOUT WHEN THIS AUTOBIO-GRAPHICAL MANGA BEGINS.
BY THE WAY, MY REAL NAME IS...
HEY!
HAYASHI AKIKO!
MUNCH
MUNCH
Milk
YOU COMIN' TO ART CLUB OR WHAT?
LAC
TWIRL
TWIRL
TWIRL
TUG
TUG
SHWFF

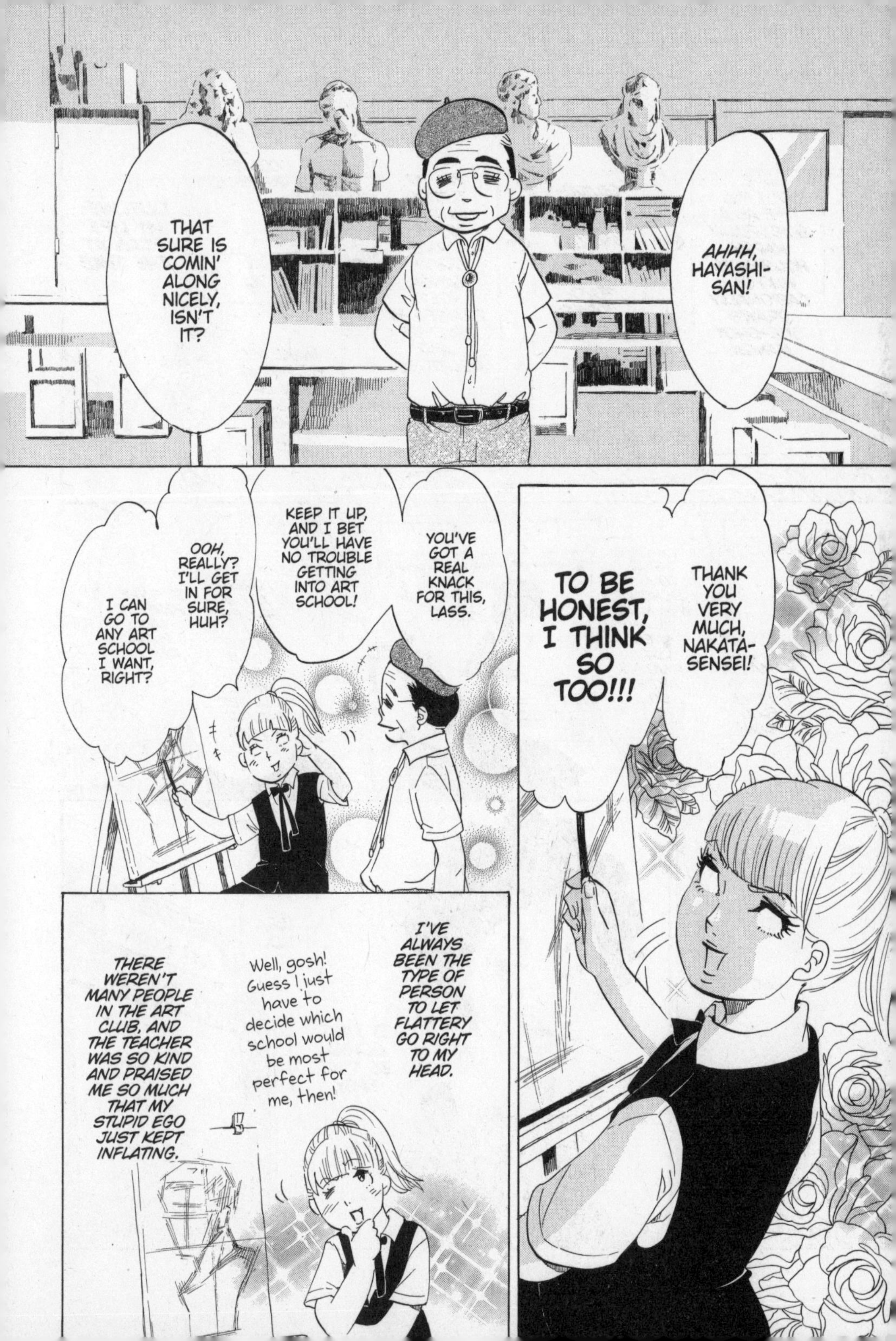
AHHH, HAYASHI-SAN!
THAT SURE IS COMIN' ALONG NICELY, ISN'T IT?
YOU'VE GOT A REAL KNACK FOR THIS, LASS.
KEEP IT UP, AND I BET YOU'LL HAVE NO TROUBLE GETTING INTO ART SCHOOL!
OOH, REALLY? I'LL GET IN FOR SURE, HUH?
I CAN GO TO ANY ART SCHOOL I WANT, RIGHT?
THANK YOU VERY MUCH, NAKATA-SENSEI!
TO BE HONEST, I THINK SO TOO!!!
I'VE ALWAYS BEEN THE TYPE OF PERSON TO LET FLATTERY GO RIGHT TO MY HEAD.
Well, gosh! Guess I just have to decide which school would be most perfect for me, then!
THERE WEREN'T MANY PEOPLE IN THE ART CLUB, AND THE TEACHER WAS SO KIND AND PRAISED ME SO MUCH THAT MY STUPID EGO JUST KEPT INFLATING.

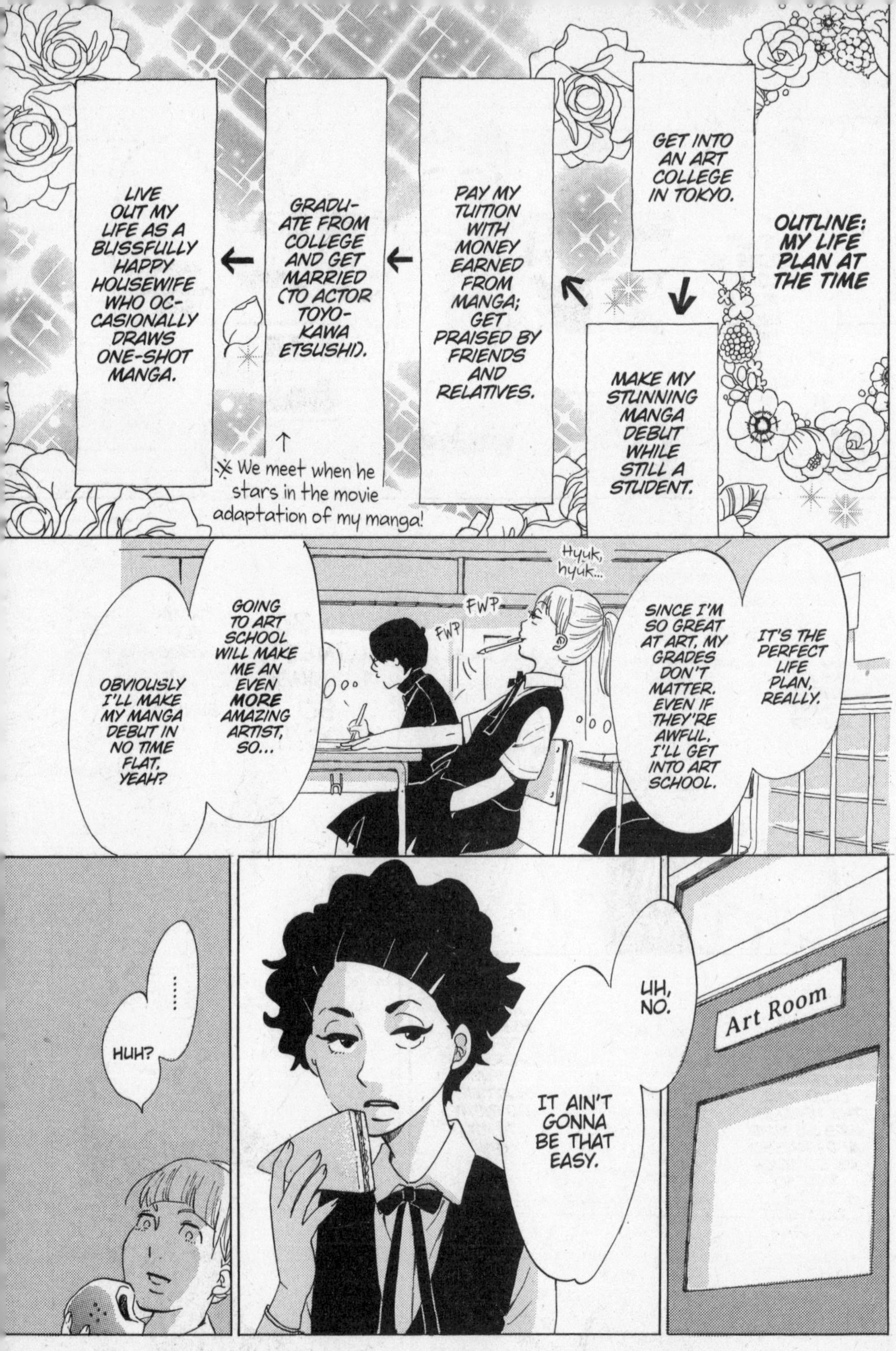
OUTLINE: MY LIFE PLAN AT THE TIME
GET INTO AN ART COLLEGE IN TOKYO.
MAKE MY STUNNING MANGA DEBUT WHILE STILL A STUDENT.
PAY MY TUITION WITH MONEY EARNED FROM MANGA; GET PRAISED BY FRIENDS AND RELATIVES.
GRADUATE FROM COLLEGE AND GET MARRIED (TO ACTOR TOYOKAWA ETSUSHI).
※ We meet when he stars in the movie adaptation of my manga!
LIVE OUT MY LIFE AS A BLISSFULLY HAPPY HOUSEWIFE WHO OCCASIONALLY DRAWS ONE-SHOT MANGA.
IT'S THE PERFECT LIFE PLAN, REALLY.
SINCE I'M SO GREAT AT ART, MY GRADES DON'T MATTER. EVEN IF THEY'RE AWFUL, I'LL GET INTO ART SCHOOL.
Hyuk, hyuk...
FWP
FWP
GOING TO ART SCHOOL WILL MAKE ME AN EVEN MORE AMAZING ARTIST, SO...
OBVIOUSLY I'LL MAKE MY MANGA DEBUT IN NO TIME FLAT, YEAH?
Art Room
UH, NO.
IT AIN'T GONNA BE THAT EASY.
......
HUH?

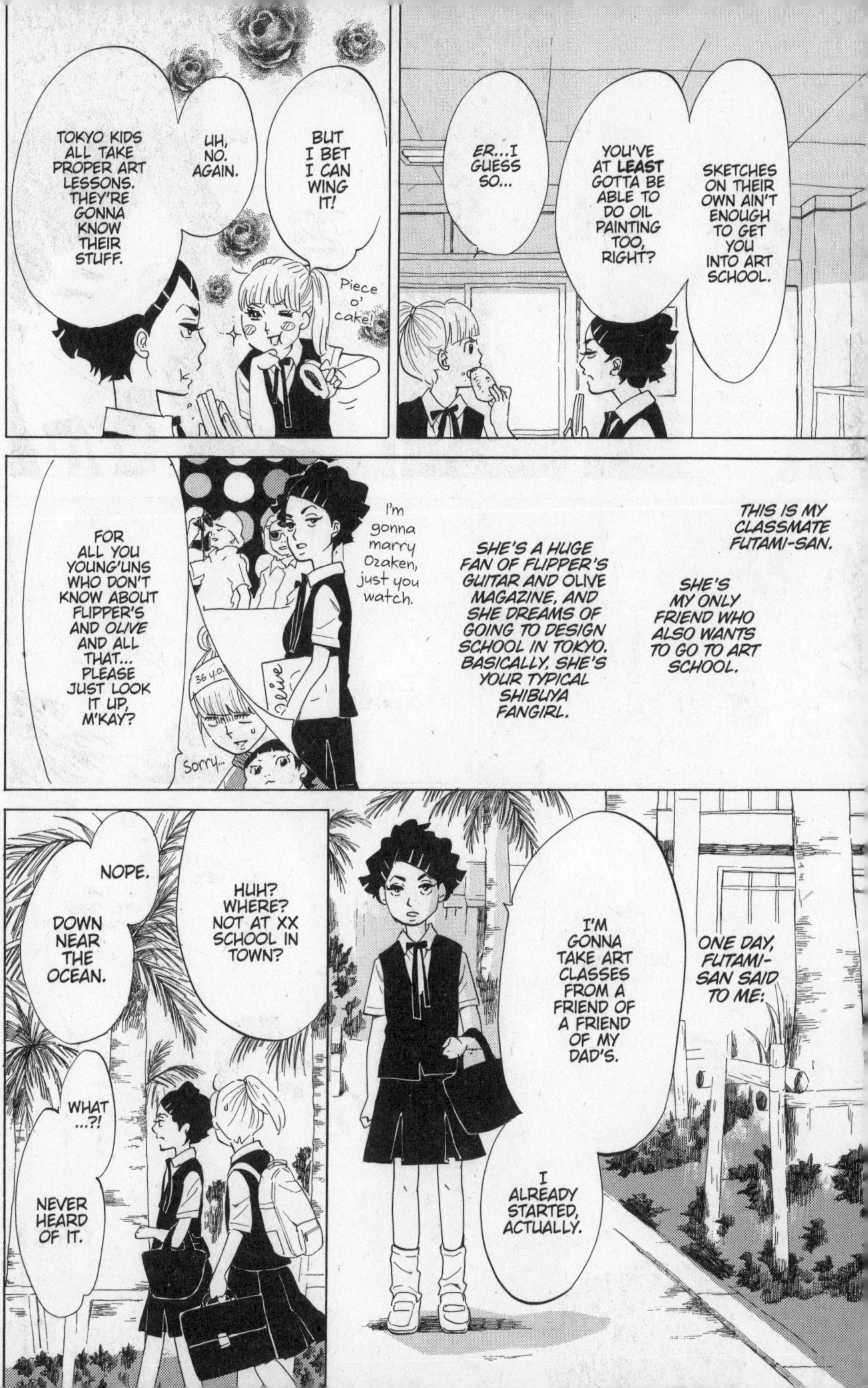
SKETCHES ON THEIR OWN AIN'T ENOUGH TO GET YOU INTO ART SCHOOL.
YOU'VE AT **LEAST** GOTTA BE ABLE TO DO OIL PAINTING TOO, RIGHT?
ER...I GUESS SO...
BUT I BET I CAN WING IT!
UH, NO. AGAIN.
TOKYO KIDS ALL TAKE PROPER ART LESSONS. THEY'RE GONNA KNOW THEIR STUFF.
Piece o' cake!
THIS IS MY CLASSMATE FUTAMI-SAN.
SHE'S MY ONLY FRIEND WHO ALSO WANTS TO GO TO ART SCHOOL.
SHE'S A HUGE FAN OF FLIPPER'S GUITAR AND OLIVE MAGAZINE, AND SHE DREAMS OF GOING TO DESIGN SCHOOL IN TOKYO. BASICALLY, SHE'S YOUR TYPICAL SHIBUYA FANGIRL.
I'm gonna marry Ozaken, just you watch.
FOR ALL YOU YOUNG'UNS WHO DON'T KNOW ABOUT FLIPPER'S AND *OLIVE* AND ALL THAT... PLEASE JUST LOOK IT UP, M'KAY?
36 y.o.
Sorry...
ONE DAY, FUTAMI-SAN SAID TO ME:
I'M GONNA TAKE ART CLASSES FROM A FRIEND OF A FRIEND OF MY DAD'S.
I ALREADY STARTED, ACTUALLY.
HUH? WHERE? NOT AT XX SCHOOL IN TOWN?
NOPE.
DOWN NEAR THE OCEAN.
WHAT ...?!
NEVER HEARD OF IT.

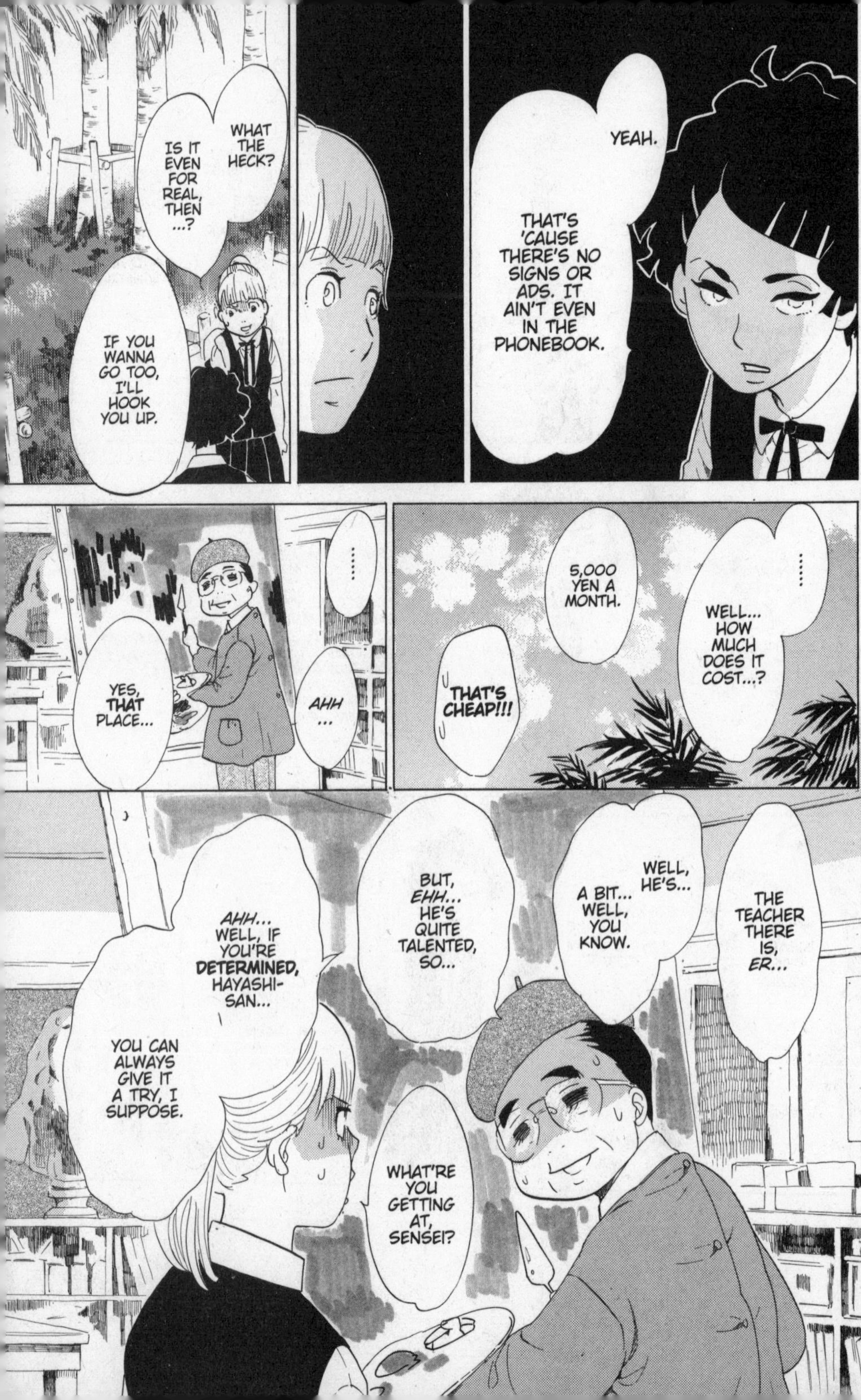
YEAH.
THAT'S 'CAUSE THERE'S NO SIGNS OR ADS. IT AIN'T EVEN IN THE PHONEBOOK.
WHAT THE HECK? IS IT EVEN FOR REAL, THEN ...?
IF YOU WANNA GO TOO, I'LL HOOK YOU UP.
...... WELL... HOW MUCH DOES IT COST...?
5,000 YEN A MONTH.
THAT'S CHEAP!!!
......
AHH ...
YES, THAT PLACE...
THE TEACHER THERE IS, ER...
WELL, HE'S... A BIT... WELL, YOU KNOW.
BUT, EHH... HE'S QUITE TALENTED, SO...
AHH... WELL, IF YOU'RE DETERMINED, HAYASHI-SAN...
YOU CAN ALWAYS GIVE IT A TRY, I SUPPOSE.
WHAT'RE YOU GETTING AT, SENSEI?

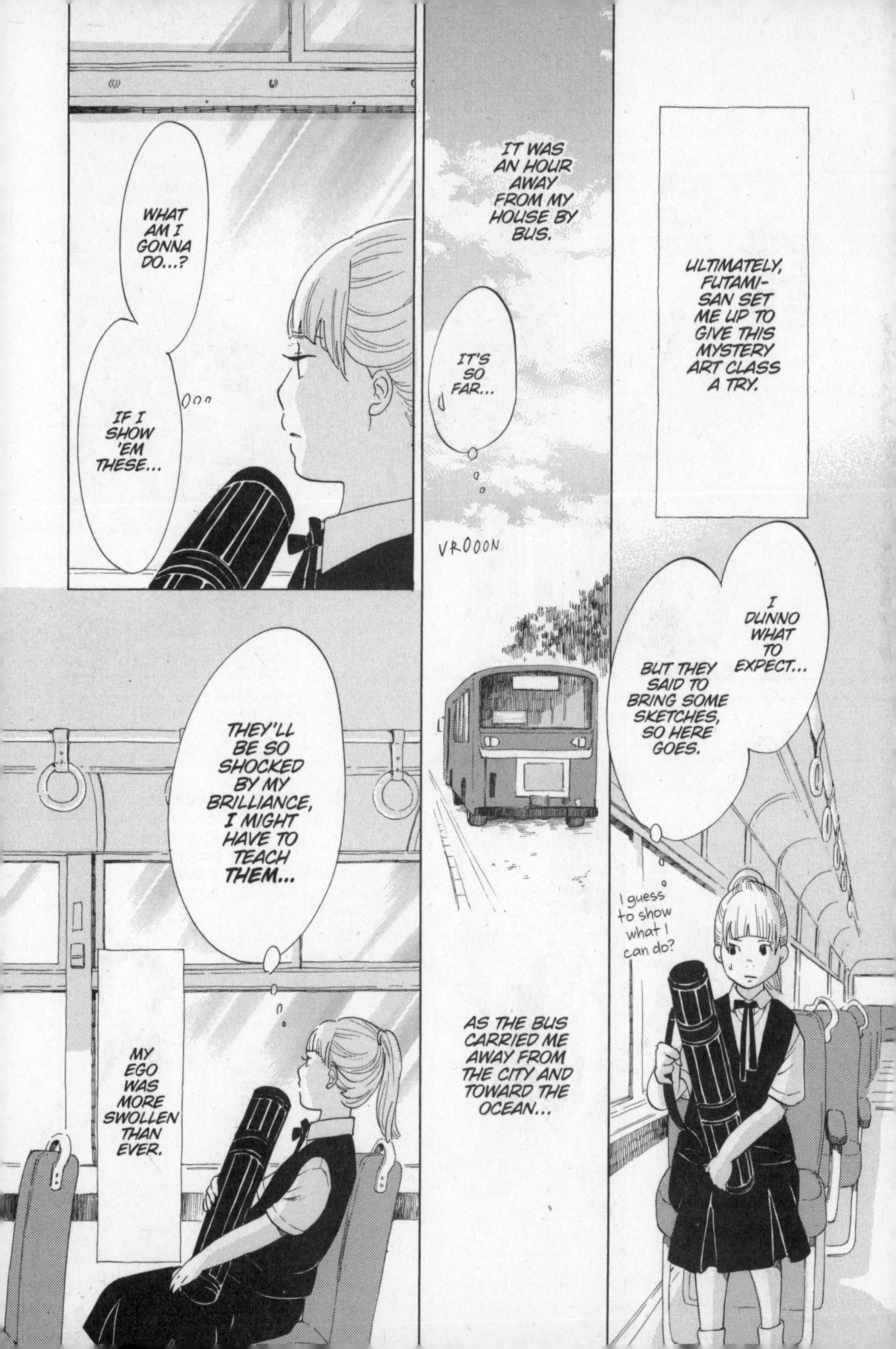
ULTIMATELY, FUTAMI-SAN SET ME UP TO GIVE THIS MYSTERY ART CLASS A TRY.
I DUNNO WHAT TO EXPECT...
BUT THEY SAID TO BRING SOME SKETCHES, SO HERE GOES.
I guess to show what I can do?
IT WAS AN HOUR AWAY FROM MY HOUSE BY BUS.
IT'S SO FAR...
VROOON
AS THE BUS CARRIED ME AWAY FROM THE CITY AND TOWARD THE OCEAN...
WHAT AM I GONNA DO...?
IF I SHOW 'EM THESE...
THEY'LL BE SO SHOCKED BY MY BRILLIANCE, I MIGHT HAVE TO TEACH THEM...
MY EGO WAS MORE SWOLLEN THAN EVER.

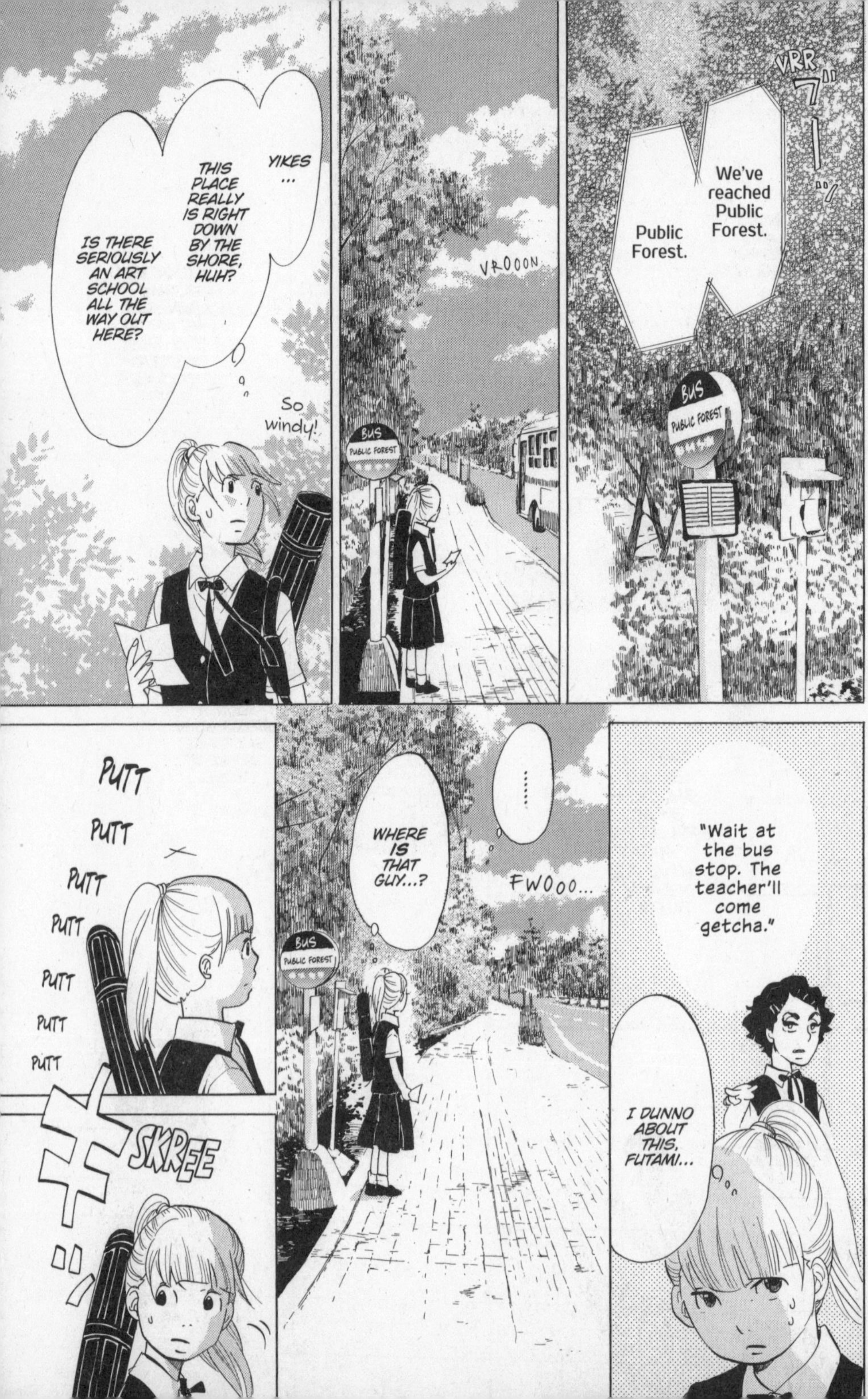
VRR
We've reached Public Forest.
Public Forest.
VROOON
YIKES...
THIS PLACE REALLY IS RIGHT DOWN BY THE SHORE, HUH?
IS THERE SERIOUSLY AN ART SCHOOL ALL THE WAY OUT HERE?
So windy!
"Wait at the bus stop. The teacher'll come getcha."
I DUNNO ABOUT THIS, FUTAMI...
......
WHERE IS THAT GUY...?
FWOOO...
BUS
PUBLIC FOREST
PUTT PUTT PUTT PUTT PUTT PUTT PUTT
SKREE

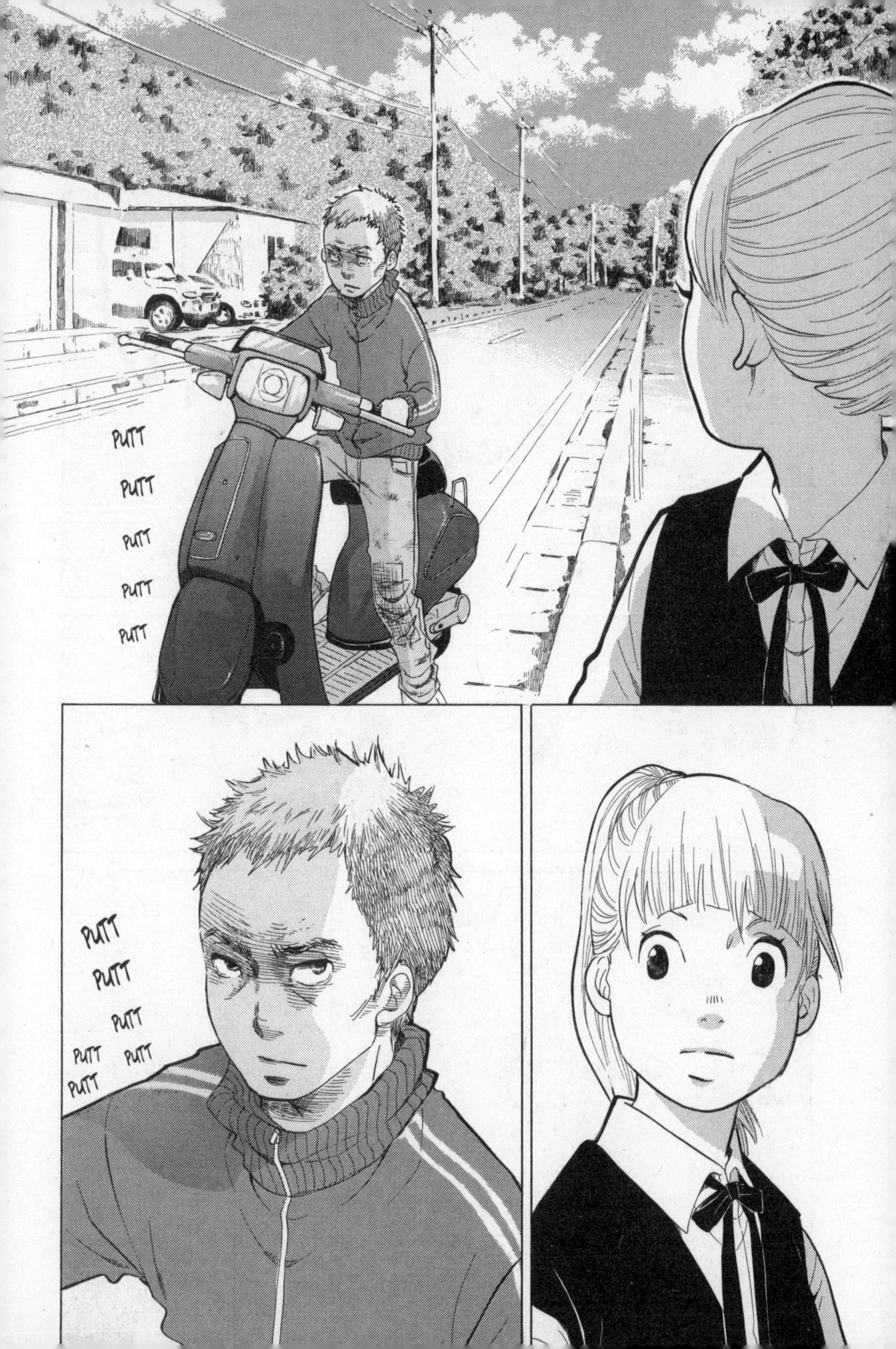
PUTT
PUTT
PUTT
PUTT
PUTT
PUTT
PUTT
PUTT
PUTT PUTT
PUTT

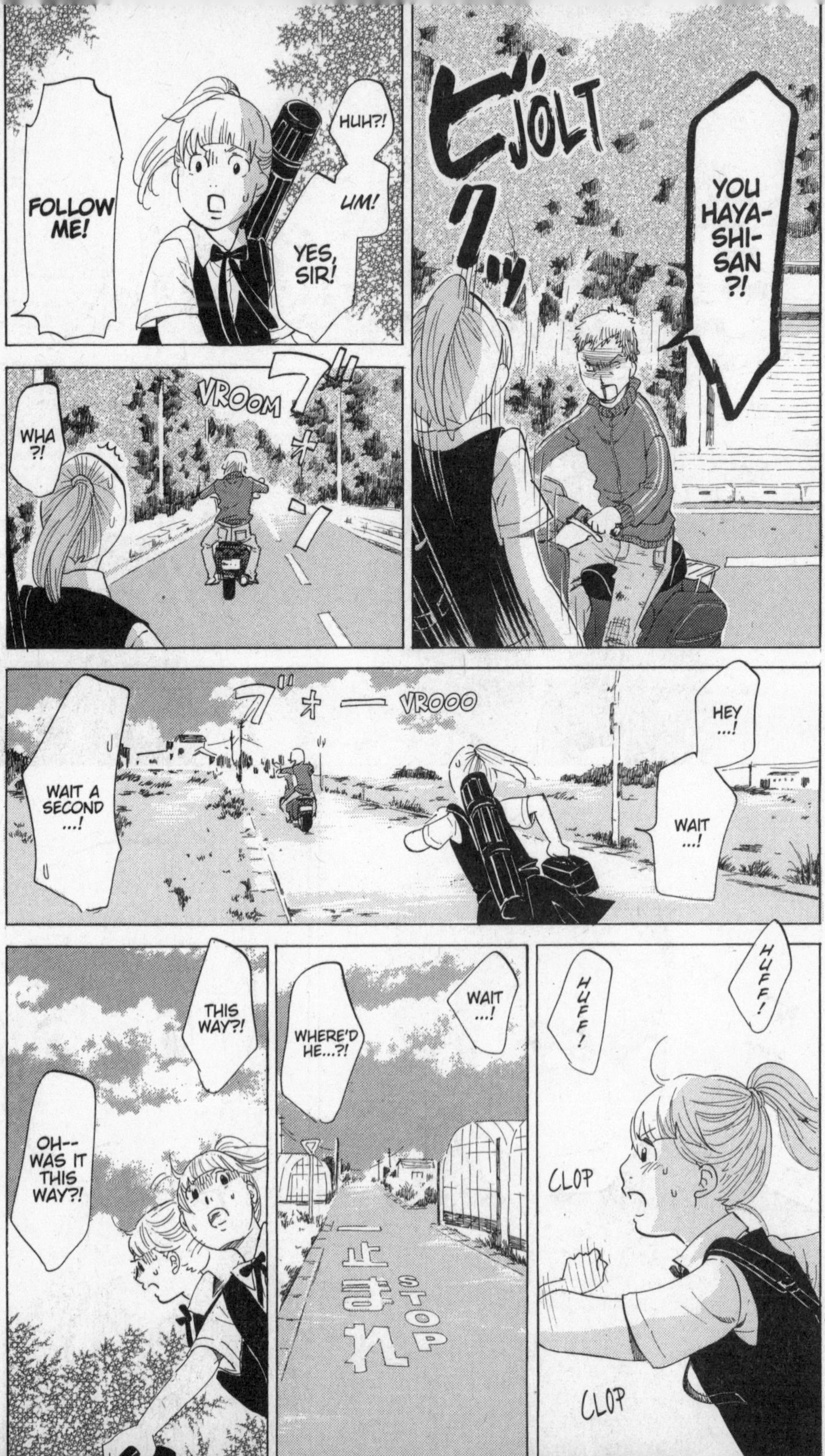
JOLT
YOU HAYA-SHI-SAN?!
HUH?!
UM!
YES, SIR!
FOLLOW ME!
VROOM
WHA?!
HEY...!
WAIT...!
VROOO
WAIT A SECOND...!
HUFF!
HUFF!
CLOP
CLOP
WAIT...!
WHERE'D HE...?!
止まれ STOP
THIS WAY?!
OH--WAS IT THIS WAY?!

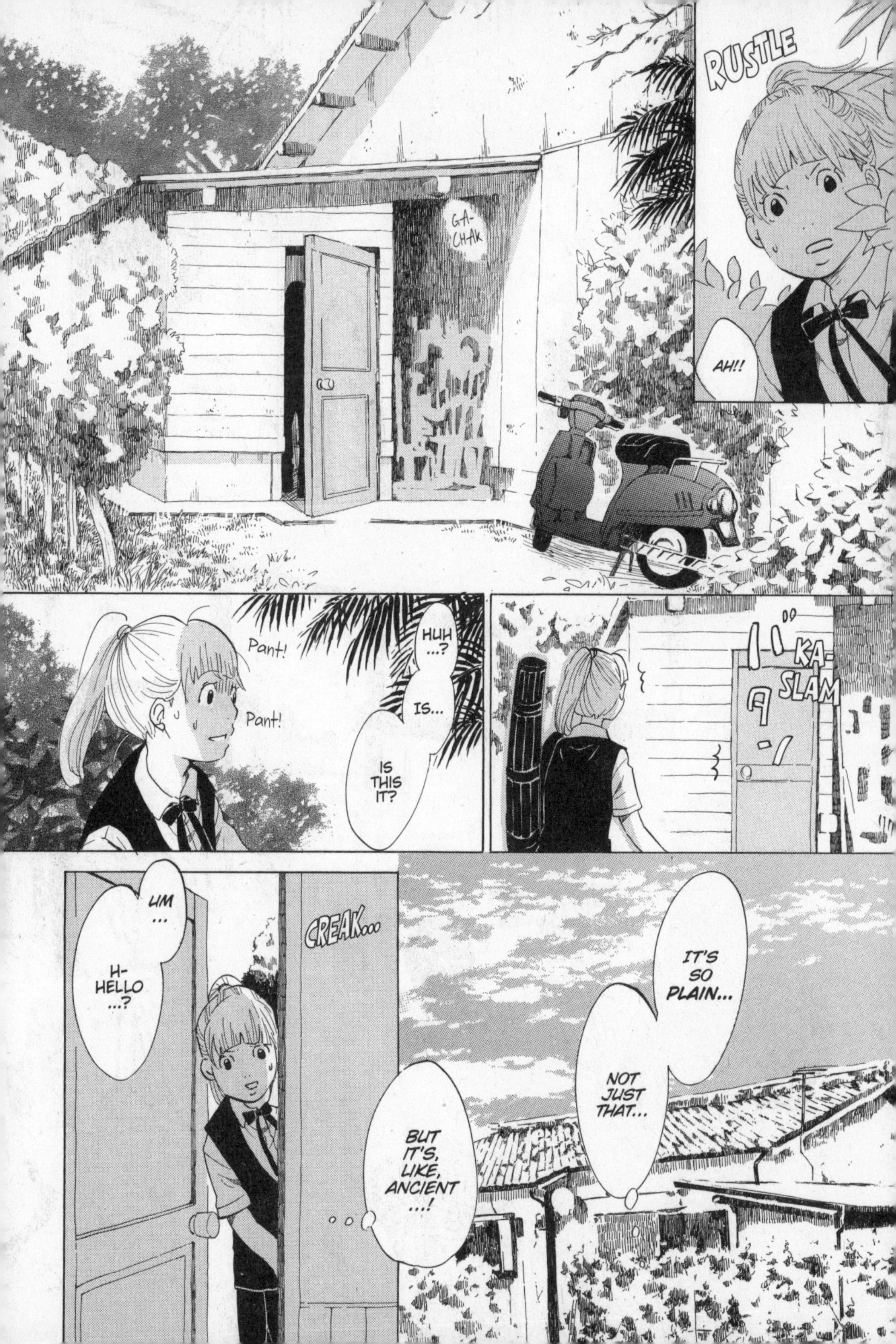
RUSTLE
AH!!
GA-CHAK
KA-SLAM
HUH ...?
IS...
IS THIS IT?
Pant!
Pant!
IT'S SO PLAIN...
NOT JUST THAT...
BUT IT'S, LIKE, ANCIENT ...!
CREAK...
UM ...
H-HELLO ...?

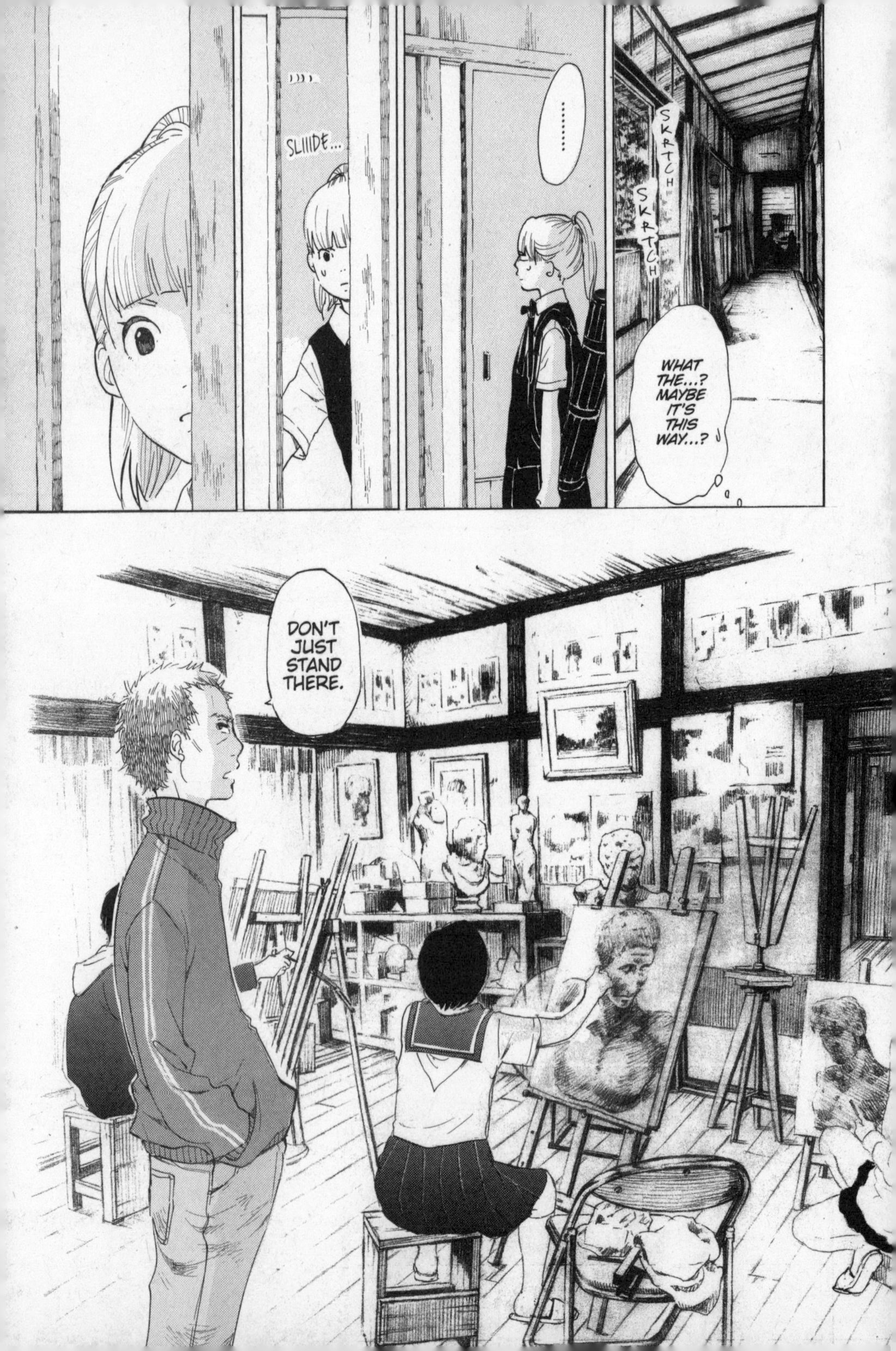
SKRTCH
SKRTCH
WHAT THE...? MAYBE IT'S THIS WAY...?
......
SLIIDE...
DON'T JUST STAND THERE.

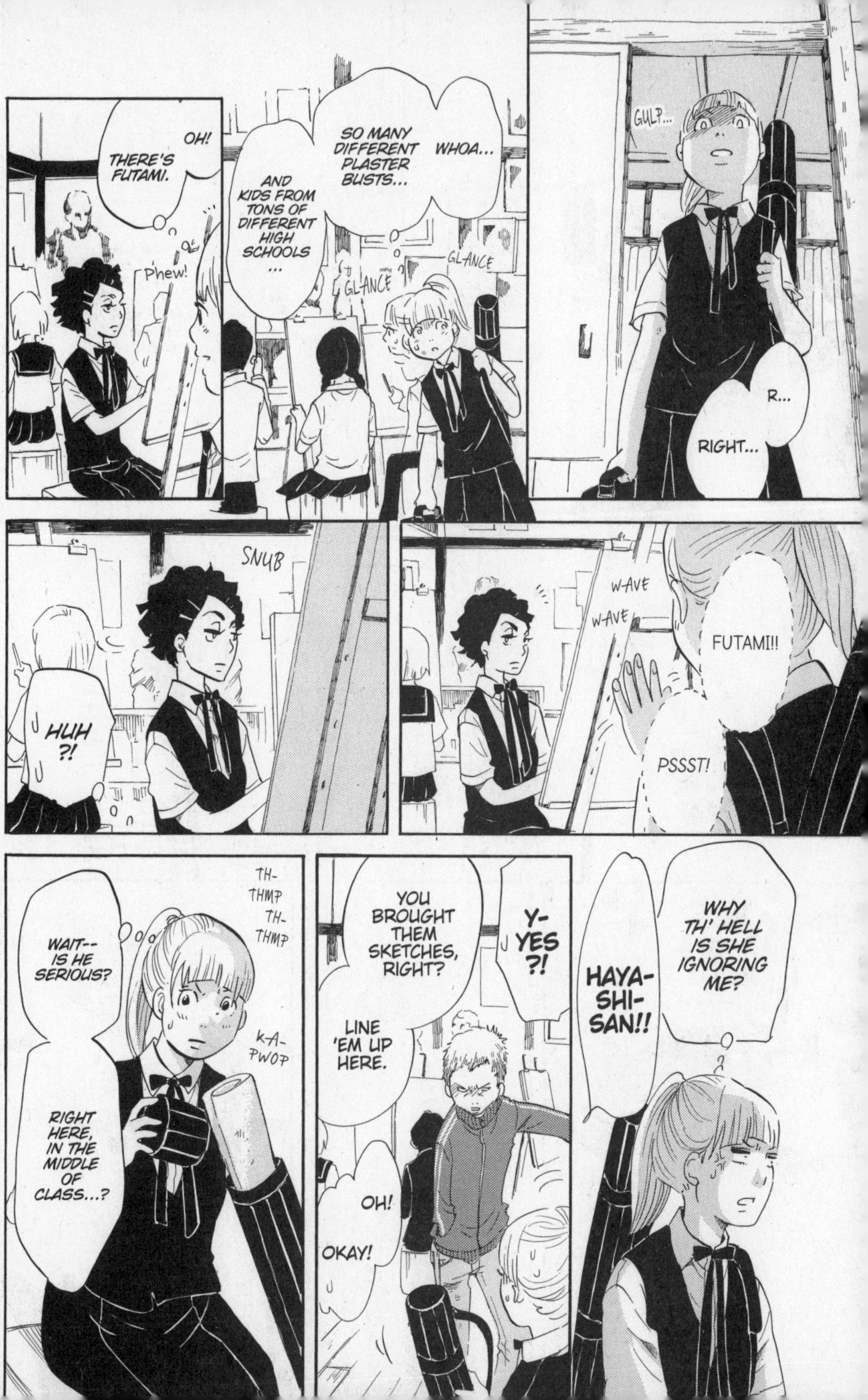
GULP...
R...
RIGHT...
WHOA...
SO MANY DIFFERENT PLASTER BUSTS...
AND KIDS FROM TONS OF DIFFERENT HIGH SCHOOLS...
GLANCE
GLANCE
OH!
THERE'S FUTAMI.
Phew!
WAVE
WAVE
FUTAMI!!
PSSST!
SNUB
HUH?!
WHY TH' HELL IS SHE IGNORING ME?
HAYA-SHI-SAN!!
Y-YES?!
YOU BROUGHT THEM SKETCHES, RIGHT?
LINE 'EM UP HERE.
OH!
OKAY!
WAIT-- IS HE SERIOUS?
TH-THMP
TH-THMP
KA-PWOP
RIGHT HERE, IN THE MIDDLE OF CLASS...?

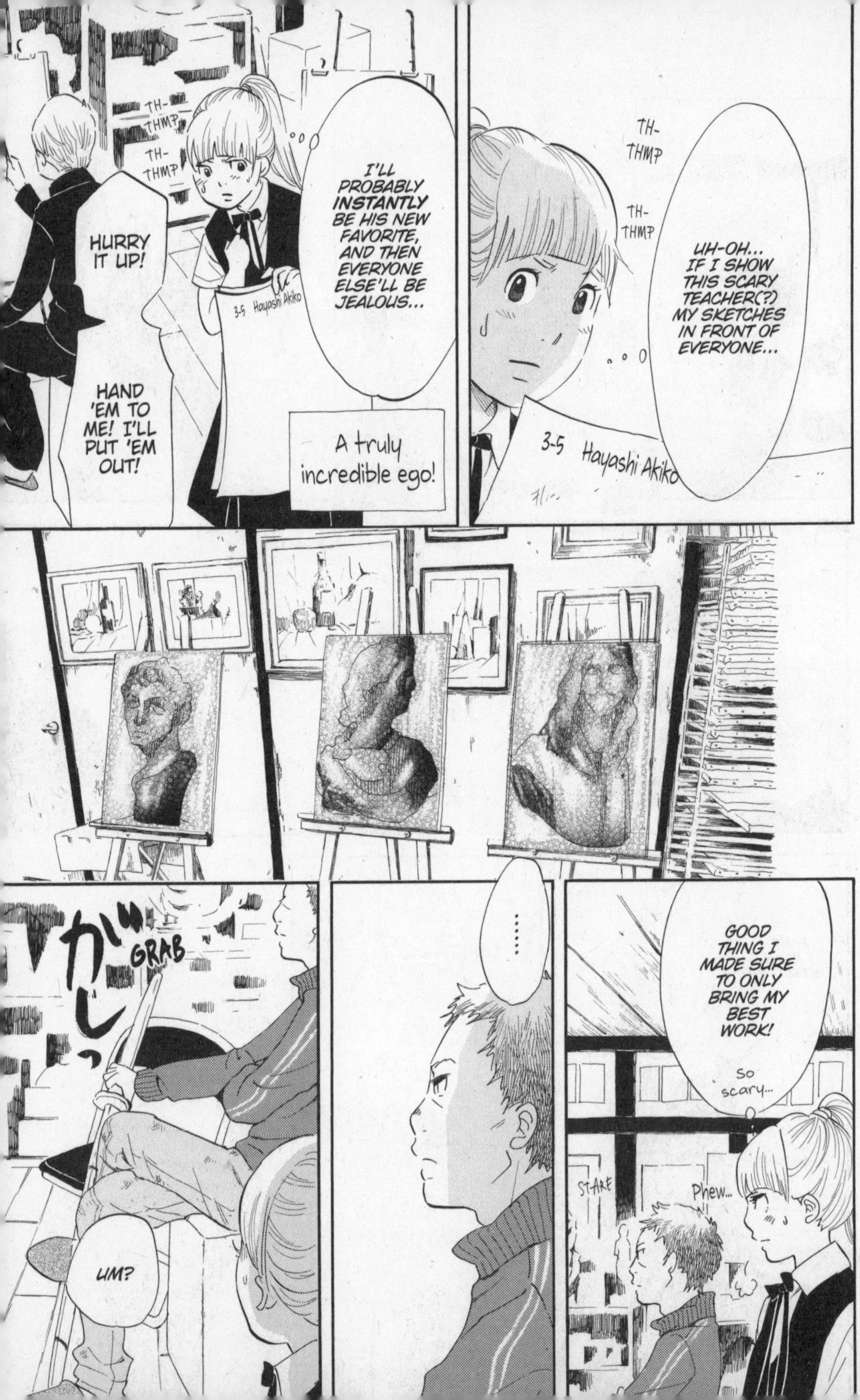
TH-THMP
TH-THMP
UH-OH... IF I SHOW THIS SCARY TEACHER(?) MY SKETCHES IN FRONT OF EVERYONE...
3-5 Hayashi Akiko
I'LL PROBABLY INSTANTLY BE HIS NEW FAVORITE, AND THEN EVERYONE ELSE'LL BE JEALOUS...
A truly incredible ego!
TH-THMP
TH-THMP
HURRY IT UP!
HAND 'EM TO ME! I'LL PUT 'EM OUT!
3-5 Hayashi Akiko
GOOD THING I MADE SURE TO ONLY BRING MY BEST WORK!
So scary...
Phew...
STARE
......
かしっ
GRAB
UM?

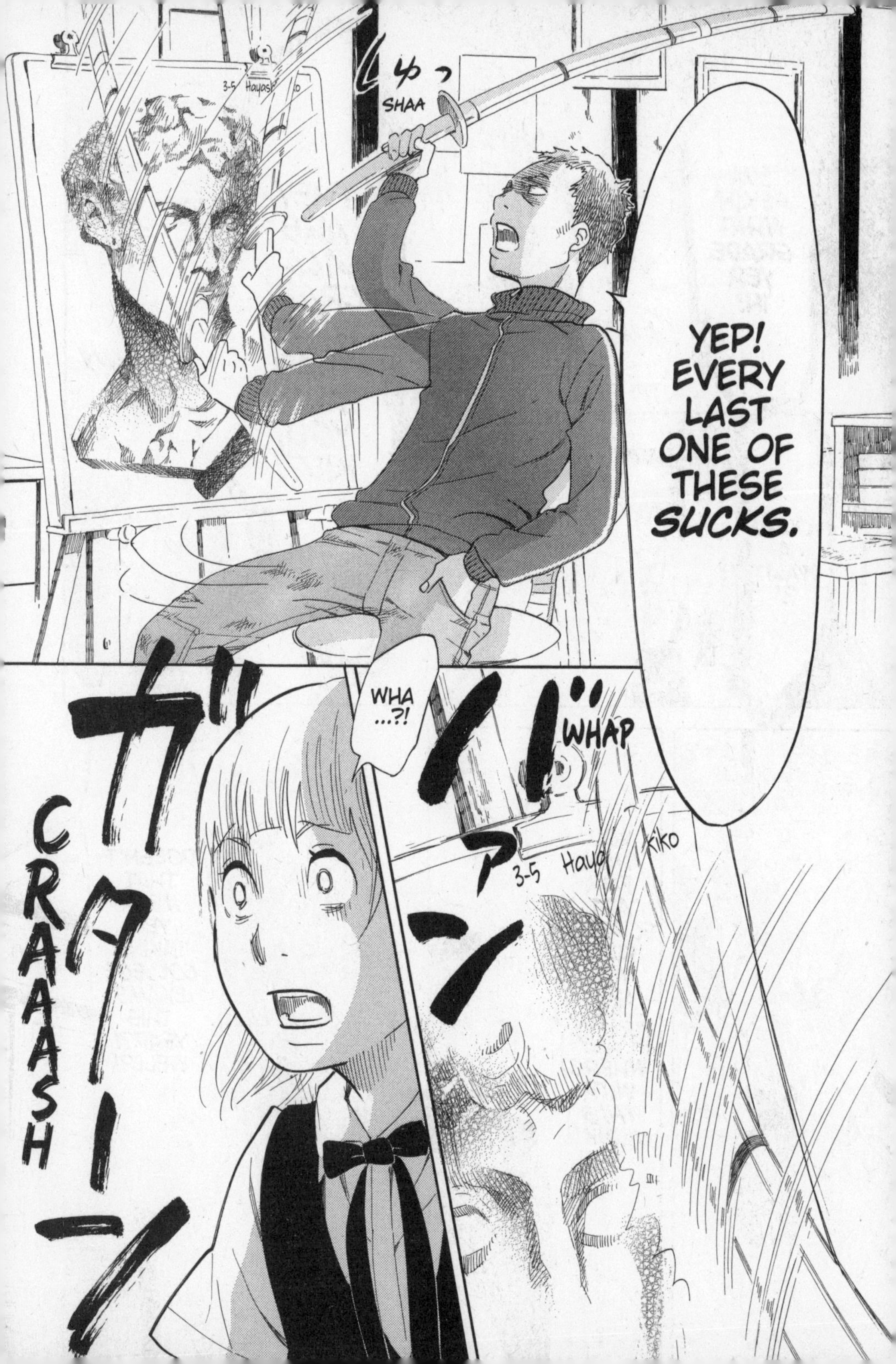

YEP! EVERY LAST ONE OF THESE SUCKS.
SHAA
WHAP
WHA ...?!
CRAAASH

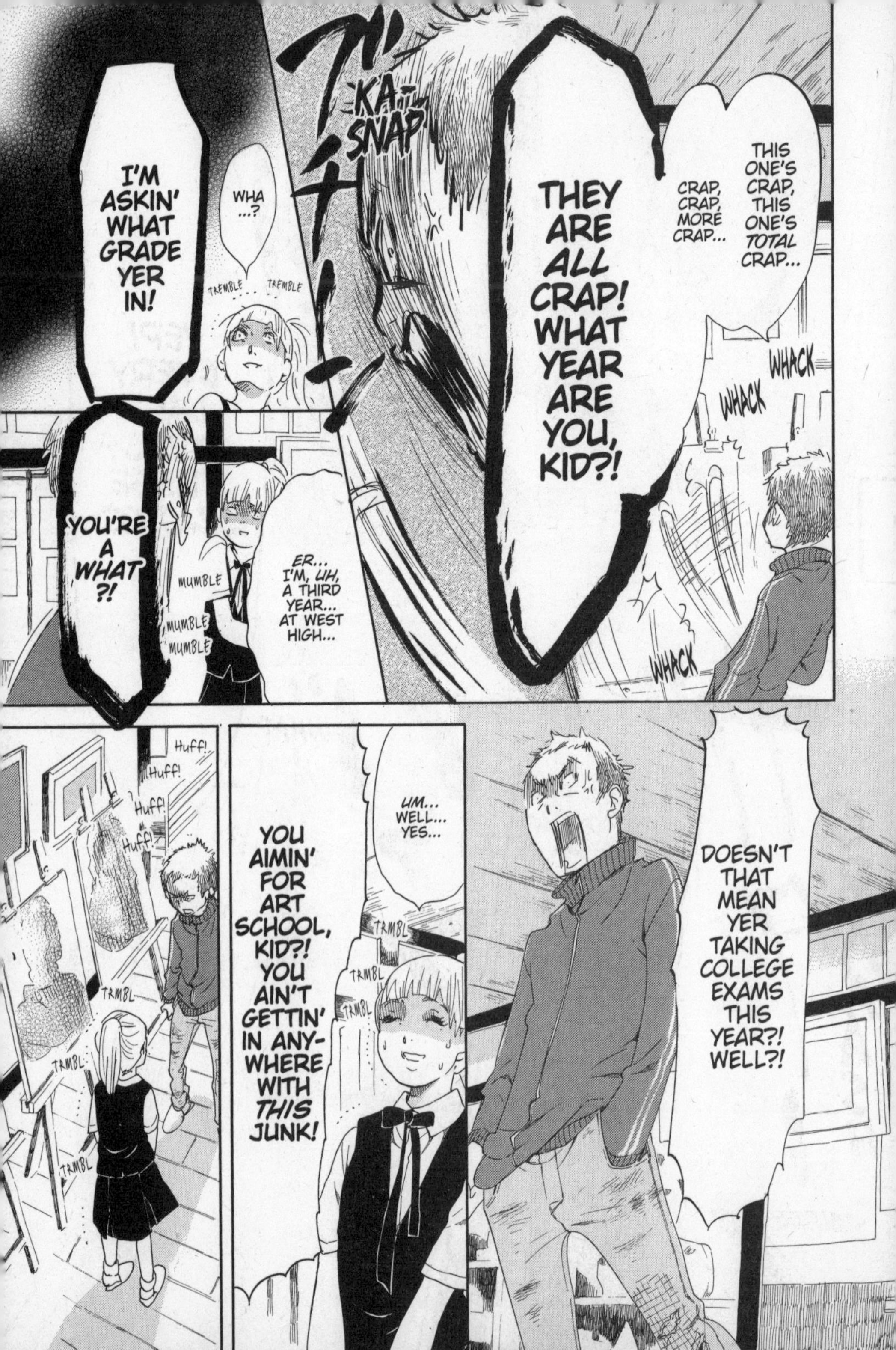
THIS ONE'S CRAP, THIS ONE'S TOTAL CRAP...
CRAP, CRAP, MORE CRAP...
WHACK
WHACK
THEY ARE ALL CRAP! WHAT YEAR ARE YOU, KID?!
KA-SNAP
WHACK
WHA ...?
I'M ASKIN' WHAT GRADE YER IN!
TREMBLE TREMBLE
ER... I'M, UH, A THIRD YEAR... AT WEST HIGH...
YOU'RE A WHAT?!
MUMBLE
MUMBLE
MUMBLE
DOESN'T THAT MEAN YER TAKING COLLEGE EXAMS THIS YEAR?! WELL?!
UM... WELL... YES...
YOU AIMIN' FOR ART SCHOOL, KID?! YOU AIN'T GETTIN' IN ANY-WHERE WITH THIS JUNK!
TRMBL
TRMBL
TRMBL
Huff!
Huff!
Huff!
Huff!
TRMBL
TRMBL
TRMBL

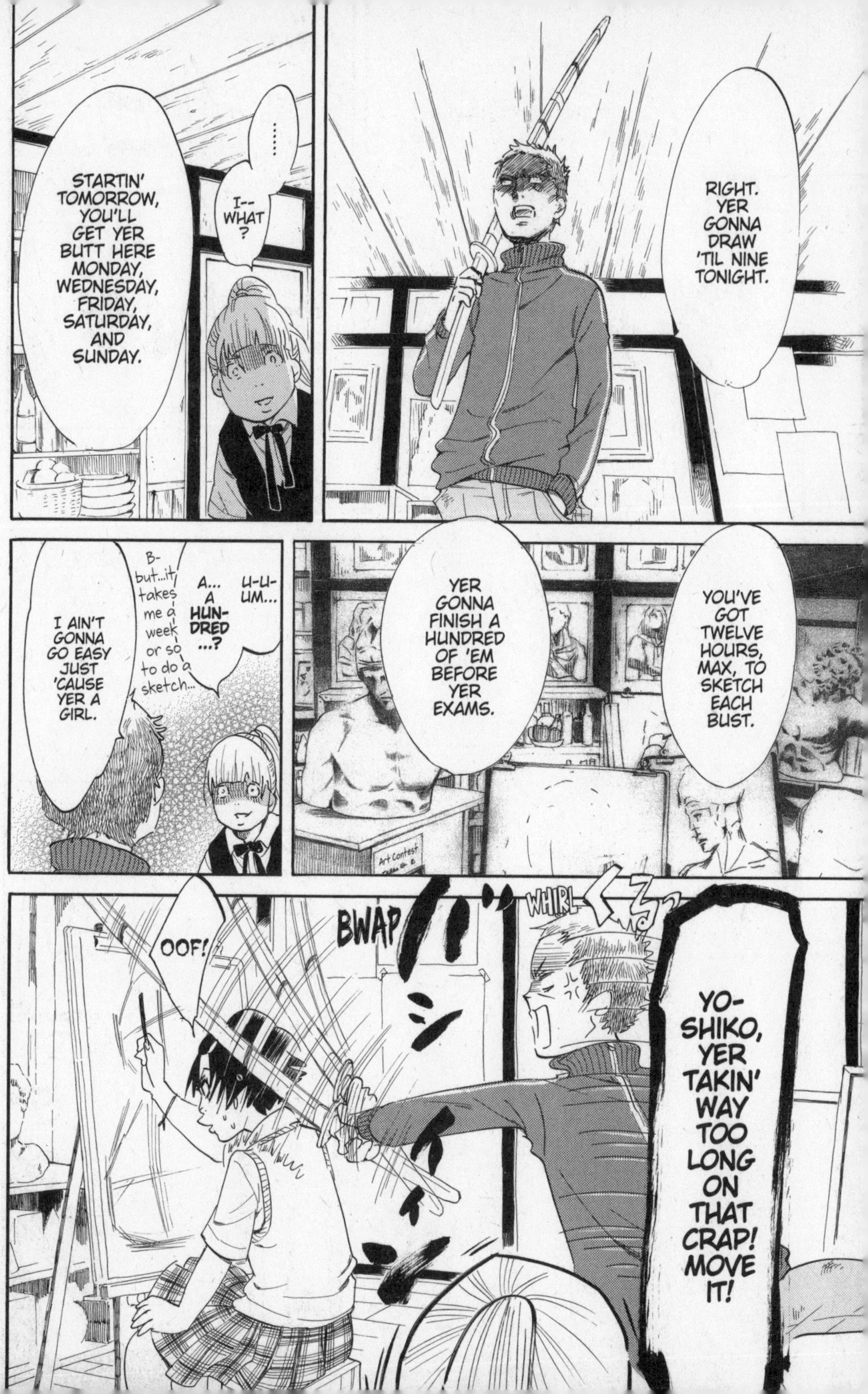
RIGHT. YER GONNA DRAW 'TIL NINE TONIGHT.
......
I-- WHAT?
STARTIN' TOMORROW, YOU'LL GET YER BUTT HERE MONDAY, WEDNESDAY, FRIDAY, SATURDAY, AND SUNDAY.
YOU'VE GOT TWELVE HOURS, MAX, TO SKETCH EACH BUST.
YER GONNA FINISH A HUNDRED OF 'EM BEFORE YER EXAMS.
Art Contest
U-U-UM...
A... A HUNDRED ...?
B-but...it takes me a week or so to do a sketch...
I AIN'T GONNA GO EASY JUST 'CAUSE YER A GIRL.
WHIRL
YO-SHIKO, YER TAKIN' WAY TOO LONG ON THAT CRAP! MOVE IT!
BWAP
OOF!

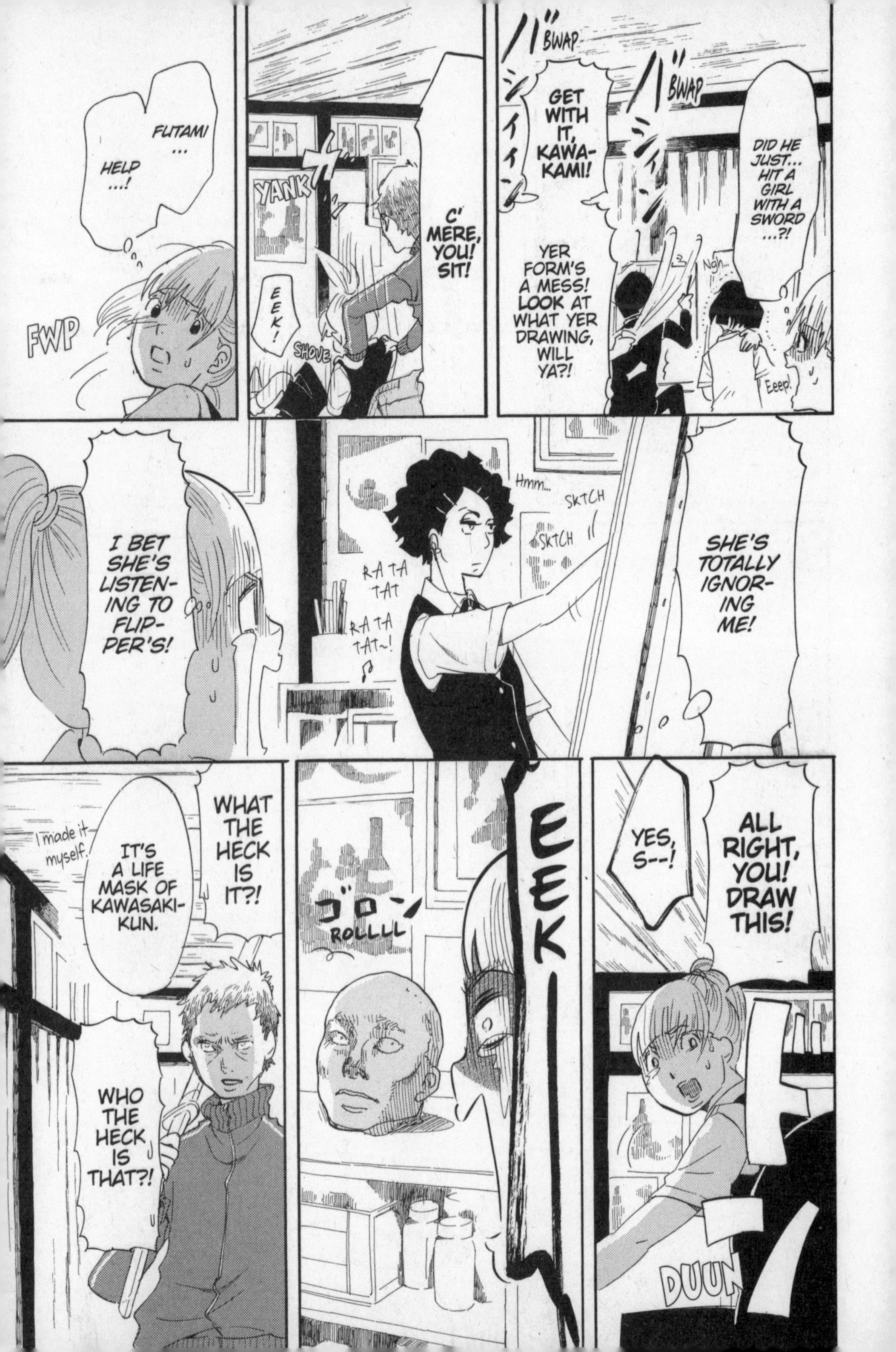
BWAP
BWAP
GET WITH IT, KAWA-KAMI!
DID HE JUST... HIT A GIRL WITH A SWORD...?!
YER FORM'S A MESS! LOOK AT WHAT YER DRAWING, WILL YA?!
Ngh...
Eeep.
YANK
C' MERE, YOU! SIT!
EEK!
SHOVE
FUTAMI...
HELP...!
FWP
SHE'S TOTALLY IGNOR-ING ME!
Hmm...
SKTCH
SKTCH
RATATAT
RATATAT~!
I BET SHE'S LISTEN-ING TO FLIP-PER'S!
ALL RIGHT, YOU! DRAW THIS!
YES, S--!
DUUN
EEK
ROLLLL
WHAT THE HECK IS IT?!
IT'S A LIFE MASK OF KAWASAKI-KUN.
I made it myself.
WHO THE HECK IS THAT?!

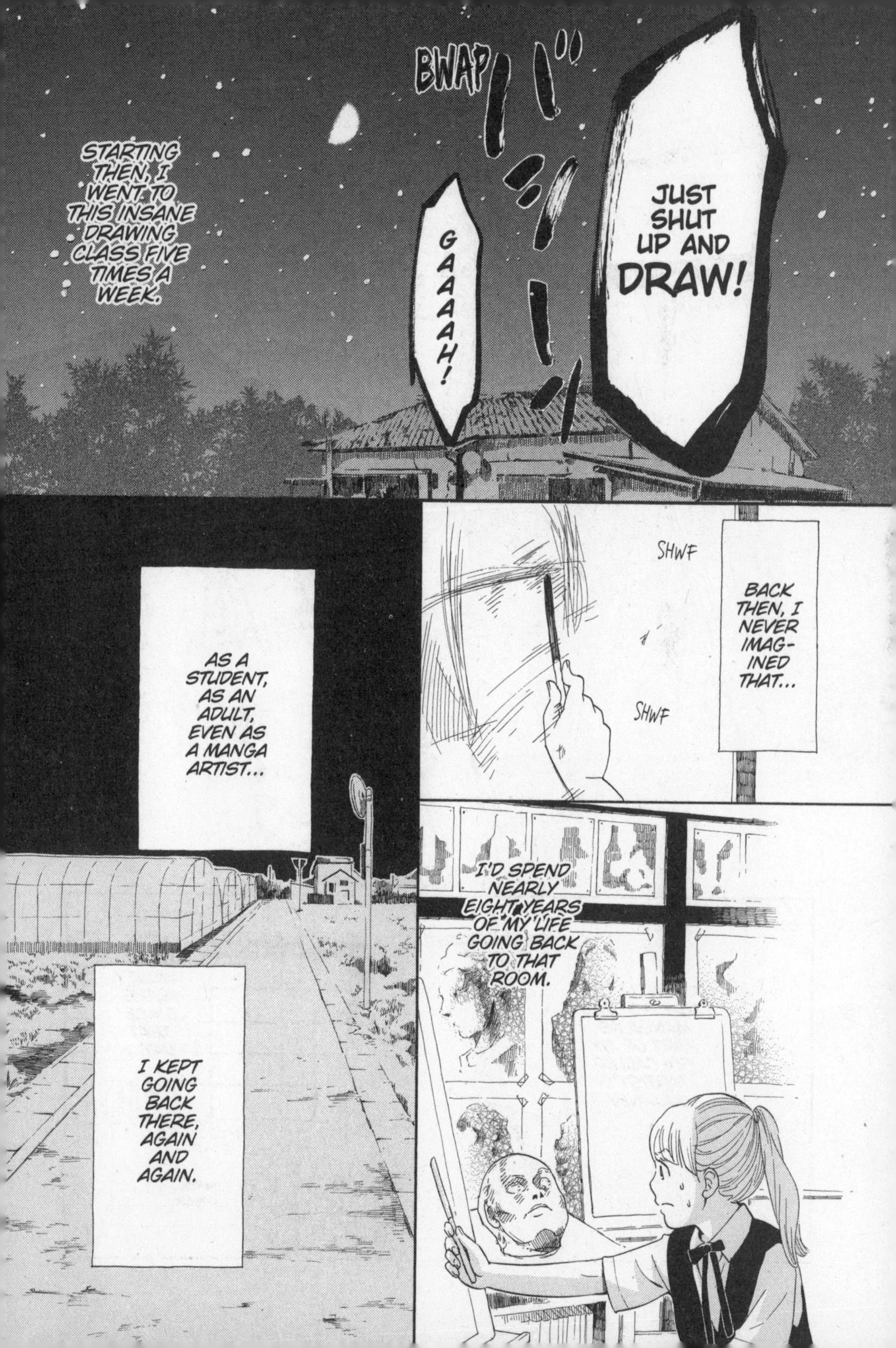
BWAP
JUST SHUT UP AND DRAW!
GAAAAAH!
STARTING THEN, I WENT TO THIS INSANE DRAWING CLASS FIVE TIMES A WEEK.
BACK THEN, I NEVER IMAG-INED THAT...
SHWF
SHWF
I'D SPEND NEARLY EIGHT YEARS OF MY LIFE GOING BACK TO THAT ROOM.
AS A STUDENT, AS AN ADULT, EVEN AS A MANGA ARTIST...
I KEPT GOING BACK THERE, AGAIN AND AGAIN.

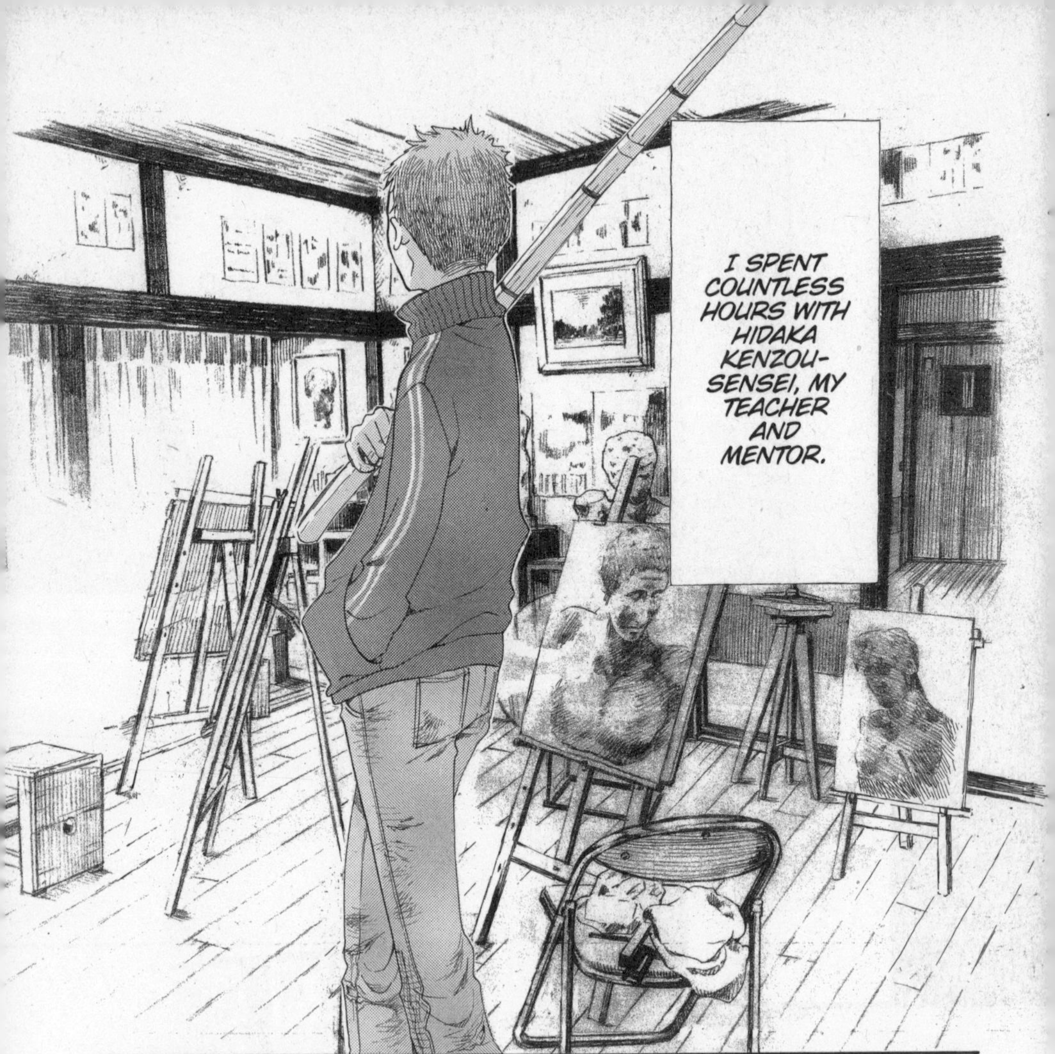
I SPENT COUNTLESS HOURS WITH HIDAKA KENZOU-SENSEI, MY TEACHER AND MENTOR.

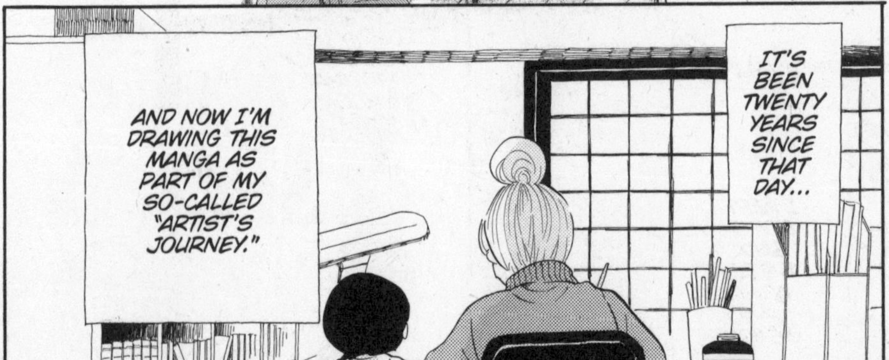
IT'S BEEN TWENTY YEARS SINCE THAT DAY...
AND NOW I'M DRAWING THIS MANGA AS PART OF MY SO-CALLED "ARTIST'S JOURNEY."

Blank
Canvas
My So-Called
Artist's Journey

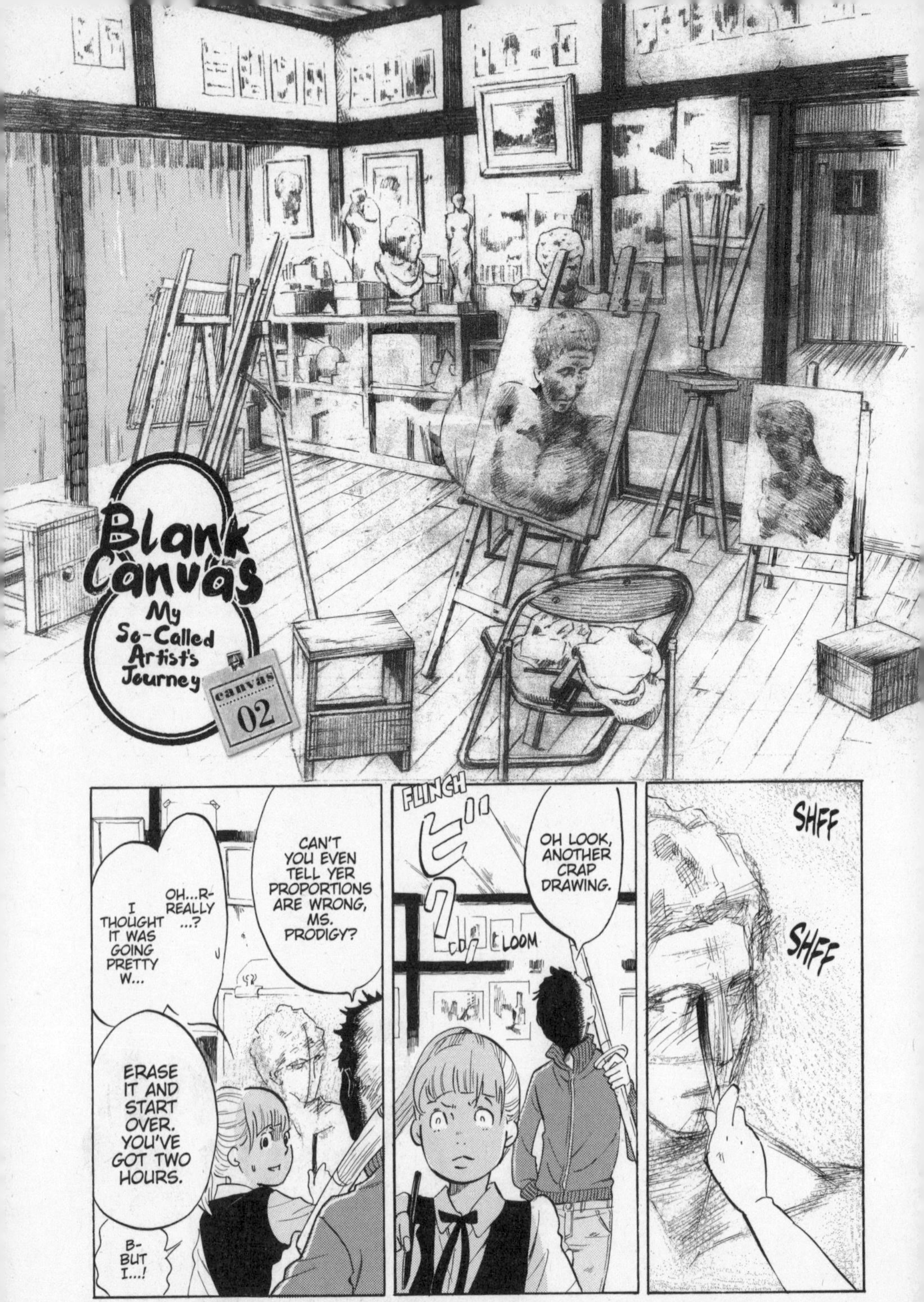
Blank Canvas
My So-Called Artist's Journey
canvas 02
SHFF
SHFF
FLINCH
OH LOOK, ANOTHER CRAP DRAWING.
LOOM
CAN'T YOU EVEN TELL YER PROPORTIONS ARE WRONG, MS. PRODIGY?
OH...R-REALLY ...?
I THOUGHT IT WAS GOING PRETTY W...
ERASE IT AND START OVER. YOU'VE GOT TWO HOURS.
B-BUT I...!

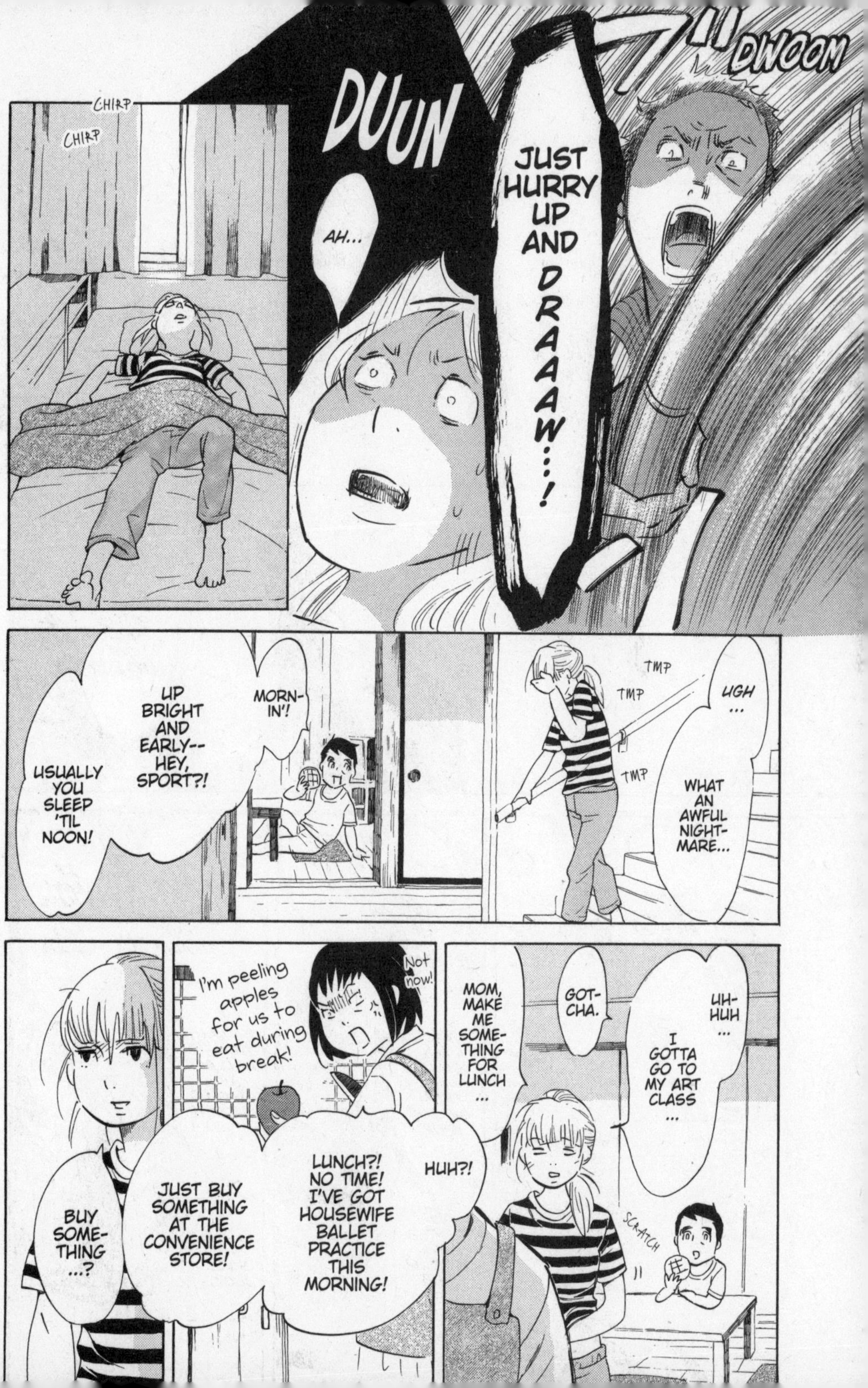
DWOOM
JUST HURRY UP AND DRAAAAW...!
DUUN
AH...
CHIRP
CHIRP
UGH...
WHAT AN AWFUL NIGHTMARE...
TMP
TMP
TMP
MORN-IN'!
UP BRIGHT AND EARLY--HEY, SPORT?!
USUALLY YOU SLEEP 'TIL NOON!
UH-HUH...
I GOTTA GO TO MY ART CLASS...
GOT-CHA.
MOM, MAKE ME SOMETHING FOR LUNCH...
HUH?!
SCRATCH
Not now!
I'm peeling apples for us to eat during break!
LUNCH?! NO TIME! I'VE GOT HOUSEWIFE BALLET PRACTICE THIS MORNING!
JUST BUY SOMETHING AT THE CONVENIENCE STORE!
BUY SOMETHING...?

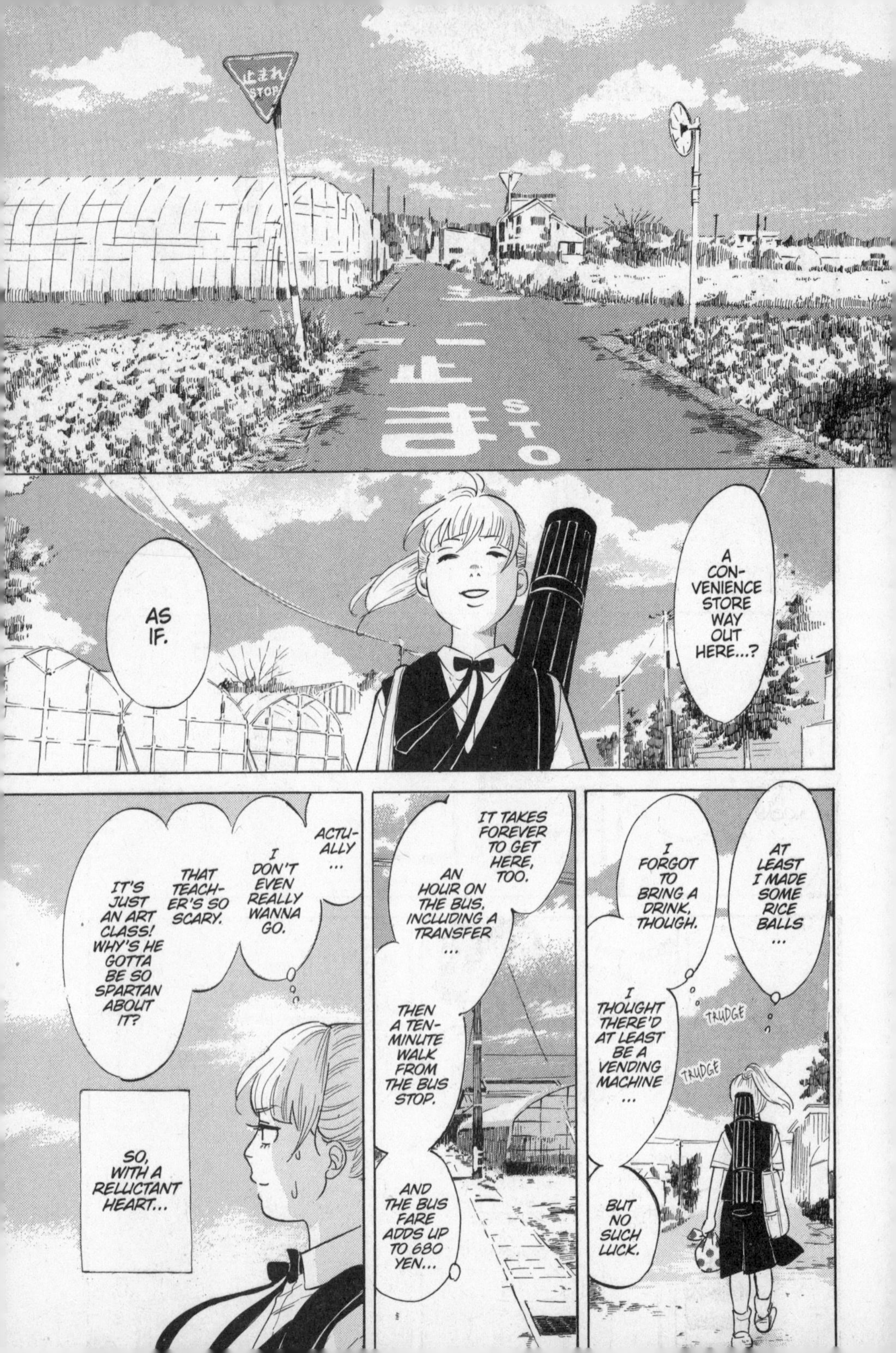
止まれ STOP
止まれ STOP
A CON-VENIENCE STORE WAY OUT HERE...?
AS IF.
AT LEAST I MADE SOME RICE BALLS...
I FORGOT TO BRING A DRINK, THOUGH.
TRUDGE
TRUDGE
I THOUGHT THERE'D AT LEAST BE A VENDING MACHINE...
BUT NO SUCH LUCK.
IT TAKES FOREVER TO GET HERE, TOO.
AN HOUR ON THE BUS, INCLUDING A TRANSFER...
THEN A TEN-MINUTE WALK FROM THE BUS STOP.
AND THE BUS FARE ADDS UP TO 680 YEN...
ACTU-ALLY...
I DON'T EVEN REALLY WANNA GO.
THAT TEACH-ER'S SO SCARY.
IT'S JUST AN ART CLASS! WHY'S HE GOTTA BE SO SPARTAN ABOUT IT?
SO, WITH A RELUCTANT HEART...

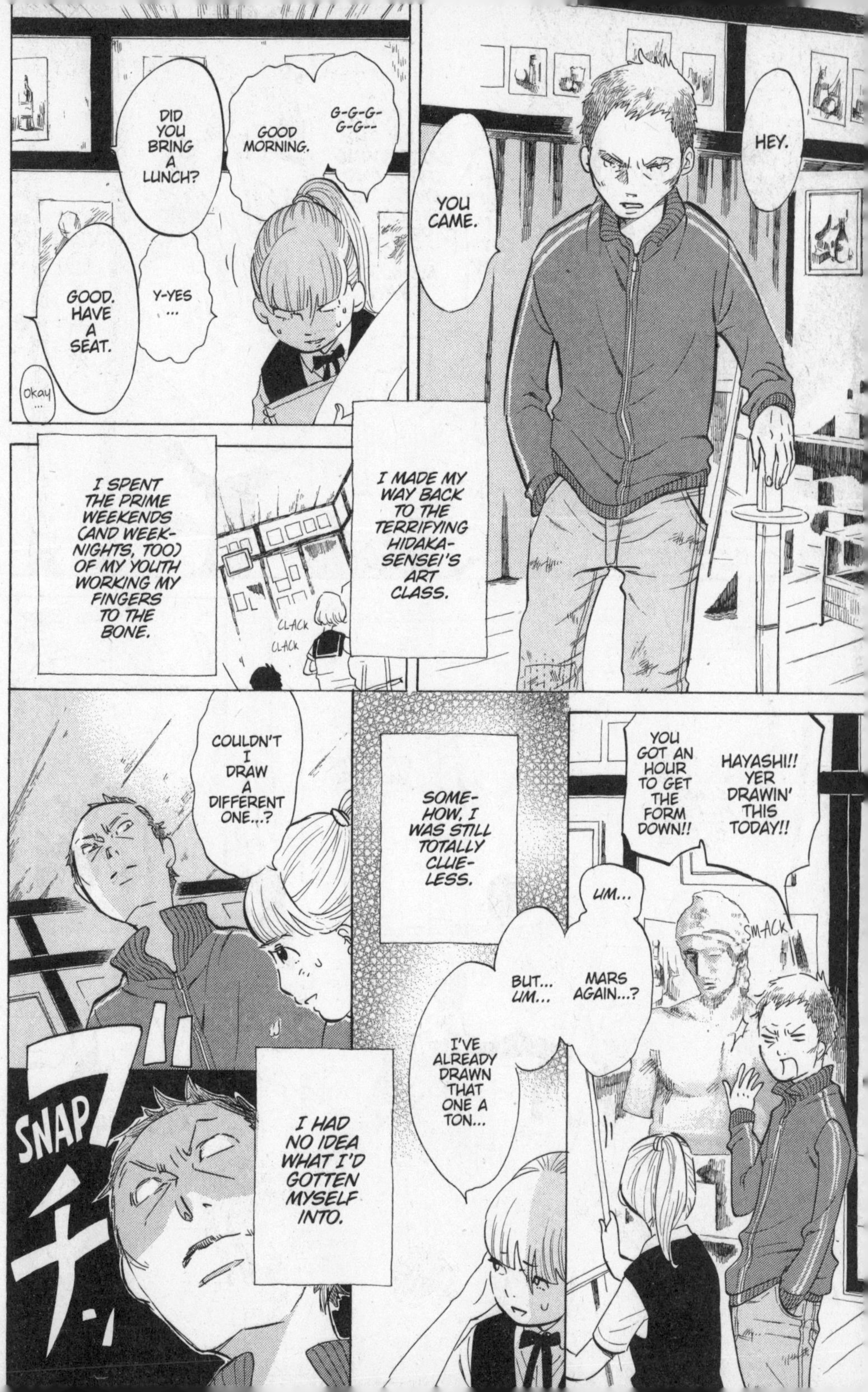
HEY.
YOU CAME.
I MADE MY WAY BACK TO THE TERRIFYING HIDAKA-SENSEI'S ART CLASS.
G-G-G-G-G--
GOOD MORNING.
DID YOU BRING A LUNCH?
Y-YES...
GOOD. HAVE A SEAT.
Okay...
I SPENT THE PRIME WEEKENDS (AND WEEK-NIGHTS, TOO) OF MY YOUTH WORKING MY FINGERS TO THE BONE.
CLACK
CLACK
HAYASHI!! YER DRAWIN' THIS TODAY!!
YOU GOT AN HOUR TO GET THE FORM DOWN!!
SMACK
UM...
MARS AGAIN...?
BUT... UM...
I'VE ALREADY DRAWN THAT ONE A TON...
SOME-HOW, I WAS STILL TOTALLY CLUE-LESS.
COULDN'T I DRAW A DIFFERENT ONE...?
SNAP
I HAD NO IDEA WHAT I'D GOTTEN MYSELF INTO.

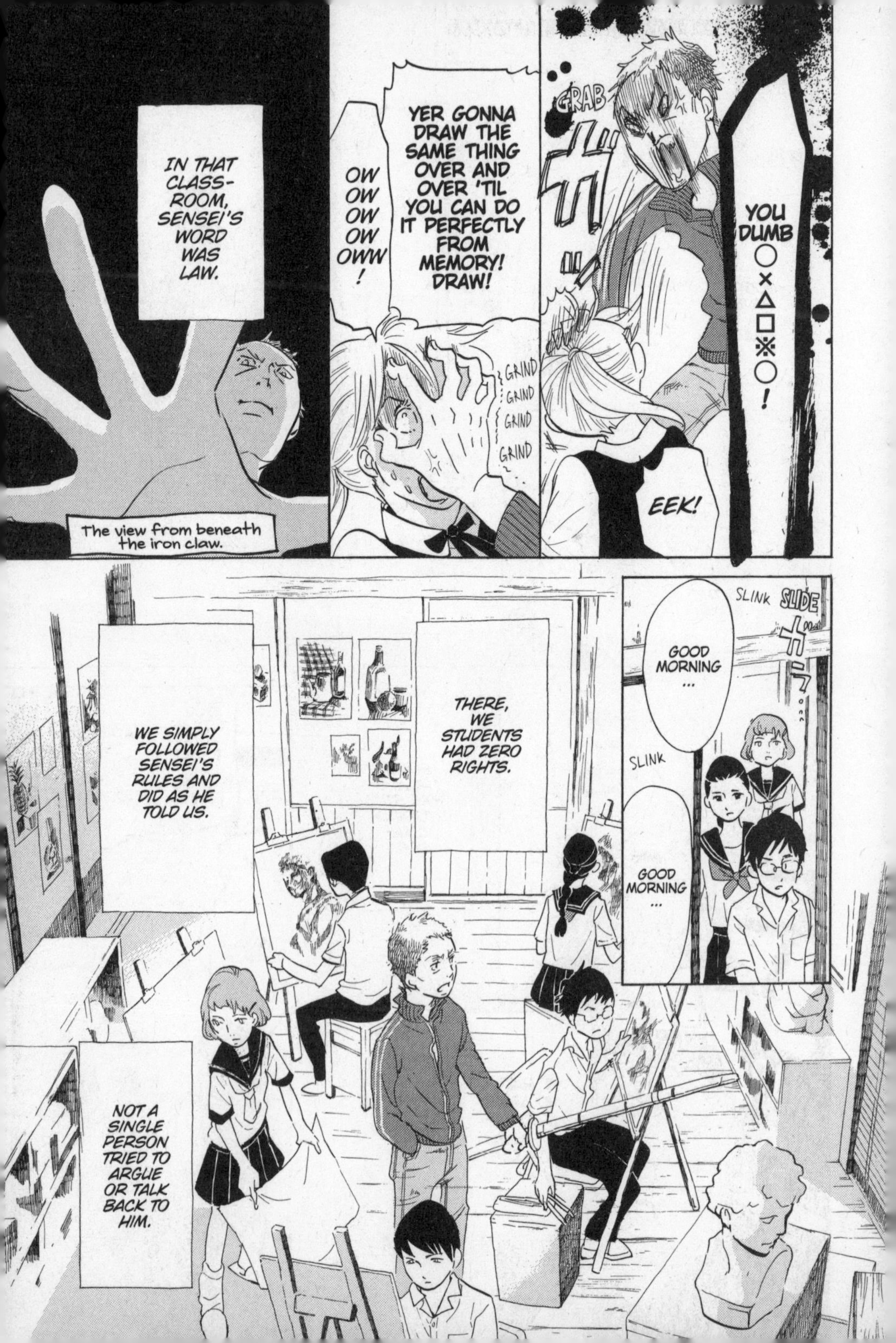
GRAB
YOU DUMB ○×△□※○!
EEK!
YER GONNA DRAW THE SAME THING OVER AND OVER 'TIL YOU CAN DO IT PERFECTLY FROM MEMORY! DRAW!
OW OW OW OW OWW!
GRIND GRIND GRIND GRIND
IN THAT CLASSROOM, SENSEI'S WORD WAS LAW.
The view from beneath the iron claw.
SLIDE
SLINK
GOOD MORNING...
SLINK
GOOD MORNING...
THERE, WE STUDENTS HAD ZERO RIGHTS.
WE SIMPLY FOLLOWED SENSEI'S RULES AND DID AS HE TOLD US.
NOT A SINGLE PERSON TRIED TO ARGUE OR TALK BACK TO HIM.

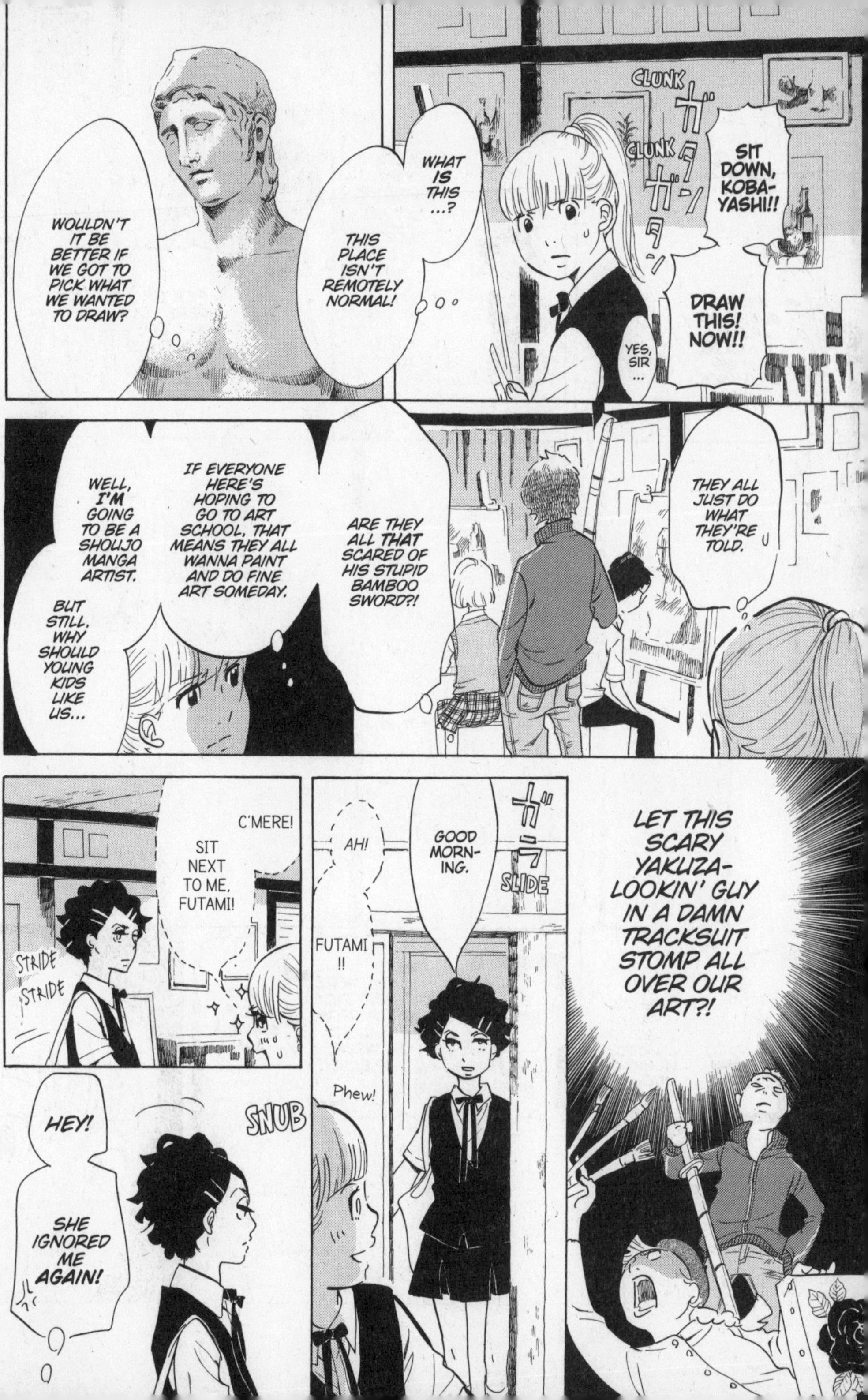
SIT DOWN, KOBA-YASHI!!
CLUNK
CLUNK
DRAW THIS! NOW!!
YES, SIR...
WHAT IS THIS ...?
THIS PLACE ISN'T REMOTELY NORMAL!
WOULDN'T IT BE BETTER IF WE GOT TO PICK WHAT WE WANTED TO DRAW?
THEY ALL JUST DO WHAT THEY'RE TOLD.
ARE THEY ALL THAT SCARED OF HIS STUPID BAMBOO SWORD?!
IF EVERYONE HERE'S HOPING TO GO TO ART SCHOOL, THAT MEANS THEY ALL WANNA PAINT AND DO FINE ART SOMEDAY.
WELL, I'M GOING TO BE A SHOUJO MANGA ARTIST.
BUT STILL, WHY SHOULD YOUNG KIDS LIKE US...
LET THIS SCARY YAKUZA-LOOKIN' GUY IN A DAMN TRACKSUIT STOMP ALL OVER OUR ART?!
SLIDE
GOOD MORN-ING.
AH!
FUTAMI !!
Phew!
C'MERE!
SIT NEXT TO ME, FUTAMI!
STRIDE
STRIDE
SNUB
HEY!
SHE IGNORED ME AGAIN!

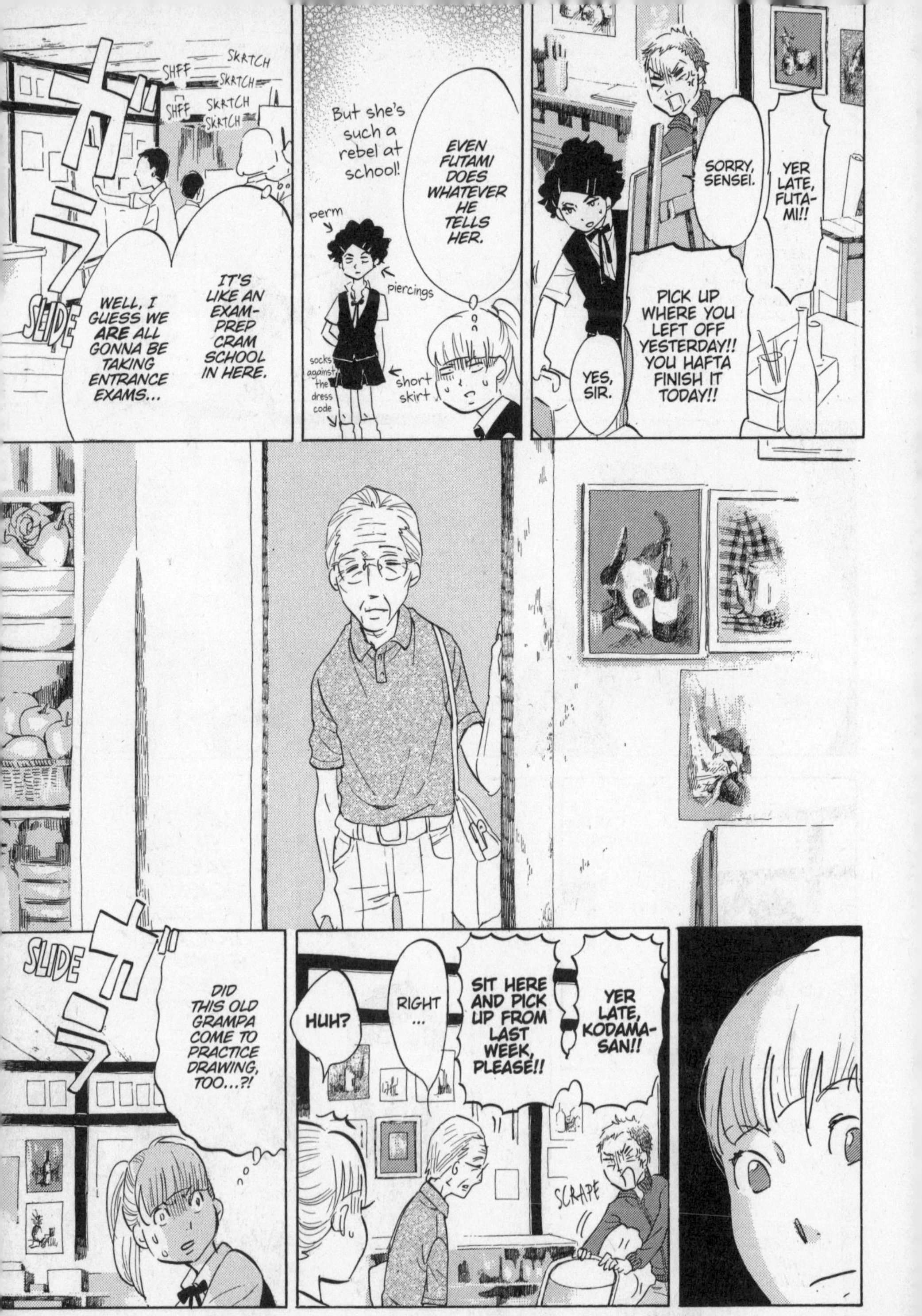
YER LATE, FUTAMI!!
SORRY, SENSEI.
PICK UP WHERE YOU LEFT OFF YESTERDAY!! YOU HAFTA FINISH IT TODAY!!
YES, SIR.
EVEN FUTAMI DOES WHATEVER HE TELLS HER.
But she's such a rebel at school!
perm
piercings
socks against the dress code
short skirt
SKRTCH
SKRTCH
SHFF
SKRTCH
SHFF
SKRTCH
SLIDE
IT'S LIKE AN EXAM-PREP CRAM SCHOOL IN HERE.
WELL, I GUESS WE ARE ALL GONNA BE TAKING ENTRANCE EXAMS...
YER LATE, KODAMA-SAN!!
SIT HERE AND PICK UP FROM LAST WEEK, PLEASE!!
RIGHT ...
HUH?
SCRAPE
SLIDE
DID THIS OLD GRAMPA COME TO PRACTICE DRAWING, TOO...?!

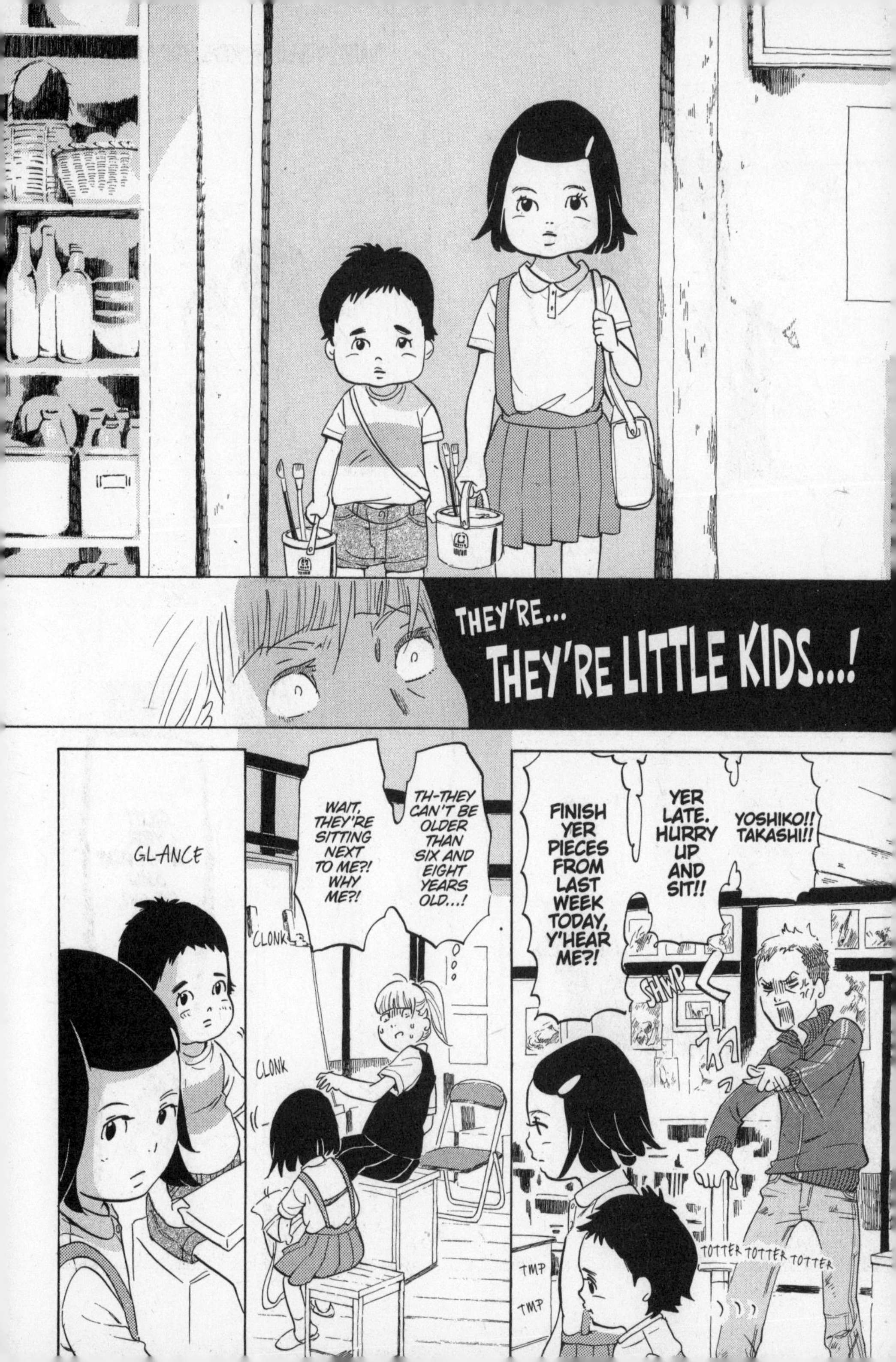
THEY'RE...
THEY'RE LITTLE KIDS...!
YOSHIKO!! TAKASHI!!
YER LATE. HURRY UP AND SIT!!
FINISH YER PIECES FROM LAST WEEK TODAY, Y'HEAR ME?!
SHWP
TOTTER TOTTER TOTTER
TMP
TMP
TH-THEY CAN'T BE OLDER THAN SIX AND EIGHT YEARS OLD...!
WAIT, THEY'RE SITTING NEXT TO ME?! WHY ME?!
CLONK
CLONK
GLANCE

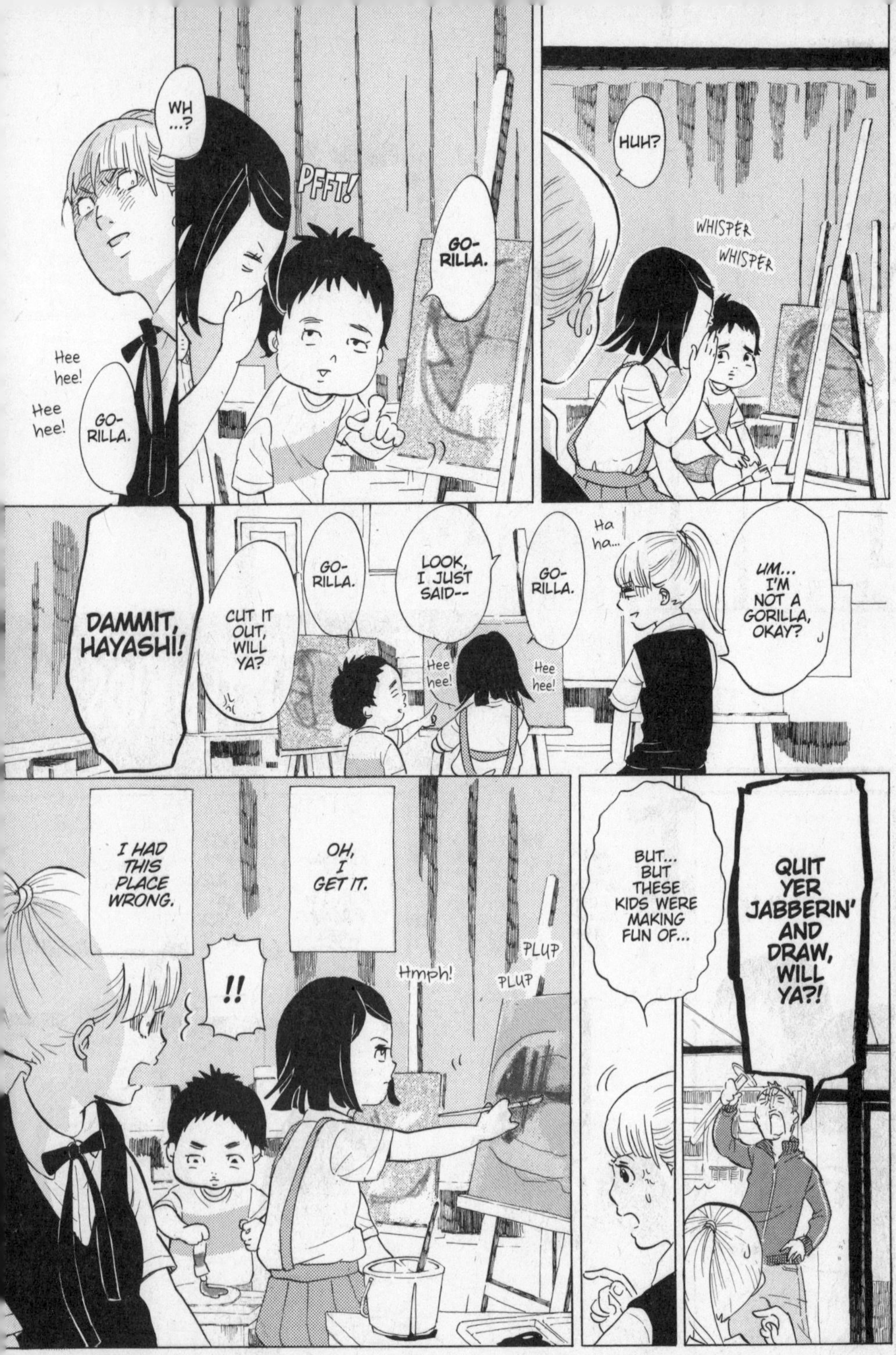
HUH?
WHISPER
WHISPER
GO-RILLA.
PFFT!
WH ...?
Hee hee!
Hee hee!
GO-RILLA.
UM... I'M NOT A GORILLA, OKAY?
Ha ha...
GO-RILLA.
LOOK, I JUST SAID--
GO-RILLA.
Hee hee!
Hee hee!
CUT IT OUT, WILL YA?
DAMMIT, HAYASHI!
QUIT YER JABBERIN' AND DRAW, WILL YA?!
BUT... BUT THESE KIDS WERE MAKING FUN OF...
OH, I GET IT.
I HAD THIS PLACE WRONG.
PLUP
PLUP
Hmph!
!!

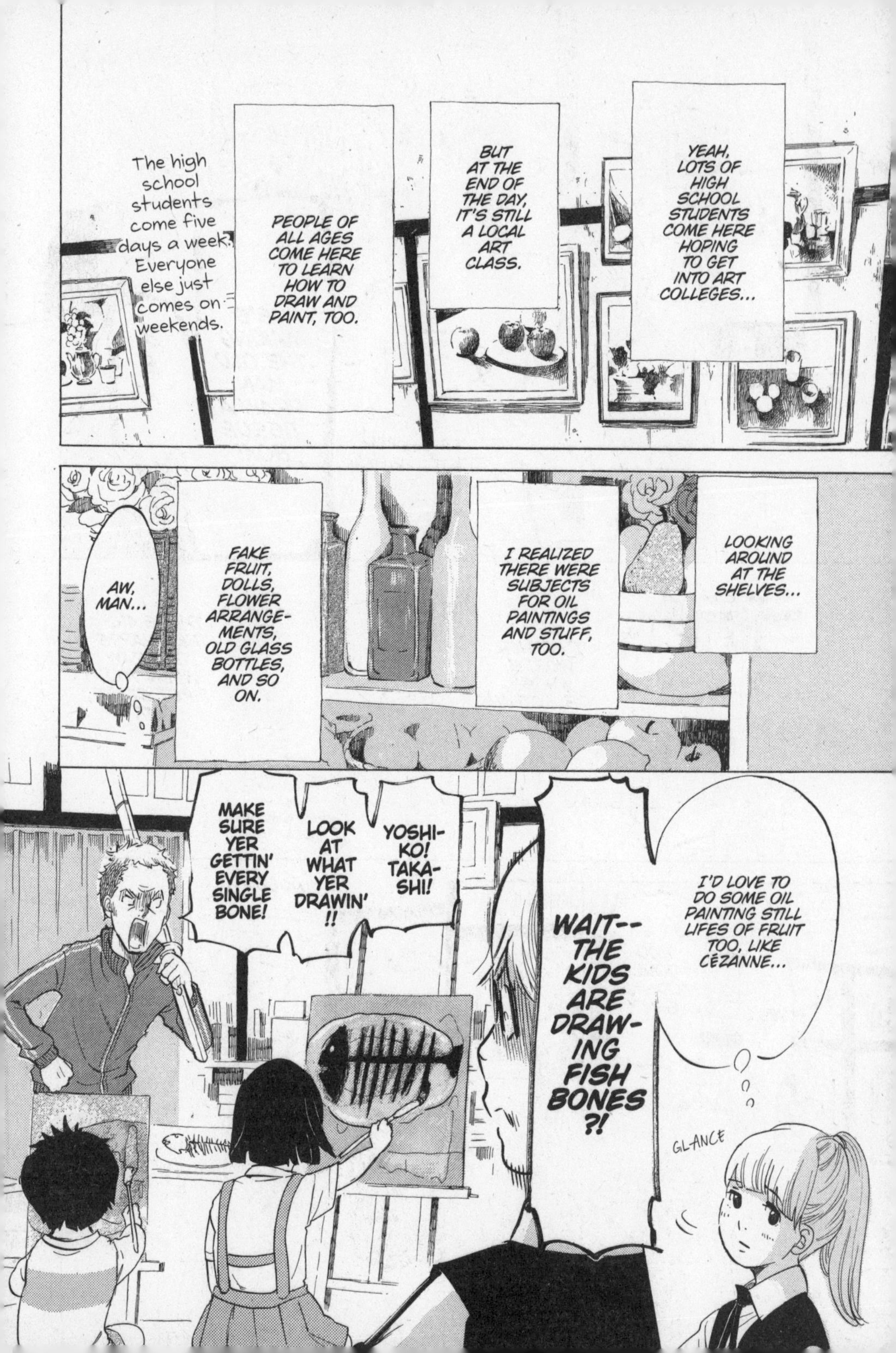
YEAH, LOTS OF HIGH SCHOOL STUDENTS COME HERE HOPING TO GET INTO ART COLLEGES...
BUT AT THE END OF THE DAY, IT'S STILL A LOCAL ART CLASS.
PEOPLE OF ALL AGES COME HERE TO LEARN HOW TO DRAW AND PAINT, TOO.
The high school students come five days a week. Everyone else just comes on weekends.
LOOKING AROUND AT THE SHELVES...
I REALIZED THERE WERE SUBJECTS FOR OIL PAINTINGS AND STUFF, TOO.
FAKE FRUIT, DOLLS, FLOWER ARRANGE-MENTS, OLD GLASS BOTTLES, AND SO ON.
AW, MAN...
I'D LOVE TO DO SOME OIL PAINTING STILL LIFES OF FRUIT TOO, LIKE CÉZANNE...
GLANCE
WAIT--THE KIDS ARE DRAW-ING FISH BONES?!
YOSHI-KO! TAKA-SHI!
LOOK AT WHAT YER DRAWIN'!!
MAKE SURE YER GETTIN' EVERY SINGLE BONE!

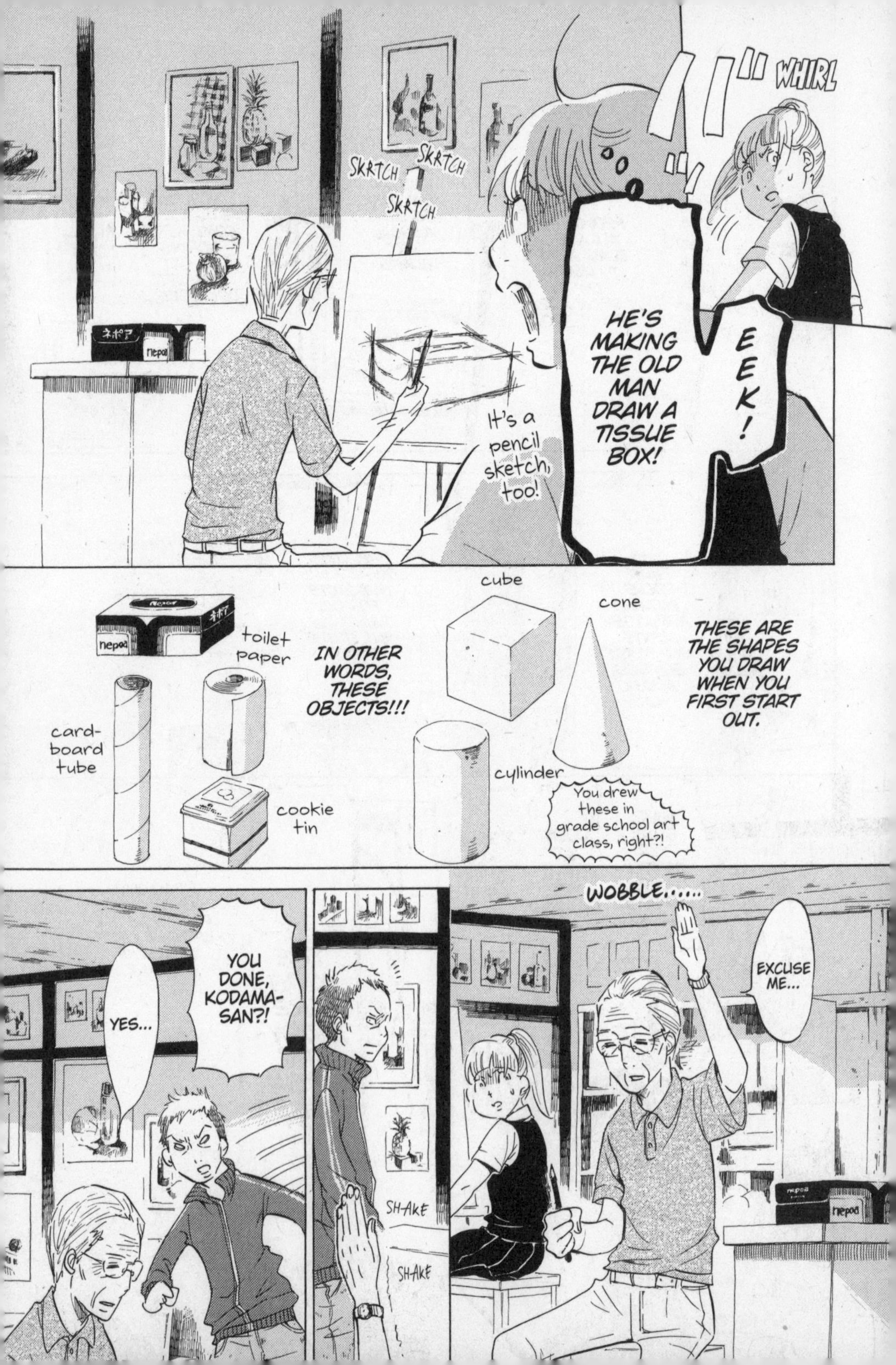

WHIRL
EEK!
HE'S MAKING THE OLD MAN DRAW A TISSUE BOX!
It's a pencil sketch, too!
SKRTCH
SKRTCH
SKRTCH
THESE ARE THE SHAPES YOU DRAW WHEN YOU FIRST START OUT.
cone
cube
IN OTHER WORDS, THESE OBJECTS!!!
toilet paper
card-board tube
cylinder
You drew these in grade school art class, right?!
cookie tin
WOBBLE.....
EXCUSE ME...
SHAKE
SHAKE
YOU DONE, KODAMA-SAN?!
YES...

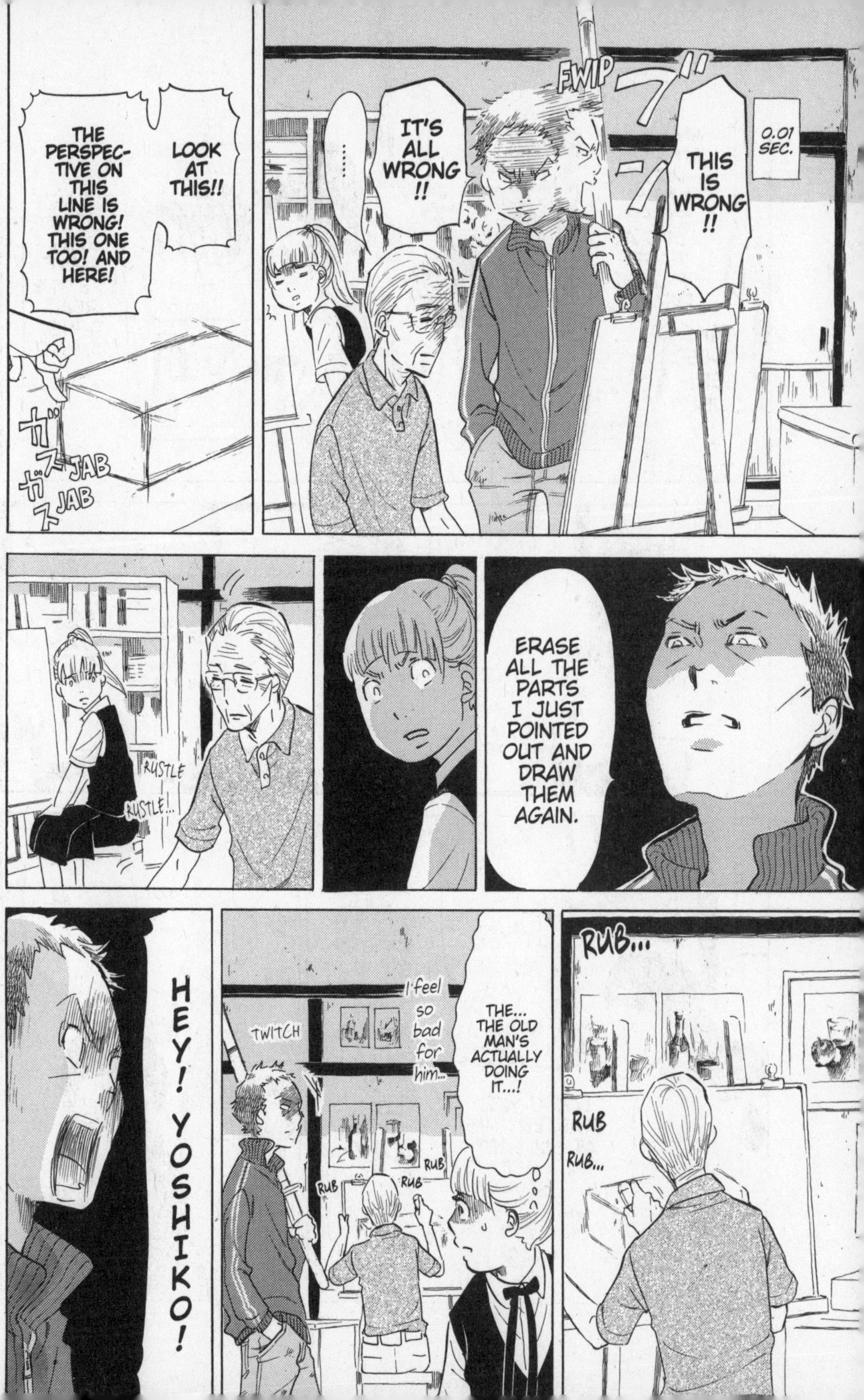
0.01 SEC.
THIS IS WRONG!!
FWIP
IT'S ALL WRONG!!
......
LOOK AT THIS!!
THE PERSPEC-TIVE ON THIS LINE IS WRONG! THIS ONE TOO! AND HERE!
JAB
JAB
ERASE ALL THE PARTS I JUST POINTED OUT AND DRAW THEM AGAIN.
RUSTLE
RUSTLE...
RUB...
RUB
RUB...
THE... THE OLD MAN'S ACTUALLY DOING IT...!
I feel so bad for him...
TWITCH
RUB
RUB
RUB
HEY! YOSHIKO!

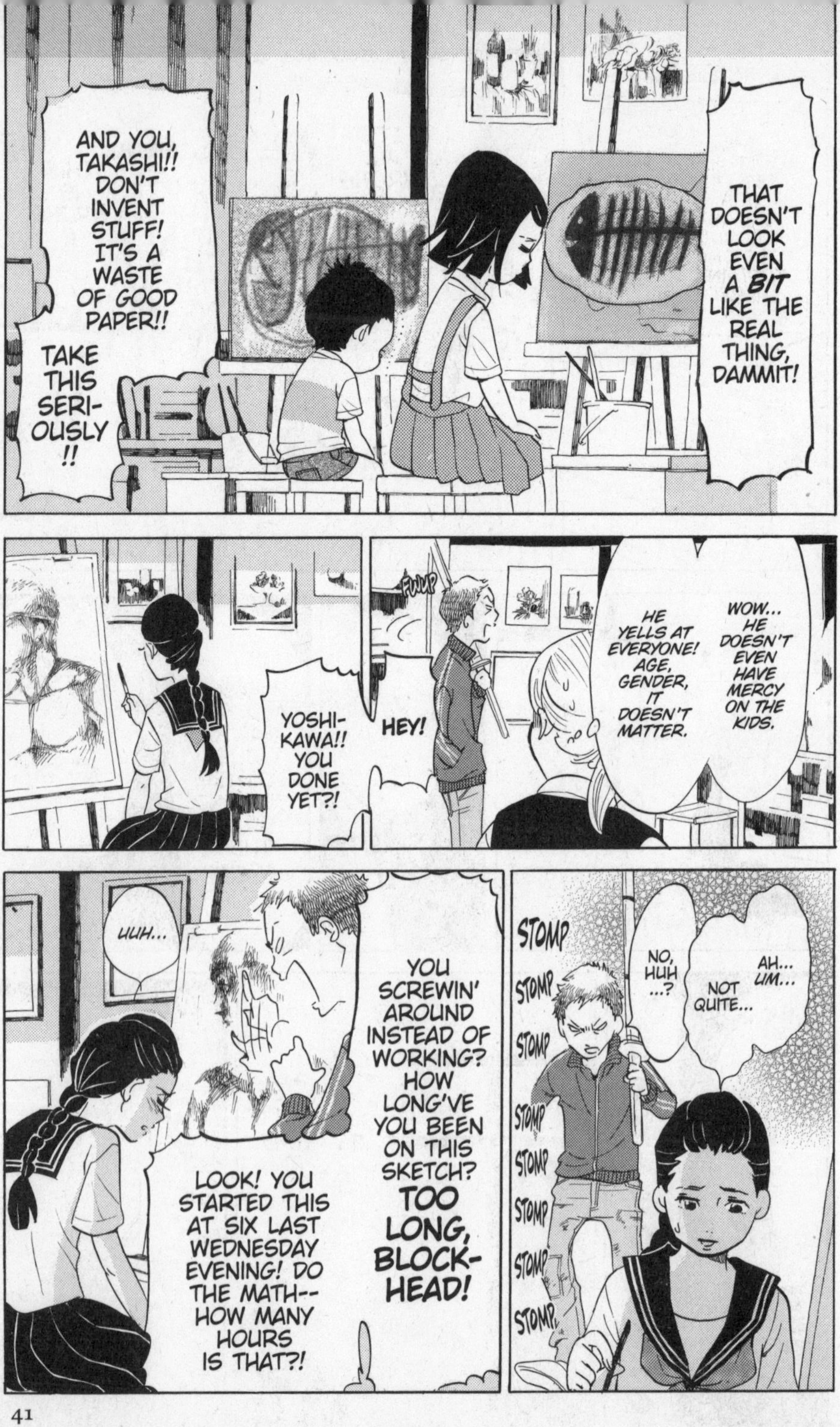
THAT DOESN'T LOOK EVEN A *BIT* LIKE THE REAL THING, DAMMIT!
AND YOU, TAKASHI!! DON'T INVENT STUFF! IT'S A WASTE OF GOOD PAPER!!
TAKE THIS SERI-OUSLY!!
WOW... HE DOESN'T EVEN HAVE MERCY ON THE KIDS.
HE YELLS AT EVERYONE! AGE, GENDER, IT DOESN'T MATTER.
HEY!
YOSHI-KAWA!! YOU DONE YET?!
STOMP
AH... UM... NOT QUITE...
NO, HUH ...?
STOMP STOMP STOMP STOMP STOMP STOMP
YOU SCREWIN' AROUND INSTEAD OF WORKING? HOW LONG'VE YOU BEEN ON THIS SKETCH? **TOO LONG, BLOCK-HEAD!**
LOOK! YOU STARTED THIS AT SIX LAST WEDNESDAY EVENING! DO THE MATH-- HOW MANY HOURS IS THAT?!
UUH...

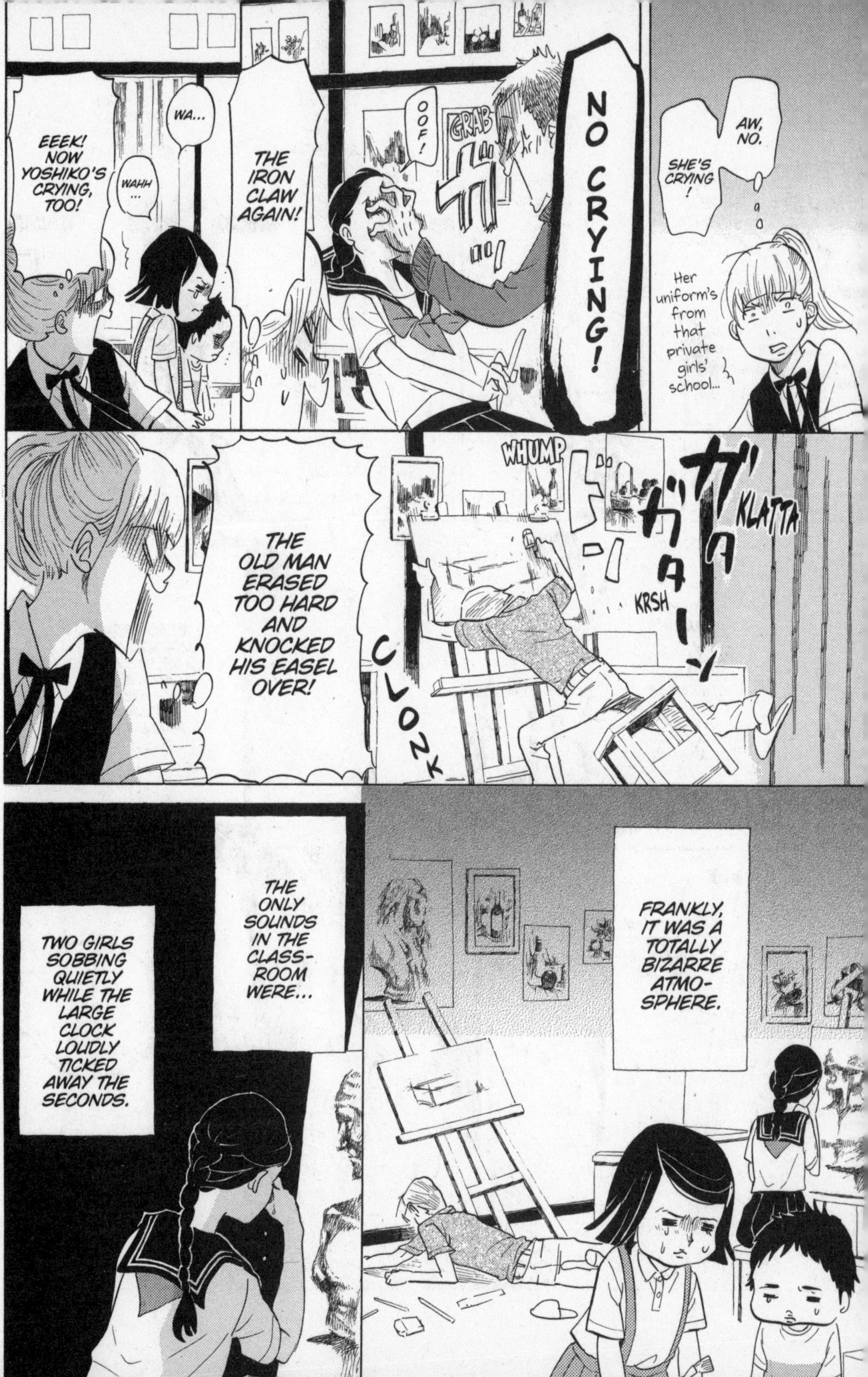
AW, NO.
SHE'S CRYING!
Her uniform's from that private girls' school...
NO CRYING!
GRAB
OOF!
THE IRON CLAW AGAIN!
WA...
WAHH...
EEEK! NOW YOSHIKO'S CRYING, TOO!
WHUMP
KLATTA
KRSH
CLONK
THE OLD MAN ERASED TOO HARD AND KNOCKED HIS EASEL OVER!
FRANKLY, IT WAS A TOTALLY BIZARRE ATMO-SPHERE.
THE ONLY SOUNDS IN THE CLASS-ROOM WERE...
TWO GIRLS SOBBING QUIETLY WHILE THE LARGE CLOCK LOUDLY TICKED AWAY THE SECONDS.

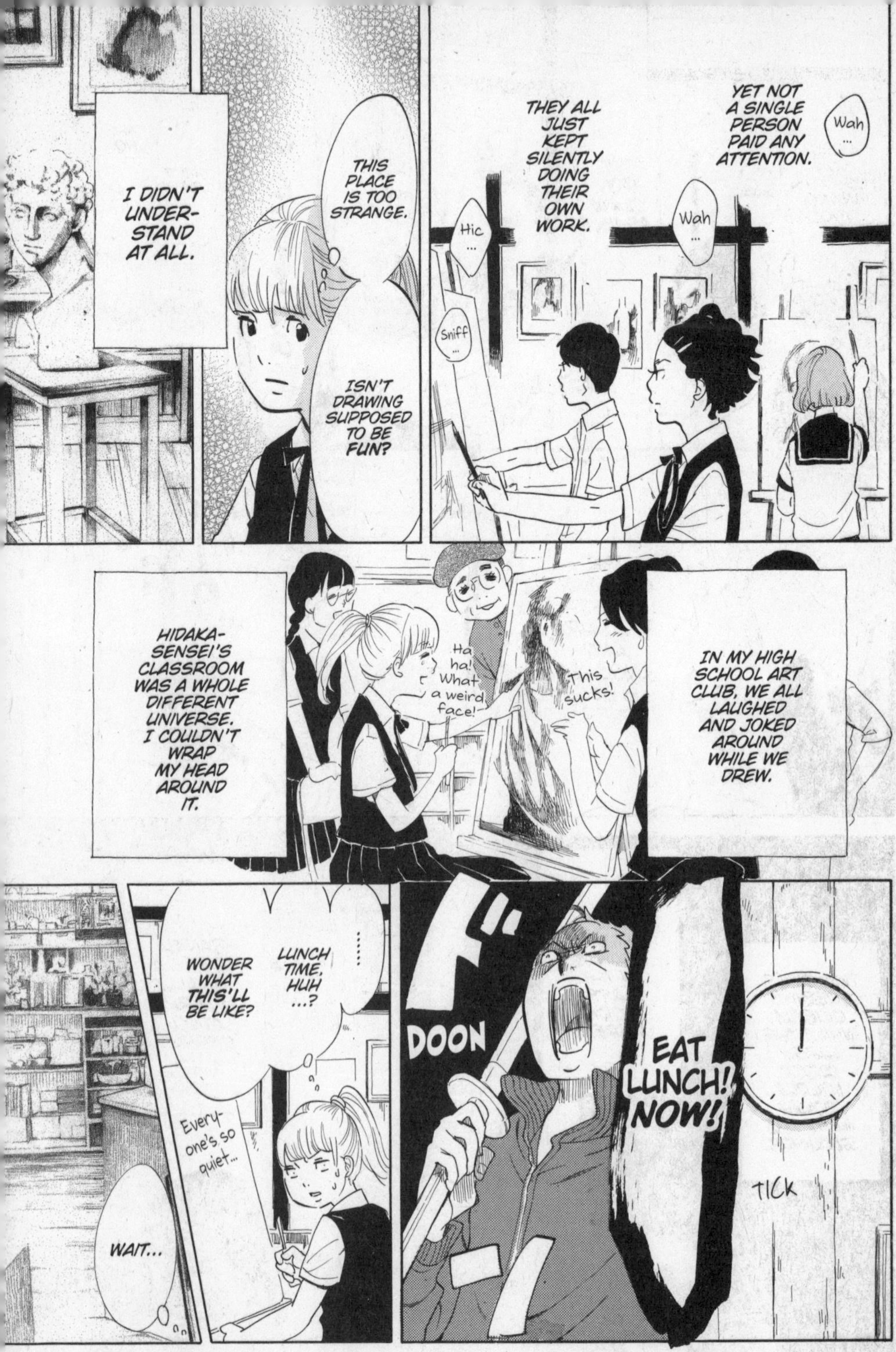

YET NOT A SINGLE PERSON PAID ANY ATTENTION.
Wah ...
THEY ALL JUST KEPT SILENTLY DOING THEIR OWN WORK.
Wah ...
Hic ...
Sniff ...
THIS PLACE IS TOO STRANGE.
ISN'T DRAWING SUPPOSED TO BE FUN?
I DIDN'T UNDER-STAND AT ALL.
IN MY HIGH SCHOOL ART CLUB, WE ALL LAUGHED AND JOKED AROUND WHILE WE DREW.
This sucks!
Ha ha! What a weird face!
HIDAKA-SENSEI'S CLASSROOM WAS A WHOLE DIFFERENT UNIVERSE. I COULDN'T WRAP MY HEAD AROUND IT.
EAT LUNCH! NOW!
DOON
TICK
......
LUNCH TIME, HUH ...?
WONDER WHAT THIS'LL BE LIKE?
Every-one's so quiet...
WAIT...

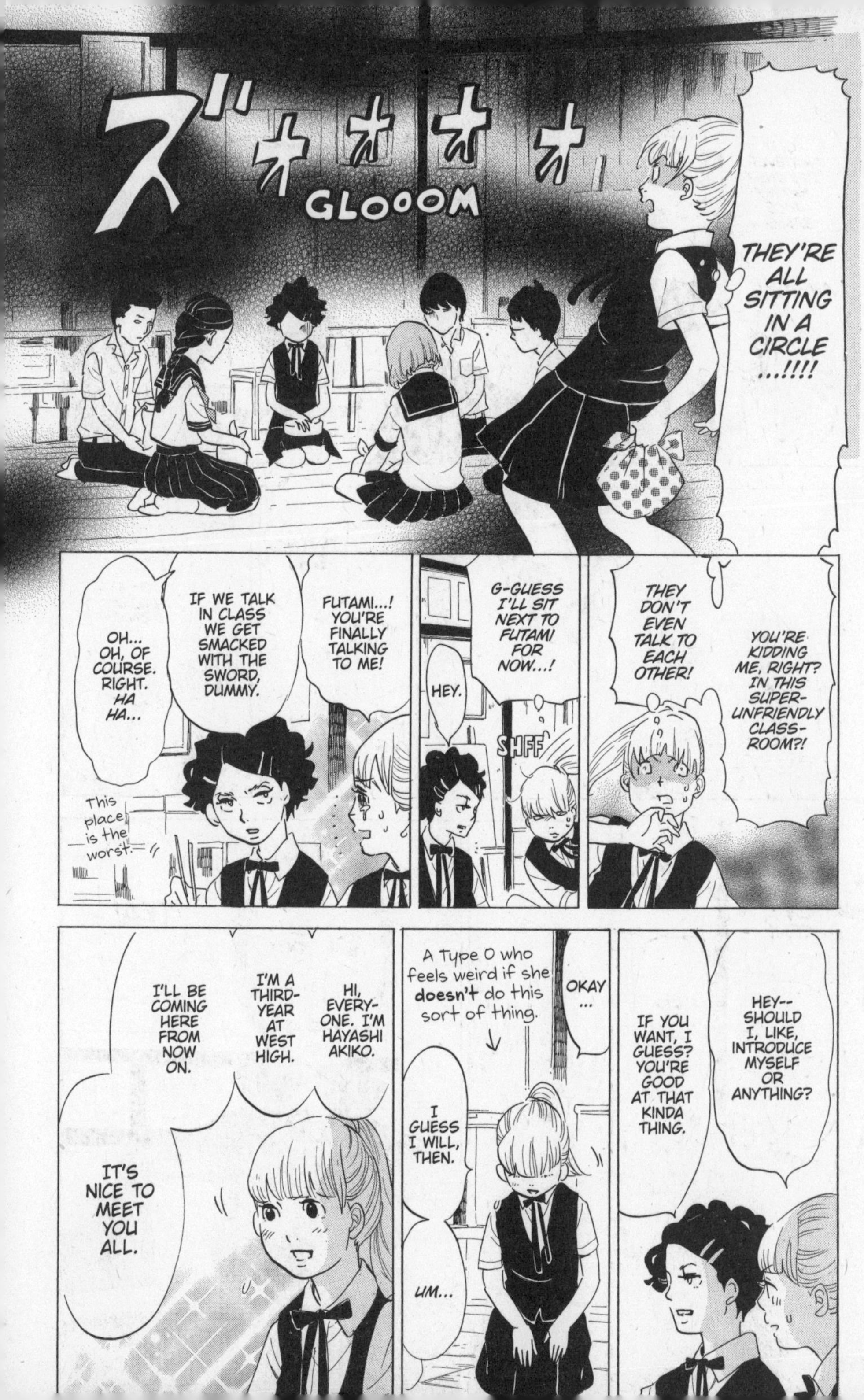
THEY'RE ALL SITTING IN A CIRCLE ...!!!!
ズォォォォ
GLOOOM
YOU'RE KIDDING ME, RIGHT? IN THIS SUPER-UNFRIENDLY CLASSROOM?!
THEY DON'T EVEN TALK TO EACH OTHER!
G-GUESS I'LL SIT NEXT TO FUTAMI FOR NOW...!
SHFF
HEY.
FUTAMI...! YOU'RE FINALLY TALKING TO ME!
IF WE TALK IN CLASS WE GET SMACKED WITH THE SWORD, DUMMY.
OH... OH, OF COURSE. RIGHT. HA HA...
This place is the worst.
HEY-- SHOULD I, LIKE, INTRODUCE MYSELF OR ANYTHING?
IF YOU WANT, I GUESS? YOU'RE GOOD AT THAT KINDA THING.
OKAY ...
A Type O who feels weird if she **doesn't** do this sort of thing.
I GUESS I WILL, THEN.
UM...
HI, EVERY-ONE. I'M HAYASHI AKIKO.
I'M A THIRD-YEAR AT WEST HIGH.
I'LL BE COMING HERE FROM NOW ON.
IT'S NICE TO MEET YOU ALL.

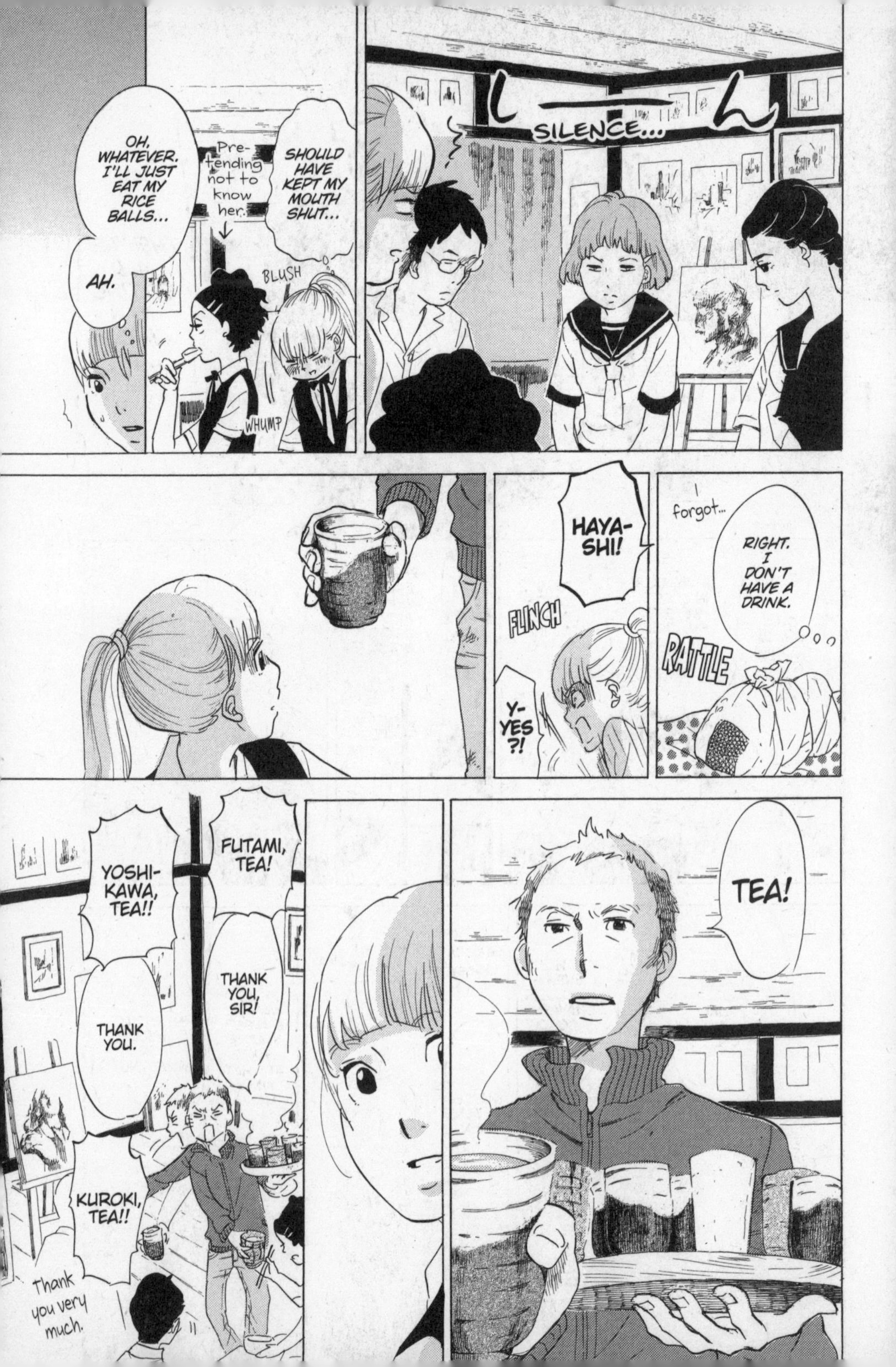
しーん
SILENCE...
SHOULD HAVE KEPT MY MOUTH SHUT...
BLUSH
Pretending not to know her.
OH, WHATEVER. I'LL JUST EAT MY RICE BALLS...
AH.
WHUMP
I forgot...
RIGHT. I DON'T HAVE A DRINK.
RATTLE
HAYA-SHI!
FLINCH
Y-YES?!
TEA!
FUTAMI, TEA!
YOSHI-KAWA, TEA!!
THANK YOU, SIR!
THANK YOU.
KUROKI, TEA!!
Thank you very much.

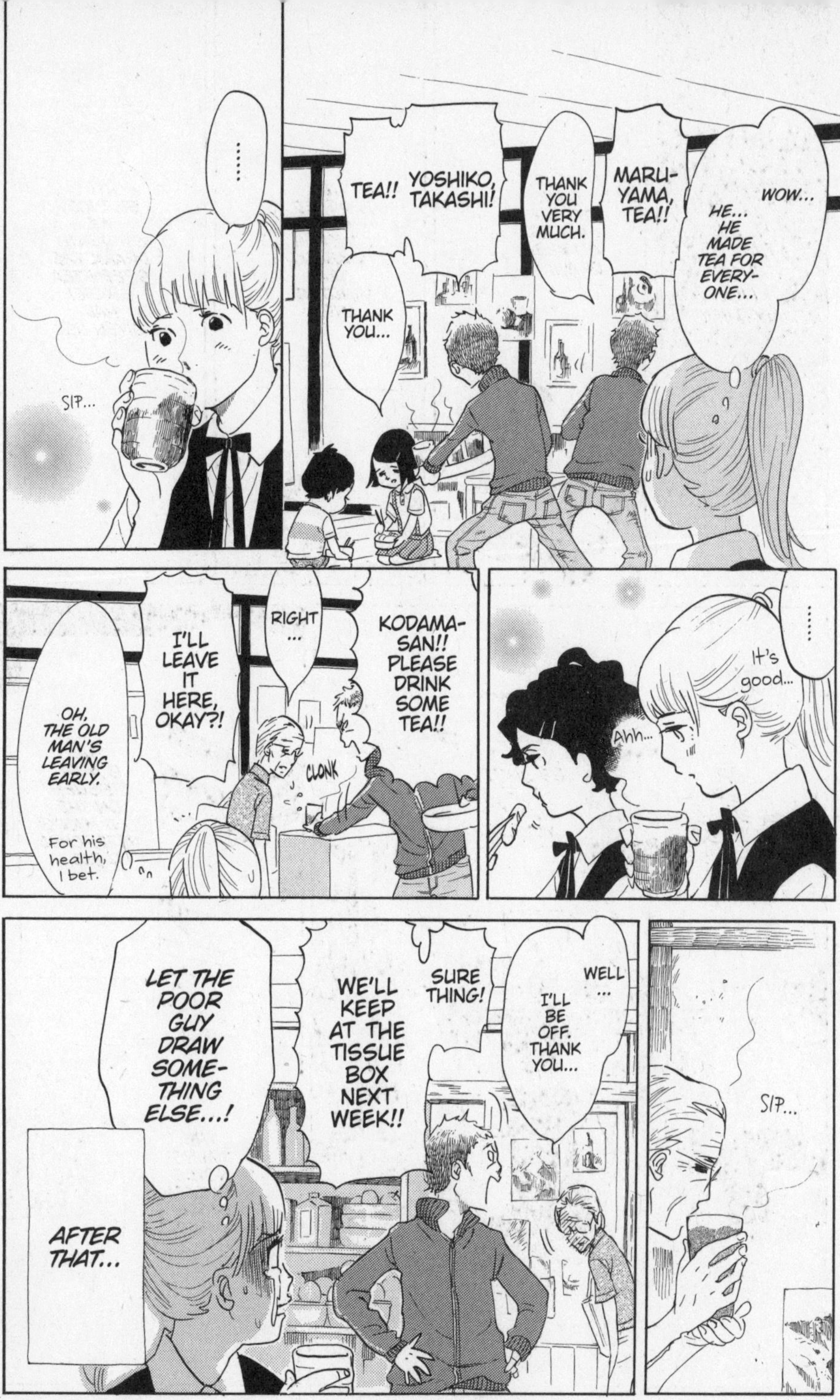
WOW... HE... HE MADE TEA FOR EVERYONE...
MARU-YAMA, TEA!!
THANK YOU VERY MUCH.
YOSHIKO, TAKASHI!
TEA!!
THANK YOU...
......
SIP...
......
It's good...
Ahh...
KODAMA-SAN!! PLEASE DRINK SOME TEA!!
RIGHT...
I'LL LEAVE IT HERE, OKAY?!
CLONK
OH, THE OLD MAN'S LEAVING EARLY.
For his health, I bet.
SIP...
WELL... I'LL BE OFF. THANK YOU...
SURE THING!
WE'LL KEEP AT THE TISSUE BOX NEXT WEEK!!
LET THE POOR GUY DRAW SOMETHING ELSE...!
AFTER THAT...

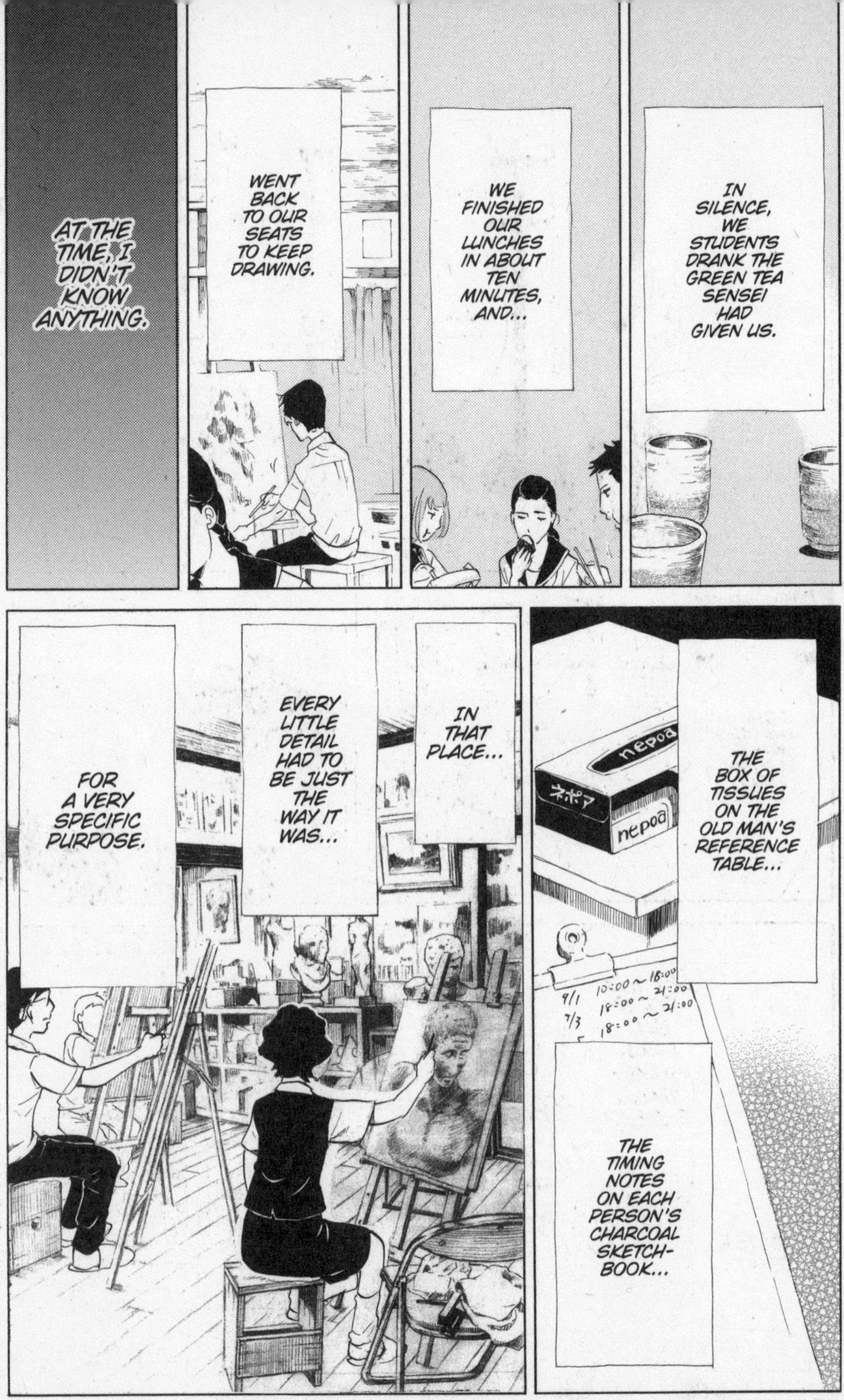
IN SILENCE, WE STUDENTS DRANK THE GREEN TEA SENSEI HAD GIVEN US.
WE FINISHED OUR LUNCHES IN ABOUT TEN MINUTES, AND...
WENT BACK TO OUR SEATS TO KEEP DRAWING.
AT THE TIME, I DIDN'T KNOW ANYTHING.
THE BOX OF TISSUES ON THE OLD MAN'S REFERENCE TABLE...
nepoa
ネポア
nepoa
THE TIMING NOTES ON EACH PERSON'S CHARCOAL SKETCH-BOOK...
IN THAT PLACE...
EVERY LITTLE DETAIL HAD TO BE JUST THE WAY IT WAS...
FOR A VERY SPECIFIC PURPOSE.

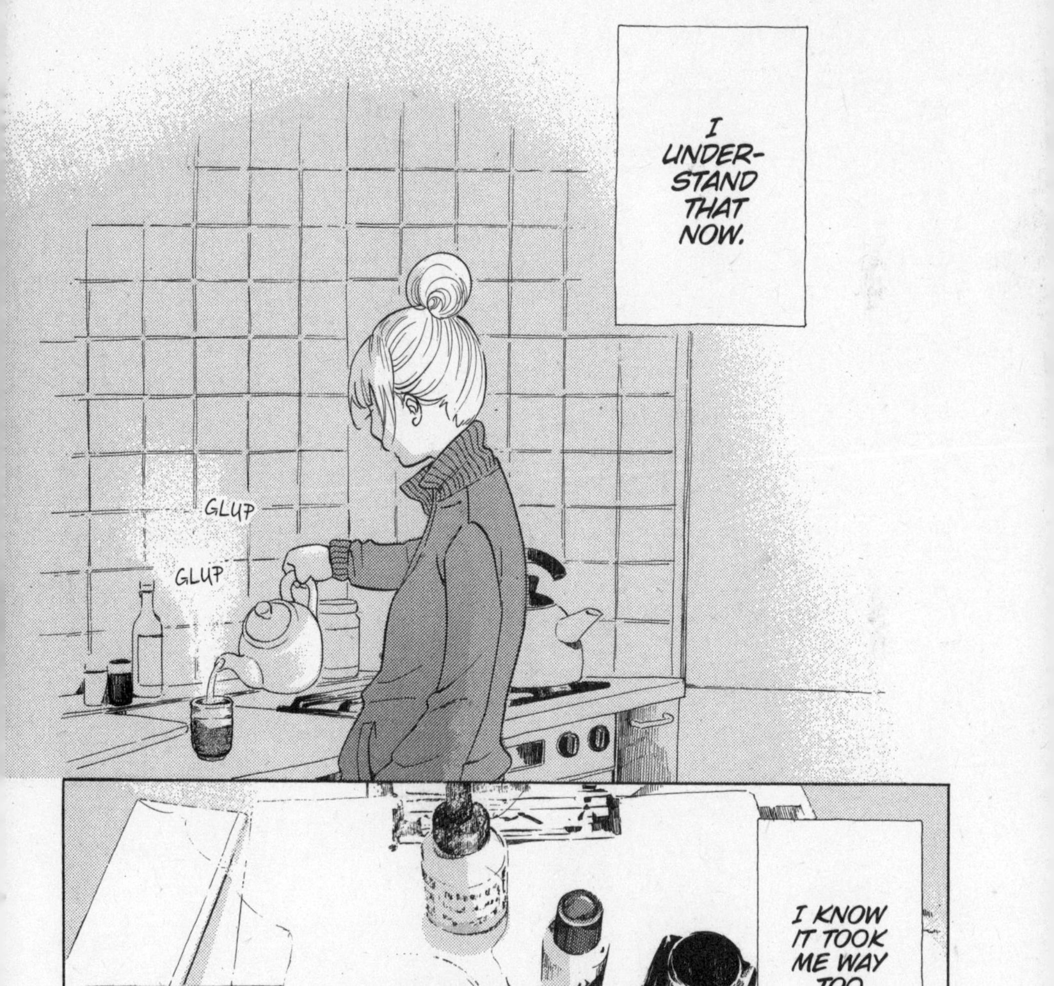
I UNDER-STAND THAT NOW.
GLUP
GLUP

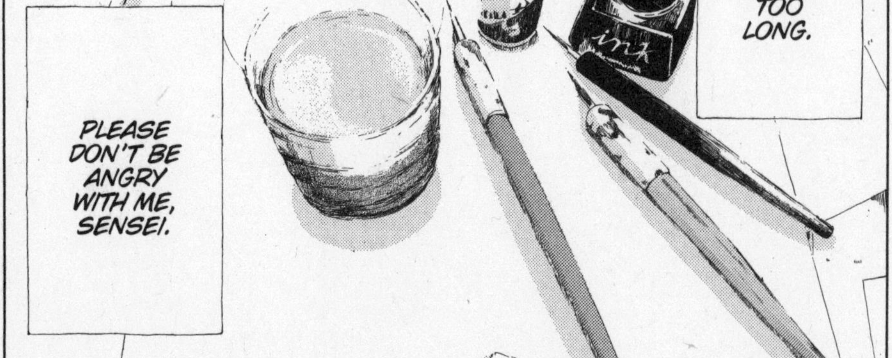
I KNOW IT TOOK ME WAY TOO LONG.
PLEASE DON'T BE ANGRY WITH ME, SENSEI.

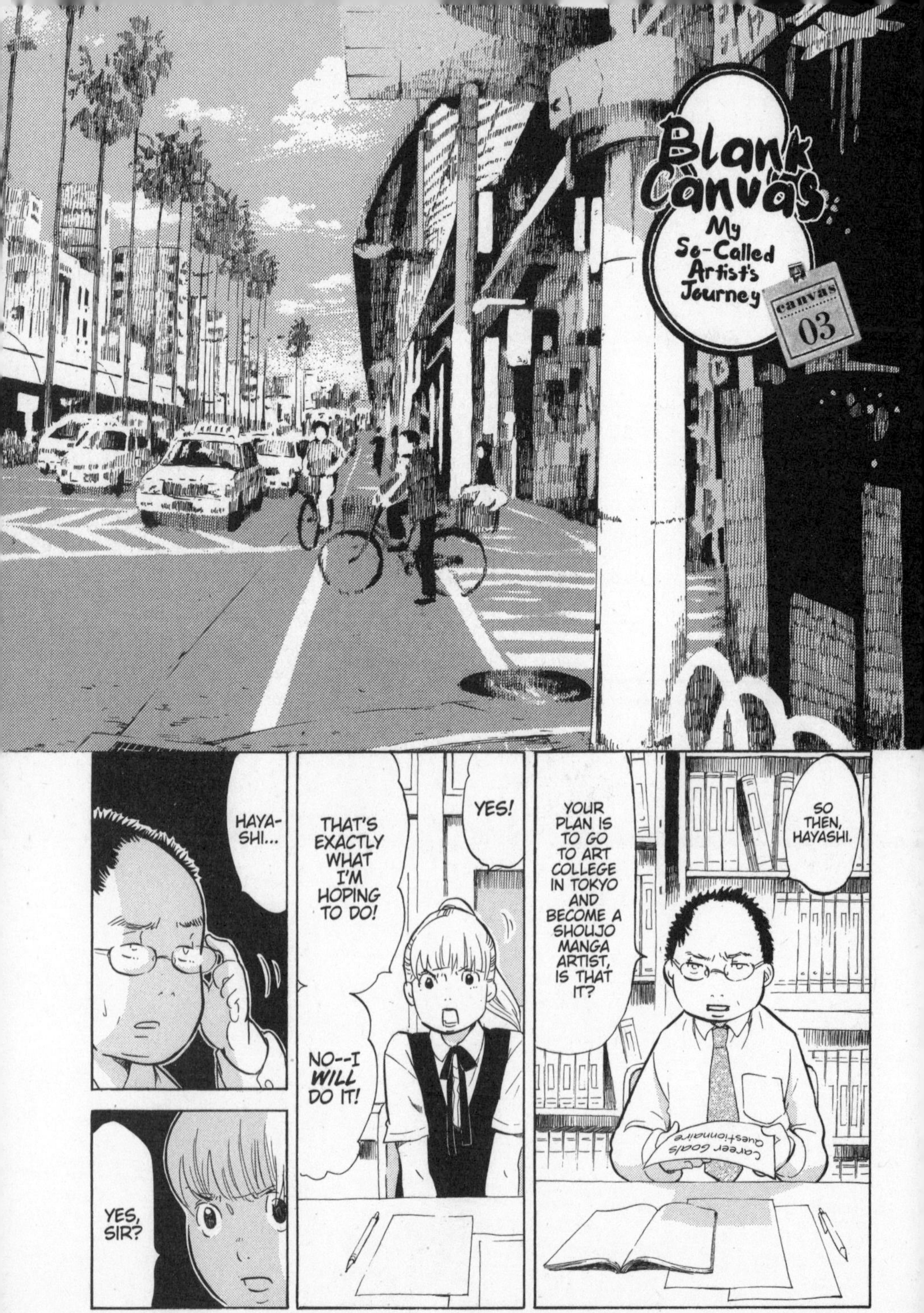
Blank Canvas
My So-Called Artist's Journey
canvas 03
SO THEN, HAYASHI.
YOUR PLAN IS TO GO TO ART COLLEGE IN TOKYO AND BECOME A SHOUJO MANGA ARTIST, IS THAT IT?
Career Goals Questionnaire
YES!
THAT'S EXACTLY WHAT I'M HOPING TO DO!
NO--I **WILL** DO IT!
HAYA-SHI...
YES, SIR?

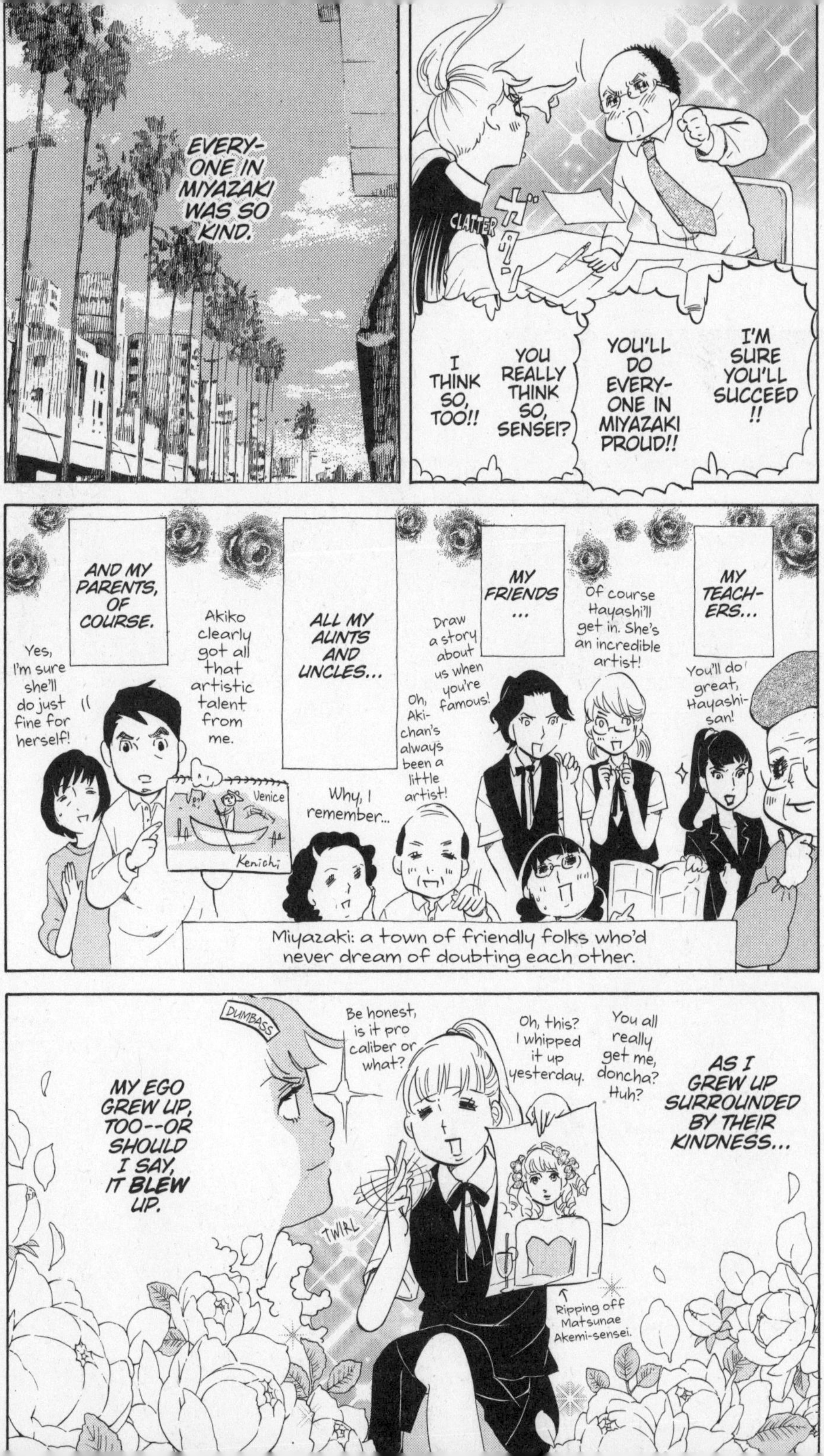

I'M SURE YOU'LL SUCCEED !!
YOU'LL DO EVERY-ONE IN MIYAZAKI PROUD!!
YOU REALLY THINK SO, SENSEI?
I THINK SO, TOO!!
CLATTER
EVERY-ONE IN MIYAZAKI WAS SO KIND.
MY TEACHERS...
You'll do great, Hayashi-san!
MY FRIENDS...
Of course Hayashi'll get in. She's an incredible artist!
Draw a story about us when you're famous!
ALL MY AUNTS AND UNCLES...
Oh, Aki-chan's always been a little artist!
Why, I remember...
AND MY PARENTS, OF COURSE.
Akiko clearly got all that artistic talent from me.
Yes, I'm sure she'll do just fine for herself!
Venice
Kenichi
Miyazaki: a town of friendly folks who'd never dream of doubting each other.
AS I GREW UP SURROUNDED BY THEIR KINDNESS...
You all really get me, doncha? Huh?
Oh, this? I whipped it up yesterday.
Be honest, is it pro caliber or what?
DUMBASS
MY EGO GREW UP, TOO--OR SHOULD I SAY, IT BLEW UP.
TWIRL
Ripping off Matsunae Akemi-sensei.

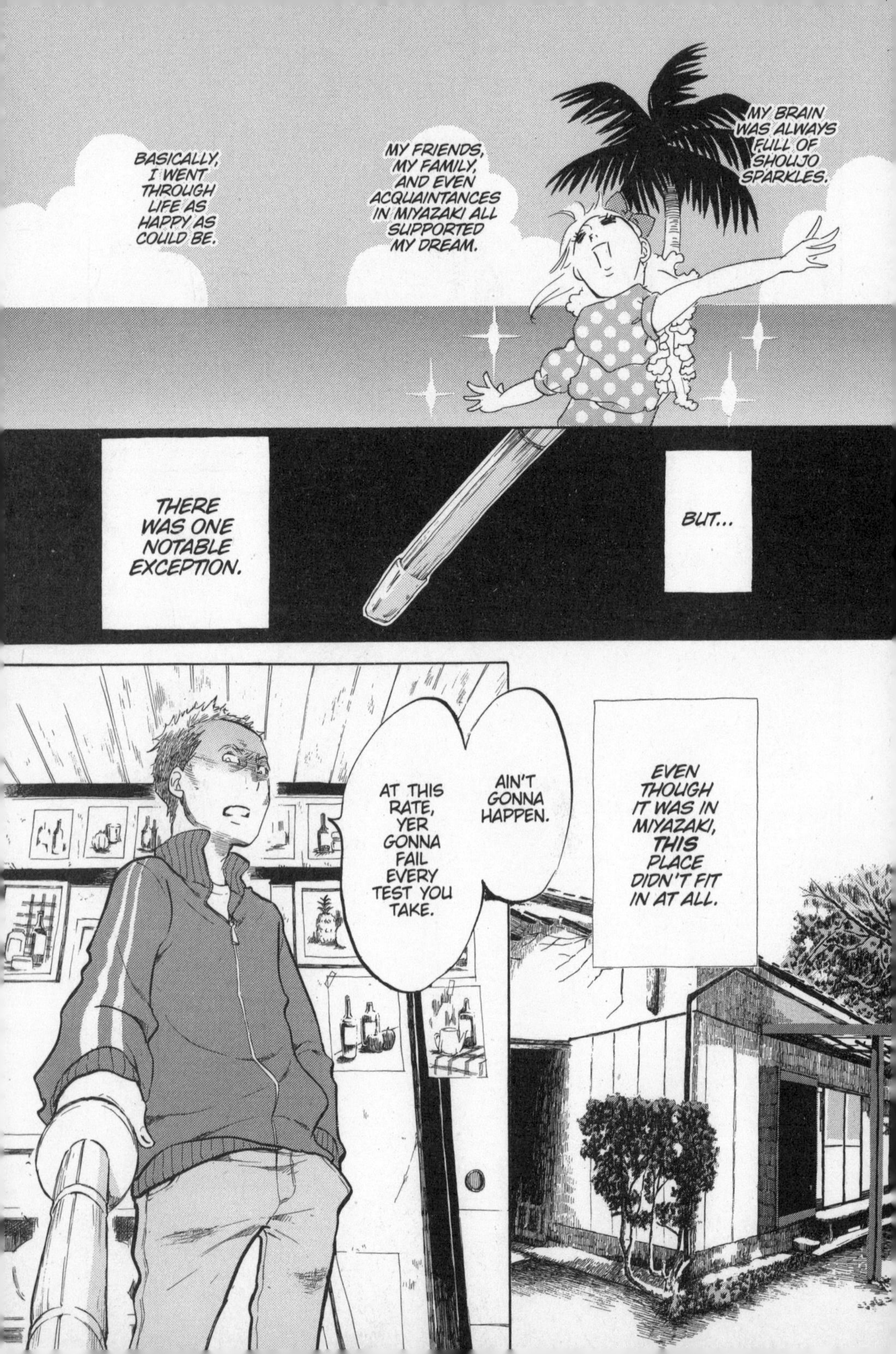
MY BRAIN WAS ALWAYS FULL OF SHOUJO SPARKLES.
MY FRIENDS, MY FAMILY, AND EVEN ACQUAINTANCES IN MIYAZAKI ALL SUPPORTED MY DREAM.
BASICALLY, I WENT THROUGH LIFE AS HAPPY AS COULD BE.
BUT...
THERE WAS ONE NOTABLE EXCEPTION.
EVEN THOUGH IT WAS IN MIYAZAKI, THIS PLACE DIDN'T FIT IN AT ALL.
AIN'T GONNA HAPPEN.
AT THIS RATE, YER GONNA FAIL EVERY TEST YOU TAKE.

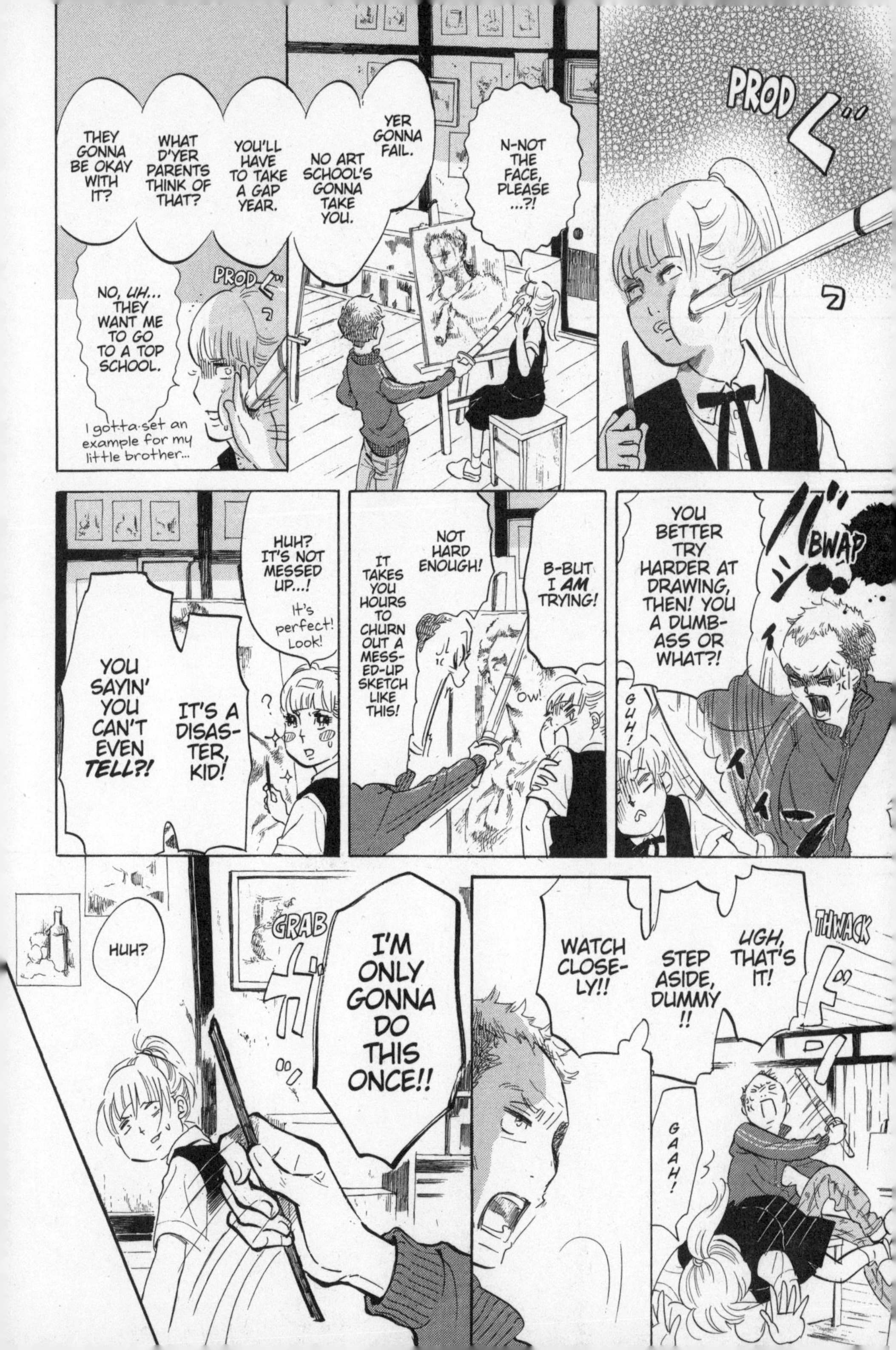

PROD
N-NOT THE FACE, PLEASE ...?!
YER GONNA FAIL.
NO ART SCHOOL'S GONNA TAKE YOU.
YOU'LL HAVE TO TAKE A GAP YEAR.
WHAT D'YER PARENTS THINK OF THAT?
THEY GONNA BE OKAY WITH IT?
PROD
NO, *UH*... THEY WANT ME TO GO TO A TOP SCHOOL.
I gotta set an example for my little brother...
BWAP
YOU BETTER TRY HARDER AT DRAWING, THEN! YOU A DUMBASS OR WHAT?!
GUH!
B-BUT I **AM** TRYING!
NOT HARD ENOUGH!
IT TAKES YOU HOURS TO CHURN OUT A MESSED-UP SKETCH LIKE THIS!
Ow!
HUH? IT'S NOT MESSED UP...!
It's perfect! Look!
IT'S A DISASTER, KID!
YOU SAYIN' YOU CAN'T EVEN ***TELL?!***
THWACK
UGH, THAT'S IT!
STEP ASIDE, DUMMY!!
WATCH CLOSELY!!
GAAH!
I'M ONLY GONNA DO THIS ONCE!!
GRAB
HUH?

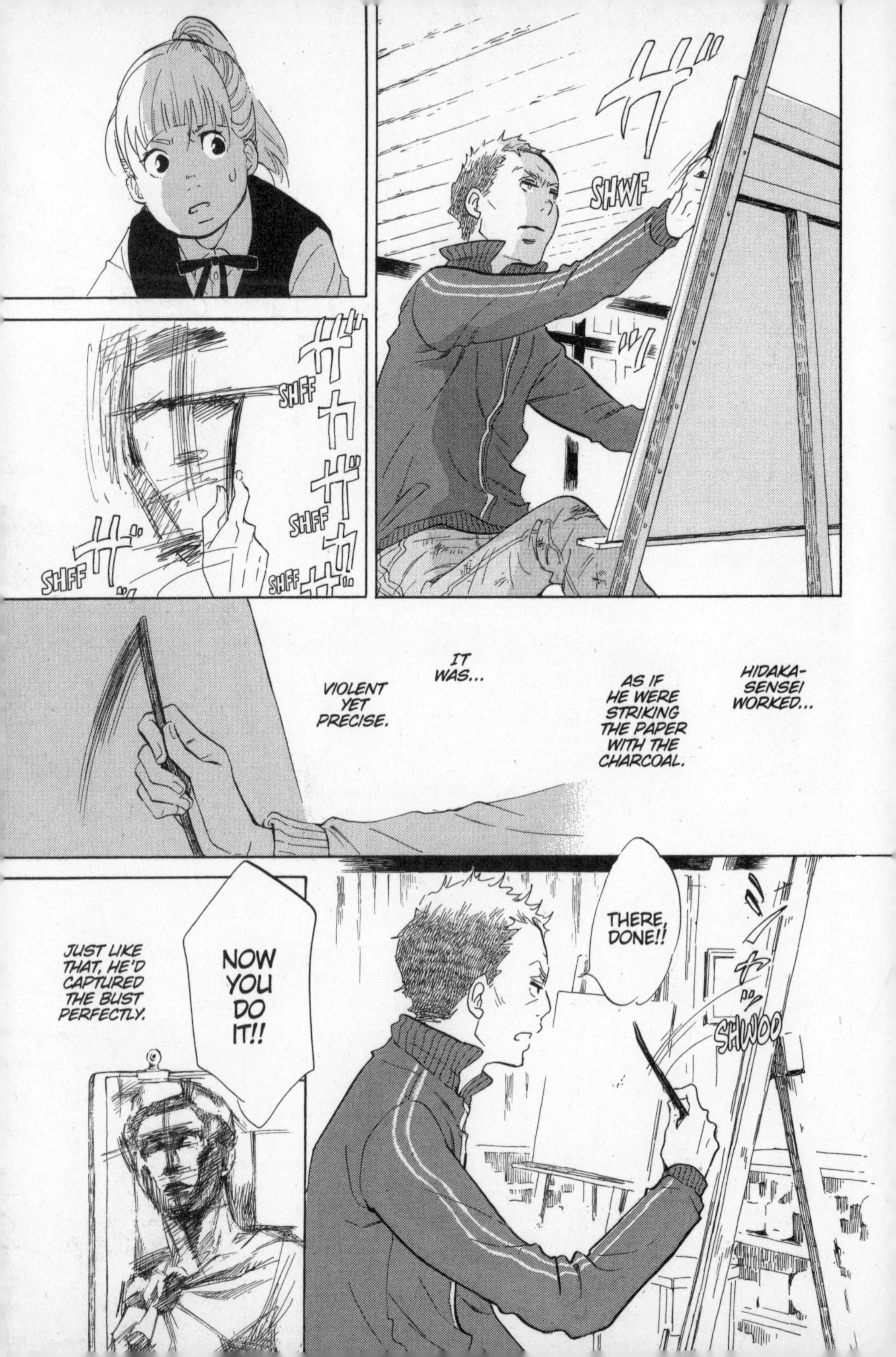
SHWF
SHFF
SHFF
SHFF
SHFF
HIDAKA-SENSEI WORKED...
AS IF HE WERE STRIKING THE PAPER WITH THE CHARCOAL.
IT WAS...
VIOLENT YET PRECISE.
THERE, DONE!!
SHWOO
NOW YOU DO IT!!
JUST LIKE THAT, HE'D CAPTURED THE BUST PERFECTLY.

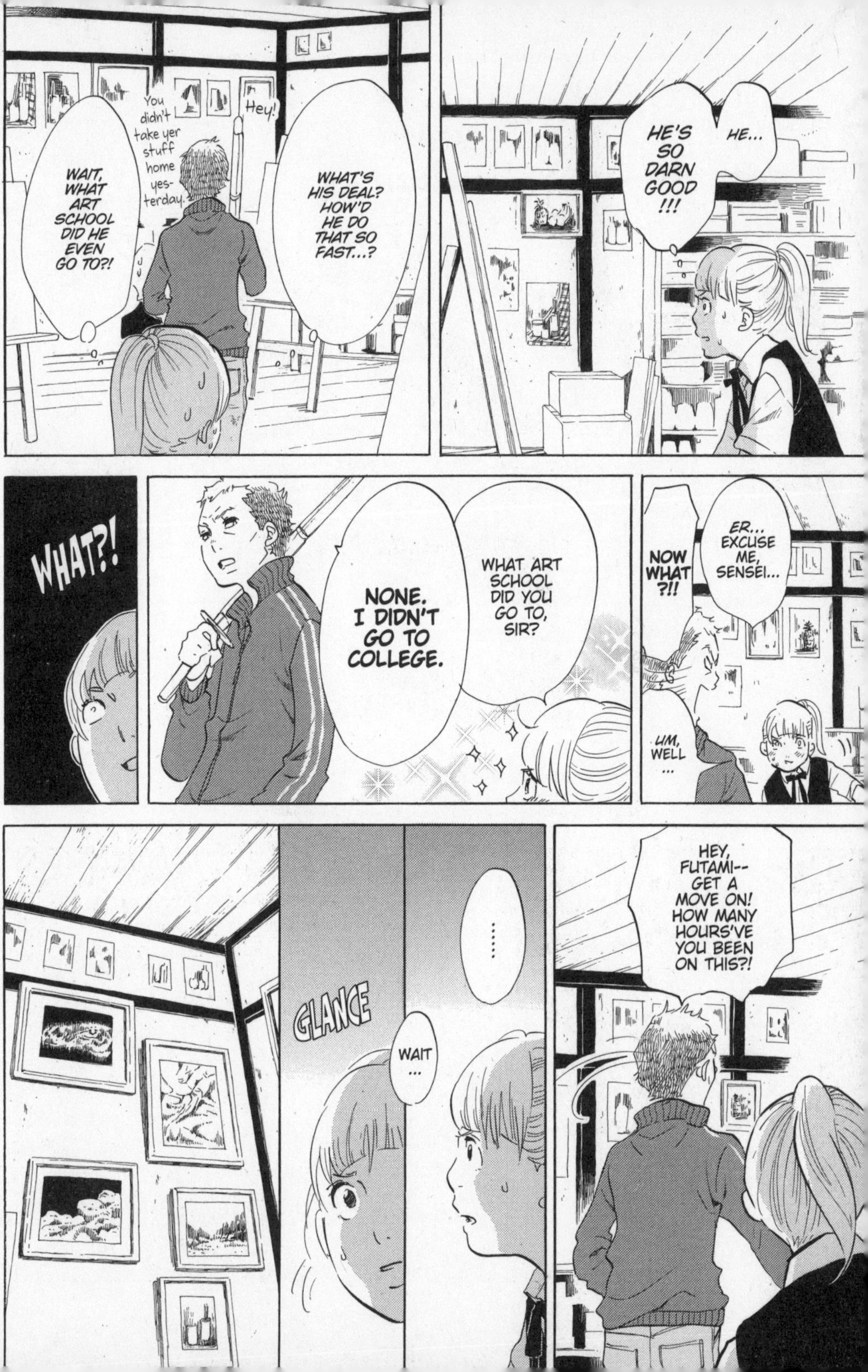
HE...
HE'S SO DARN GOOD !!!
Hey!
WHAT'S HIS DEAL? HOW'D HE DO THAT SO FAST...?
You didn't take yer stuff home yes-terday.
WAIT, WHAT ART SCHOOL DID HE EVEN GO TO?!
ER... EXCUSE ME, SENSEI...
NOW WHAT ?!!
UM, WELL ...
WHAT ART SCHOOL DID YOU GO TO, SIR?
NONE. I DIDN'T GO TO COLLEGE.
WHAT?!
HEY, FUTAMI-- GET A MOVE ON! HOW MANY HOURS'VE YOU BEEN ON THIS?!
......
GLANCE
WAIT ...

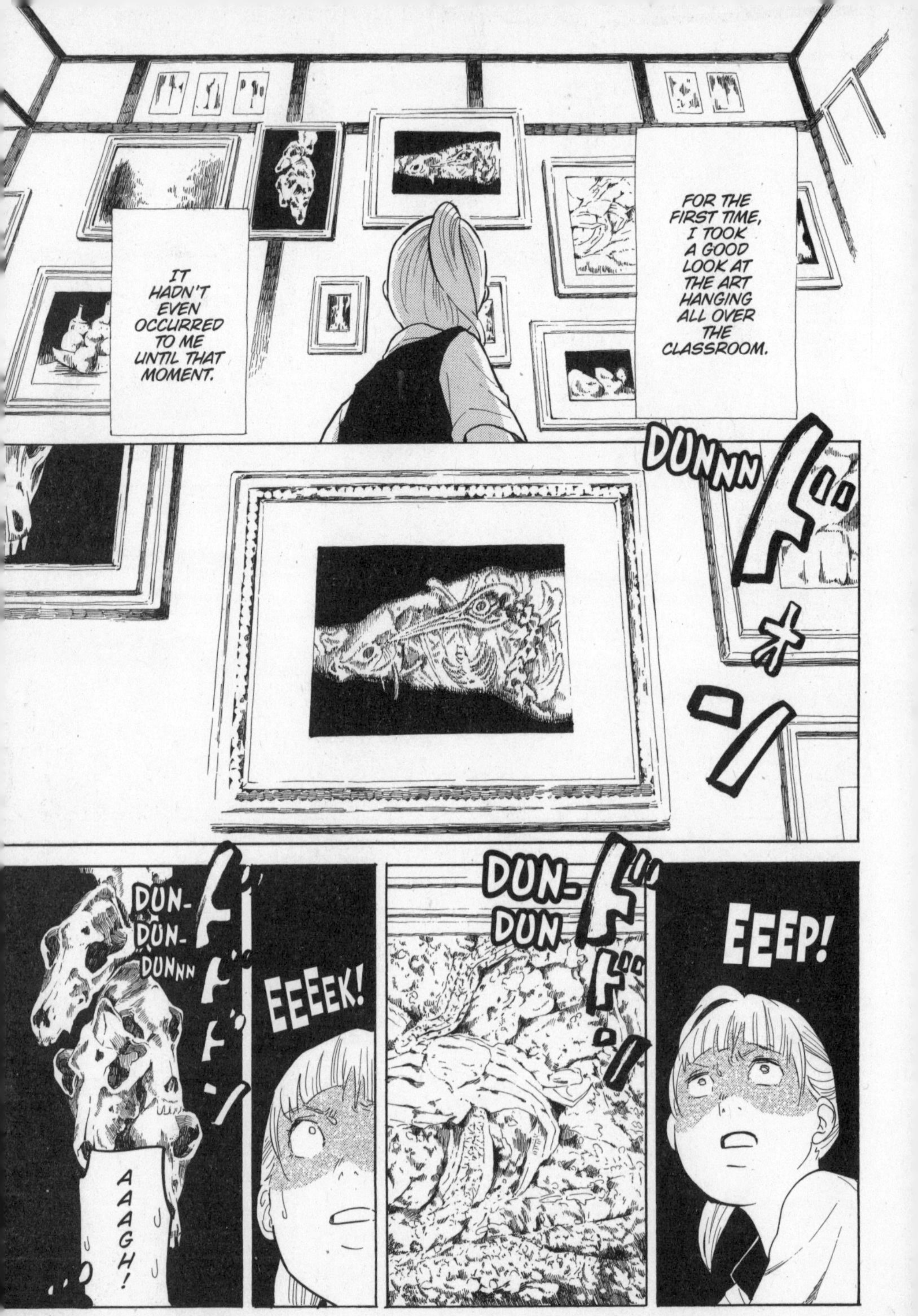
FOR THE FIRST TIME, I TOOK A GOOD LOOK AT THE ART HANGING ALL OVER THE CLASSROOM.
IT HADN'T EVEN OCCURRED TO ME UNTIL THAT MOMENT.
DUNNN
EEEP!
DUN-DUN
EEEEK!
DUN-DUN-DUNNN
AAAGH!

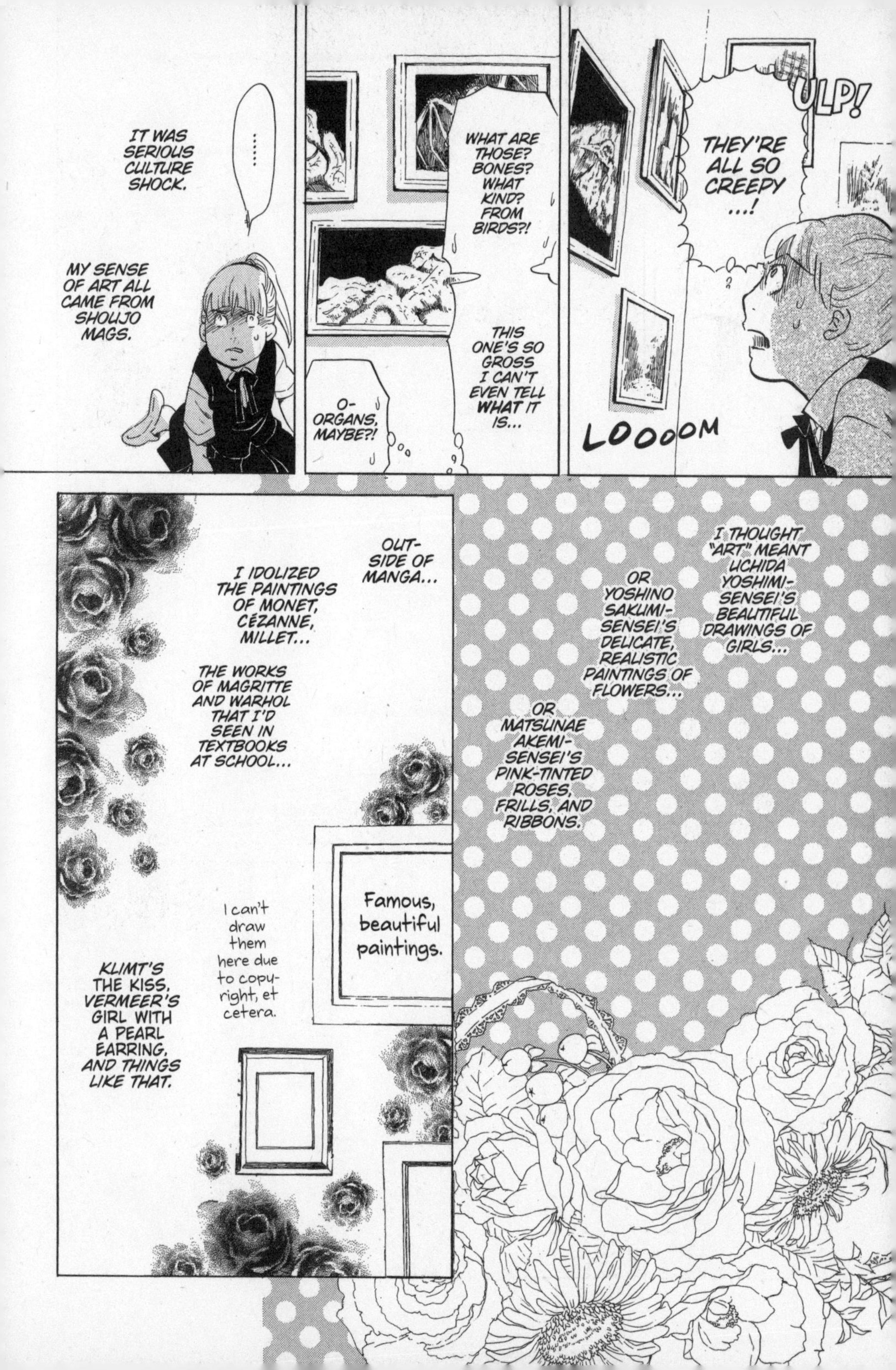
ULP!
THEY'RE ALL SO CREEPY ...!
LOOOOM
WHAT ARE THOSE? BONES? WHAT KIND? FROM BIRDS?!
THIS ONE'S SO GROSS I CAN'T EVEN TELL WHAT IT IS...
O-ORGANS, MAYBE?!
......
IT WAS SERIOUS CULTURE SHOCK.
MY SENSE OF ART ALL CAME FROM SHOUJO MAGS.
I THOUGHT "ART" MEANT UCHIDA YOSHIMI-SENSEI'S BEAUTIFUL DRAWINGS OF GIRLS...
OR YOSHINO SAKUMI-SENSEI'S DELICATE, REALISTIC PAINTINGS OF FLOWERS...
OR MATSUNAE AKEMI-SENSEI'S PINK-TINTED ROSES, FRILLS, AND RIBBONS.
OUTSIDE OF MANGA...
I IDOLIZED THE PAINTINGS OF MONET, CÉZANNE, MILLET...
THE WORKS OF MAGRITTE AND WARHOL THAT I'D SEEN IN TEXTBOOKS AT SCHOOL...
Famous, beautiful paintings.
I can't draw them here due to copy-right, et cetera.
KLIMT'S THE KISS, VERMEER'S GIRL WITH A PEARL EARRING, AND THINGS LIKE THAT.

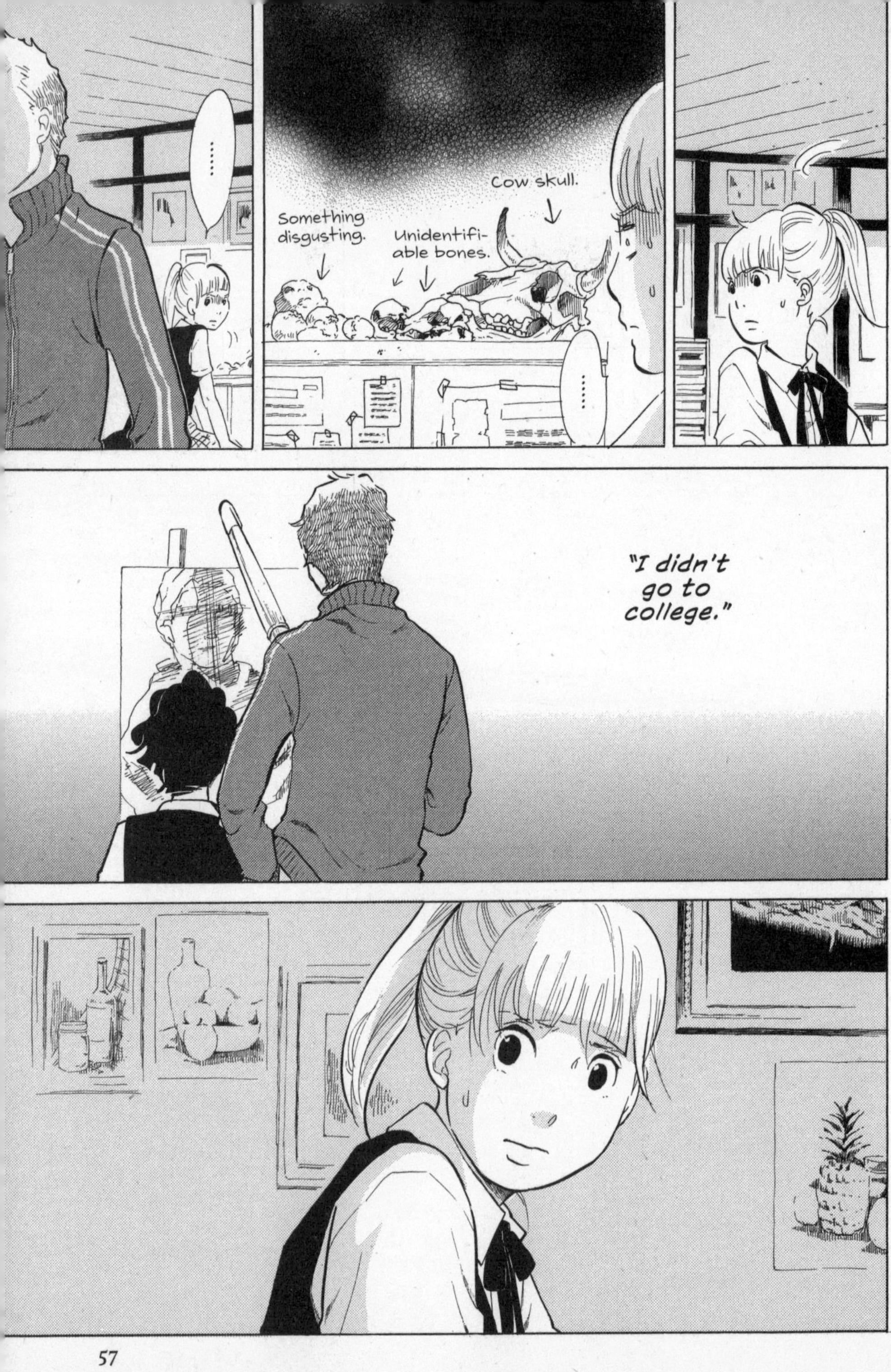
Cow skull.
Unidentifiable bones.
Something disgusting.
……
……
"I didn't go to college."

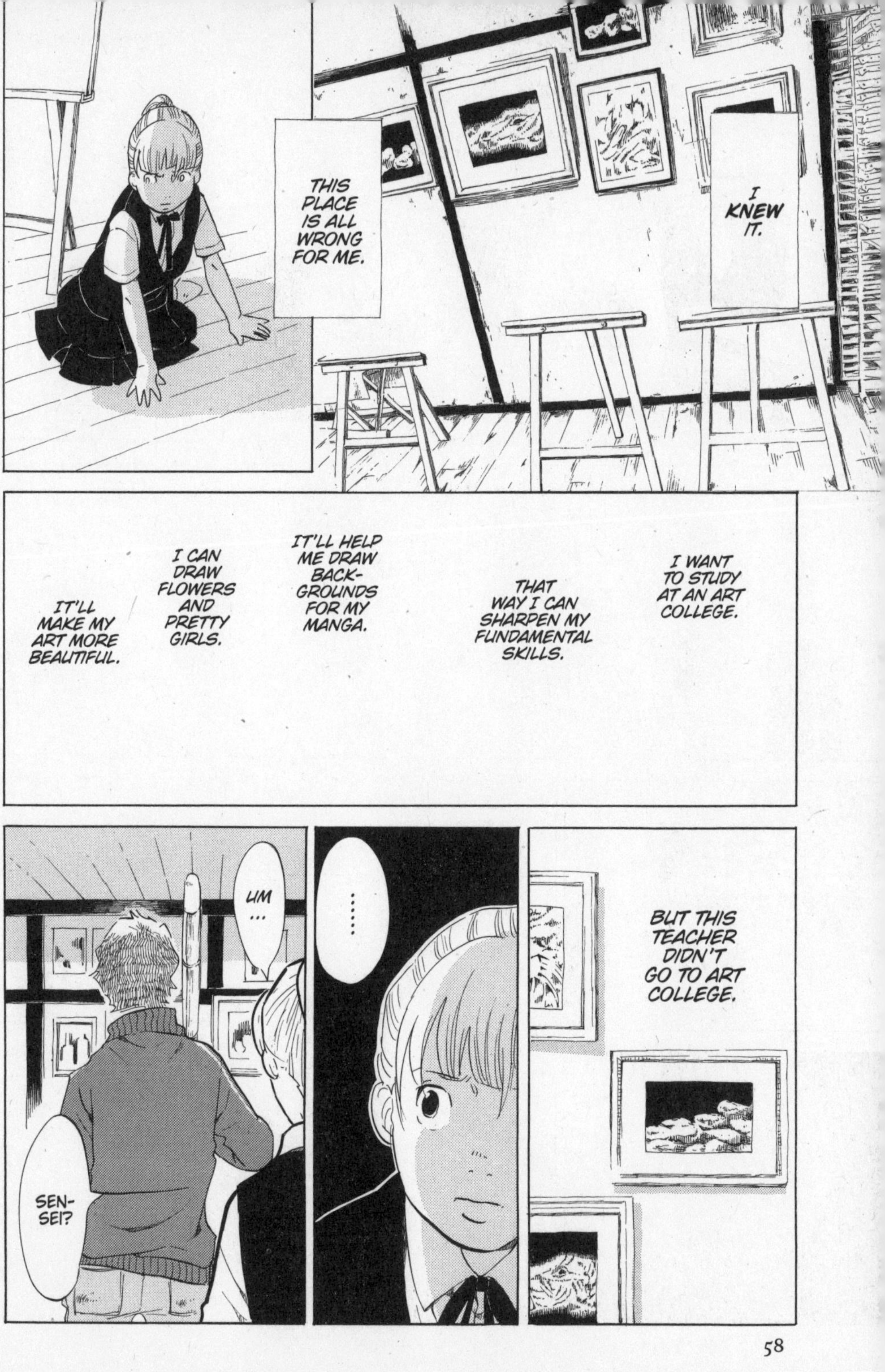
I KNEW IT.
THIS PLACE IS ALL WRONG FOR ME.
I WANT TO STUDY AT AN ART COLLEGE.
THAT WAY I CAN SHARPEN MY FUNDAMENTAL SKILLS.
IT'LL HELP ME DRAW BACK-GROUNDS FOR MY MANGA.
I CAN DRAW FLOWERS AND PRETTY GIRLS.
IT'LL MAKE MY ART MORE BEAUTIFUL.
BUT THIS TEACHER DIDN'T GO TO ART COLLEGE.
......
UM...
SEN-SEI?

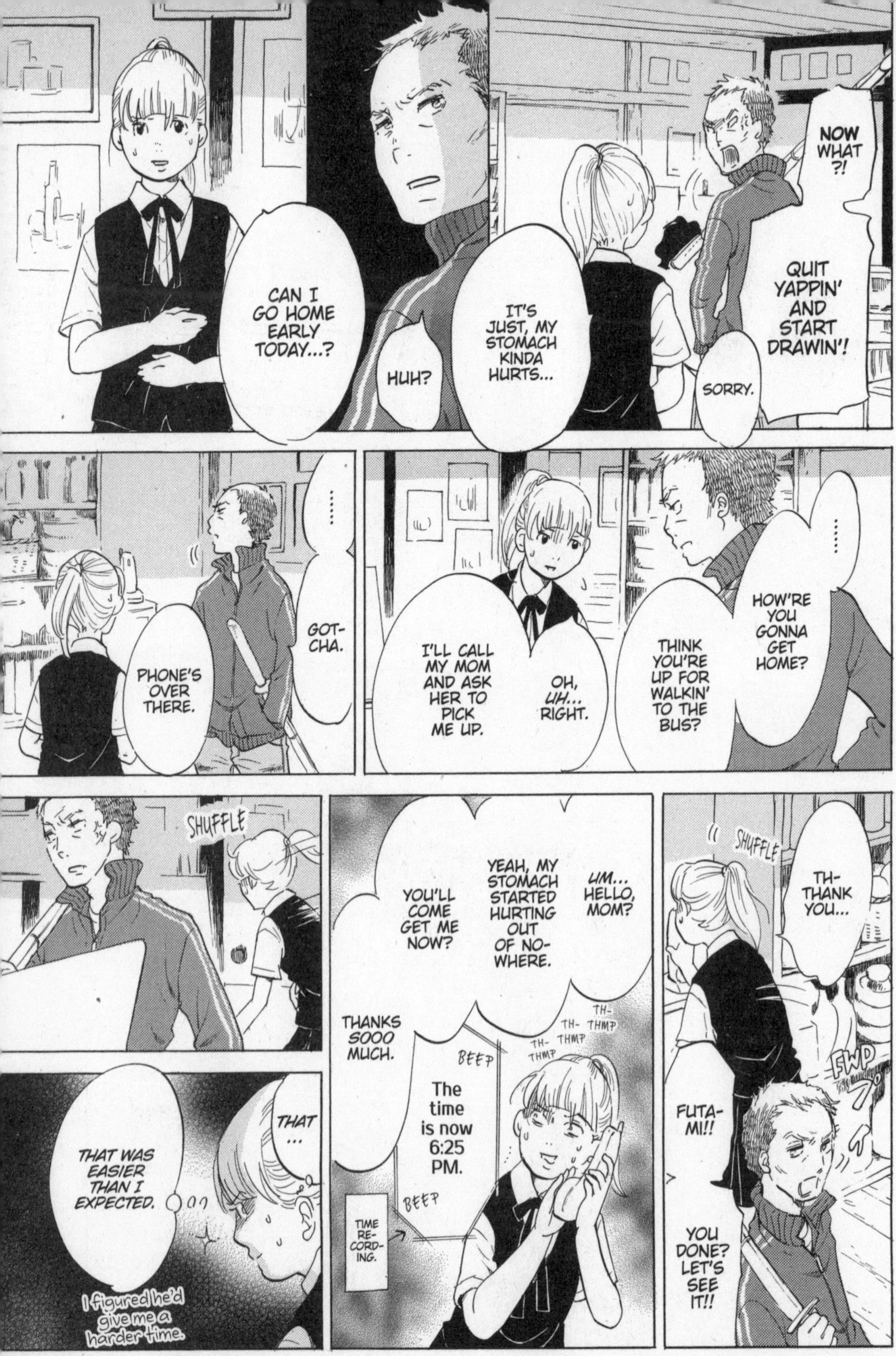
NOW WHAT?!
QUIT YAPPIN' AND START DRAWIN'!
SORRY.
IT'S JUST, MY STOMACH KINDA HURTS...
HUH?
CAN I GO HOME EARLY TODAY...?
......
HOW'RE YOU GONNA GET HOME?
THINK YOU'RE UP FOR WALKIN' TO THE BUS?
OH, UH... RIGHT.
I'LL CALL MY MOM AND ASK HER TO PICK ME UP.
......
GOT-CHA.
PHONE'S OVER THERE.
SHUFFLE
TH-THANK YOU...
FWP
FUTAMI!!
YOU DONE? LET'S SEE IT!!
UM... HELLO, MOM?
YEAH, MY STOMACH STARTED HURTING OUT OF NO-WHERE.
YOU'LL COME GET ME NOW?
TH-THMP TH-THMP TH-THMP
THANKS SOOO MUCH.
BEEP
The time is now 6:25 PM.
BEEP
TIME RE-CORD-ING.
SHUFFLE
THAT...
THAT WAS EASIER THAN I EXPECTED.
I figured he'd give me a harder time.

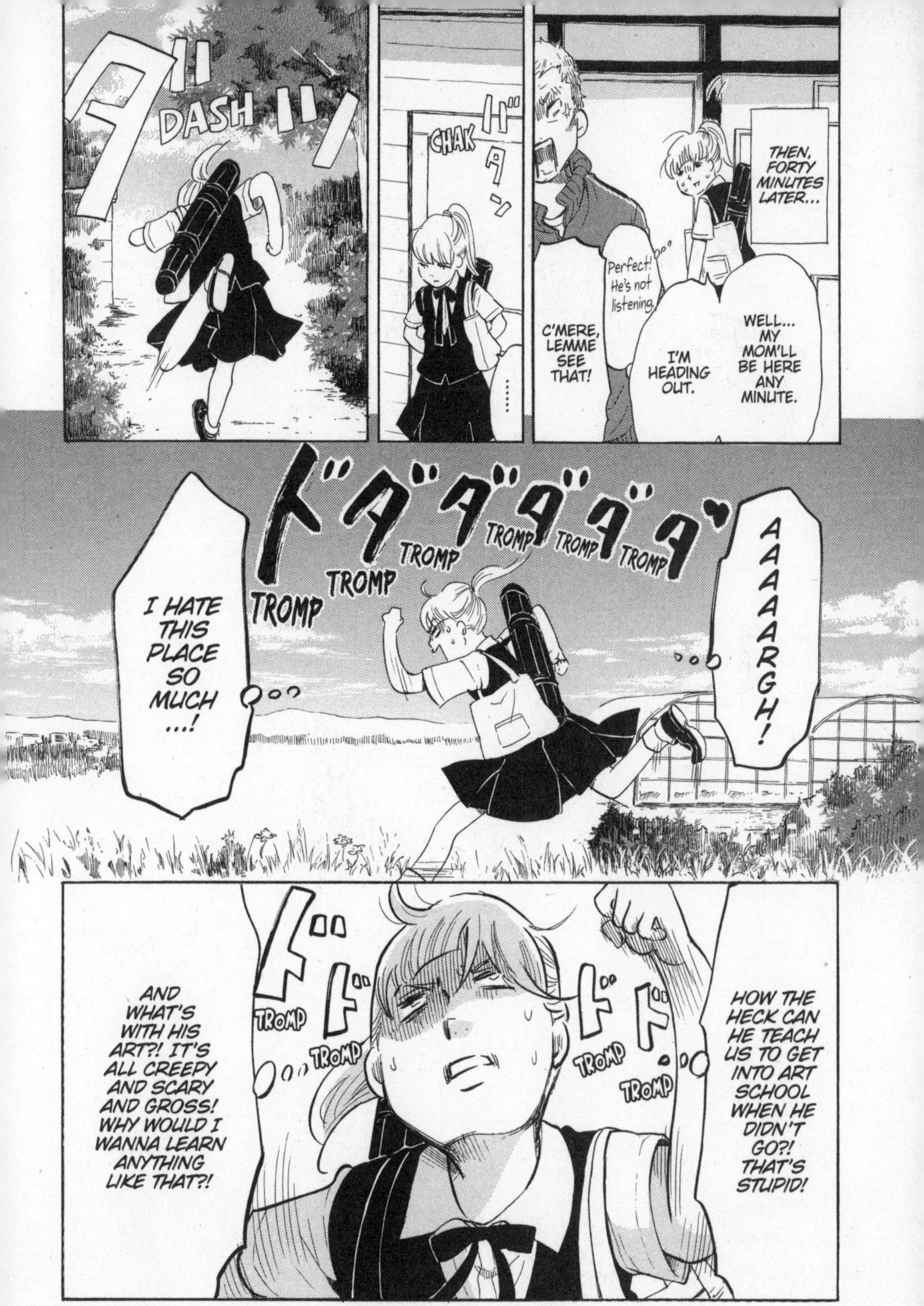
THEN, FORTY MINUTES LATER...
WELL... MY MOM'LL BE HERE ANY MINUTE.
I'M HEADING OUT.
Perfect! He's not listening.
C'MERE, LEMME SEE THAT!
CHAK
......
DASH
AAAAARGH!
TROMP TROMP TROMP TROMP TROMP TROMP
I HATE THIS PLACE SO MUCH...!
HOW THE HECK CAN HE TEACH US TO GET INTO ART SCHOOL WHEN HE DIDN'T GO?! THAT'S STUPID!
TROMP TROMP TROMP TROMP
AND WHAT'S WITH HIS ART?! IT'S ALL CREEPY AND SCARY AND GROSS! WHY WOULD I WANNA LEARN ANYTHING LIKE THAT?!

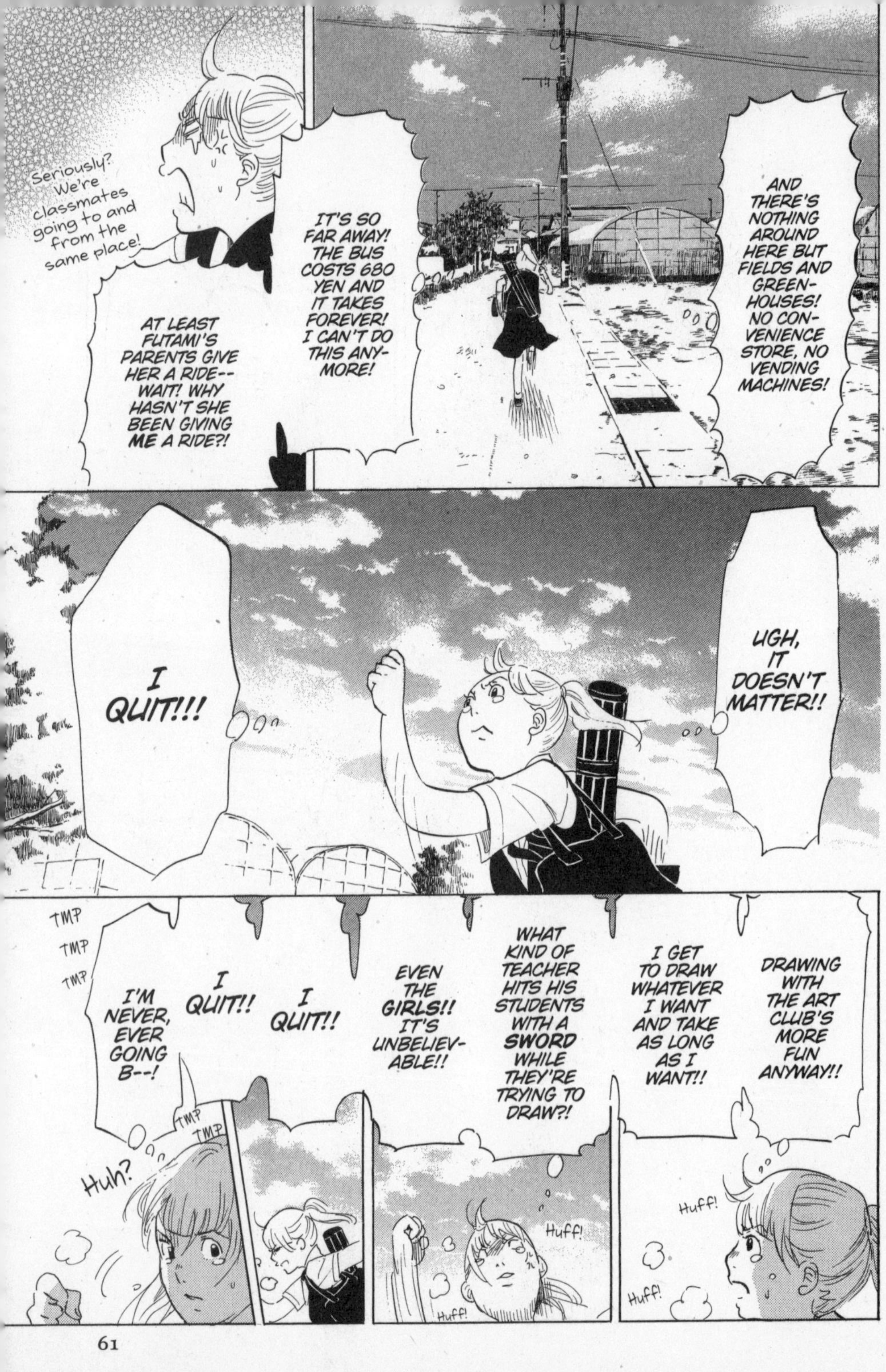
AND THERE'S NOTHING AROUND HERE BUT FIELDS AND GREEN-HOUSES! NO CON-VENIENCE STORE, NO VENDING MACHINES!
IT'S SO FAR AWAY! THE BUS COSTS 680 YEN AND IT TAKES FOREVER! I CAN'T DO THIS ANY-MORE!
AT LEAST FUTAMI'S PARENTS GIVE HER A RIDE-- WAIT! WHY HASN'T SHE BEEN GIVING **ME** A RIDE?!
Seriously? We're classmates going to and from the same place!
UGH, IT DOESN'T MATTER!!
I QUIT!!!
DRAWING WITH THE ART CLUB'S MORE FUN ANYWAY!!
I GET TO DRAW WHATEVER I WANT AND TAKE AS LONG AS I WANT!!
Huff!
Huff!
WHAT KIND OF TEACHER HITS HIS STUDENTS WITH A **SWORD** WHILE THEY'RE TRYING TO DRAW?!
EVEN THE **GIRLS!!** IT'S UNBELIEV-ABLE!!
Huff!
Huff!
I QUIT!!
I QUIT!!
I'M NEVER, EVER GOING B--!
TMP
TMP
TMP
TMP
TMP
Huh?

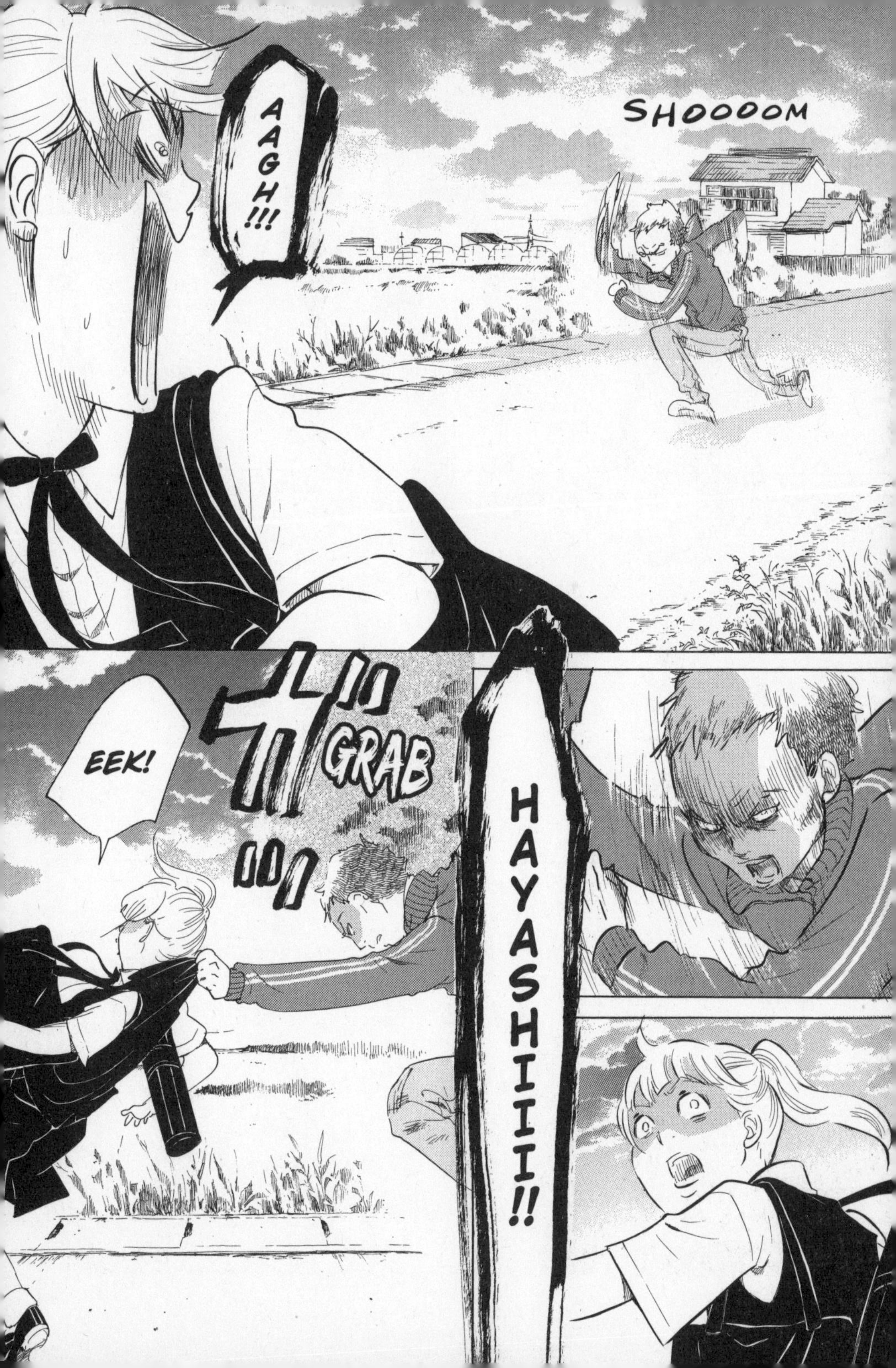
SHOOOOM
AAGH!!!
HAYASHIIII!!
GRAB
EEK!

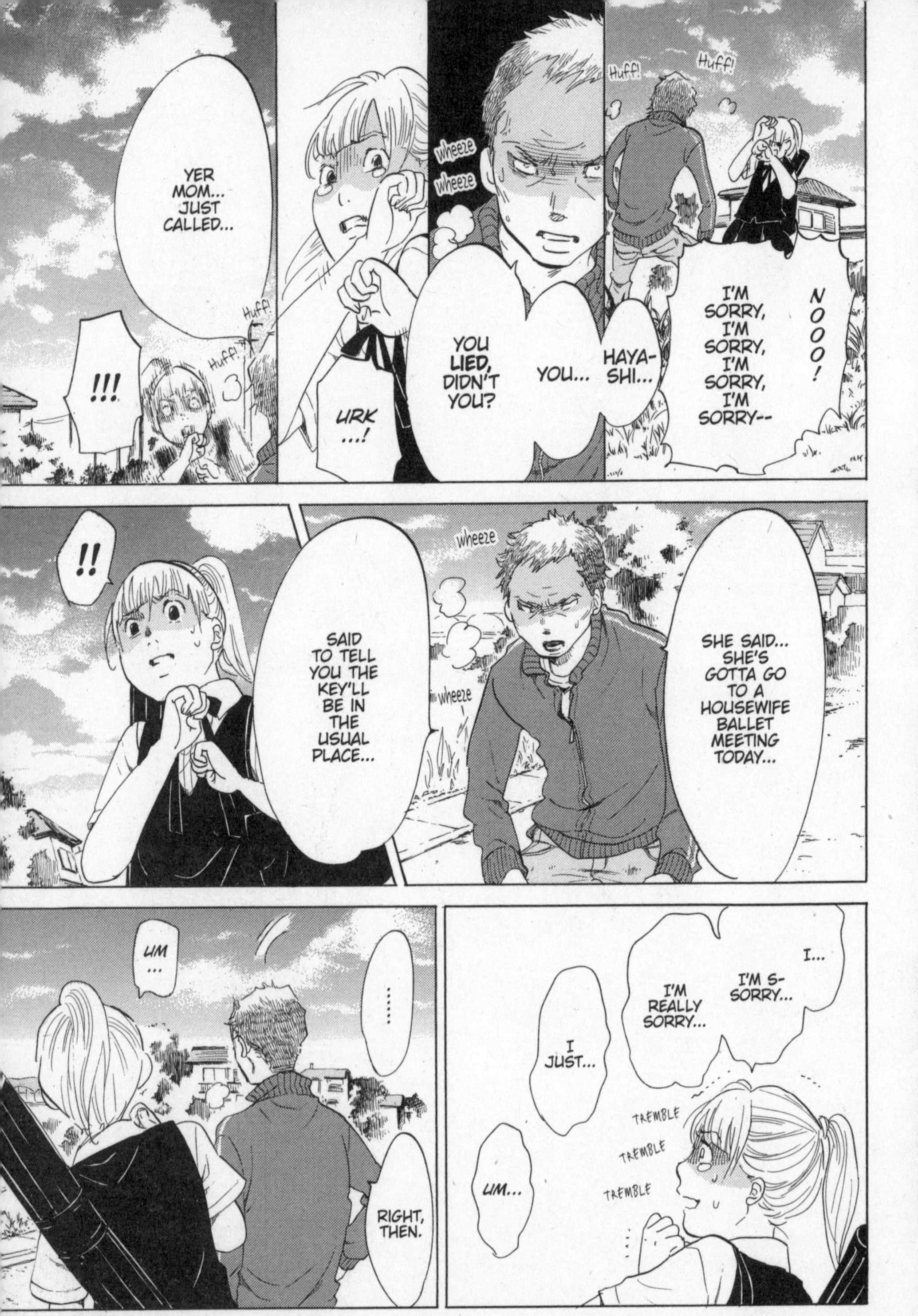
Huff!
Huff!
NOOOO!
I'M SORRY, I'M SORRY, I'M SORRY, I'M SORRY--
wheeze
wheeze
HAYA-SHI...
YOU...
YOU LIED, DIDN'T YOU?
URK...!
YER MOM... JUST CALLED...
Huff!
Huff!
!!!
wheeze
SHE SAID... SHE'S GOTTA GO TO A HOUSEWIFE BALLET MEETING TODAY...
wheeze
SAID TO TELL YOU THE KEY'LL BE IN THE USUAL PLACE...
!!
I...
I'M S-SORRY...
I'M REALLY SORRY...
I JUST...
TREMBLE
TREMBLE
TREMBLE
UM...
......
UM...
RIGHT, THEN.

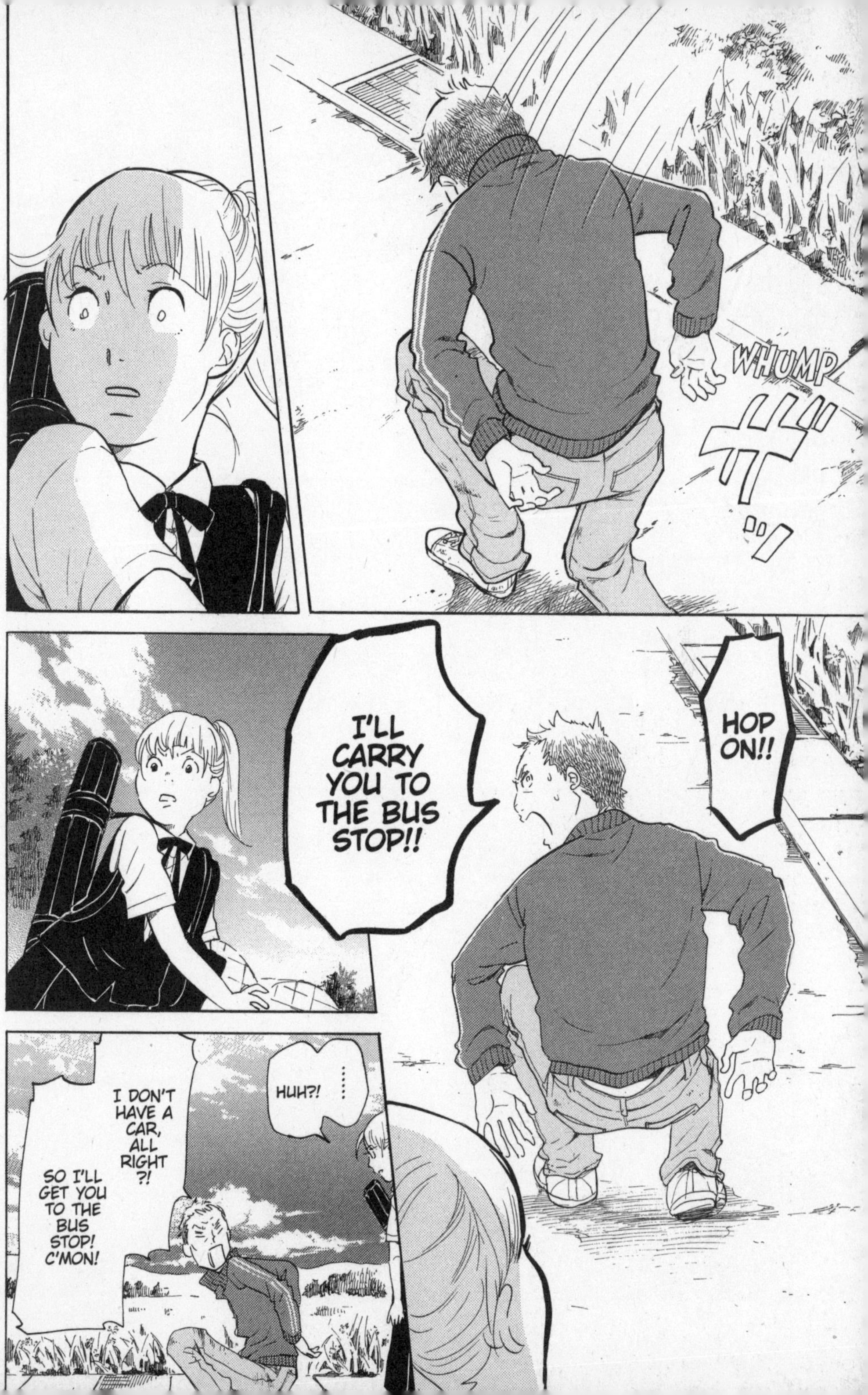
WHUMP
ザッ
HOP ON!!
I'LL CARRY YOU TO THE BUS STOP!!
...... HUH?!
I DON'T HAVE A CAR, ALL RIGHT ?!
SO I'LL GET YOU TO THE BUS STOP! C'MON!

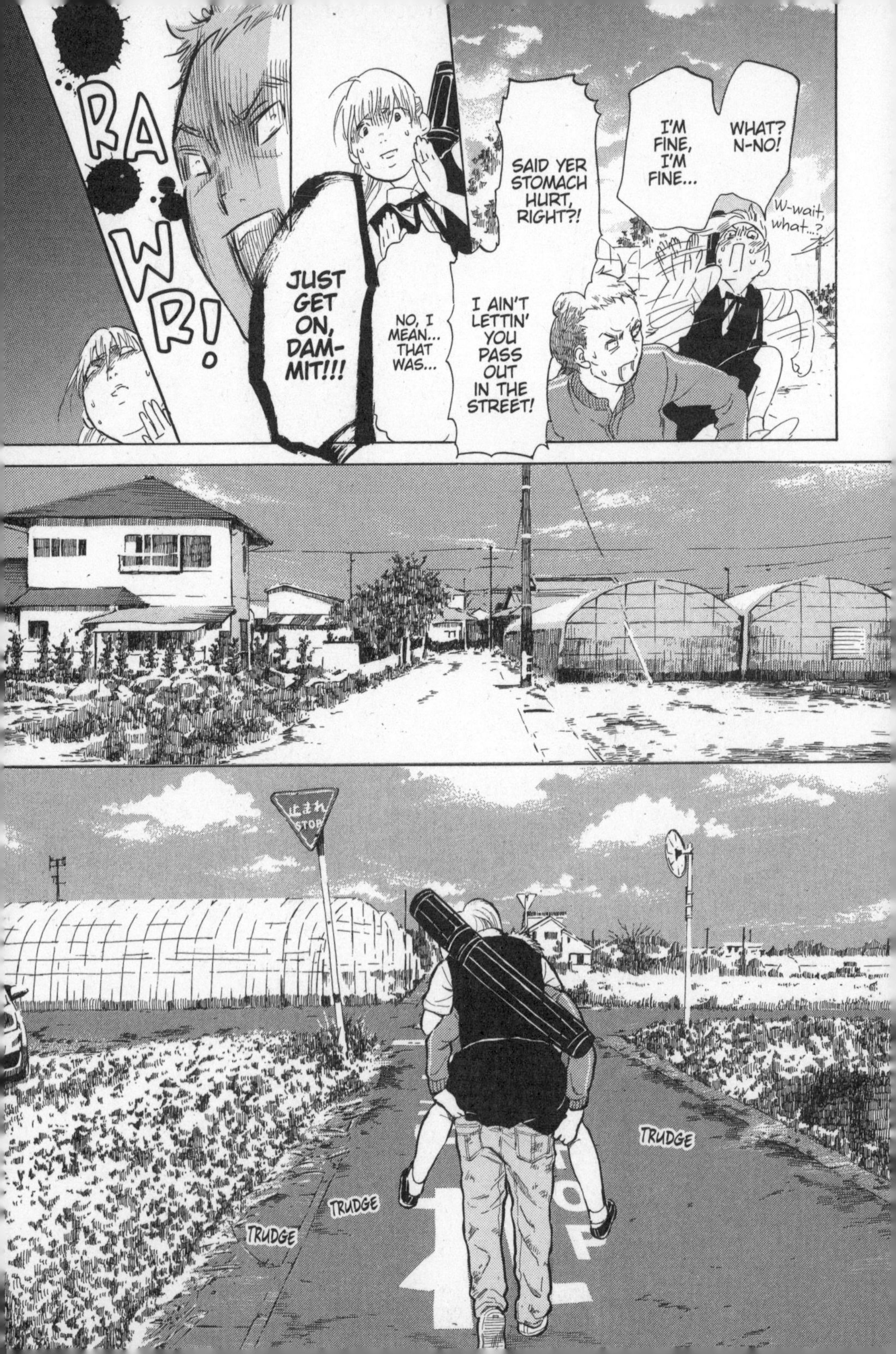
WHAT? N-NO!
I'M FINE, I'M FINE...
W-wait, what...?
SAID YER STOMACH HURT, RIGHT?!
I AIN'T LETTIN' YOU PASS OUT IN THE STREET!
NO, I MEAN... THAT WAS...
JUST GET ON, DAMMIT!!!
RAWR!
止まれ
STOP
TRUDGE
TRUDGE
TRUDGE

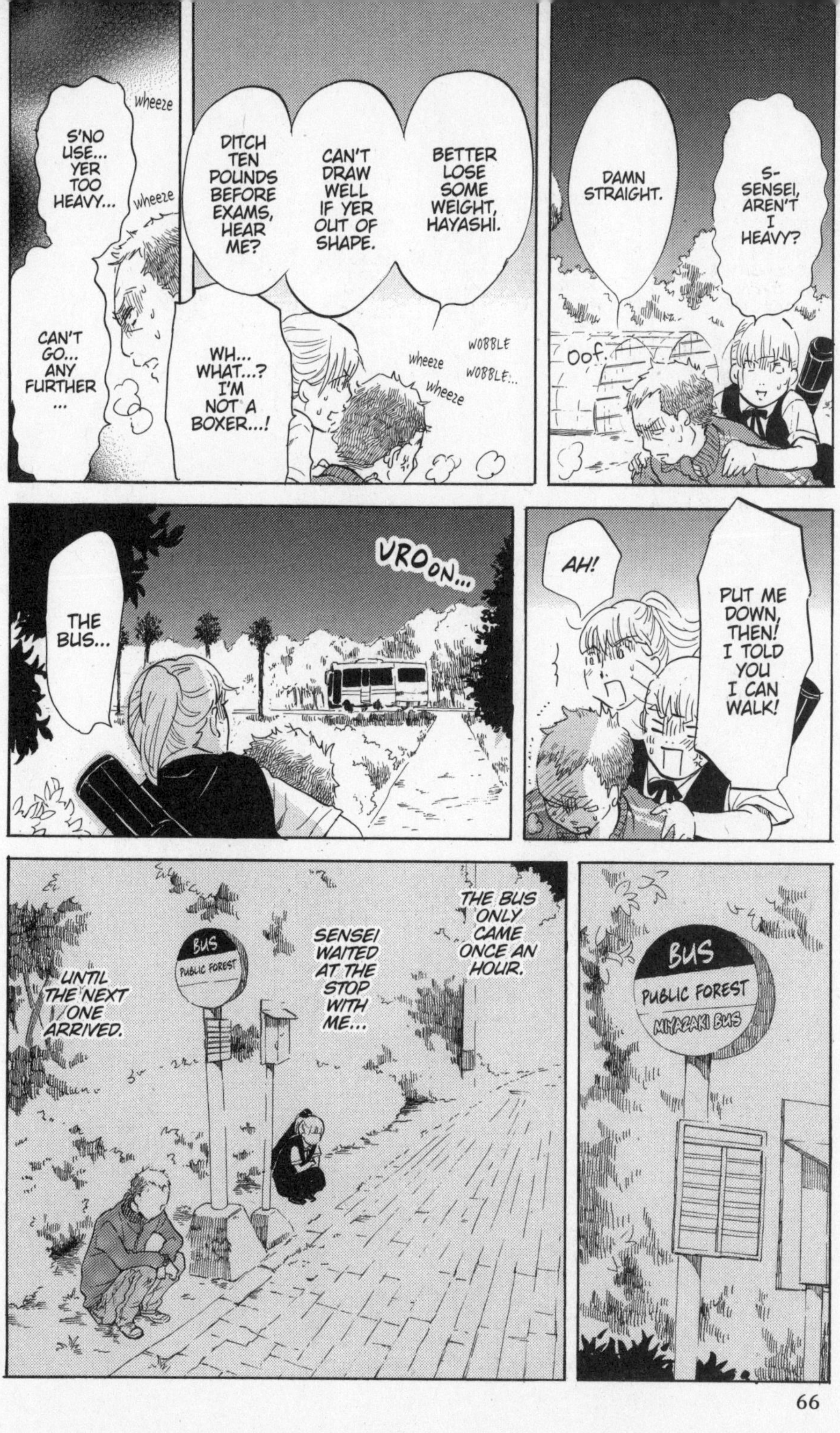
S-SENSEI, AREN'T I HEAVY?
DAMN STRAIGHT.
Oof.
BETTER LOSE SOME WEIGHT, HAYASHI.
CAN'T DRAW WELL IF YER OUT OF SHAPE.
DITCH TEN POUNDS BEFORE EXAMS, HEAR ME?
WOBBLE WOBBLE...
wheeze
wheeze
WH... WHAT...? I'M NOT A BOXER...!
wheeze
S'NO USE... YER TOO HEAVY...
wheeze
CAN'T GO... ANY FURTHER...
AH!
PUT ME DOWN, THEN! I TOLD YOU I CAN WALK!
VROOon...
THE BUS...
BUS
PUBLIC FOREST
MIYAZAKI BUS
THE BUS ONLY CAME ONCE AN HOUR.
SENSEI WAITED AT THE STOP WITH ME...
UNTIL THE NEXT ONE ARRIVED.
BUS
PUBLIC FOREST

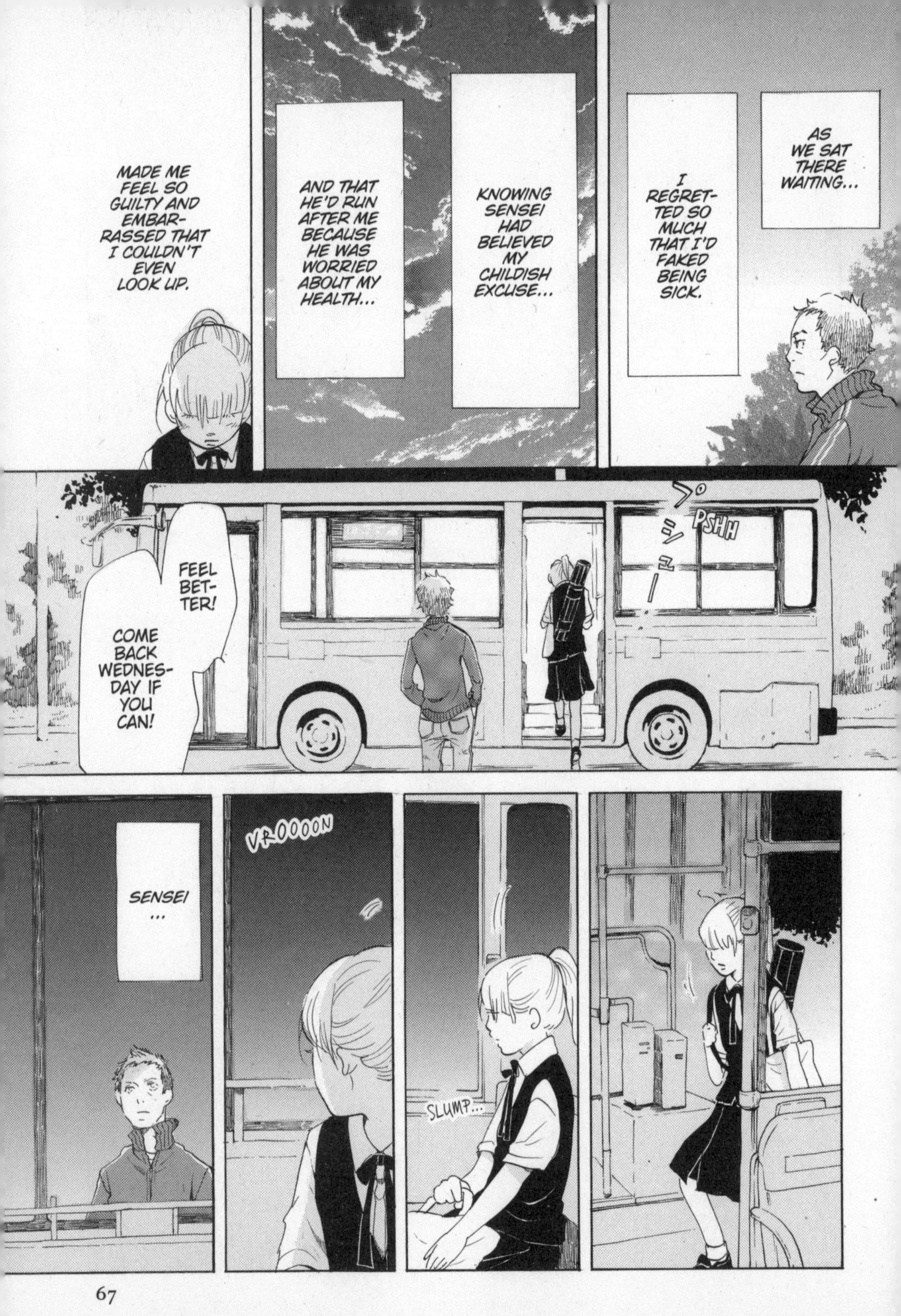
AS WE SAT THERE WAITING...
I REGRETTED SO MUCH THAT I'D FAKED BEING SICK.
KNOWING SENSEI HAD BELIEVED MY CHILDISH EXCUSE...
AND THAT HE'D RUN AFTER ME BECAUSE HE WAS WORRIED ABOUT MY HEALTH...
MADE ME FEEL SO GUILTY AND EMBARRASSED THAT I COULDN'T EVEN LOOK UP.
プシュー
PSHH
FEEL BETTER!
COME BACK WEDNESDAY IF YOU CAN!
SLUMP...
VROOOON
SENSEI ...

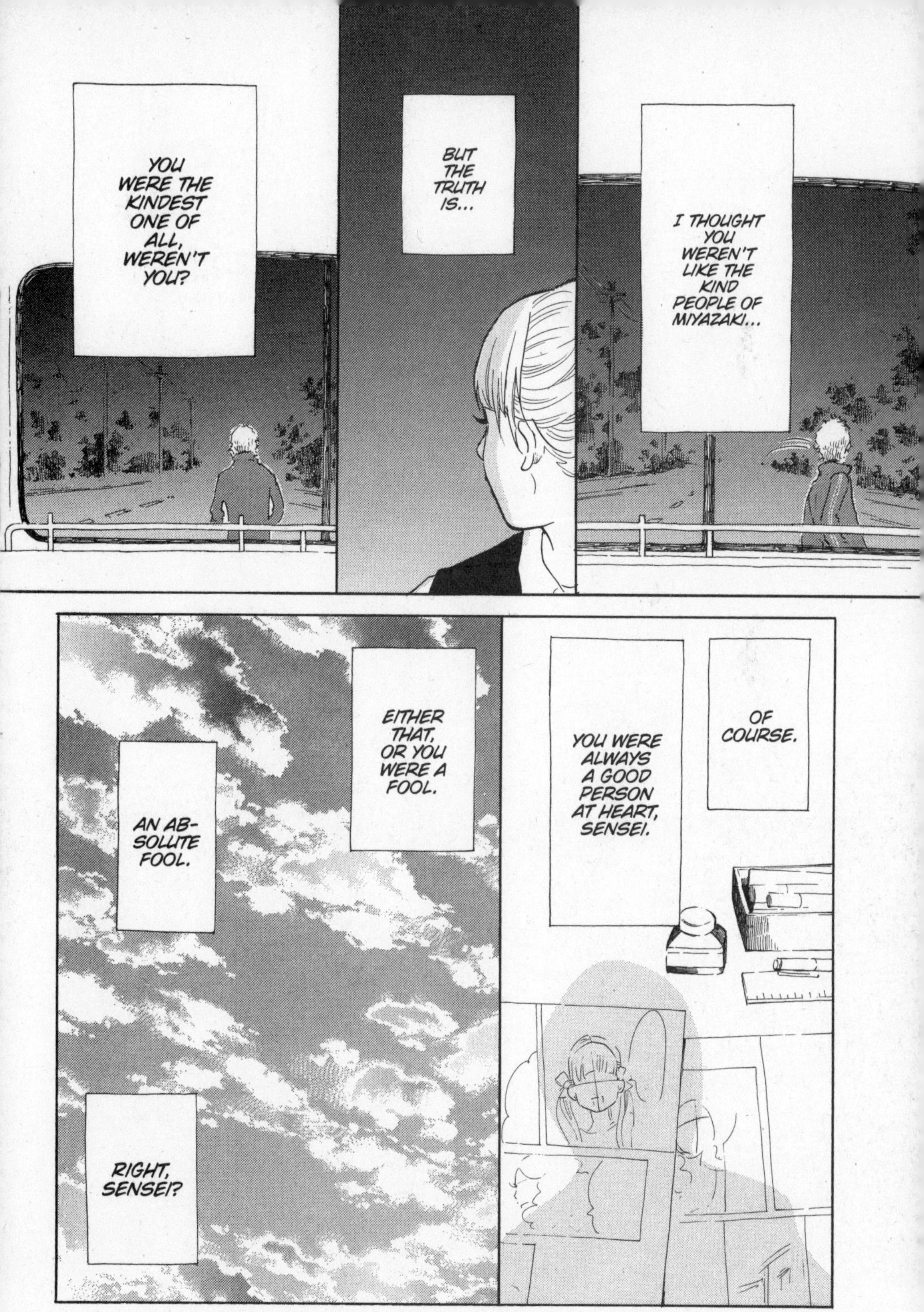
I THOUGHT YOU WEREN'T LIKE THE KIND PEOPLE OF MIYAZAKI...
BUT THE TRUTH IS...
YOU WERE THE KINDEST ONE OF ALL, WEREN'T YOU?
OF COURSE.
YOU WERE ALWAYS A GOOD PERSON AT HEART, SENSEI.
EITHER THAT, OR YOU WERE A FOOL.
AN ABSOLUTE FOOL.
RIGHT, SENSEI?

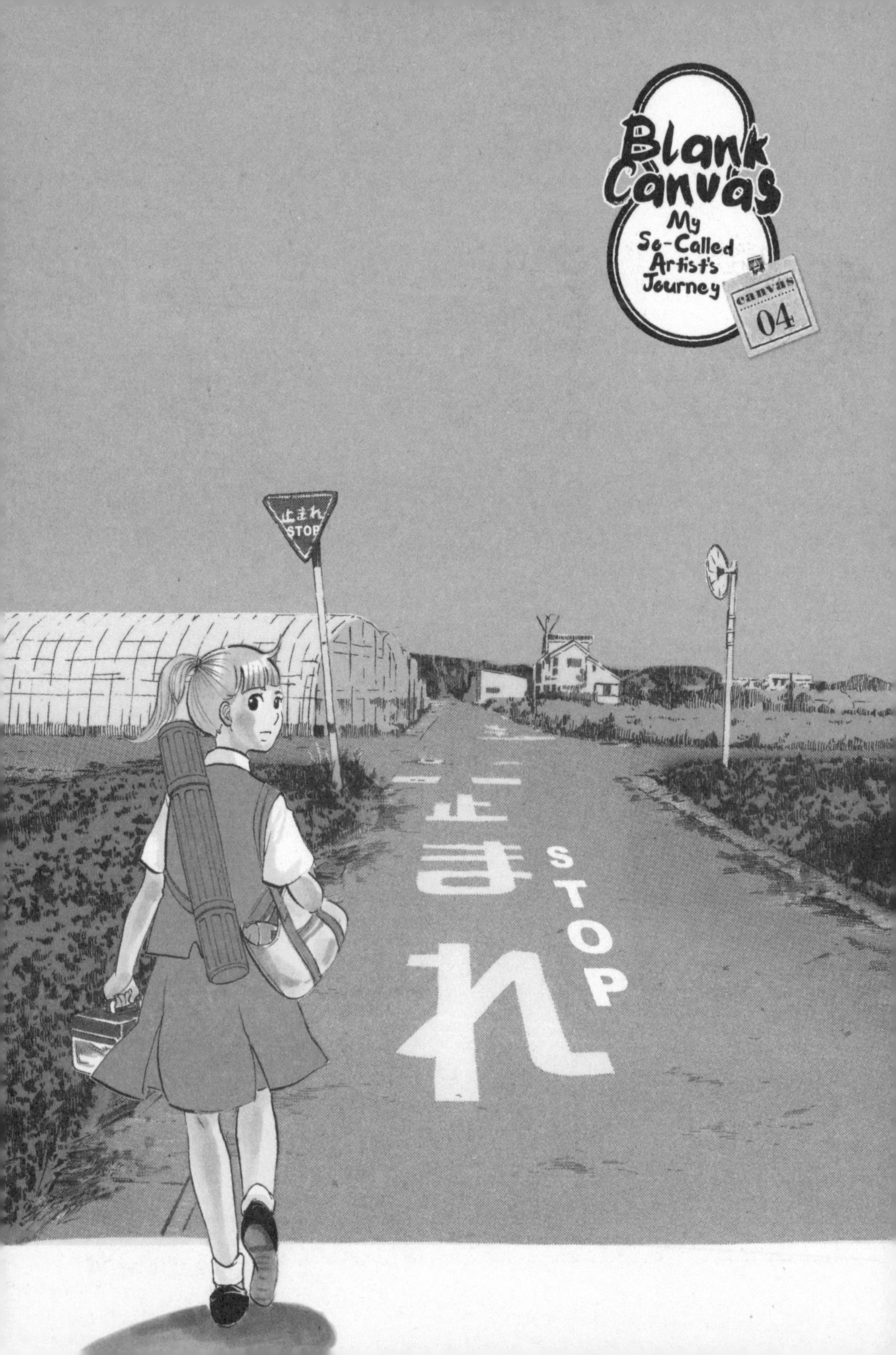
Blank Canvas
My So-Called Artist's Journey
canvas
04
止まれ
STOP
止まれ
STOP

Blank
Canvas
My So-Called
Artist's Journey

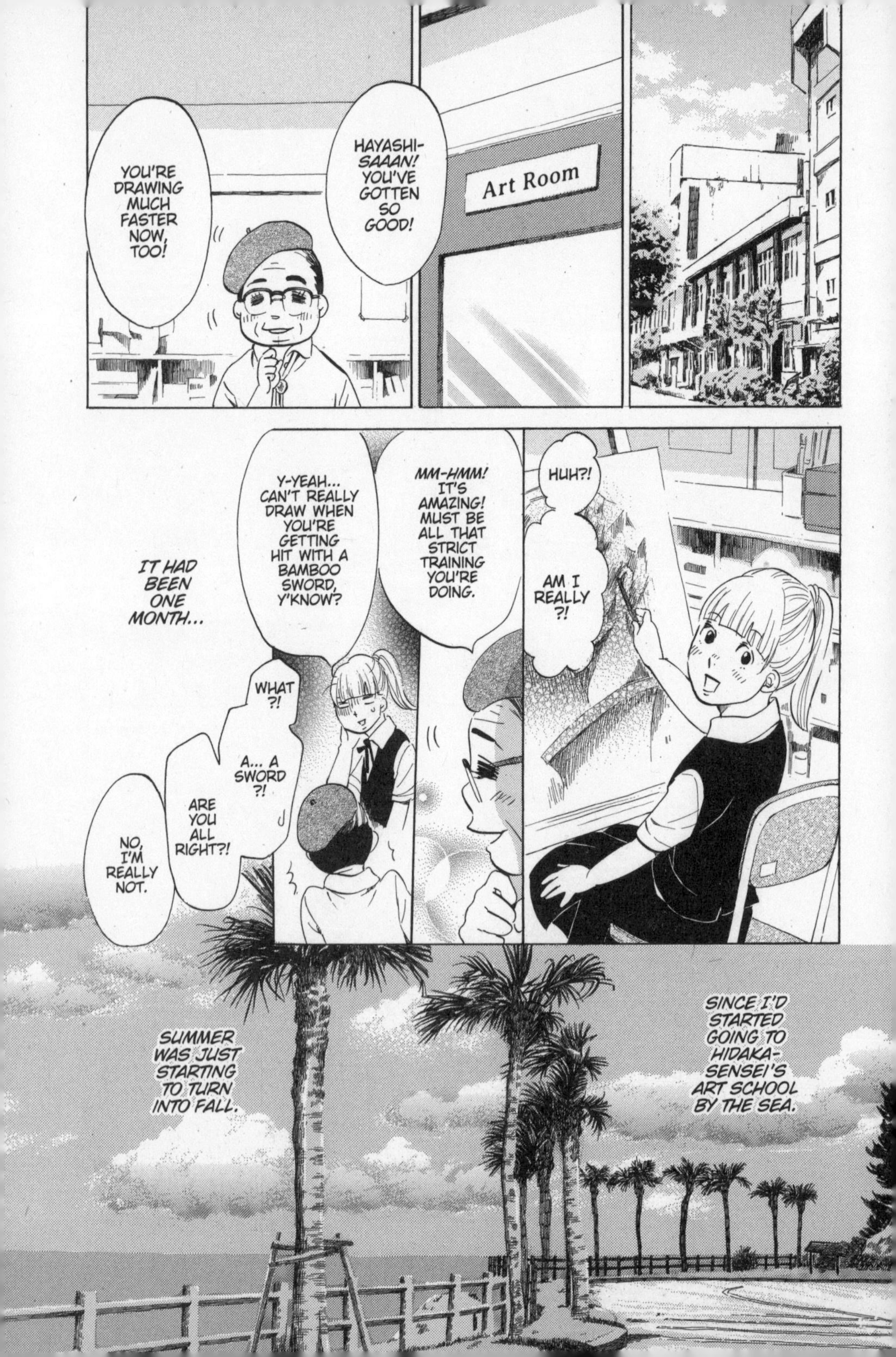
Art Room
HAYASHI-SAAAN! YOU'VE GOTTEN SO GOOD!
YOU'RE DRAWING MUCH FASTER NOW, TOO!
HUH?!
AM I REALLY?!
MM-HMM! IT'S AMAZING! MUST BE ALL THAT STRICT TRAINING YOU'RE DOING.
Y-YEAH... CAN'T REALLY DRAW WHEN YOU'RE GETTING HIT WITH A BAMBOO SWORD, Y'KNOW?
WHAT?!
A... A SWORD?!
ARE YOU ALL RIGHT?!
NO, I'M REALLY NOT.
IT HAD BEEN ONE MONTH...
SINCE I'D STARTED GOING TO HIDAKA-SENSEI'S ART SCHOOL BY THE SEA.
SUMMER WAS JUST STARTING TO TURN INTO FALL.

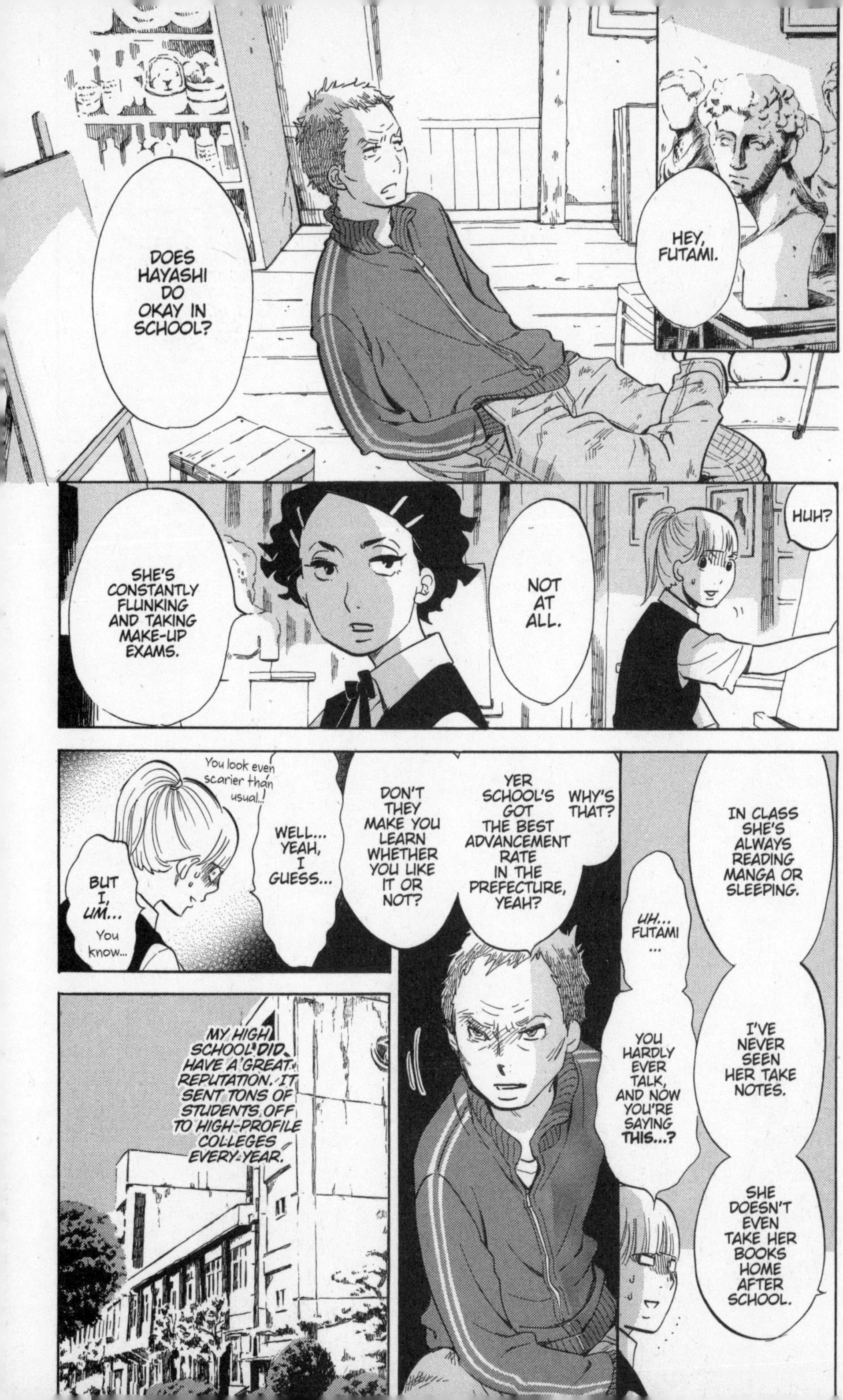
HEY, FUTAMI.
DOES HAYASHI DO OKAY IN SCHOOL?
HUH?
NOT AT ALL.
SHE'S CONSTANTLY FLUNKING AND TAKING MAKE-UP EXAMS.
IN CLASS SHE'S ALWAYS READING MANGA OR SLEEPING.
I'VE NEVER SEEN HER TAKE NOTES.
SHE DOESN'T EVEN TAKE HER BOOKS HOME AFTER SCHOOL.
UH... FUTAMI ...
YOU HARDLY EVER TALK, AND NOW YOU'RE SAYING THIS...?
WHY'S THAT?
YER SCHOOL'S GOT THE BEST ADVANCEMENT RATE IN THE PREFECTURE, YEAH?
DON'T THEY MAKE YOU LEARN WHETHER YOU LIKE IT OR NOT?
WELL... YEAH, I GUESS...
You look even scarier than usual...!
BUT I, UM...
You know...
MY HIGH SCHOOL DID HAVE A GREAT REPUTATION. IT SENT TONS OF STUDENTS OFF TO HIGH-PROFILE COLLEGES EVERY YEAR.

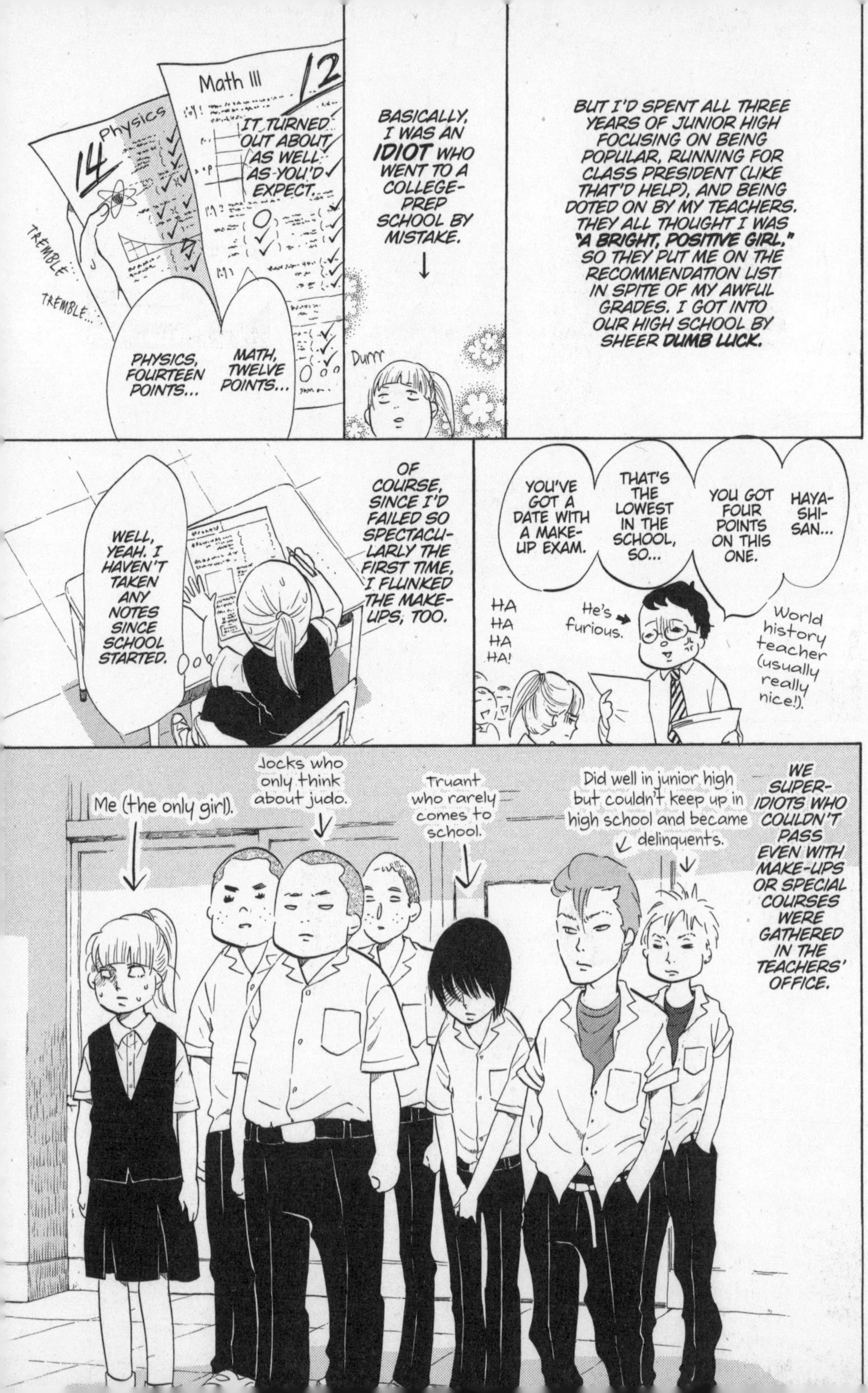
BUT I'D SPENT ALL THREE YEARS OF JUNIOR HIGH FOCUSING ON BEING POPULAR, RUNNING FOR CLASS PRESIDENT (LIKE THAT'D HELP), AND BEING DOTED ON BY MY TEACHERS. THEY ALL THOUGHT I WAS "A BRIGHT, POSITIVE GIRL," SO THEY PUT ME ON THE RECOMMENDATION LIST IN SPITE OF MY AWFUL GRADES. I GOT INTO OUR HIGH SCHOOL BY SHEER DUMB LUCK.
BASICALLY, I WAS AN IDIOT WHO WENT TO A COLLEGE-PREP SCHOOL BY MISTAKE.
Durrr
Math III
12
Physics
14
IT TURNED OUT ABOUT AS WELL AS YOU'D EXPECT.
MATH, TWELVE POINTS...
PHYSICS, FOURTEEN POINTS...
TREMBLE
TREMBLE...
HAYA-SHI-SAN...
YOU GOT FOUR POINTS ON THIS ONE.
THAT'S THE LOWEST IN THE SCHOOL, SO...
YOU'VE GOT A DATE WITH A MAKE-UP EXAM.
World history teacher (usually really nice!).
He's furious.
HA HA HA HA!
OF COURSE, SINCE I'D FAILED SO SPECTACULARLY THE FIRST TIME, I FLUNKED THE MAKE-UPS, TOO.
WELL, YEAH. I HAVEN'T TAKEN ANY NOTES SINCE SCHOOL STARTED.
WE SUPER-IDIOTS WHO COULDN'T PASS EVEN WITH MAKE-UPS OR SPECIAL COURSES WERE GATHERED IN THE TEACHERS' OFFICE.
Did well in junior high but couldn't keep up in high school and became delinquents.
Truant who rarely comes to school.
Jocks who only think about judo.
Me (the only girl).

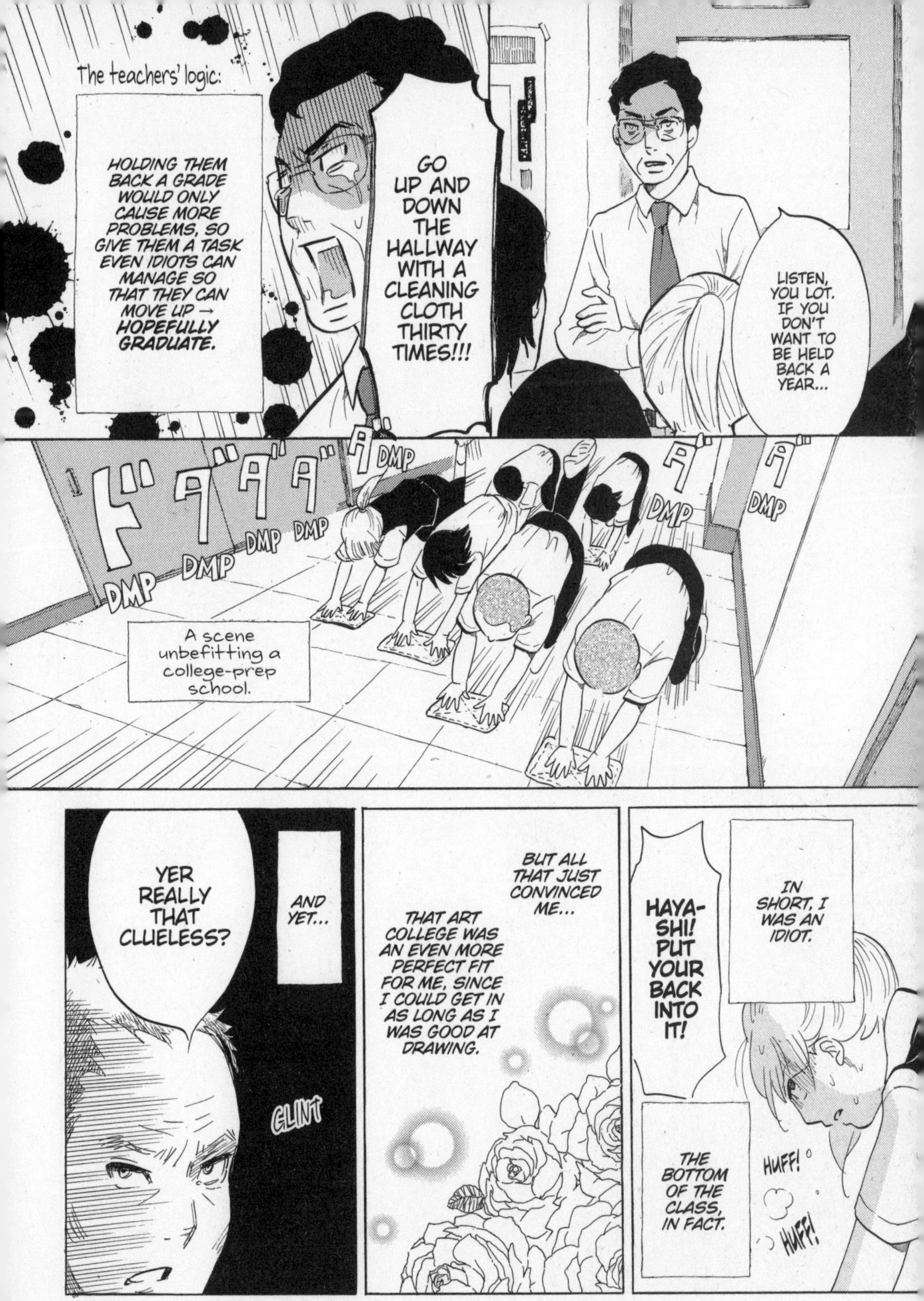

LISTEN, YOU LOT. IF YOU DON'T WANT TO BE HELD BACK A YEAR...
GO UP AND DOWN THE HALLWAY WITH A CLEANING CLOTH THIRTY TIMES!!!
The teachers' logic:
HOLDING THEM BACK A GRADE WOULD ONLY CAUSE MORE PROBLEMS, SO GIVE THEM A TASK EVEN IDIOTS CAN MANAGE SO THAT THEY CAN MOVE UP → HOPEFULLY GRADUATE.
DMP DMP DMP
DMP DMP DMP DMP DMP
A scene unbefitting a college-prep school.
IN SHORT, I WAS AN IDIOT.
HAYA-SHI! PUT YOUR BACK INTO IT!
THE BOTTOM OF THE CLASS, IN FACT.
HUFF!
HUFF!
BUT ALL THAT JUST CONVINCED ME...
THAT ART COLLEGE WAS AN EVEN MORE PERFECT FIT FOR ME, SINCE I COULD GET IN AS LONG AS I WAS GOOD AT DRAWING.
AND YET...
YER REALLY THAT CLUELESS?
GLINT

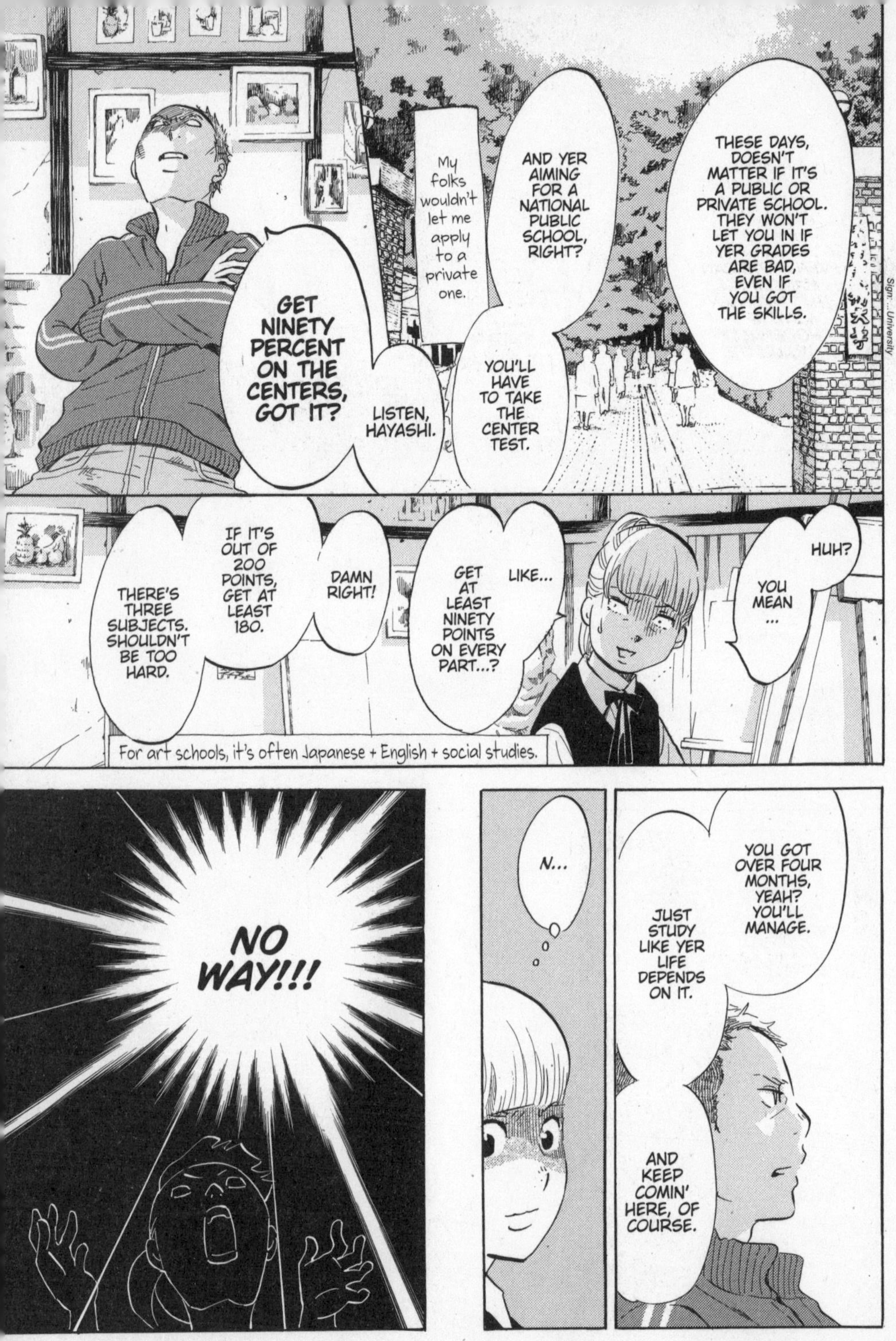

Sign: ...University
THESE DAYS, DOESN'T MATTER IF IT'S A PUBLIC OR PRIVATE SCHOOL. THEY WON'T LET YOU IN IF YER GRADES ARE BAD, EVEN IF YOU GOT THE SKILLS.
AND YER AIMING FOR A NATIONAL PUBLIC SCHOOL, RIGHT?
My folks wouldn't let me apply to a private one.
YOU'LL HAVE TO TAKE THE CENTER TEST.
LISTEN, HAYASHI.
GET NINETY PERCENT ON THE CENTERS, GOT IT?
HUH?
YOU MEAN ...
LIKE...
GET AT LEAST NINETY POINTS ON EVERY PART...?
DAMN RIGHT!
IF IT'S OUT OF 200 POINTS, GET AT LEAST 180.
THERE'S THREE SUBJECTS. SHOULDN'T BE TOO HARD.
For art schools, it's often Japanese + English + social studies.
YOU GOT OVER FOUR MONTHS, YEAH? YOU'LL MANAGE.
JUST STUDY LIKE YER LIFE DEPENDS ON IT.
AND KEEP COMIN' HERE, OF COURSE.
N...
NO WAY!!!

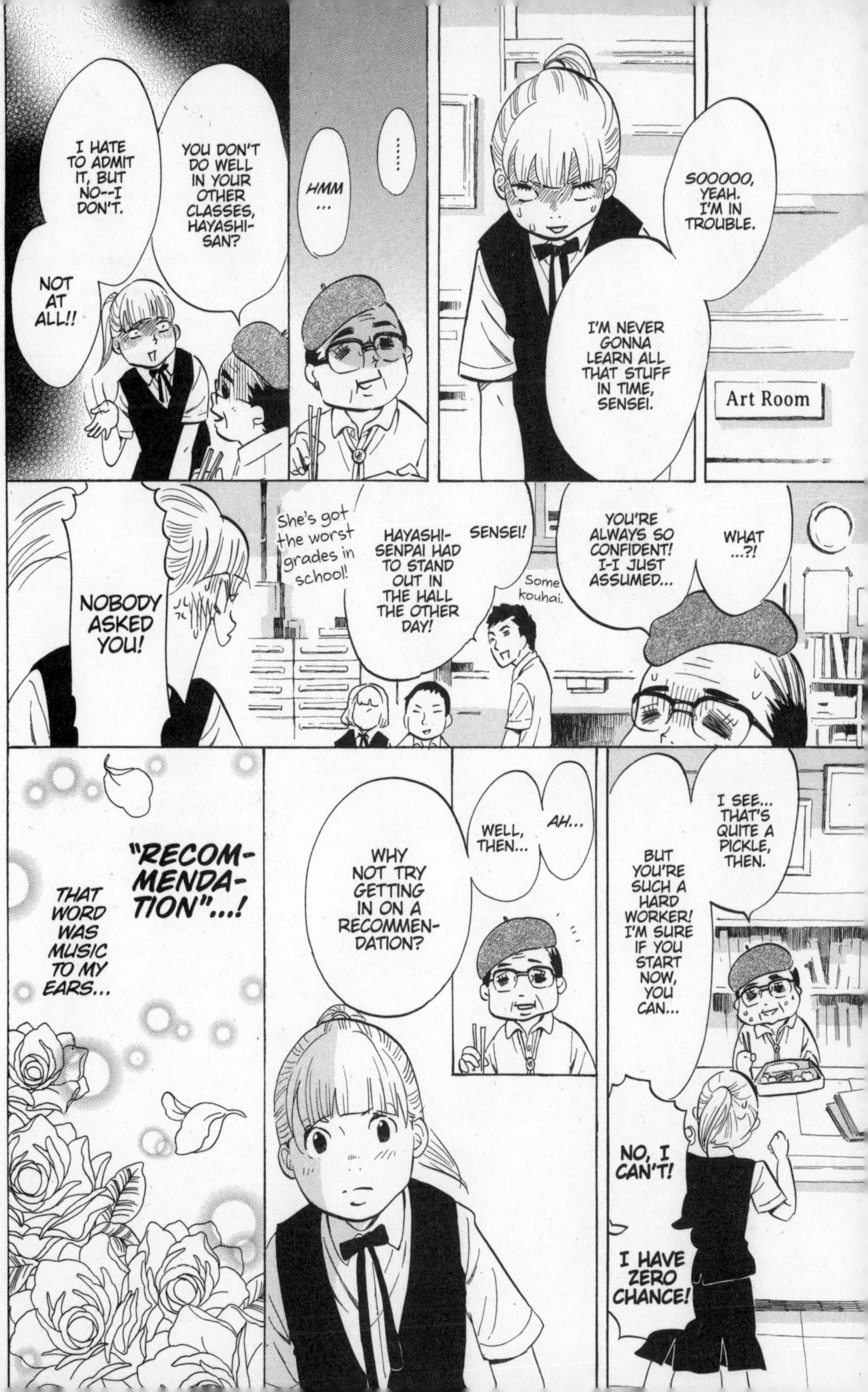
SOOOOO, YEAH. I'M IN TROUBLE.
I'M NEVER GONNA LEARN ALL THAT STUFF IN TIME, SENSEI.
Art Room
......
HMM...
YOU DON'T DO WELL IN YOUR OTHER CLASSES, HAYASHI-SAN?
I HATE TO ADMIT IT, BUT NO--I DON'T.
NOT AT ALL!!
WHAT...?!
YOU'RE ALWAYS SO CONFIDENT! I-I JUST ASSUMED...
SENSEI!
HAYASHI-SENPAI HAD TO STAND OUT IN THE HALL THE OTHER DAY!
Some kouhai.
She's got the worst grades in school!
NOBODY ASKED YOU!
I SEE... THAT'S QUITE A PICKLE, THEN.
BUT YOU'RE SUCH A HARD WORKER! I'M SURE IF YOU START NOW, YOU CAN...
NO, I CAN'T!
I HAVE ZERO CHANCE!
AH...
WELL, THEN...
WHY NOT TRY GETTING IN ON A RECOMMEN-DATION?
"RECOMMEN-MENDA-TION"...!
THAT WORD WAS MUSIC TO MY EARS...

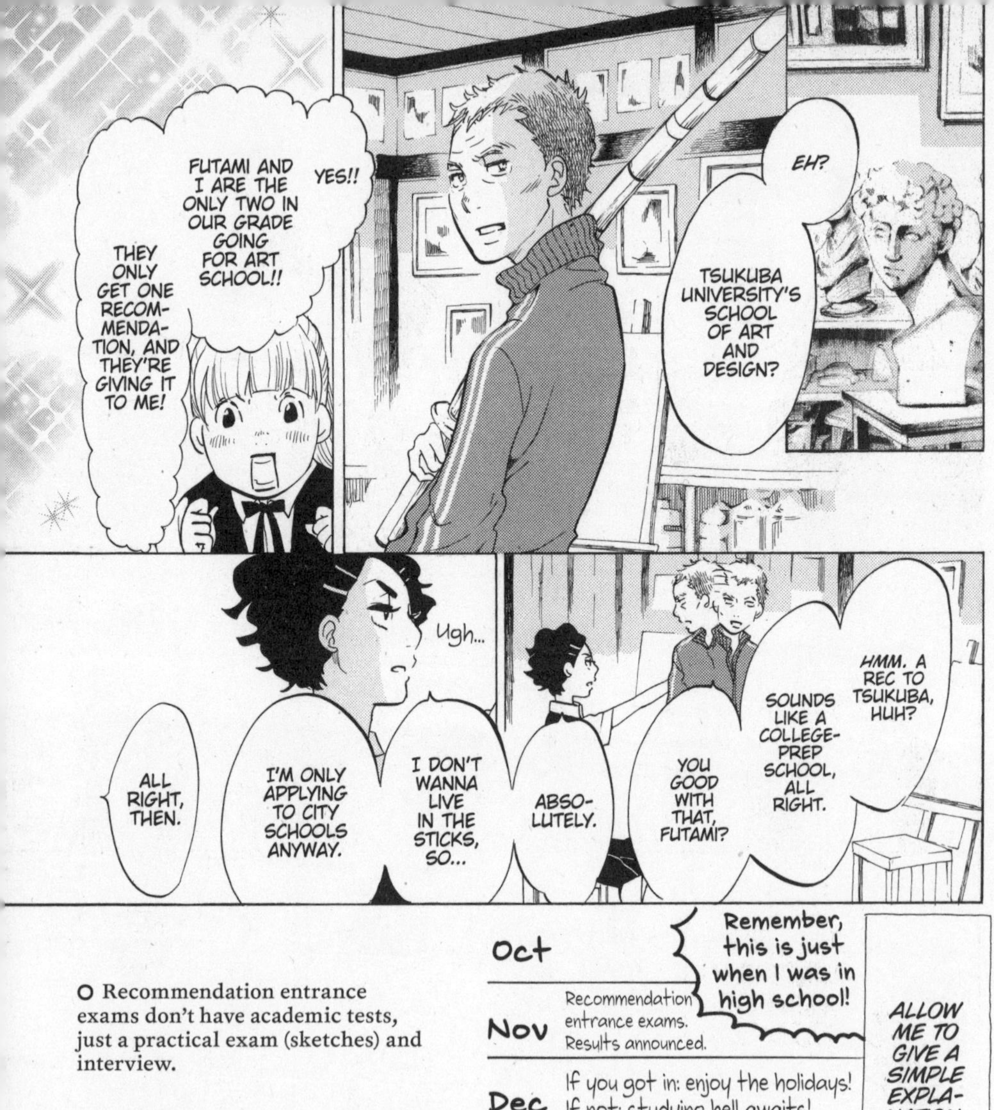
EH?
TSUKUBA UNIVERSITY'S SCHOOL OF ART AND DESIGN?
YES!!
FUTAMI AND I ARE THE ONLY TWO IN OUR GRADE GOING FOR ART SCHOOL!!
THEY ONLY GET ONE RECOMMENDATION, AND THEY'RE GIVING IT TO ME!
HMM. A REC TO TSUKUBA, HUH?
SOUNDS LIKE A COLLEGE-PREP SCHOOL, ALL RIGHT.
YOU GOOD WITH THAT, FUTAMI?
ABSOLUTELY.
I DON'T WANNA LIVE IN THE STICKS, SO...
I'M ONLY APPLYING TO CITY SCHOOLS ANYWAY.
Ugh...
ALL RIGHT, THEN.

ALLOW ME TO GIVE A SIMPLE EXPLANATION.

Remember, this is just when I was in high school!

Oct	
Nov	Recommendation entrance exams. Results announced.
Dec	If you got in: enjoy the holidays! If not: studying hell awaits!
Jan	Center Test.
Feb	Private school entrance exams. Public school A block.
Mar	B block. C block (1st half of month).
Apr	If you got in somewhere, rejoice--you're a college student!!

- Recommendation entrance exams don't have academic tests, just a practical exam (sketches) and interview.
- Acceptance rates are lower than ordinary entrance exams.
- Students who work hard on the student council, clubs, et cetera tend to get recommendations.
- Being president of the art club is the only thing Akiko works hard at, so she got a pretty good deal here.

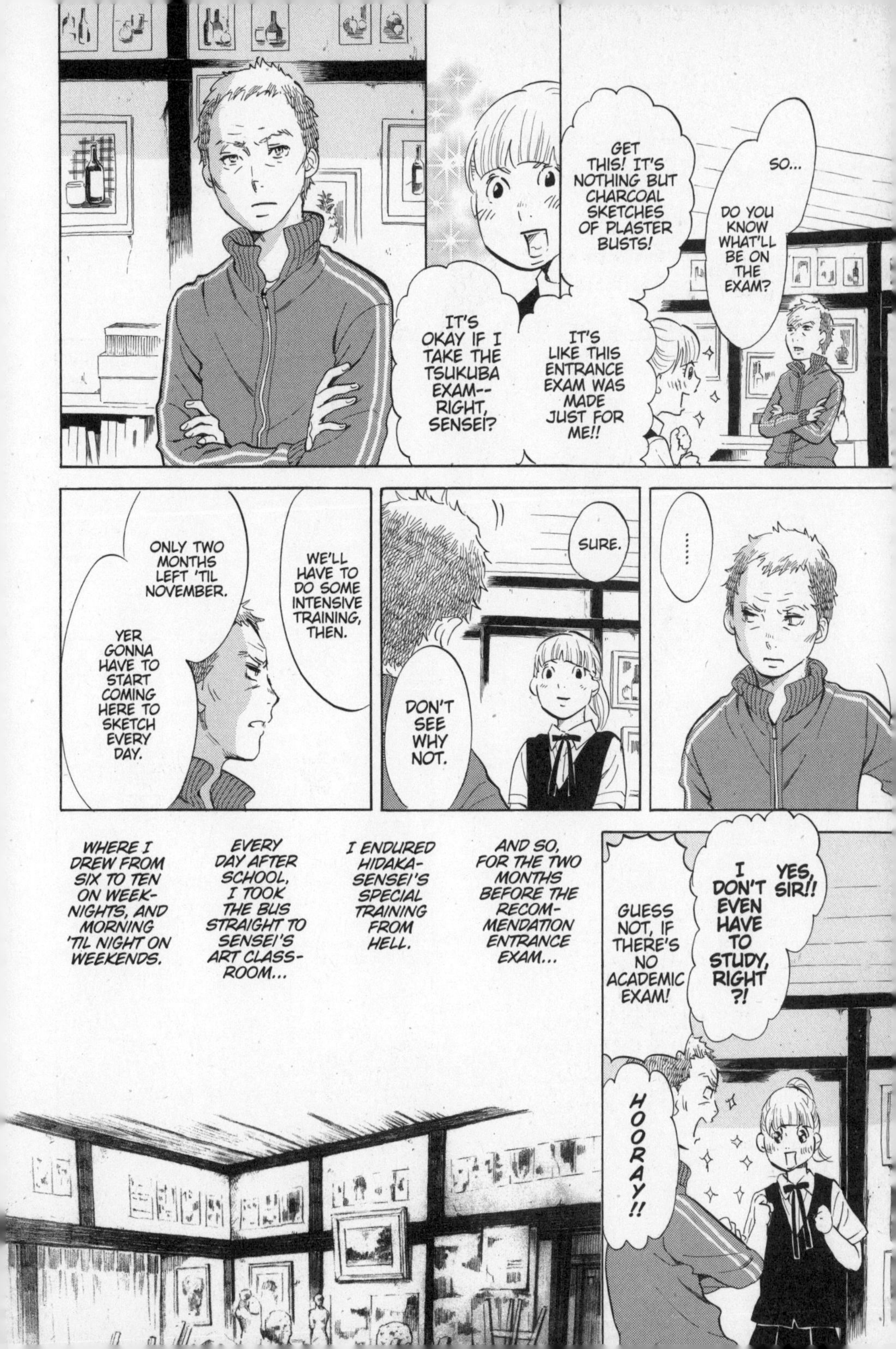
SO...
DO YOU KNOW WHAT'LL BE ON THE EXAM?
GET THIS! IT'S NOTHING BUT CHARCOAL SKETCHES OF PLASTER BUSTS!
IT'S LIKE THIS ENTRANCE EXAM WAS MADE JUST FOR ME!!
IT'S OKAY IF I TAKE THE TSUKUBA EXAM--RIGHT, SENSEI?
......
SURE.
DON'T SEE WHY NOT.
WE'LL HAVE TO DO SOME INTENSIVE TRAINING, THEN.
ONLY TWO MONTHS LEFT 'TIL NOVEMBER.
YER GONNA HAVE TO START COMING HERE TO SKETCH EVERY DAY.
YES, SIR!!
I DON'T EVEN HAVE TO STUDY, RIGHT?!
GUESS NOT, IF THERE'S NO ACADEMIC EXAM!
HOORAY!!
AND SO, FOR THE TWO MONTHS BEFORE THE RECOMMENDATION ENTRANCE EXAM...
I ENDURED HIDAKA-SENSEI'S SPECIAL TRAINING FROM HELL.
EVERY DAY AFTER SCHOOL, I TOOK THE BUS STRAIGHT TO SENSEI'S ART CLASSROOM...
WHERE I DREW FROM SIX TO TEN ON WEEKNIGHTS, AND MORNING 'TIL NIGHT ON WEEKENDS.

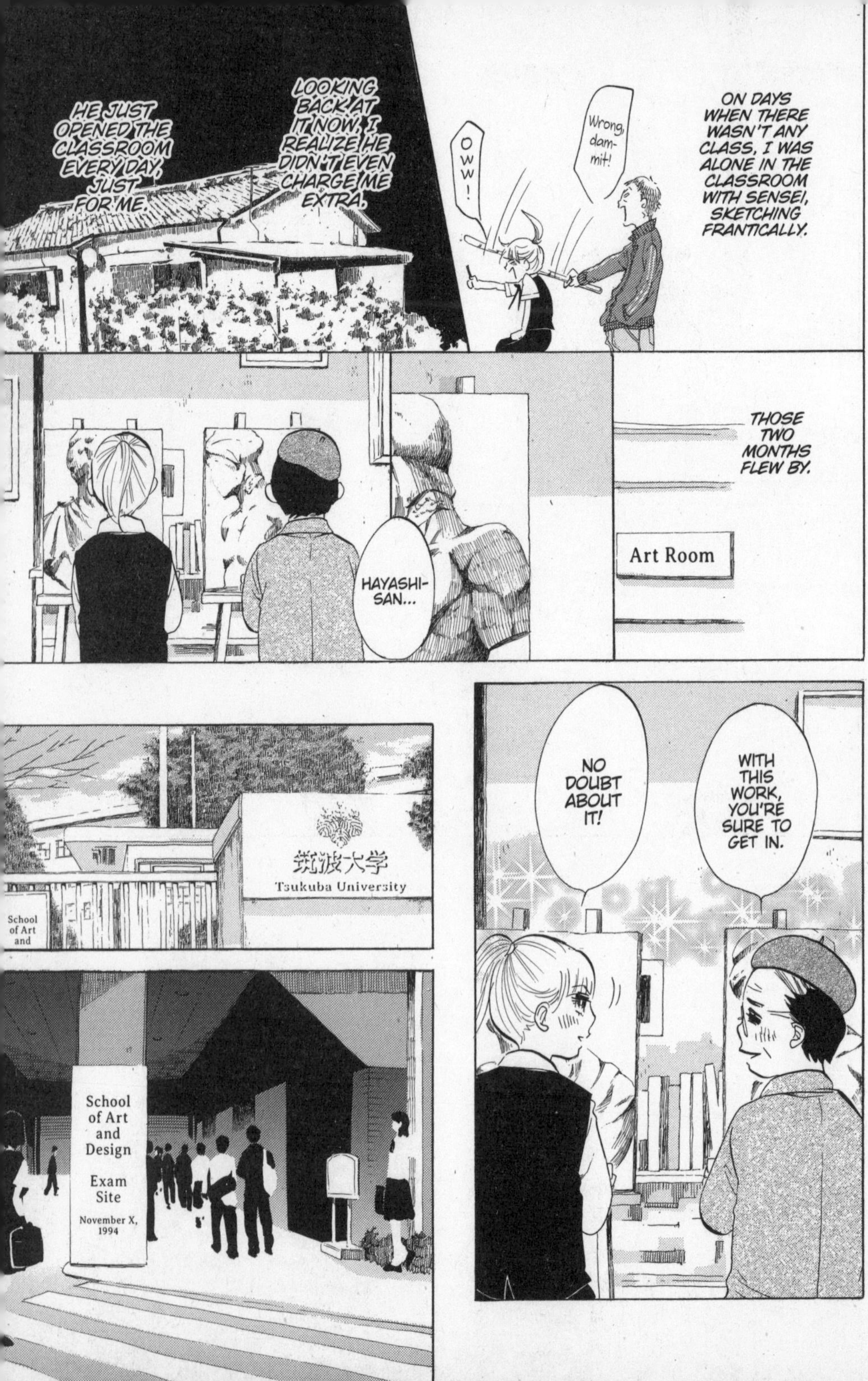
ON DAYS WHEN THERE WASN'T ANY CLASS, I WAS ALONE IN THE CLASSROOM WITH SENSEI, SKETCHING FRANTICALLY.
Wrong, dammit!
OWW!
LOOKING BACK AT IT NOW, I REALIZE HE DIDN'T EVEN CHARGE ME EXTRA.
HE JUST OPENED THE CLASSROOM EVERY DAY, JUST FOR ME.
THOSE TWO MONTHS FLEW BY.
Art Room
HAYASHI-SAN...
WITH THIS WORK, YOU'RE SURE TO GET IN.
NO DOUBT ABOUT IT!
筑波大学
Tsukuba University
School of Art and
School of Art and Design Exam Site
November X, 1994

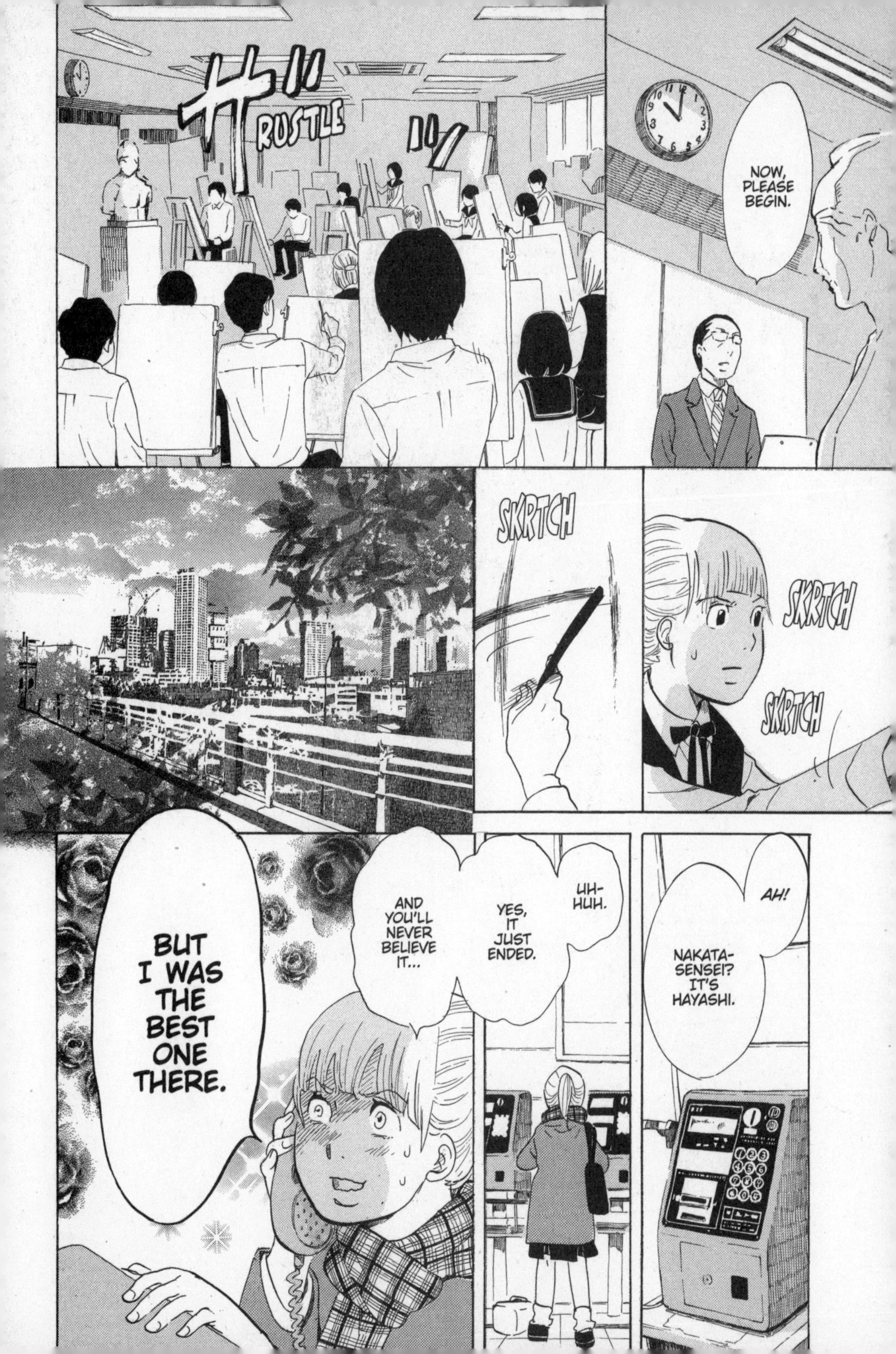
NOW, PLEASE BEGIN.
RUSTLE
SKRTCH
SKRTCH
SKRTCH
AH!
NAKATA-SENSEI? IT'S HAYASHI.
UH-HUH.
YES, IT JUST ENDED.
AND YOU'LL NEVER BELIEVE IT...
BUT I WAS THE BEST ONE THERE.

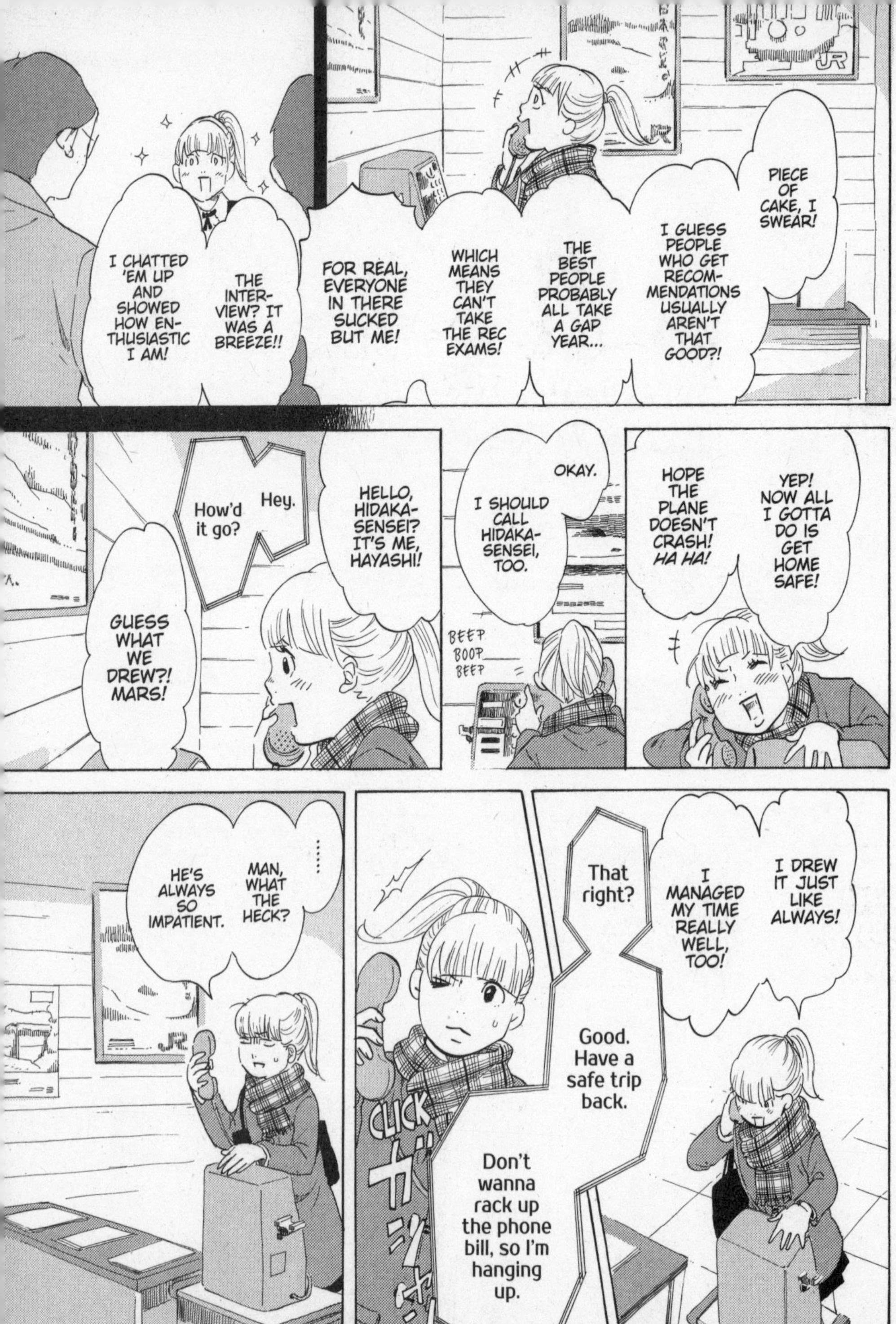
PIECE OF CAKE, I SWEAR!
I GUESS PEOPLE WHO GET RECOMMENDATIONS USUALLY AREN'T THAT GOOD?!
THE BEST PEOPLE PROBABLY ALL TAKE A GAP YEAR...
WHICH MEANS THEY CAN'T TAKE THE REC EXAMS!
FOR REAL, EVERYONE IN THERE SUCKED BUT ME!
THE INTERVIEW? IT WAS A BREEZE!!
I CHATTED 'EM UP AND SHOWED HOW ENTHUSIASTIC I AM!
YEP! NOW ALL I GOTTA DO IS GET HOME SAFE!
HOPE THE PLANE DOESN'T CRASH! HA HA!
OKAY.
I SHOULD CALL HIDAKA-SENSEI, TOO.
BEEP BOOP BEEP
HELLO, HIDAKA-SENSEI? IT'S ME, HAYASHI!
Hey.
How'd it go?
GUESS WHAT WE DREW?! MARS!
I DREW IT JUST LIKE ALWAYS!
I MANAGED MY TIME REALLY WELL, TOO!
That right?
Good. Have a safe trip back.
Don't wanna rack up the phone bill, so I'm hanging up.
CLICK
......
MAN, WHAT THE HECK?
HE'S ALWAYS SO IMPATIENT.

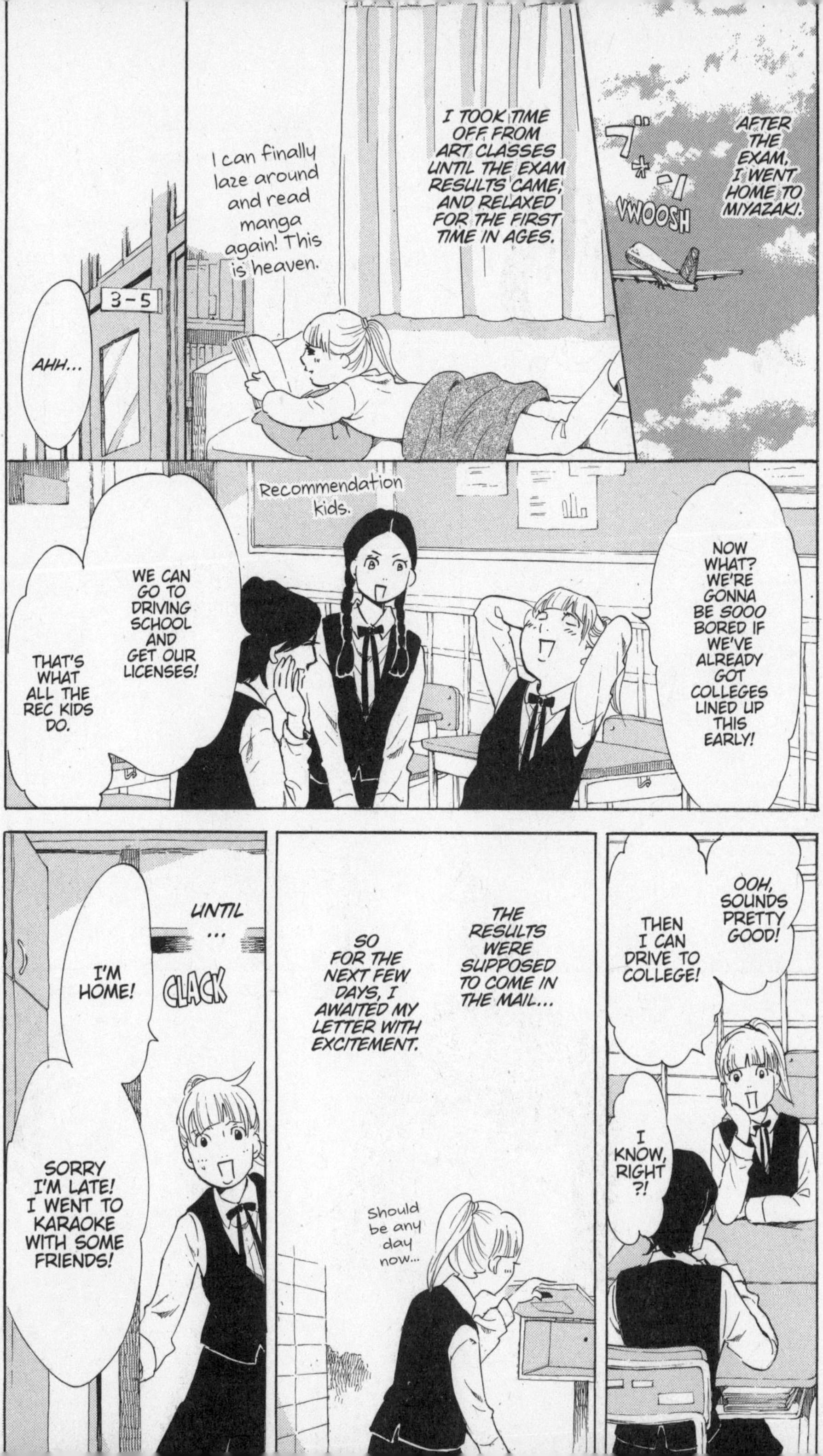
AFTER THE EXAM, I WENT HOME TO MIYAZAKI.
VWOOSH
I TOOK TIME OFF FROM ART CLASSES UNTIL THE EXAM RESULTS CAME, AND RELAXED FOR THE FIRST TIME IN AGES.
I can finally laze around and read manga again! This is heaven.
3-5
AHH...
Recommendation kids.
NOW WHAT? WE'RE GONNA BE SOOO BORED IF WE'VE ALREADY GOT COLLEGES LINED UP THIS EARLY!
WE CAN GO TO DRIVING SCHOOL AND GET OUR LICENSES!
THAT'S WHAT ALL THE REC KIDS DO.
OOH, SOUNDS PRETTY GOOD!
THEN I CAN DRIVE TO COLLEGE!
I KNOW, RIGHT?!
THE RESULTS WERE SUPPOSED TO COME IN THE MAIL...
SO FOR THE NEXT FEW DAYS, I AWAITED MY LETTER WITH EXCITEMENT.
Should be any day now...
UNTIL...
CLACK
I'M HOME!
SORRY I'M LATE! I WENT TO KARAOKE WITH SOME FRIENDS!

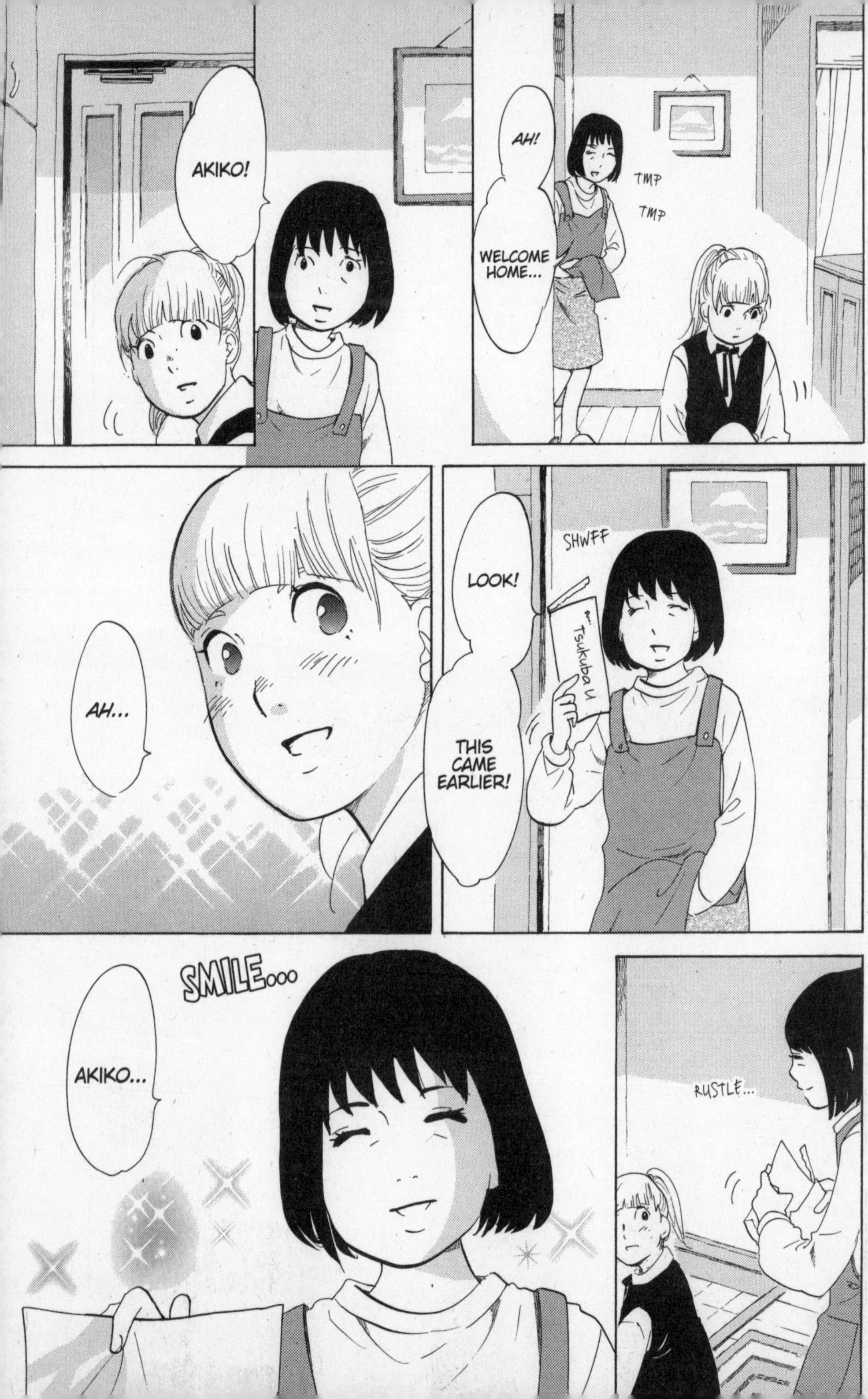
AH!
WELCOME HOME...
TMP
TMP
AKIKO!
SHWFF
LOOK!
Tsukuba U
THIS CAME EARLIER!
AH...
RUSTLE...
SMILE...
AKIKO...

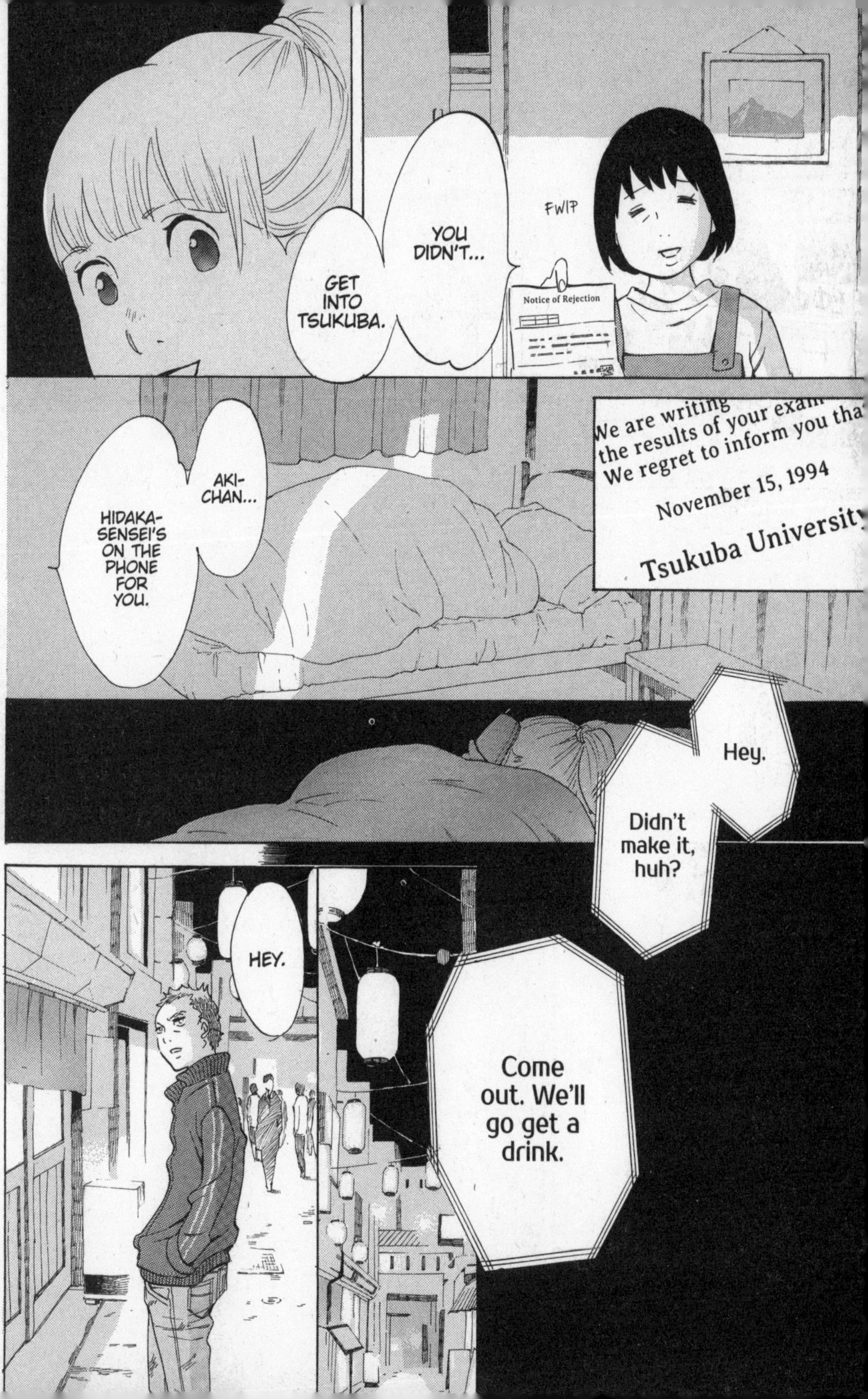
FWIP
Notice of Rejection
YOU DIDN'T...
GET INTO TSUKUBA.
We are writing
the results of your exam
We regret to inform you tha
November 15, 1994
Tsukuba University
AKI-CHAN...
HIDAKA-SENSEI'S ON THE PHONE FOR YOU.
Hey.
Didn't make it, huh?
Come out. We'll go get a drink.
HEY.

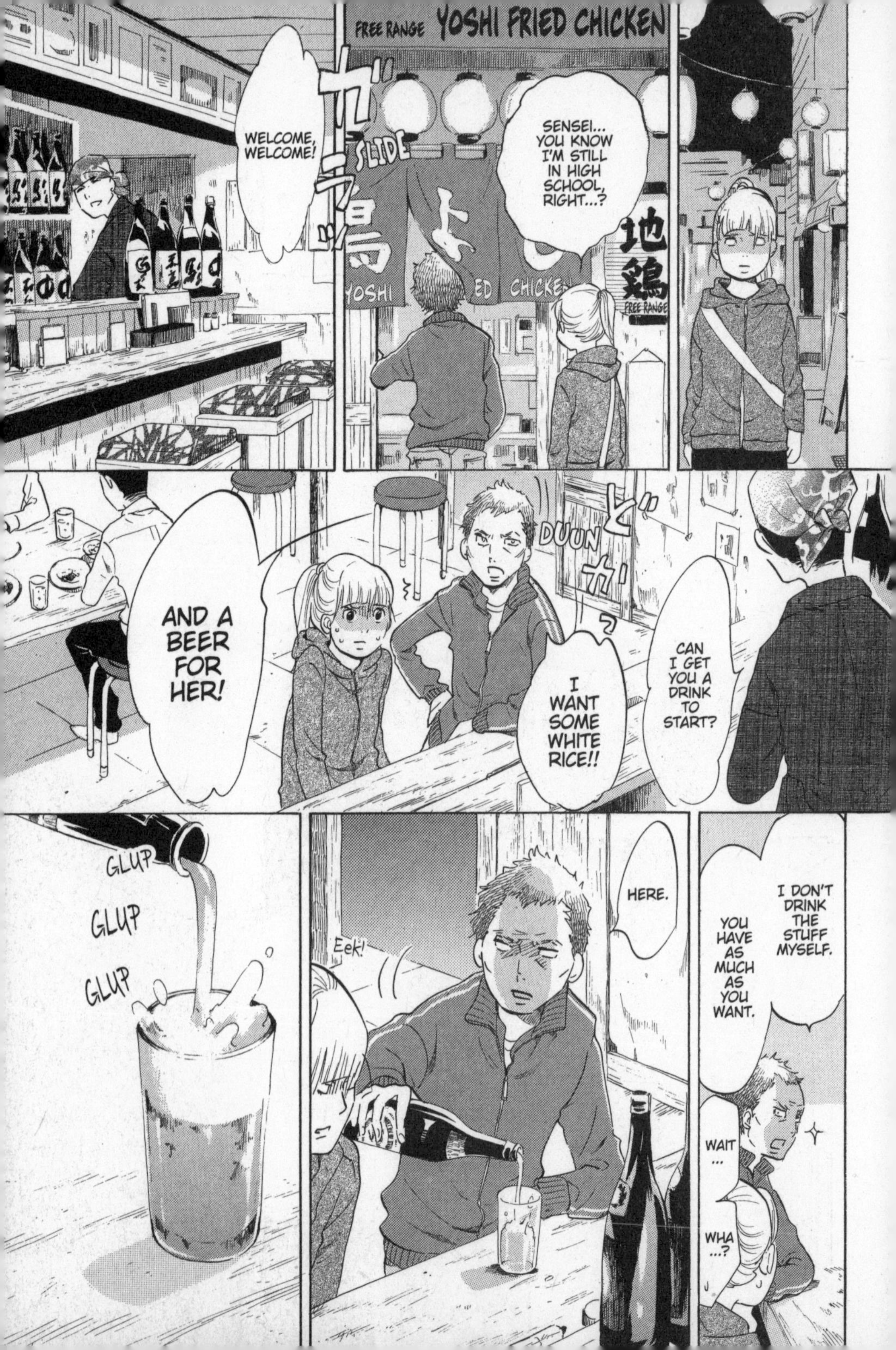
FREE RANGE YOSHI FRIED CHICKEN
SENSEI... YOU KNOW I'M STILL IN HIGH SCHOOL, RIGHT...?
地鶏
FREE RANGE
SLIDE
YOSHI ED CHICKEN
WELCOME, WELCOME!
CAN I GET YOU A DRINK TO START?
DUUN
I WANT SOME WHITE RICE!!
AND A BEER FOR HER!
I DON'T DRINK THE STUFF MYSELF.
YOU HAVE AS MUCH AS YOU WANT.
WAIT...
WHA...?
HERE.
Eek!
GLUP
GLUP
GLUP

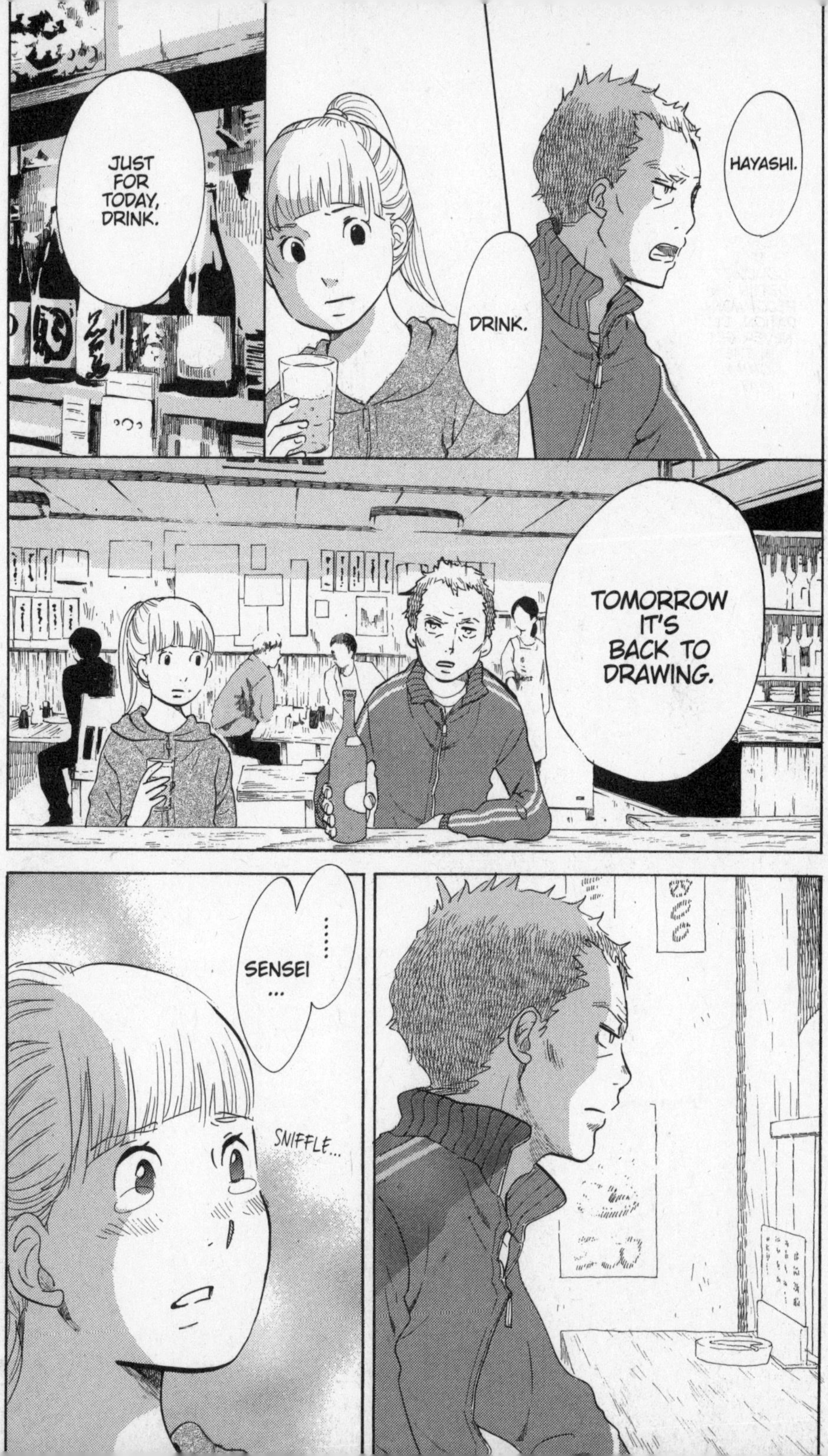
HAYASHI.
DRINK.
JUST FOR TODAY, DRINK.
TOMORROW IT'S BACK TO DRAWING.
......
SENSEI ...
SNIFFLE...

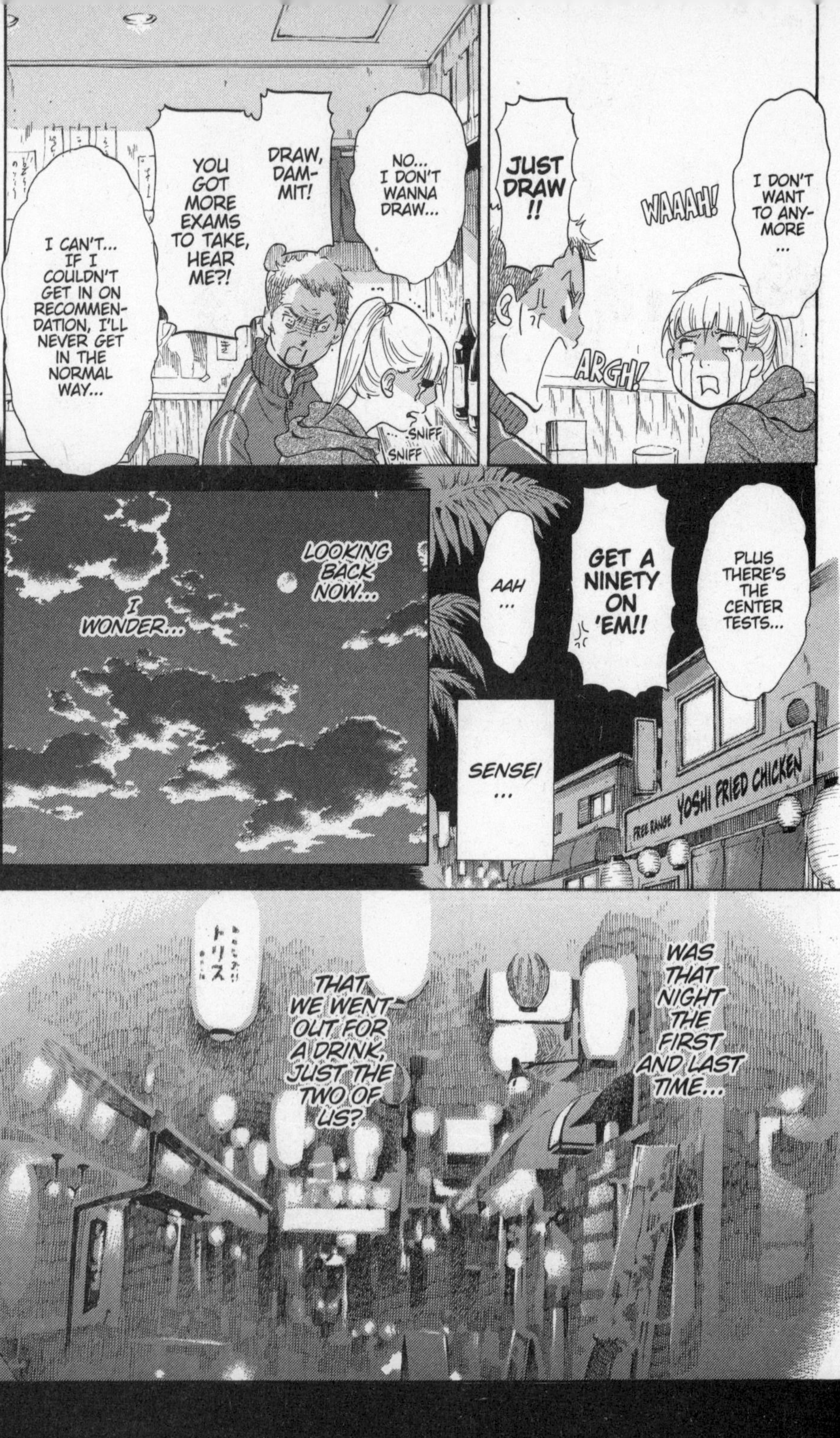
I DON'T WANT TO ANYMORE...
WAAAH!
JUST DRAW!!
ARGH!
NO... I DON'T WANNA DRAW...
DRAW, DAMMIT!
YOU GOT MORE EXAMS TO TAKE, HEAR ME?!
I CAN'T... IF I COULDN'T GET IN ON RECOMMENDATION, I'LL NEVER GET IN THE NORMAL WAY...
SNIFF
SNIFF
PLUS THERE'S THE CENTER TESTS...
GET A NINETY ON 'EM!!
AAH...
SENSEI...
FREE RANGE
YOSHI FRIED CHICKEN
LOOKING BACK NOW...
I WONDER...
WAS THAT NIGHT THE FIRST AND LAST TIME...
THAT WE WENT OUT FOR A DRINK, JUST THE TWO OF US?
トリス

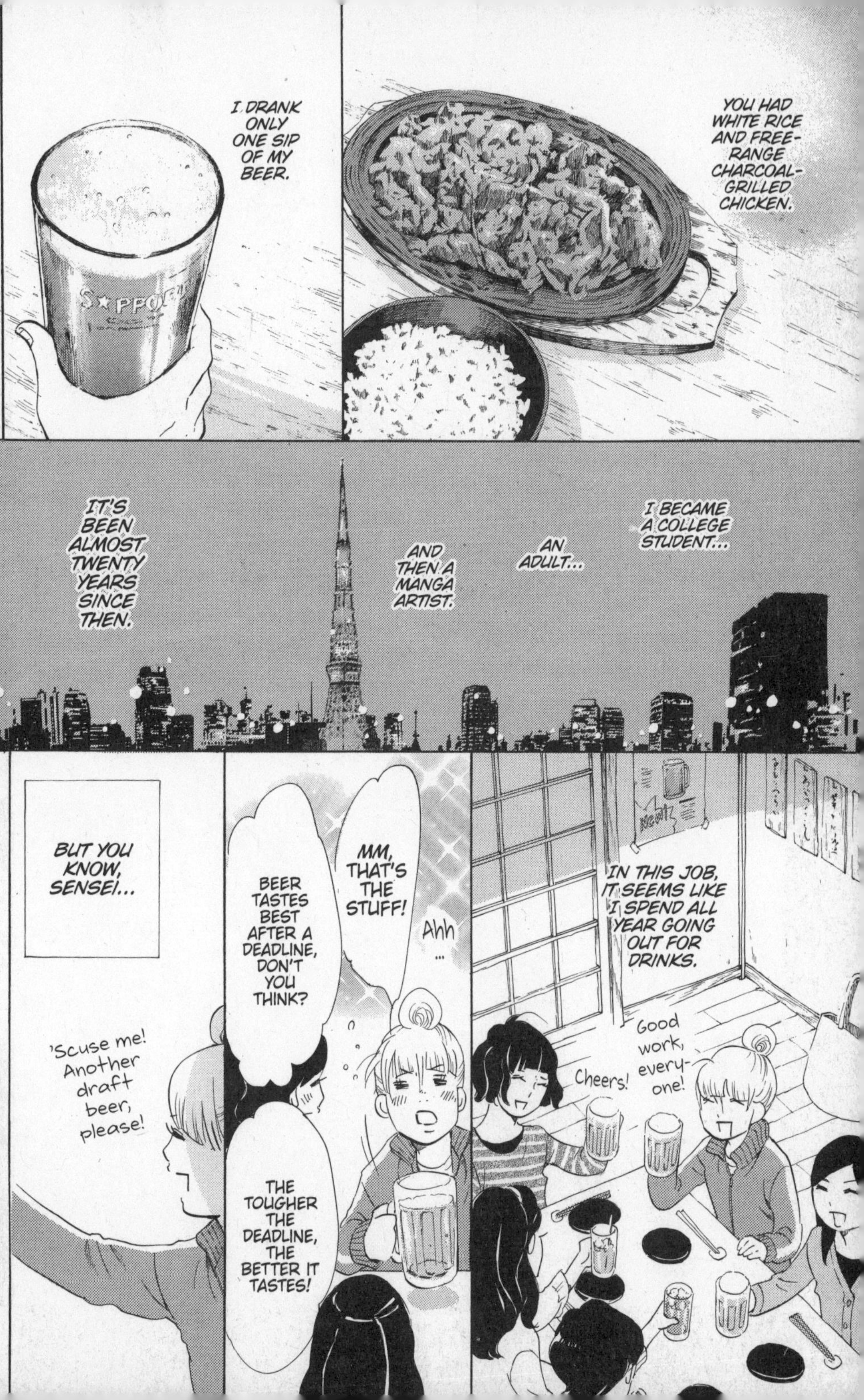
YOU HAD WHITE RICE AND FREE-RANGE CHARCOAL-GRILLED CHICKEN.
I DRANK ONLY ONE SIP OF MY BEER.
I BECAME A COLLEGE STUDENT...
AN ADULT...
AND THEN A MANGA ARTIST.
IT'S BEEN ALMOST TWENTY YEARS SINCE THEN.
IN THIS JOB, IT SEEMS LIKE I SPEND ALL YEAR GOING OUT FOR DRINKS.
Good work, every-one!
Cheers!
MM, THAT'S THE STUFF!
Ahh...
BEER TASTES BEST AFTER A DEADLINE, DON'T YOU THINK?
THE TOUGHER THE DEADLINE, THE BETTER IT TASTES!
BUT YOU KNOW, SENSEI...
'Scuse me! Another draft beer, please!

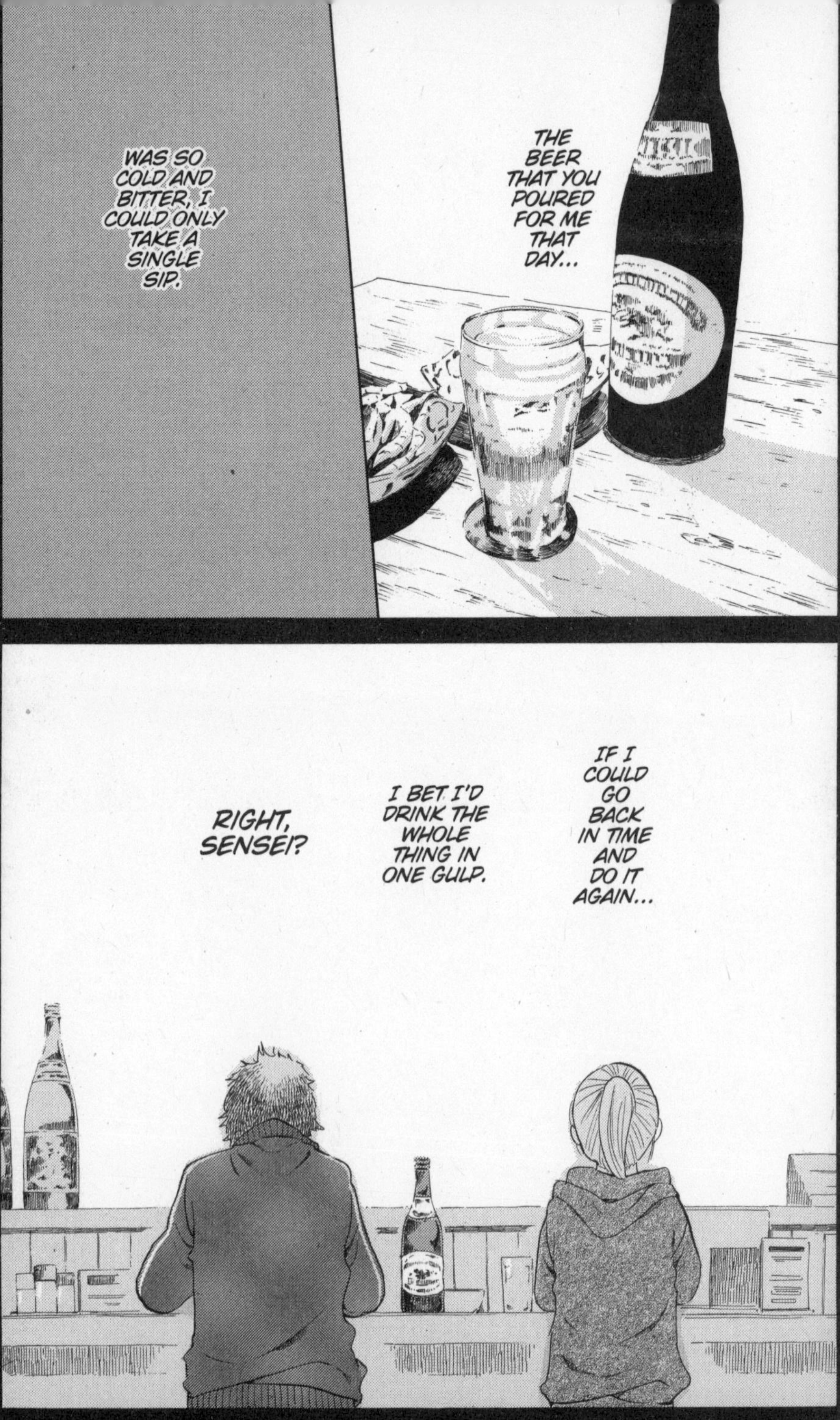
THE BEER THAT YOU POURED FOR ME THAT DAY...
WAS SO COLD AND BITTER, I COULD ONLY TAKE A SINGLE SIP.
IF I COULD GO BACK IN TIME AND DO IT AGAIN...
I BET I'D DRINK THE WHOLE THING IN ONE GULP.
RIGHT, SENSEI?

Blank Canvas

My So-Called Artist's Journey

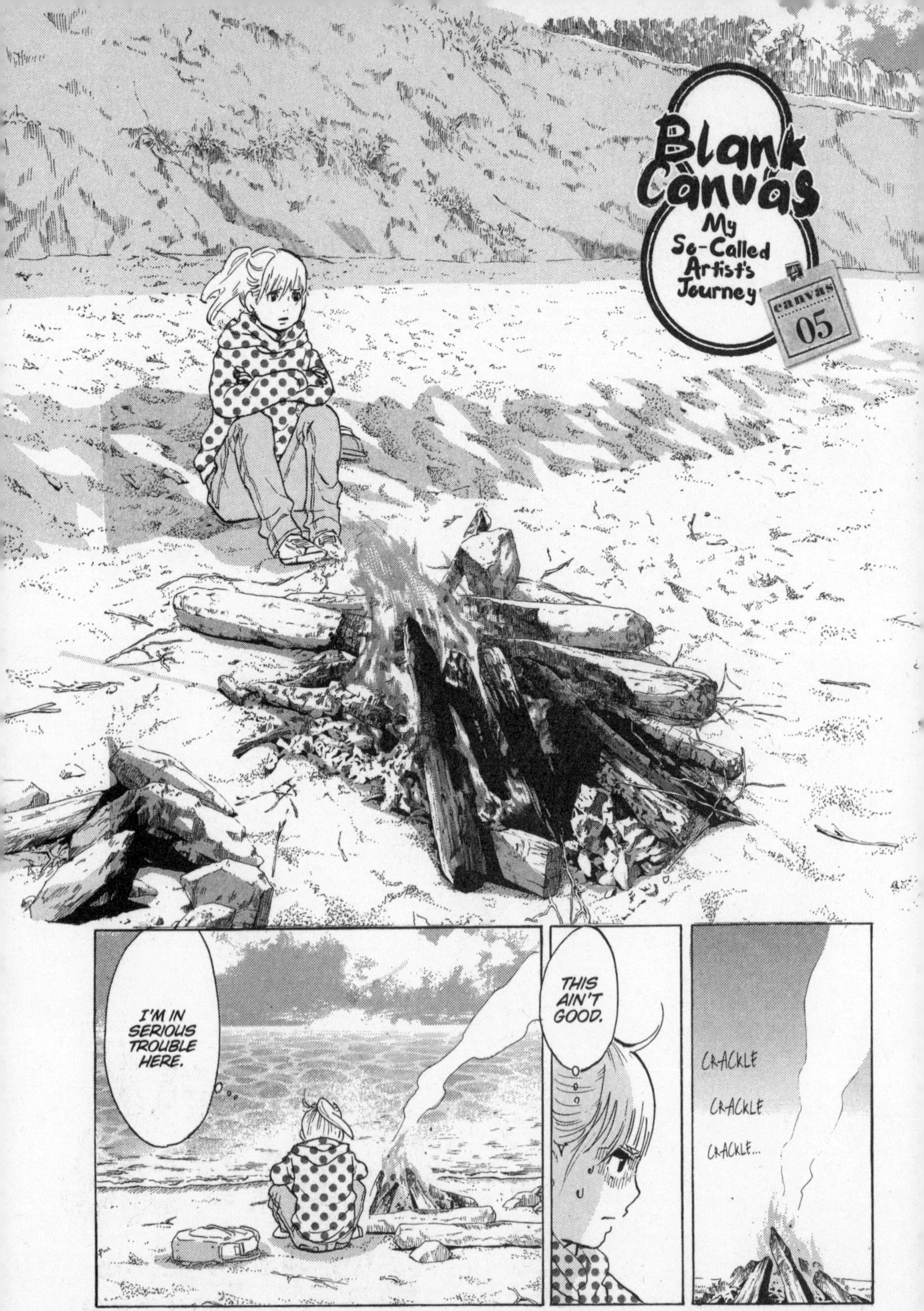
Blank Canvas
My So-Called Artist's Journey
canvas
05
CRACKLE
CRACKLE
CRACKLE...
THIS AIN'T GOOD.
I'M IN SERIOUS TROUBLE HERE.

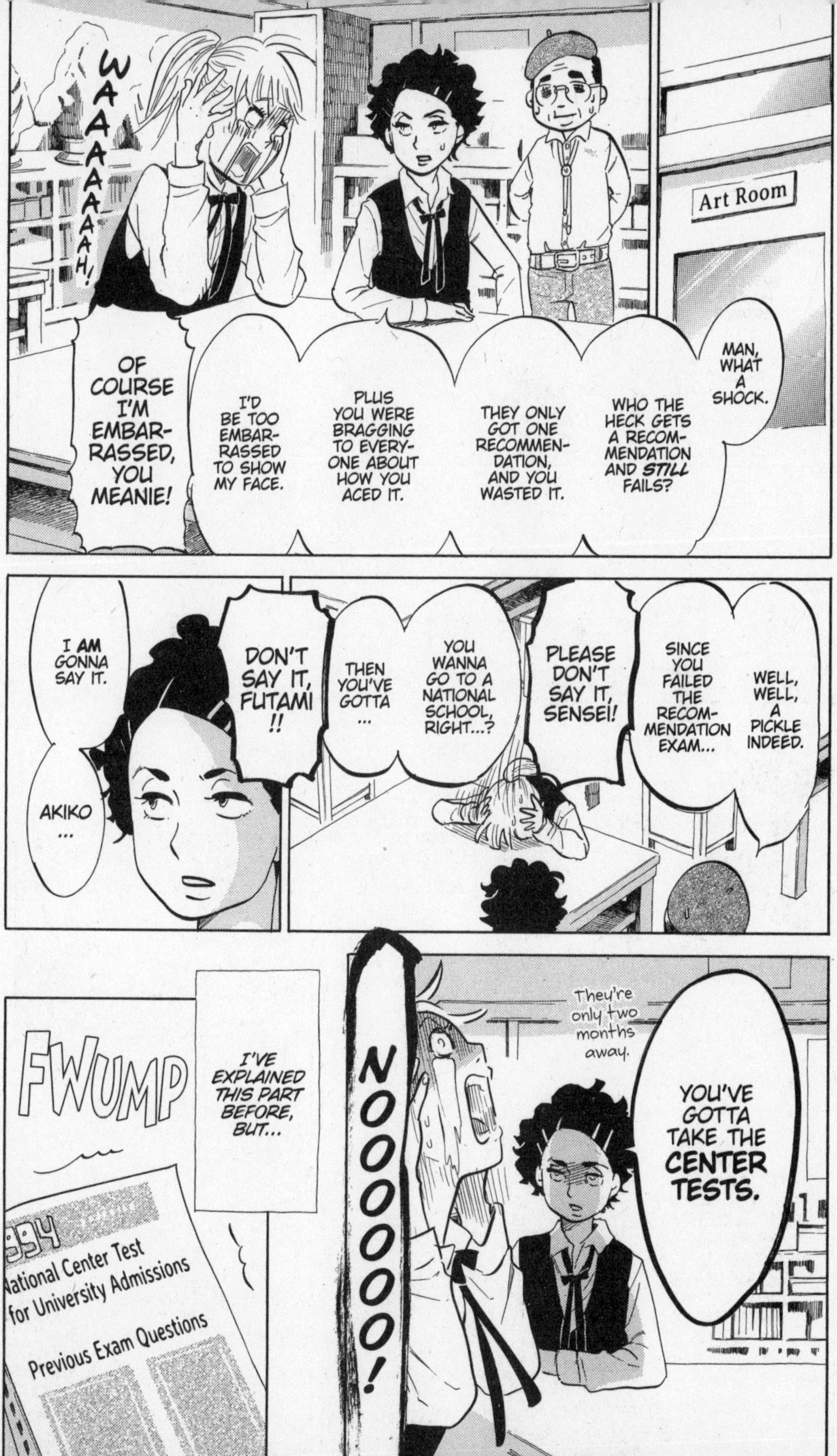
Art Room
MAN, WHAT A SHOCK.
WHO THE HECK GETS A RECOMMENDATION AND ***STILL*** FAILS?
THEY ONLY GOT ONE RECOMMENDATION, AND YOU WASTED IT.
PLUS YOU WERE BRAGGING TO EVERYONE ABOUT HOW YOU ACED IT.
I'D BE TOO EMBARRASSED TO SHOW MY FACE.
WAAAAAAAAH!
OF COURSE I'M EMBARRASSED, YOU MEANIE!
WELL, WELL, A PICKLE INDEED.
SINCE YOU FAILED THE RECOMMENDATION EXAM...
PLEASE DON'T SAY IT, SENSEI!
YOU WANNA GO TO A NATIONAL SCHOOL, RIGHT...?
THEN YOU'VE GOTTA ...
DON'T SAY IT, FUTAMI!!
I **AM** GONNA SAY IT.
AKIKO ...
YOU'VE GOTTA TAKE THE **CENTER TESTS.**
They're only two months away.
NOOOOOOO!
I'VE EXPLAINED THIS PART BEFORE, BUT...
FWUMP
994
National Center Test for University Admissions
Previous Exam Questions

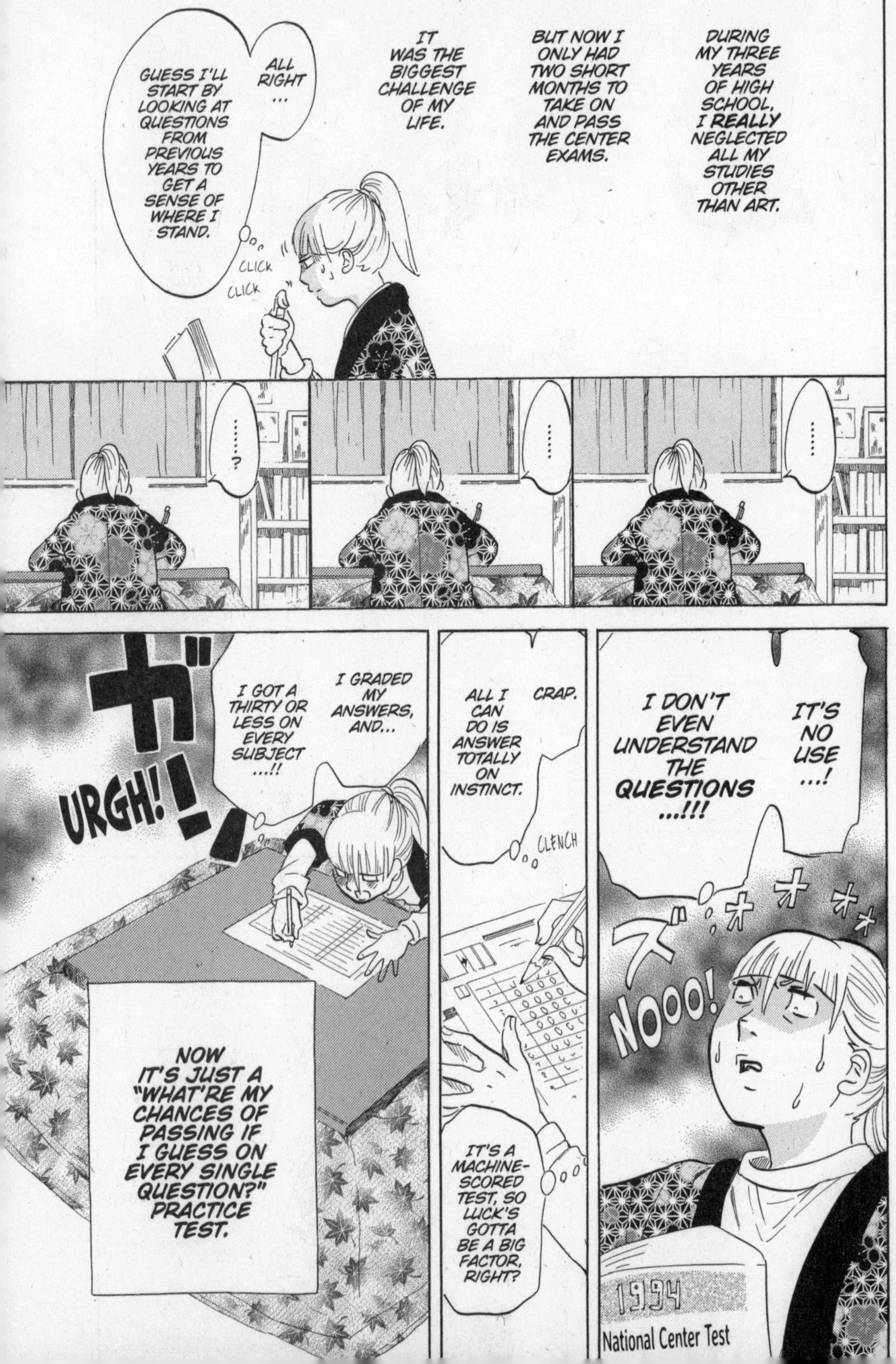
DURING MY THREE YEARS OF HIGH SCHOOL, I **REALLY** NEGLECTED ALL MY STUDIES OTHER THAN ART.
BUT NOW I ONLY HAD TWO SHORT MONTHS TO TAKE ON AND PASS THE CENTER EXAMS.
IT WAS THE BIGGEST CHALLENGE OF MY LIFE.
ALL RIGHT ...
GUESS I'LL START BY LOOKING AT QUESTIONS FROM PREVIOUS YEARS TO GET A SENSE OF WHERE I STAND.
CLICK
CLICK
......
......
......?
IT'S NO USE ...!
I DON'T EVEN UNDERSTAND THE **QUESTIONS** ...!!!
NOOO!
1994
National Center Test
CRAP.
ALL I CAN DO IS ANSWER TOTALLY ON INSTINCT.
CLENCH
IT'S A MACHINE-SCORED TEST, SO LUCK'S GOTTA BE A BIG FACTOR, RIGHT?
I GRADED MY ANSWERS, AND...
I GOT A THIRTY OR LESS ON EVERY SUBJECT ...!!
ガ
URGH!!
NOW IT'S JUST A "WHAT'RE MY CHANCES OF PASSING IF I GUESS ON EVERY SINGLE QUESTION?" PRACTICE TEST.

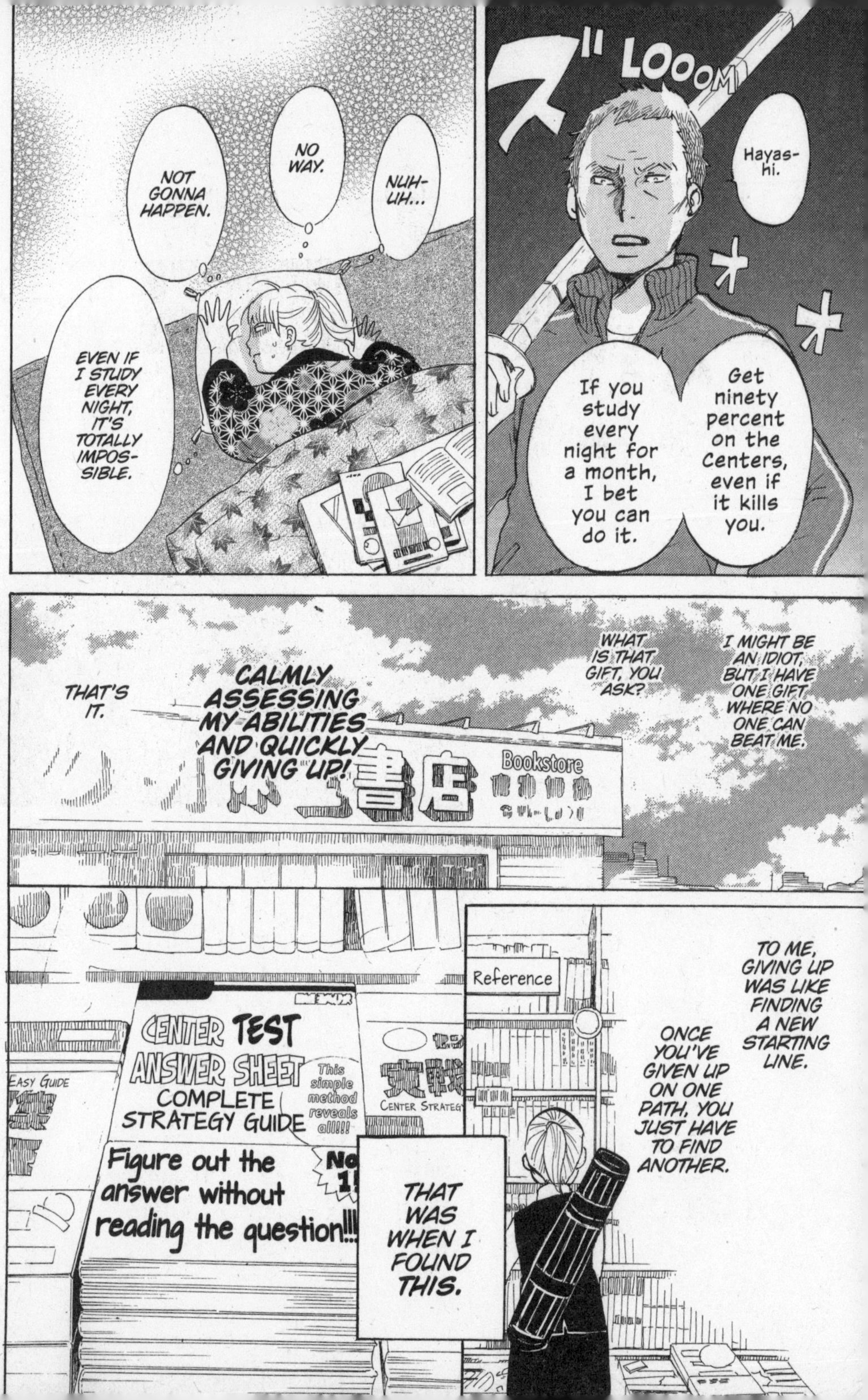
ズ" LOOOM
Hayas-hi.
Get ninety percent on the Centers, even if it kills you.
If you study every night for a month, I bet you can do it.
NUH-UH...
NO WAY.
NOT GONNA HAPPEN.
EVEN IF I STUDY EVERY NIGHT, IT'S TOTALLY IMPOS-SIBLE.
I MIGHT BE AN IDIOT, BUT I HAVE ONE GIFT WHERE NO ONE CAN BEAT ME.
WHAT IS THAT GIFT, YOU ASK?
THAT'S IT.
CALMLY ASSESSING MY ABILITIES AND QUICKLY GIVING UP!
書店
Bookstore
TO ME, GIVING UP WAS LIKE FINDING A NEW STARTING LINE.
ONCE YOU'VE GIVEN UP ON ONE PATH, YOU JUST HAVE TO FIND ANOTHER.
Reference
Center Strategy
CENTER TEST ANSWER SHEET COMPLETE STRATEGY GUIDE
This simple method reveals all!!!
Easy Guide
Figure out the answer without reading the question!!!
THAT WAS WHEN I FOUND THIS.

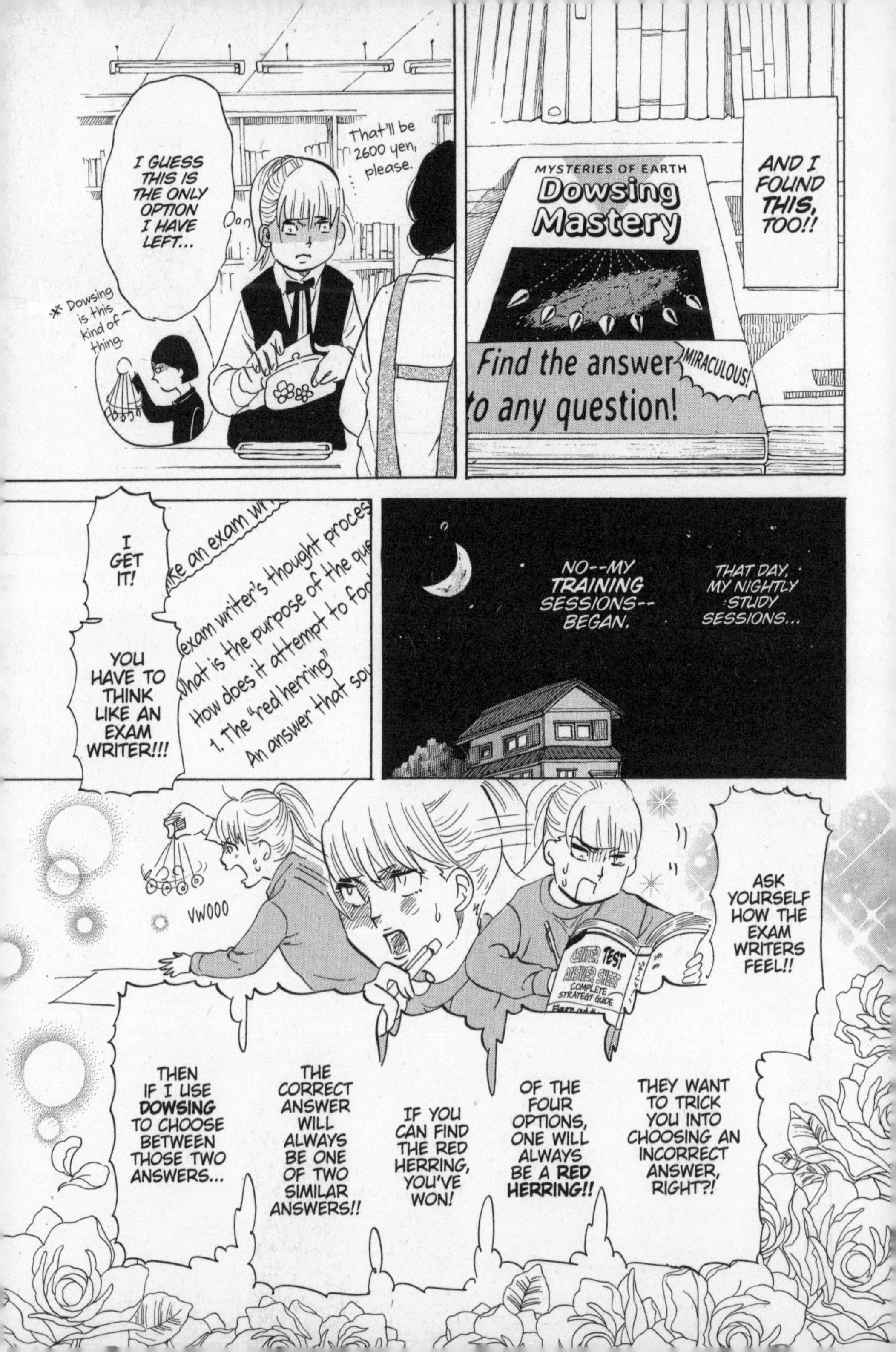

AND I FOUND THIS, TOO!!
MYSTERIES OF EARTH
Dowsing Mastery
Find the answer to any question!
MIRACULOUS!
That'll be 2600 yen, please.
I GUESS THIS IS THE ONLY OPTION I HAVE LEFT...
※ Dowsing is this kind of thing.
THAT DAY, MY NIGHTLY STUDY SESSIONS...
NO--MY TRAINING SESSIONS--BEGAN.
I GET IT!
ke an exam wr
exam writer's thought proces
hat is the purpose of the que
How does it attempt to foo
1. The "red herring"
An answer that sou
YOU HAVE TO THINK LIKE AN EXAM WRITER!!!
ASK YOURSELF HOW THE EXAM WRITERS FEEL!!
CENTER TEST ANSWER SHEET COMPLETE STRATEGY GUIDE
VWOOO
THEY WANT TO TRICK YOU INTO CHOOSING AN INCORRECT ANSWER, RIGHT?!
OF THE FOUR OPTIONS, ONE WILL ALWAYS BE A RED HERRING!!
IF YOU CAN FIND THE RED HERRING, YOU'VE WON!
THE CORRECT ANSWER WILL ALWAYS BE ONE OF TWO SIMILAR ANSWERS!!
THEN IF I USE DOWSING TO CHOOSE BETWEEN THOSE TWO ANSWERS...

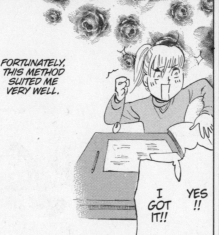

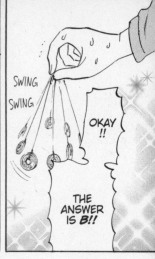

SWING
SWING
OKAY!!
THE ANSWER IS B!!
FORTUNATELY, THIS METHOD SUITED ME VERY WELL.
I GUESS THE CONCEPT OF TRYING TO PUT MYSELF IN THE EXAM WRITERS' SHOES AND THINKING ABOUT HOW THEY MIGHT TRY TO FOOL OR TRAP EXAMINEES REALLY MESHED WITH MY PERSONALITY.
YES!!
I GOT IT!!
FYI, THIS METHOD DOESN'T WORK WITH NUMBER-BASED ANSWERS!
EX. Q: Who is the author of this novel?
(a. Yoshida Soseki) (b. Natsume Soseki) (c. Natsume Akira) (d. Dazai Osamu)
Look for similar words or ideas...
The correct answer is B!!
But...
(a. 50) (b. 55) (c. 60) (d. 65)
Since numbers are just a bunch of digits, you can't look for "similar words" (because there aren't any), so there's no way to use this method.
SO IT'S NOT USEFUL FOR MATH AND SCIENCE, BUT FOR THE HUMANITIES--THINGS LIKE ART SCHOOL EXAMS--IT'S PERFECT!
FOR MY THIRD SUBJECT, IN ADDITION TO ENGLISH AND JAPANESE, I CHOSE GEOGRAPHY...
BUT THERE TURNED OUT TO BE A LOT OF NUMBERS IN THOSE ANSWERS, TOO (LIKE TEMPERATURES AND GRAPH CHOICES).
THAT MADE ME REALIZE THAT THIS METHOD WOULDN'T BE ENOUGH TO GET ME THROUGH EVERYTHING, SO I PICKED UP EVEN MORE CHEATING--ER, REFERENCE--BOOKS SPECIFICALLY FOR GEOGRAPHY.
Temp (°C)
Precip. (mm)
気温
降水量
Moscow
Cairo
Center Tests
Geography
for Dummies
One easy trick!
GEOGRAPHY
SIMPLE METHODS
FOR PASSING
Easy-to-understand key points!!
I SHOULD MENTION THAT THIS ANSWER-SHEET METHOD BECAME SUCH A WIDESPREAD PROBLEM RIGHT AROUND THEN...
THAT I'M PRETTY SURE THEY COMPLETELY OVERHAULED THE TESTS A YEAR OR TWO LATER SO IT WOULDN'T WORK ANYMORE.

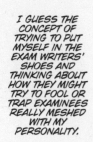

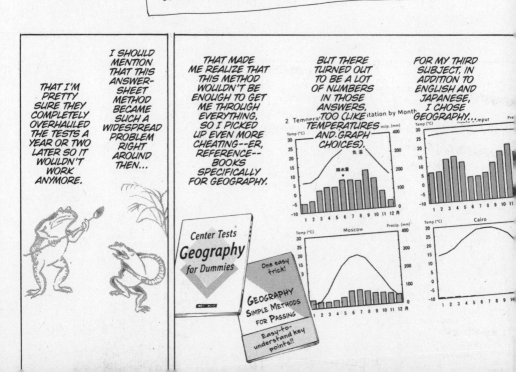

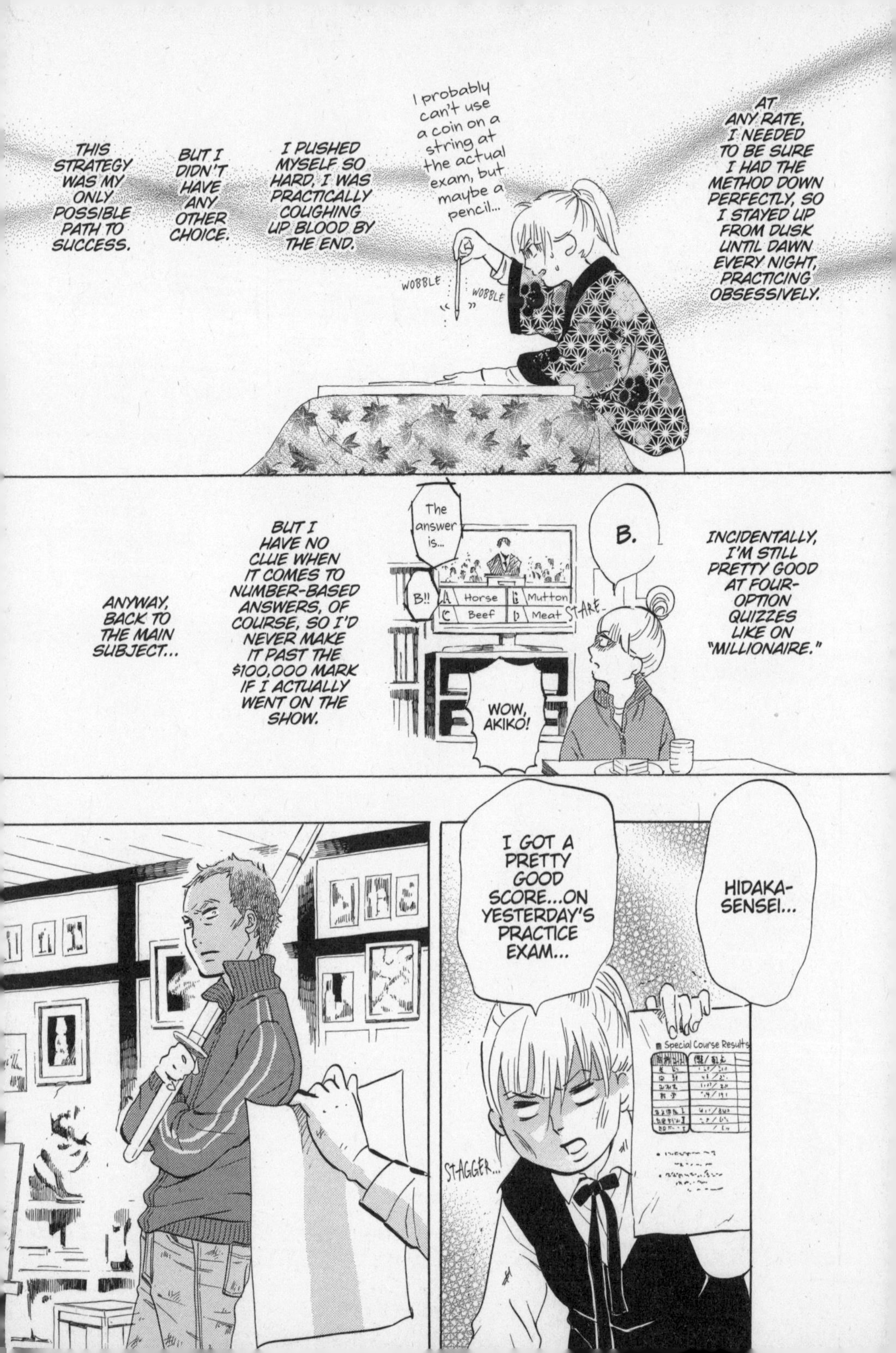
AT ANY RATE, I NEEDED TO BE SURE I HAD THE METHOD DOWN PERFECTLY, SO I STAYED UP FROM DUSK UNTIL DAWN EVERY NIGHT, PRACTICING OBSESSIVELY.
I probably can't use a coin on a string at the actual exam, but maybe a pencil...
WOBBLE
WOBBLE
I PUSHED MYSELF SO HARD, I WAS PRACTICALLY COUGHING UP BLOOD BY THE END.
BUT I DIDN'T HAVE ANY OTHER CHOICE.
THIS STRATEGY WAS MY ONLY POSSIBLE PATH TO SUCCESS.
INCIDENTALLY, I'M STILL PRETTY GOOD AT FOUR-OPTION QUIZZES LIKE ON "MILLIONAIRE."
B.
The answer is...
A Horse
B Mutton
C Beef
D Meat
STARE
B!!
WOW, AKIKO!
BUT I HAVE NO CLUE WHEN IT COMES TO NUMBER-BASED ANSWERS, OF COURSE, SO I'D NEVER MAKE IT PAST THE $100,000 MARK IF I ACTUALLY WENT ON THE SHOW.
ANYWAY, BACK TO THE MAIN SUBJECT...
HIDAKA-SENSEI...
I GOT A PRETTY GOOD SCORE...ON YESTERDAY'S PRACTICE EXAM...
Special Course Results
STAGGER...

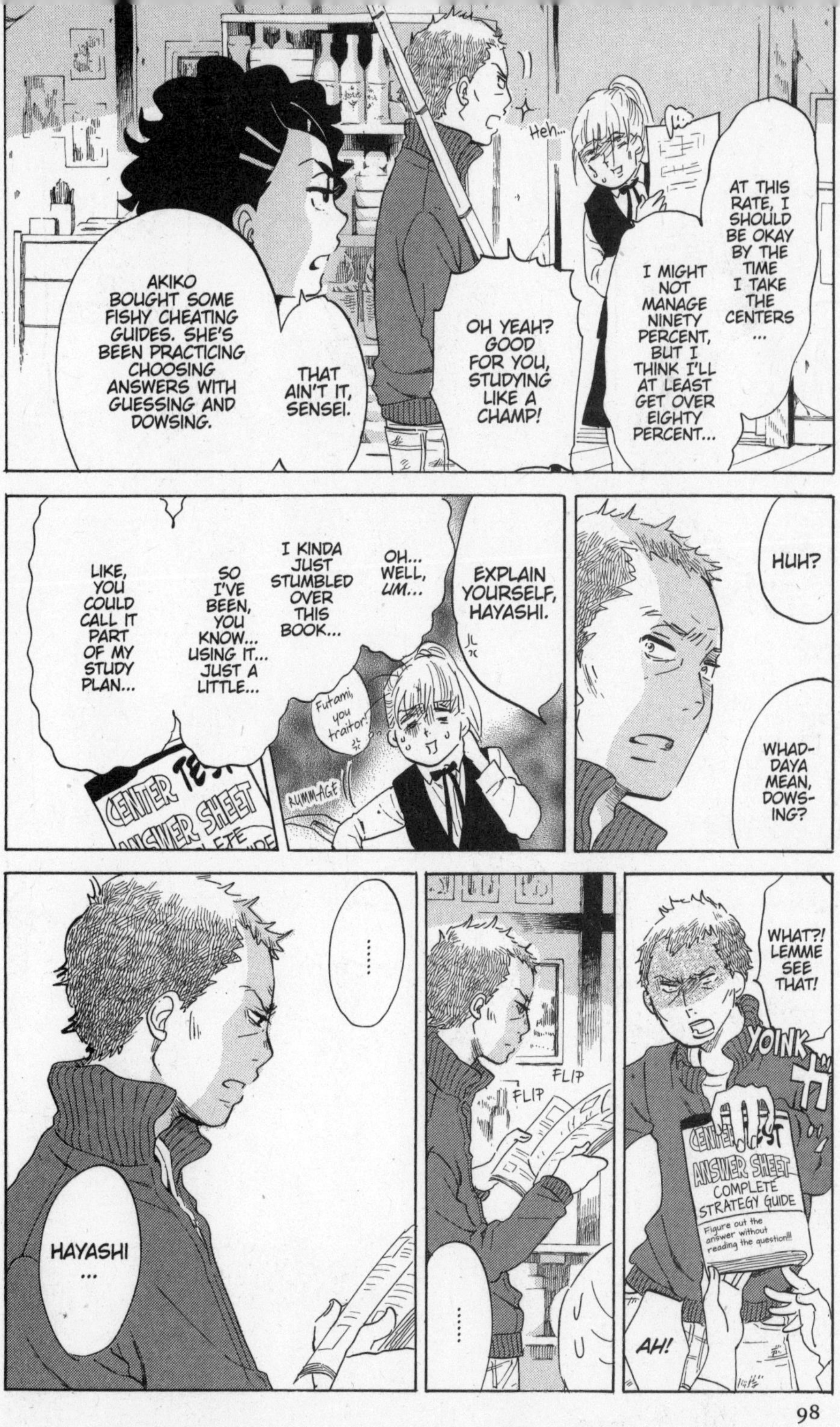
AT THIS RATE, I SHOULD BE OKAY BY THE TIME I TAKE THE CENTERS ...
I MIGHT NOT MANAGE NINETY PERCENT, BUT I THINK I'LL AT LEAST GET OVER EIGHTY PERCENT...
Heh...
OH YEAH? GOOD FOR YOU, STUDYING LIKE A CHAMP!
THAT AIN'T IT, SENSEI.
AKIKO BOUGHT SOME FISHY CHEATING GUIDES. SHE'S BEEN PRACTICING CHOOSING ANSWERS WITH GUESSING AND DOWSING.
HUH?
WHADDAYA MEAN, DOWSING?
EXPLAIN YOURSELF, HAYASHI.
OH... WELL, UM...
I KINDA JUST STUMBLED OVER THIS BOOK...
SO I'VE BEEN, YOU KNOW... USING IT... JUST A LITTLE...
LIKE, YOU COULD CALL IT PART OF MY STUDY PLAN...
Futami, you traitor!
RUMMAGE
WHAT?! LEMME SEE THAT!
YOINK
CENTER TEST ANSWER SHEET COMPLETE STRATEGY GUIDE
Figure out the answer without reading the question!!!
AH!
......
FLIP
FLIP
......
HAYASHI ...

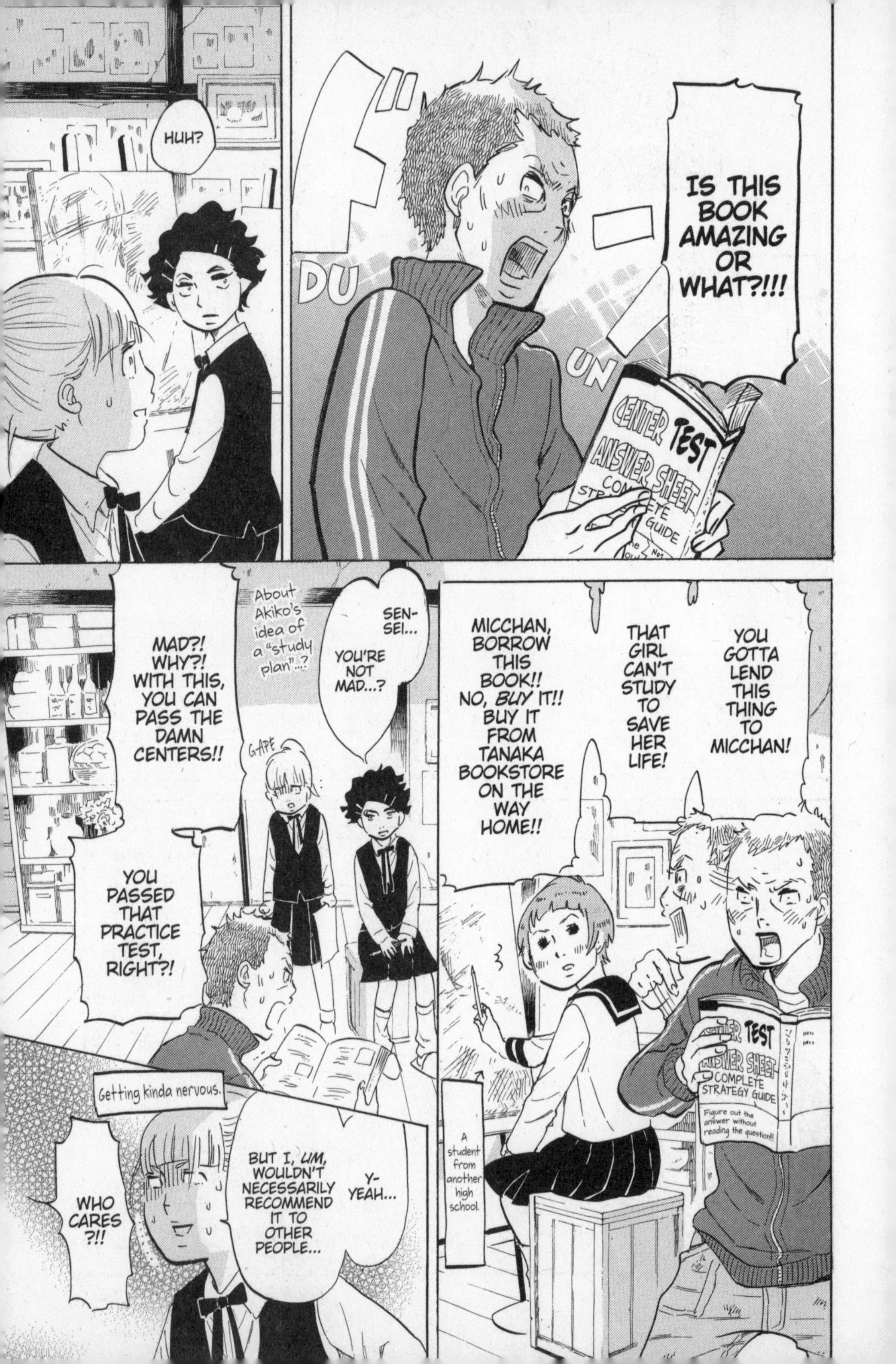
DU
UN
IS THIS BOOK AMAZING OR WHAT?!!!
CENTER TEST ANSWER SHEET
GUIDE
HUH?
YOU GOTTA LEND THIS THING TO MICCHAN!
THAT GIRL CAN'T STUDY TO SAVE HER LIFE!
MICCHAN, BORROW THIS BOOK!! NO, *BUY* IT!! BUY IT FROM TANAKA BOOKSTORE ON THE WAY HOME!!
TEST ANSWER SHEET COMPLETE STRATEGY GUIDE
Figure out the answer without reading the question!!!
A student from another high school.
SEN-SEI...
YOU'RE NOT MAD...?
About Akiko's idea of a "study plan"...?
MAD?! WHY?! WITH THIS, YOU CAN PASS THE DAMN CENTERS!!
GAPE
YOU PASSED THAT PRACTICE TEST, RIGHT?!
Getting kinda nervous.
Y-YEAH...
BUT I, *UM*, WOULDN'T NECESSARILY RECOMMEND IT TO OTHER PEOPLE...
WHO CARES?!!

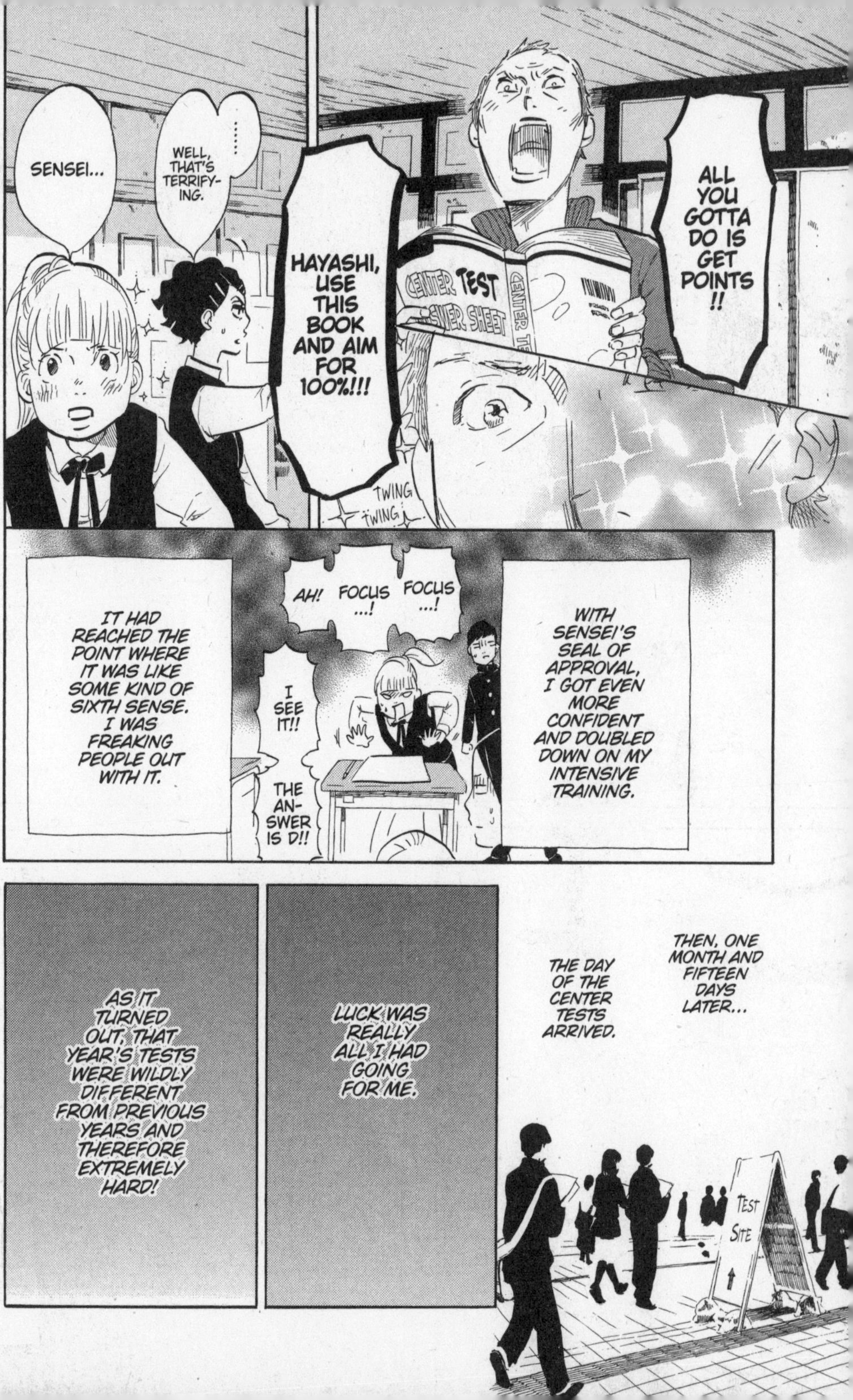
ALL YOU GOTTA DO IS GET POINTS!!
CENTER TEST
CENTER TEST
SWER SHEET
HAYASHI, USE THIS BOOK AND AIM FOR 100%!!!
......
WELL, THAT'S TERRIFYING.
SENSEI...
TWING
TWING
WITH SENSEI'S SEAL OF APPROVAL, I GOT EVEN MORE CONFIDENT AND DOUBLED DOWN ON MY INTENSIVE TRAINING.
AH! FOCUS ...! FOCUS ...!
I SEE IT!!
THE ANSWER IS D!!
IT HAD REACHED THE POINT WHERE IT WAS LIKE SOME KIND OF SIXTH SENSE. I WAS FREAKING PEOPLE OUT WITH IT.
THEN, ONE MONTH AND FIFTEEN DAYS LATER...
THE DAY OF THE CENTER TESTS ARRIVED.
TEST SITE
LUCK WAS REALLY ALL I HAD GOING FOR ME.
AS IT TURNED OUT, THAT YEAR'S TESTS WERE WILDLY DIFFERENT FROM PREVIOUS YEARS AND THEREFORE EXTREMELY HARD!

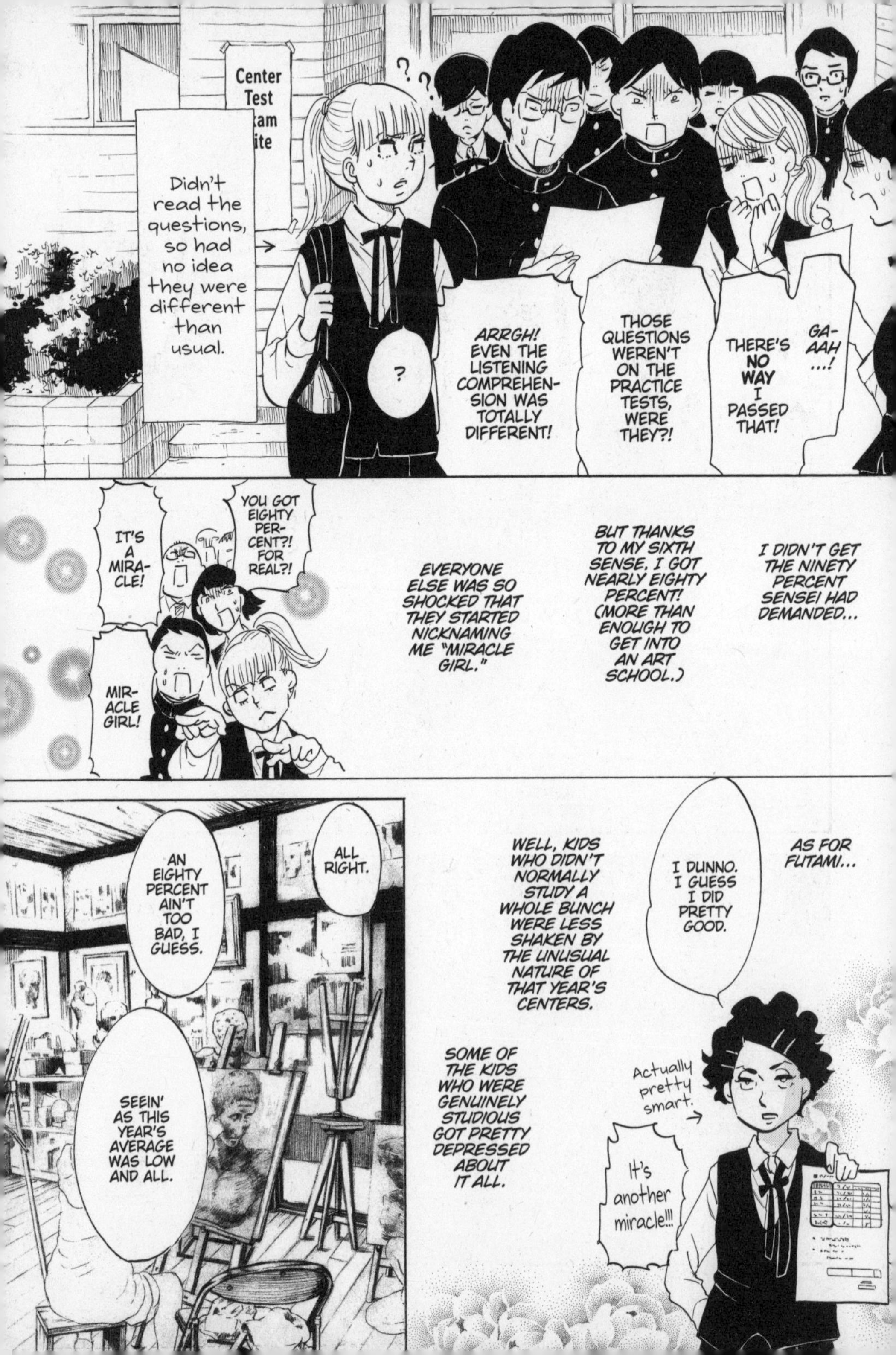
GA-AAH...!
THERE'S NO WAY I PASSED THAT!
THOSE QUESTIONS WEREN'T ON THE PRACTICE TESTS, WERE THEY?!
ARRGH! EVEN THE LISTENING COMPREHENSION WAS TOTALLY DIFFERENT!
Center Test
?
Didn't read the questions, so had no idea they were different than usual.
I DIDN'T GET THE NINETY PERCENT SENSEI HAD DEMANDED...
BUT THANKS TO MY SIXTH SENSE, I GOT NEARLY EIGHTY PERCENT! (MORE THAN ENOUGH TO GET INTO AN ART SCHOOL.)
EVERYONE ELSE WAS SO SHOCKED THAT THEY STARTED NICKNAMING ME "MIRACLE GIRL."
YOU GOT EIGHTY PERCENT?! FOR REAL?!
IT'S A MIRACLE!
MIRACLE GIRL!
AS FOR FUTAMI...
I DUNNO. I GUESS I DID PRETTY GOOD.
WELL, KIDS WHO DIDN'T NORMALLY STUDY A WHOLE BUNCH WERE LESS SHAKEN BY THE UNUSUAL NATURE OF THAT YEAR'S CENTERS.
Actually pretty smart.
SOME OF THE KIDS WHO WERE GENUINELY STUDIOUS GOT PRETTY DEPRESSED ABOUT IT ALL.
It's another miracle!!!
ALL RIGHT.
AN EIGHTY PERCENT AIN'T TOO BAD, I GUESS.
SEEIN' AS THIS YEAR'S AVERAGE WAS LOW AND ALL.

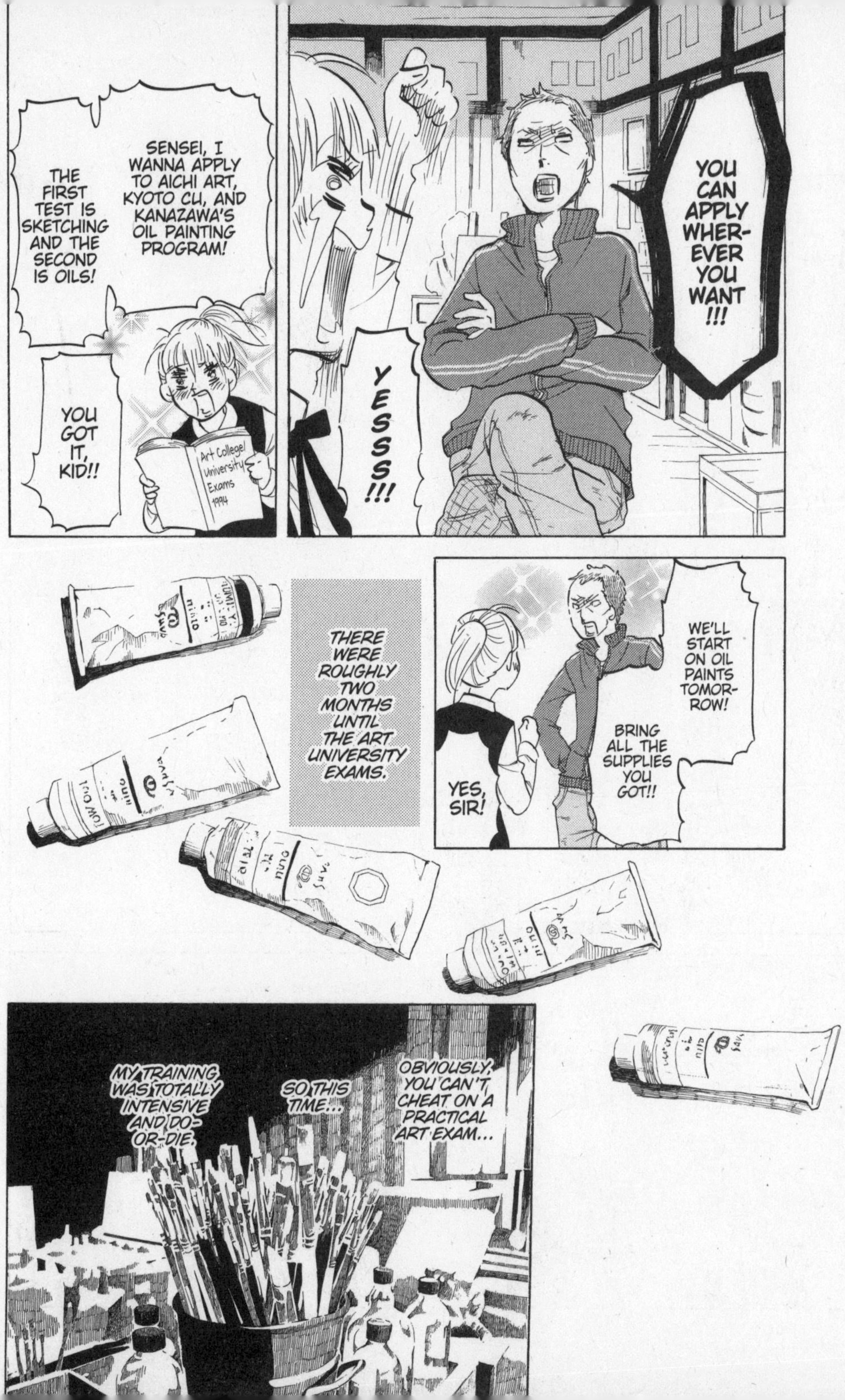
YOU CAN APPLY WHEREVER YOU WANT!!!
YESSS!!!
SENSEI, I WANNA APPLY TO AICHI ART, KYOTO CU, AND KANAZAWA'S OIL PAINTING PROGRAM!
THE FIRST TEST IS SKETCHING AND THE SECOND IS OILS!
YOU GOT IT, KID!!
Art College/University Exams 1994
WE'LL START ON OIL PAINTS TOMORROW!
BRING ALL THE SUPPLIES YOU GOT!!
YES, SIR!
THERE WERE ROUGHLY TWO MONTHS UNTIL THE ART UNIVERSITY EXAMS.
OBVIOUSLY, YOU CAN'T CHEAT ON A PRACTICAL ART EXAM...
SO THIS TIME...
MY TRAINING WAS TOTALLY INTENSIVE AND DO-OR-DIE.

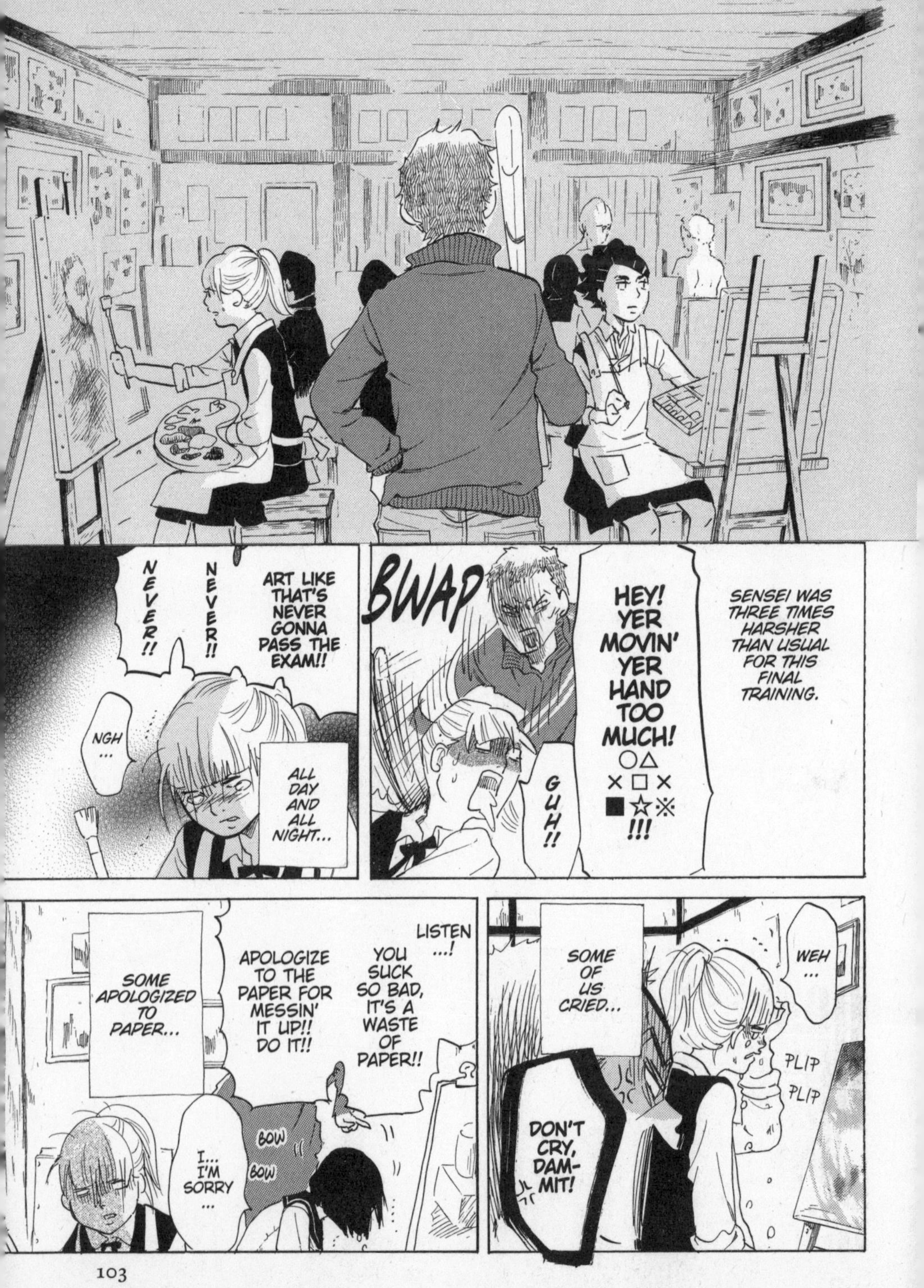
SENSEI WAS THREE TIMES HARSHER THAN USUAL FOR THIS FINAL TRAINING.
HEY! YER MOVIN' YER HAND TOO MUCH! ○△ ×□× ■☆※ !!!
BWAP
GUH!!
ART LIKE THAT'S NEVER GONNA PASS THE EXAM!!
NEVER!!
NEVER!!
NGH...
ALL DAY AND ALL NIGHT...
SOME OF US CRIED...
WEH...
PLIP
PLIP
DON'T CRY, DAM-MIT!
LISTEN...!
YOU SUCK SO BAD, IT'S A WASTE OF PAPER!!
APOLOGIZE TO THE PAPER FOR MESSIN' IT UP!! DO IT!!
SOME APOLOGIZED TO PAPER...
BOW
BOW
I... I'M SORRY...

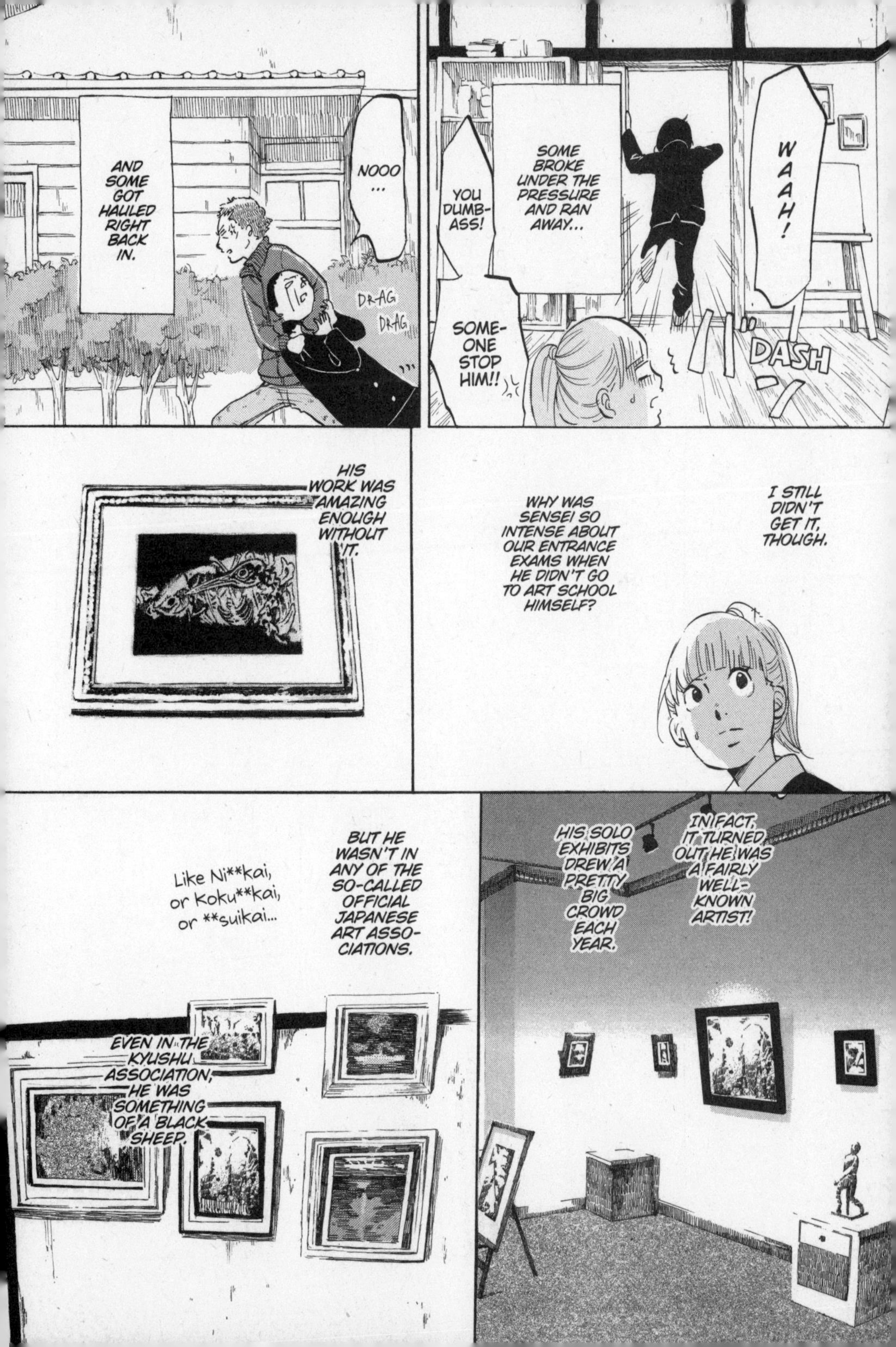
SOME BROKE UNDER THE PRESSURE AND RAN AWAY...
WAAH!
YOU DUMB-ASS!
SOME-ONE STOP HIM!!
DASH
AND SOME GOT HAULED RIGHT BACK IN.
NOOO...
DRAG
DRAG
I STILL DIDN'T GET IT, THOUGH.
WHY WAS SENSEI SO INTENSE ABOUT OUR ENTRANCE EXAMS WHEN HE DIDN'T GO TO ART SCHOOL HIMSELF?
HIS WORK WAS AMAZING ENOUGH WITHOUT IT.
IN FACT, IT TURNED OUT HE WAS A FAIRLY WELL-KNOWN ARTIST!
HIS SOLO EXHIBITS DREW A PRETTY BIG CROWD EACH YEAR.
BUT HE WASN'T IN ANY OF THE SO-CALLED OFFICIAL JAPANESE ART ASSOCIATIONS.
Like Ni**kai, or Koku**kai, or **suikai...
EVEN IN THE KYUSHU ASSOCIATION, HE WAS SOMETHING OF A BLACK SHEEP.

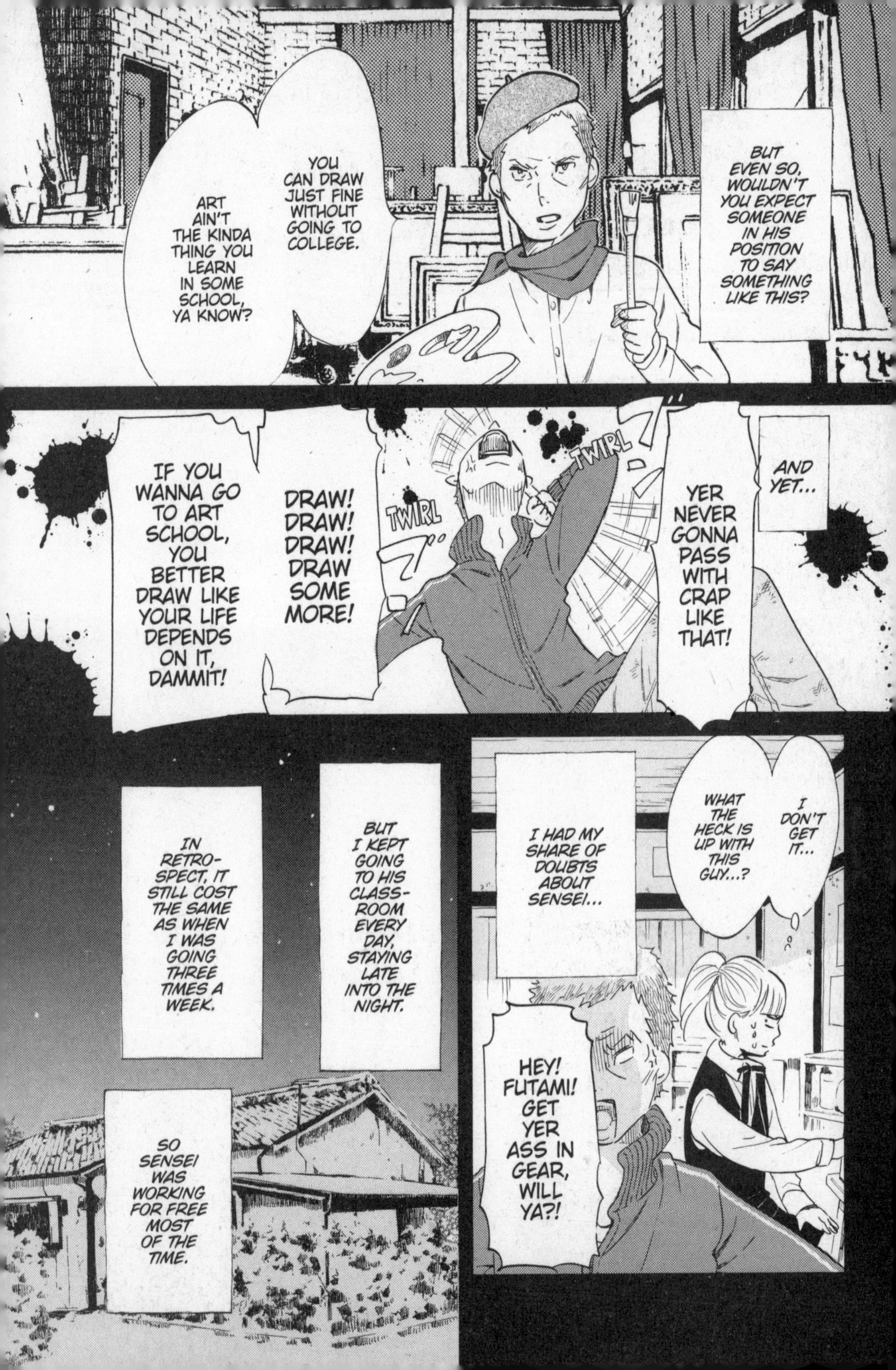
BUT EVEN SO, WOULDN'T YOU EXPECT SOMEONE IN HIS POSITION TO SAY SOMETHING LIKE THIS?
YOU CAN DRAW JUST FINE WITHOUT GOING TO COLLEGE.
ART AIN'T THE KINDA THING YOU LEARN IN SOME SCHOOL, YA KNOW?
AND YET...
YER NEVER GONNA PASS WITH CRAP LIKE THAT!
TWIRL
TWIRL
DRAW! DRAW! DRAW! DRAW SOME MORE!
IF YOU WANNA GO TO ART SCHOOL, YOU BETTER DRAW LIKE YOUR LIFE DEPENDS ON IT, DAMMIT!
I DON'T GET IT...
WHAT THE HECK IS UP WITH THIS GUY...?
I HAD MY SHARE OF DOUBTS ABOUT SENSEI...
HEY! FUTAMI! GET YER ASS IN GEAR, WILL YA?!
BUT I KEPT GOING TO HIS CLASSROOM EVERY DAY, STAYING LATE INTO THE NIGHT.
IN RETROSPECT, IT STILL COST THE SAME AS WHEN I WAS GOING THREE TIMES A WEEK.
SO SENSEI WAS WORKING FOR FREE MOST OF THE TIME.

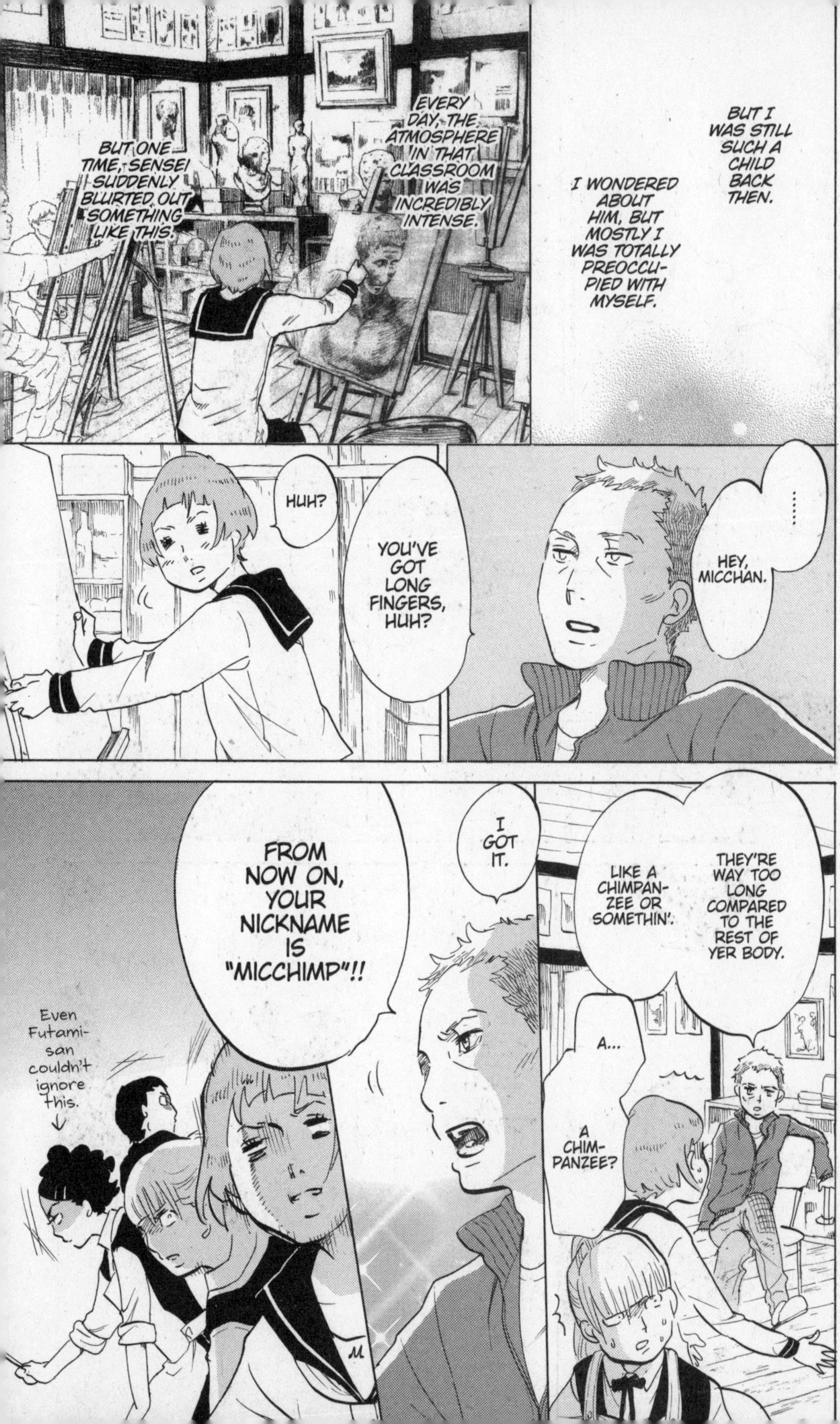

BUT I WAS STILL SUCH A CHILD BACK THEN.
I WONDERED ABOUT HIM, BUT MOSTLY I WAS TOTALLY PREOCCUPIED WITH MYSELF.
EVERY DAY, THE ATMOSPHERE IN THAT CLASSROOM WAS INCREDIBLY INTENSE.
BUT ONE TIME, SENSEI SUDDENLY BLURTED OUT SOMETHING LIKE THIS.
......
HEY, MICCHAN.
YOU'VE GOT LONG FINGERS, HUH?
HUH?
THEY'RE WAY TOO LONG COMPARED TO THE REST OF YER BODY.
LIKE A CHIMPANZEE OR SOMETHIN'.
A...
A CHIMPANZEE?
I GOT IT.
FROM NOW ON, YOUR NICKNAME IS "MICCHIMP"!!
Even Futami-san couldn't ignore this.

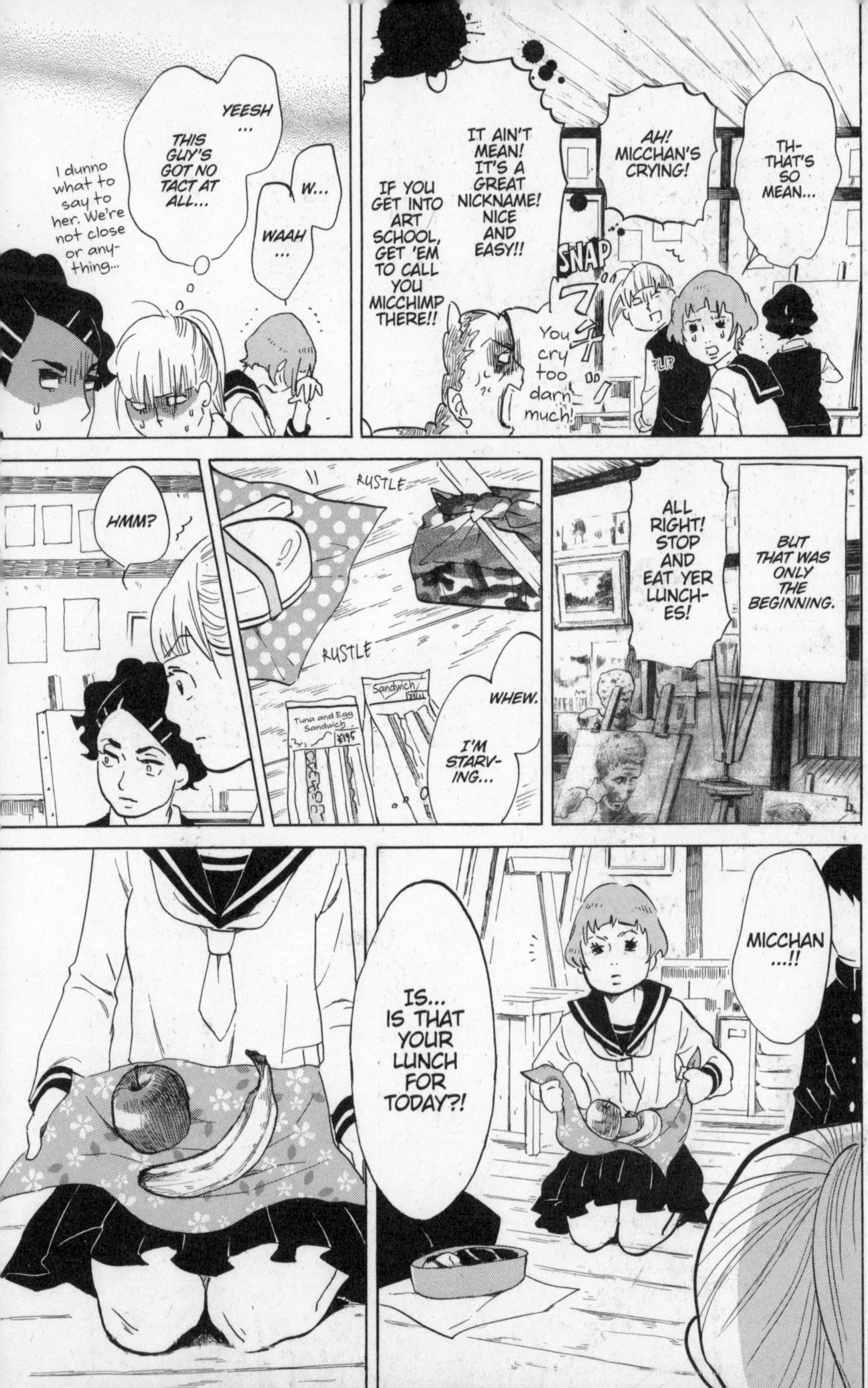
TH-THAT'S SO MEAN...
AH! MICCHAN'S CRYING!
SNAP
You cry too darn much!
IT AIN'T MEAN! IT'S A GREAT NICKNAME! NICE AND EASY!!
IF YOU GET INTO ART SCHOOL, GET 'EM TO CALL YOU MICCHIMP THERE!!
YEESH... THIS GUY'S GOT NO TACT AT ALL...
W... WAAH...
I dunno what to say to her. We're not close or any-thing...
BUT THAT WAS ONLY THE BEGINNING.
ALL RIGHT! STOP AND EAT YER LUNCH-ES!
RUSTLE
RUSTLE
Sandwich
Tuna and Egg Sandwich ¥195
WHEW.
I'M STARV-ING...
HMM?
MICCHAN...!!
IS... IS THAT YOUR LUNCH FOR TODAY?!

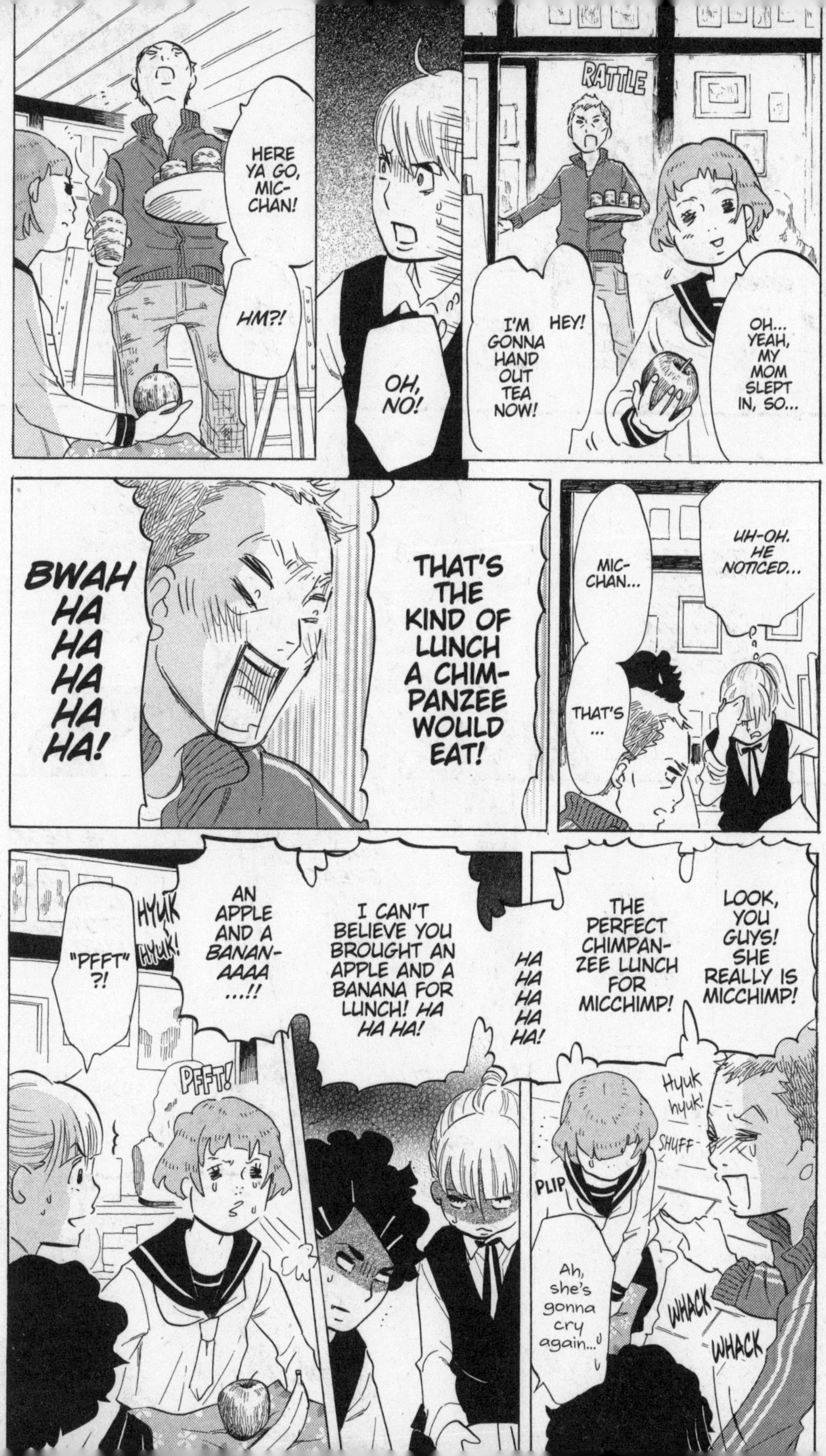
RATTLE
OH... YEAH, MY MOM SLEPT IN, SO...
HEY!
I'M GONNA HAND OUT TEA NOW!
OH, NO!
HERE YA GO, MIC-CHAN!
HM?!
UH-OH. HE NOTICED...
MIC-CHAN...
THAT'S ...
THAT'S THE KIND OF LUNCH A CHIMPANZEE WOULD EAT!
BWAH HA HA HA HA HA!
LOOK, YOU GUYS! SHE REALLY IS MICCHIMP!
THE PERFECT CHIMPANZEE LUNCH FOR MICCHIMP!
HA HA HA HA HA!
Hyuk hyuk!
SHUFF
PLIP
Ah, she's gonna cry again...
WHACK
WHACK
I CAN'T BELIEVE YOU BROUGHT AN APPLE AND A BANANA FOR LUNCH! HA HA HA!
AN APPLE AND A BANAN-AAAA ...!!
HYUK HYUK!
"PFFT" ?!
PFFT!

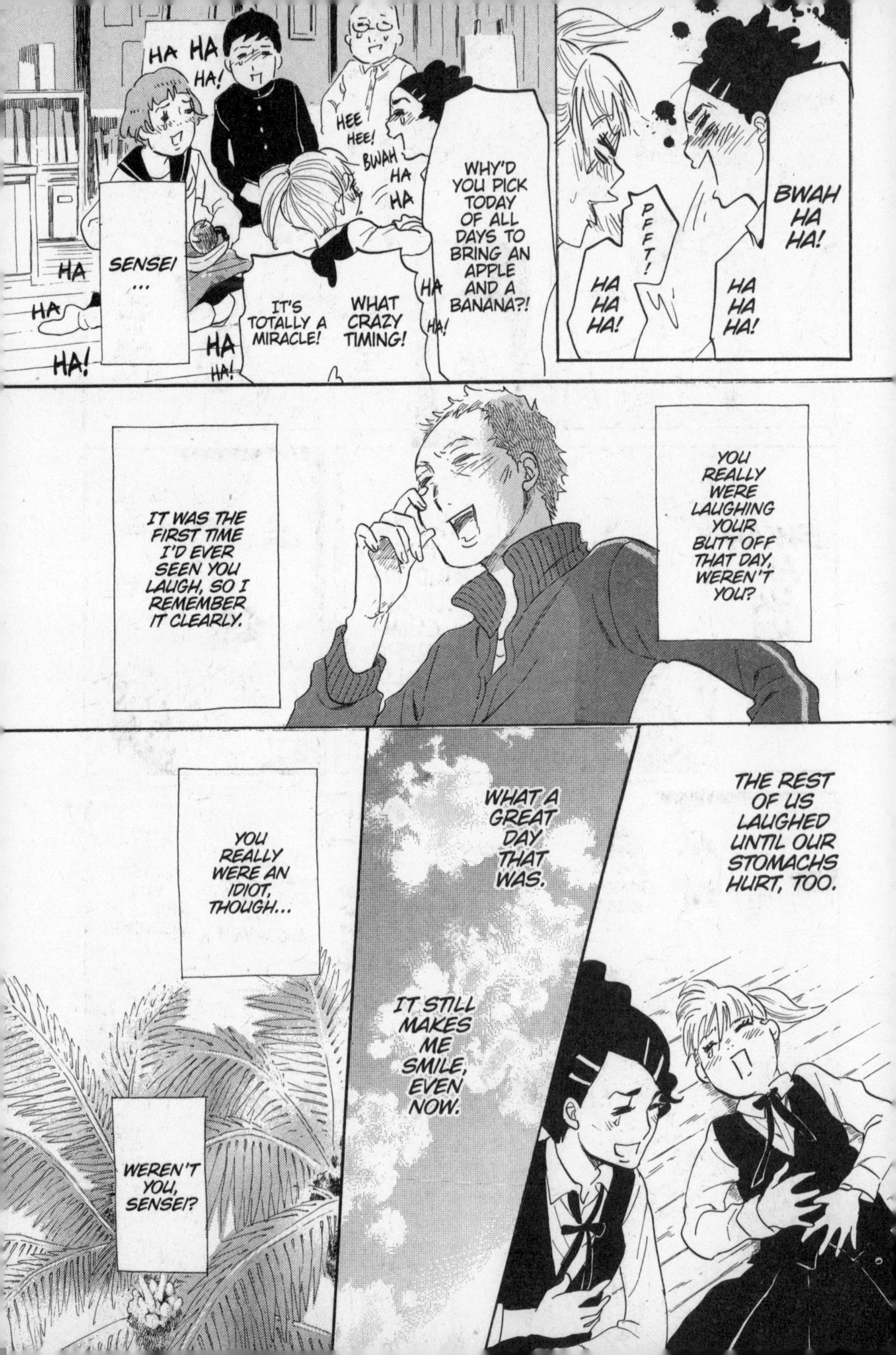
BWAH HA HA!
PFFT!
HA HA HA!
HA HA HA!
WHY'D YOU PICK TODAY OF ALL DAYS TO BRING AN APPLE AND A BANANA?!
HEE HEE!
BWAH HA HA
HA HA!
WHAT CRAZY TIMING!
IT'S TOTALLY A MIRACLE!
HA HA!
HA HA HA HA!
SENSEI ...
YOU REALLY WERE LAUGHING YOUR BUTT OFF THAT DAY, WEREN'T YOU?
IT WAS THE FIRST TIME I'D EVER SEEN YOU LAUGH, SO I REMEMBER IT CLEARLY.
THE REST OF US LAUGHED UNTIL OUR STOMACHS HURT, TOO.
WHAT A GREAT DAY THAT WAS.
IT STILL MAKES ME SMILE, EVEN NOW.
YOU REALLY WERE AN IDIOT, THOUGH...
WEREN'T YOU, SENSEI?

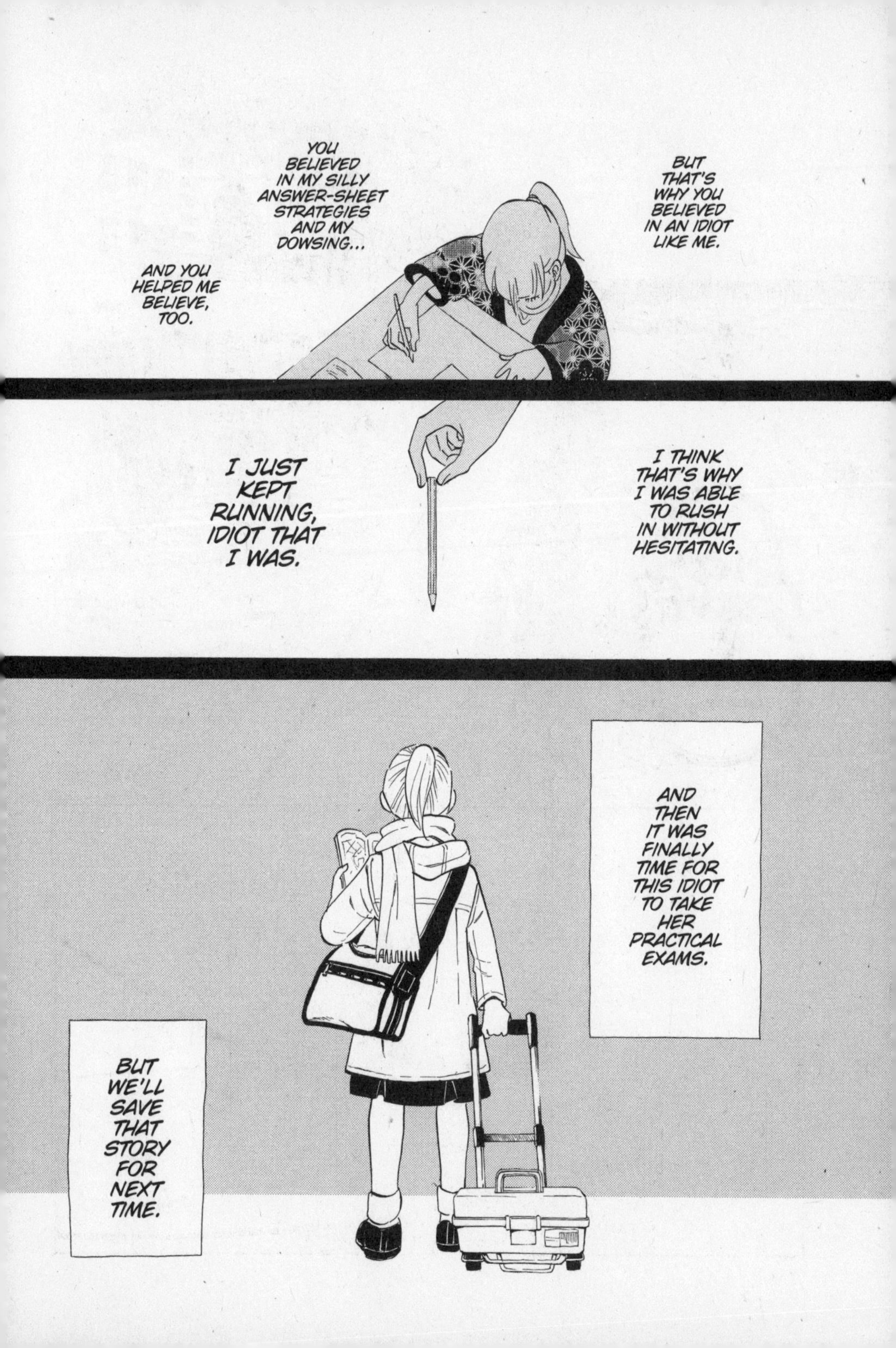
BUT THAT'S WHY YOU BELIEVED IN AN IDIOT LIKE ME.
YOU BELIEVED IN MY SILLY ANSWER-SHEET STRATEGIES AND MY DOWSING...
AND YOU HELPED ME BELIEVE, TOO.
I THINK THAT'S WHY I WAS ABLE TO RUSH IN WITHOUT HESITATING.
I JUST KEPT RUNNING, IDIOT THAT I WAS.
AND THEN IT WAS FINALLY TIME FOR THIS IDIOT TO TAKE HER PRACTICAL EXAMS.
BUT WE'LL SAVE THAT STORY FOR NEXT TIME.

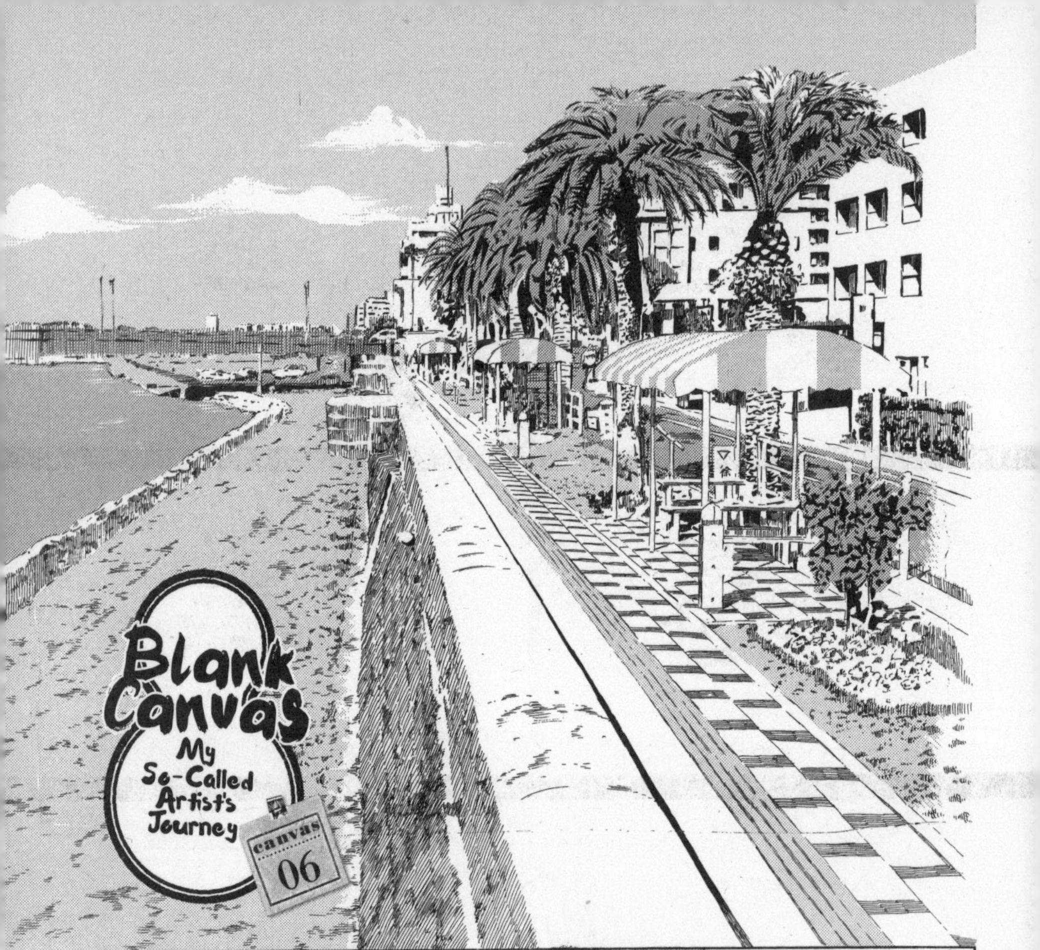
Blank Canvas
My So-Called Artist's Journey
canvas
06

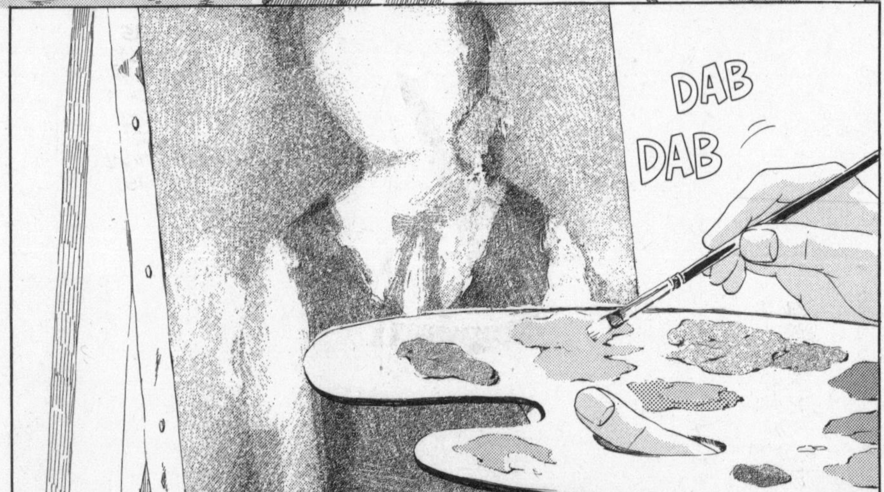
DAB DAB

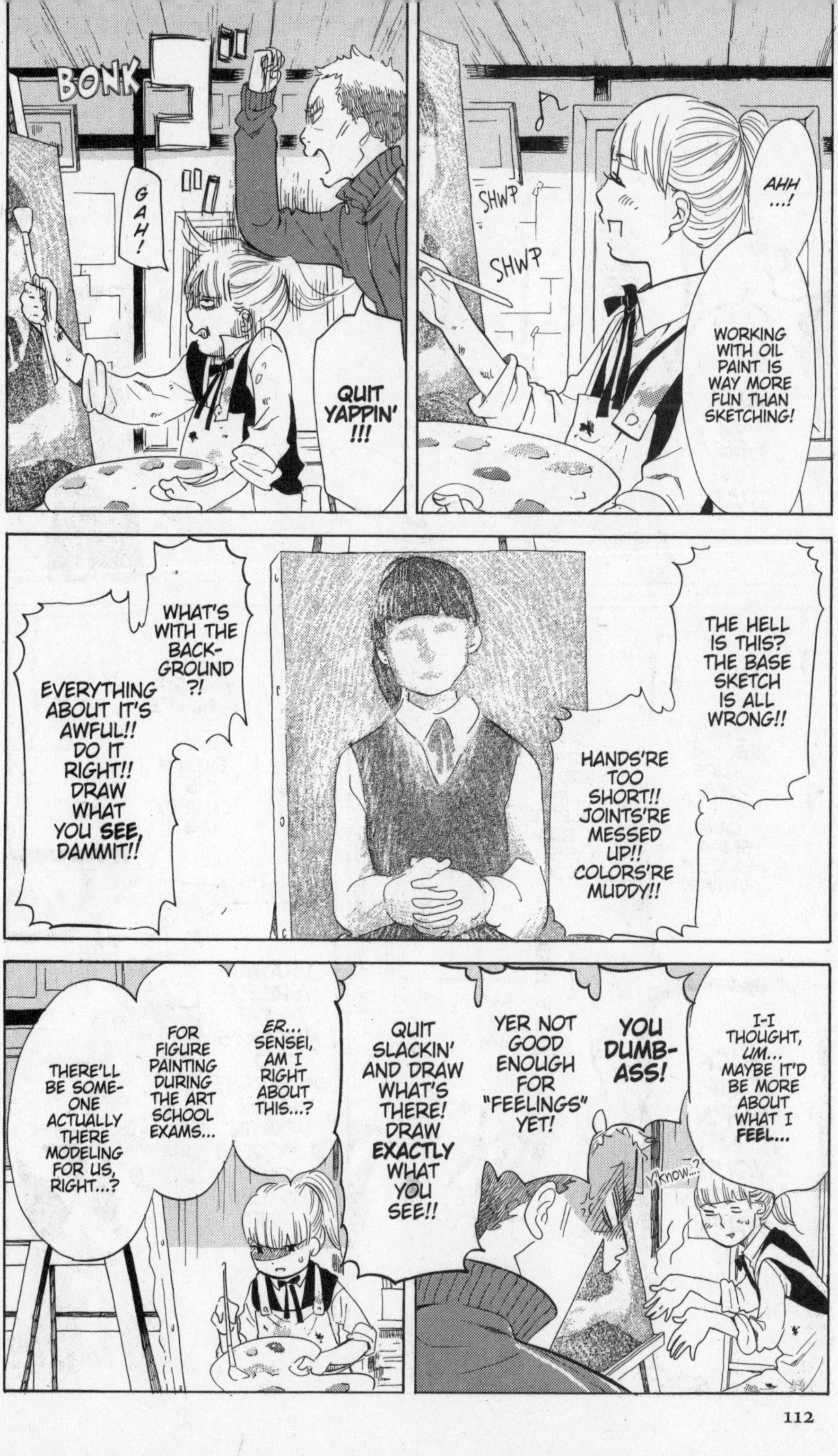
SHWP
SHWP
AHH ...!
WORKING WITH OIL PAINT IS WAY MORE FUN THAN SKETCHING!
BONK
GAH!
QUIT YAPPIN' !!!
THE HELL IS THIS? THE BASE SKETCH IS ALL WRONG!!
HANDS'RE TOO SHORT!! JOINTS'RE MESSED UP!! COLORS'RE MUDDY!!
WHAT'S WITH THE BACK-GROUND ?!
EVERYTHING ABOUT IT'S AWFUL!! DO IT RIGHT!! DRAW WHAT YOU SEE, DAMMIT!!
I-I THOUGHT, UM... MAYBE IT'D BE MORE ABOUT WHAT I FEEL...
Y'know...?
YOU DUMB-ASS!
YER NOT GOOD ENOUGH FOR "FEELINGS" YET!
QUIT SLACKIN' AND DRAW WHAT'S THERE! DRAW EXACTLY WHAT YOU SEE!!
ER... SENSEI, AM I RIGHT ABOUT THIS...?
FOR FIGURE PAINTING DURING THE ART SCHOOL EXAMS...
THERE'LL BE SOME-ONE ACTUALLY THERE MODELING FOR US, RIGHT...?

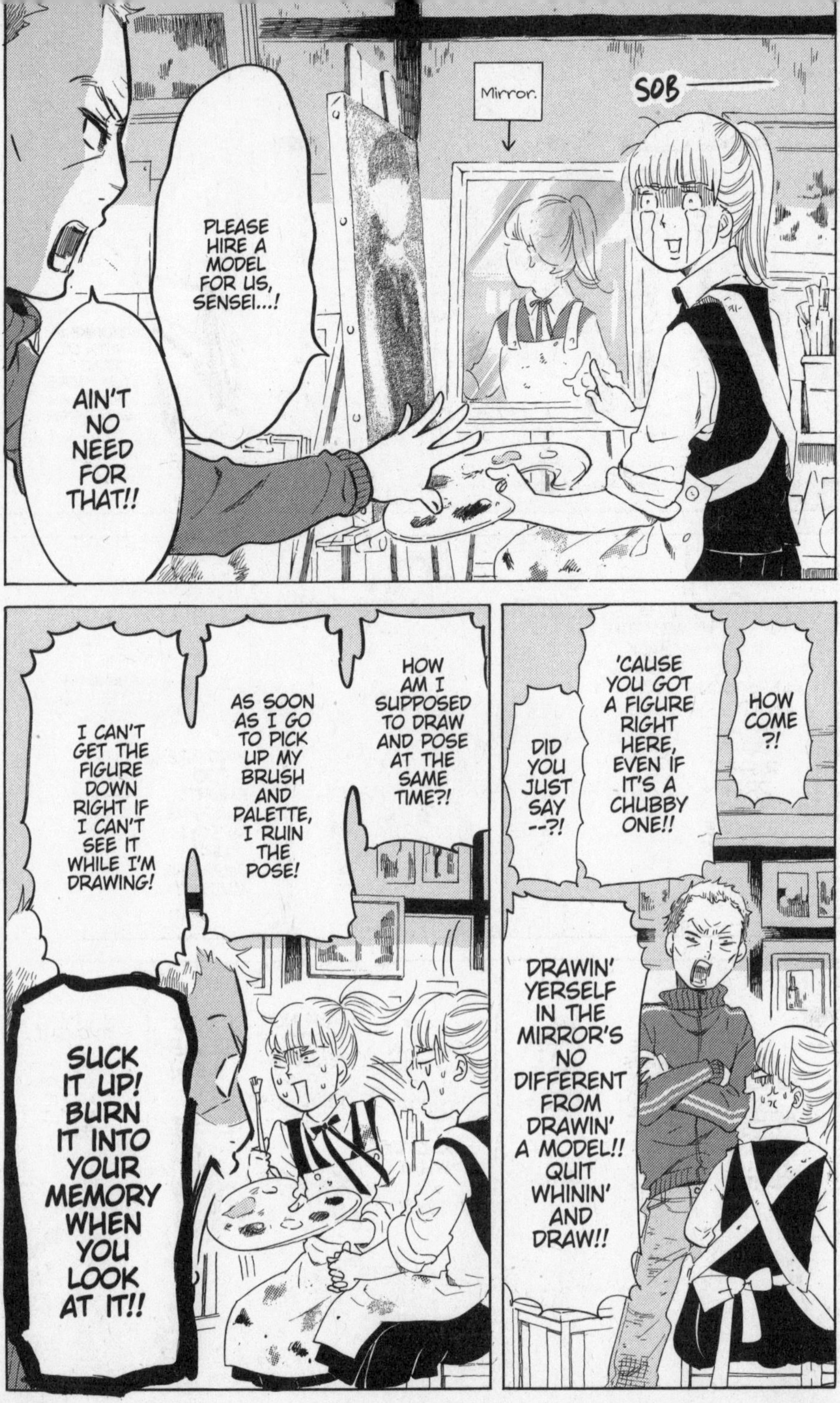
SOB
Mirror.
PLEASE HIRE A MODEL FOR US, SENSEI...!
AIN'T NO NEED FOR THAT!!
HOW COME?!
'CAUSE YOU GOT A FIGURE RIGHT HERE, EVEN IF IT'S A CHUBBY ONE!!
DID YOU JUST SAY --?!
DRAWIN' YERSELF IN THE MIRROR'S NO DIFFERENT FROM DRAWIN' A MODEL!! QUIT WHININ' AND DRAW!!
HOW AM I SUPPOSED TO DRAW AND POSE AT THE SAME TIME?!
AS SOON AS I GO TO PICK UP MY BRUSH AND PALETTE, I RUIN THE POSE!
I CAN'T GET THE FIGURE DOWN RIGHT IF I CAN'T SEE IT WHILE I'M DRAWING!
SUCK IT UP! BURN IT INTO YOUR MEMORY WHEN YOU LOOK AT IT!!

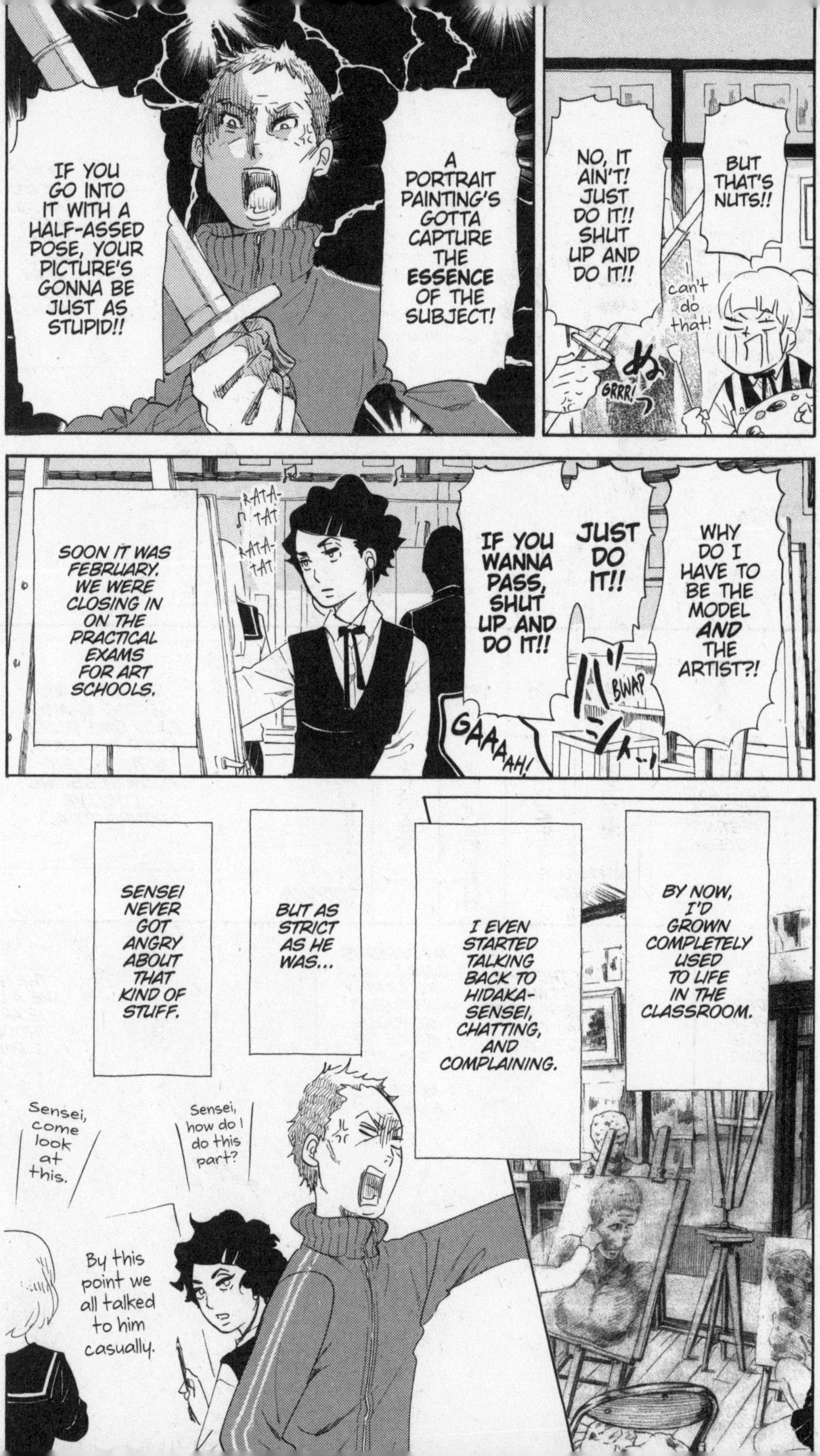
BUT THAT'S NUTS!!
NO, IT AIN'T! JUST DO IT!! SHUT UP AND DO IT!!
I can't do that!
ぬ
GRRR!
A PORTRAIT PAINTING'S GOTTA CAPTURE THE ESSENCE OF THE SUBJECT!
IF YOU GO INTO IT WITH A HALF-ASSED POSE, YOUR PICTURE'S GONNA BE JUST AS STUPID!!
WHY DO I HAVE TO BE THE MODEL AND THE ARTIST?!
JUST DO IT!!
IF YOU WANNA PASS, SHUT UP AND DO IT!!
BWAP
GAAAAH!
RATA-TAT
RATA-TAT
SOON IT WAS FEBRUARY. WE WERE CLOSING IN ON THE PRACTICAL EXAMS FOR ART SCHOOLS.
BY NOW, I'D GROWN COMPLETELY USED TO LIFE IN THE CLASSROOM.
I EVEN STARTED TALKING BACK TO HIDAKA-SENSEI, CHATTING, AND COMPLAINING.
BUT AS STRICT AS HE WAS...
SENSEI NEVER GOT ANGRY ABOUT THAT KIND OF STUFF.
Sensei, how do I do this part?
Sensei, come look at this.
By this point we all talked to him casually.

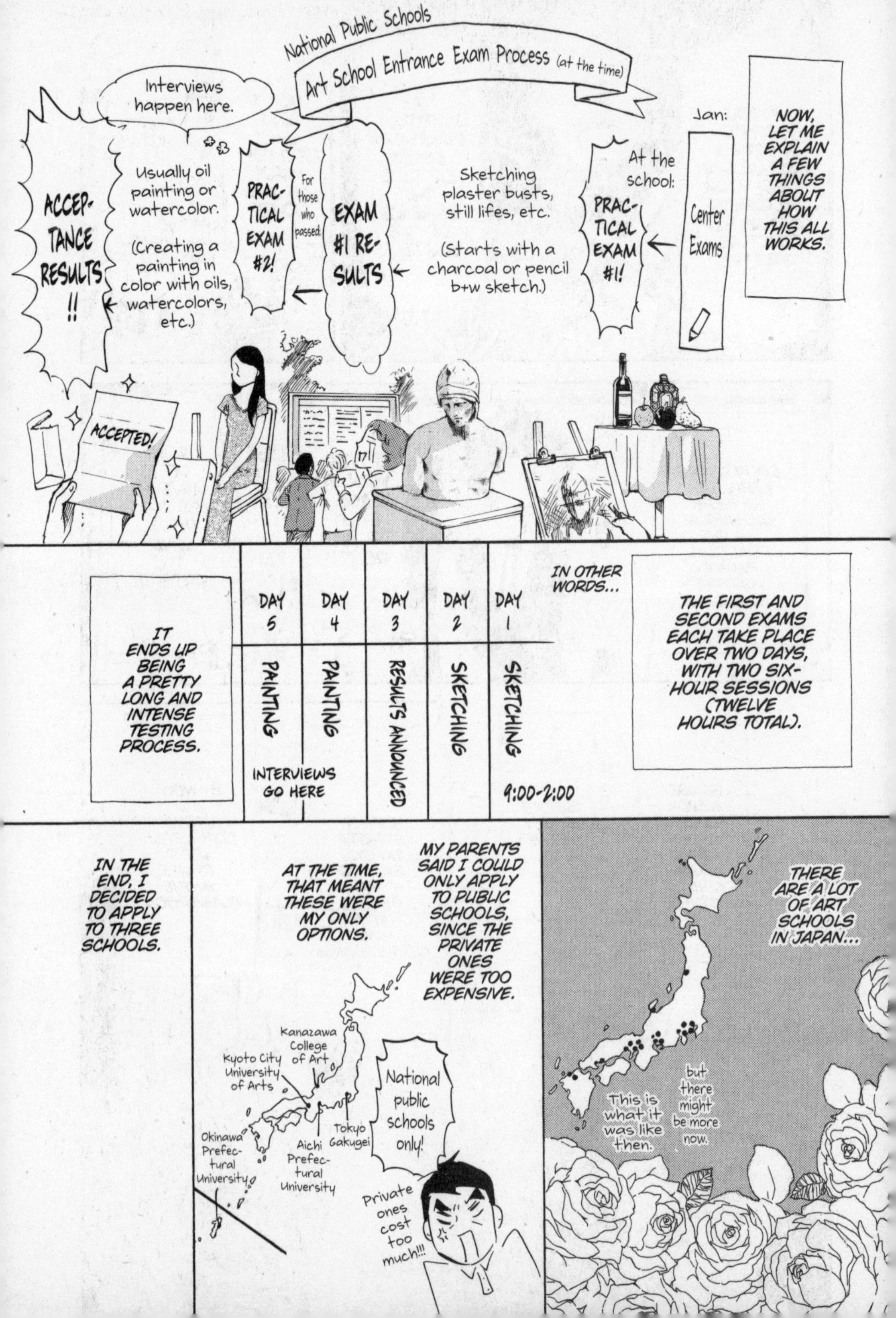
National Public Schools
Art School Entrance Exam Process (at the time)
NOW, LET ME EXPLAIN A FEW THINGS ABOUT HOW THIS ALL WORKS.
Jan:
Center Exams
At the school:
PRACTICAL EXAM #1!
Sketching plaster busts, still lifes, etc.
(Starts with a charcoal or pencil b+w sketch.)
EXAM #1 RESULTS
For those who passed:
PRACTICAL EXAM #2!
Usually oil painting or watercolor.
(Creating a painting in color with oils, watercolors, etc.)
Interviews happen here.
ACCEPTANCE RESULTS!!
ACCEPTED!
THE FIRST AND SECOND EXAMS EACH TAKE PLACE OVER TWO DAYS, WITH TWO SIX-HOUR SESSIONS (TWELVE HOURS TOTAL).
IN OTHER WORDS...
DAY 1
SKETCHING
9:00-2:00
DAY 2
SKETCHING
DAY 3
RESULTS ANNOUNCED
DAY 4
PAINTING
DAY 5
PAINTING
INTERVIEWS GO HERE
IT ENDS UP BEING A PRETTY LONG AND INTENSE TESTING PROCESS.
THERE ARE A LOT OF ART SCHOOLS IN JAPAN...
This is what it was like then.
but there might be more now.
MY PARENTS SAID I COULD ONLY APPLY TO PUBLIC SCHOOLS, SINCE THE PRIVATE ONES WERE TOO EXPENSIVE.
AT THE TIME, THAT MEANT THESE WERE MY ONLY OPTIONS.
Kanazawa College of Art
Kyoto City University of Arts
Tokyo Gakugei
Aichi Prefectural University
Okinawa Prefectural University
National public schools only!
Private ones cost too much!!!
IN THE END, I DECIDED TO APPLY TO THREE SCHOOLS.

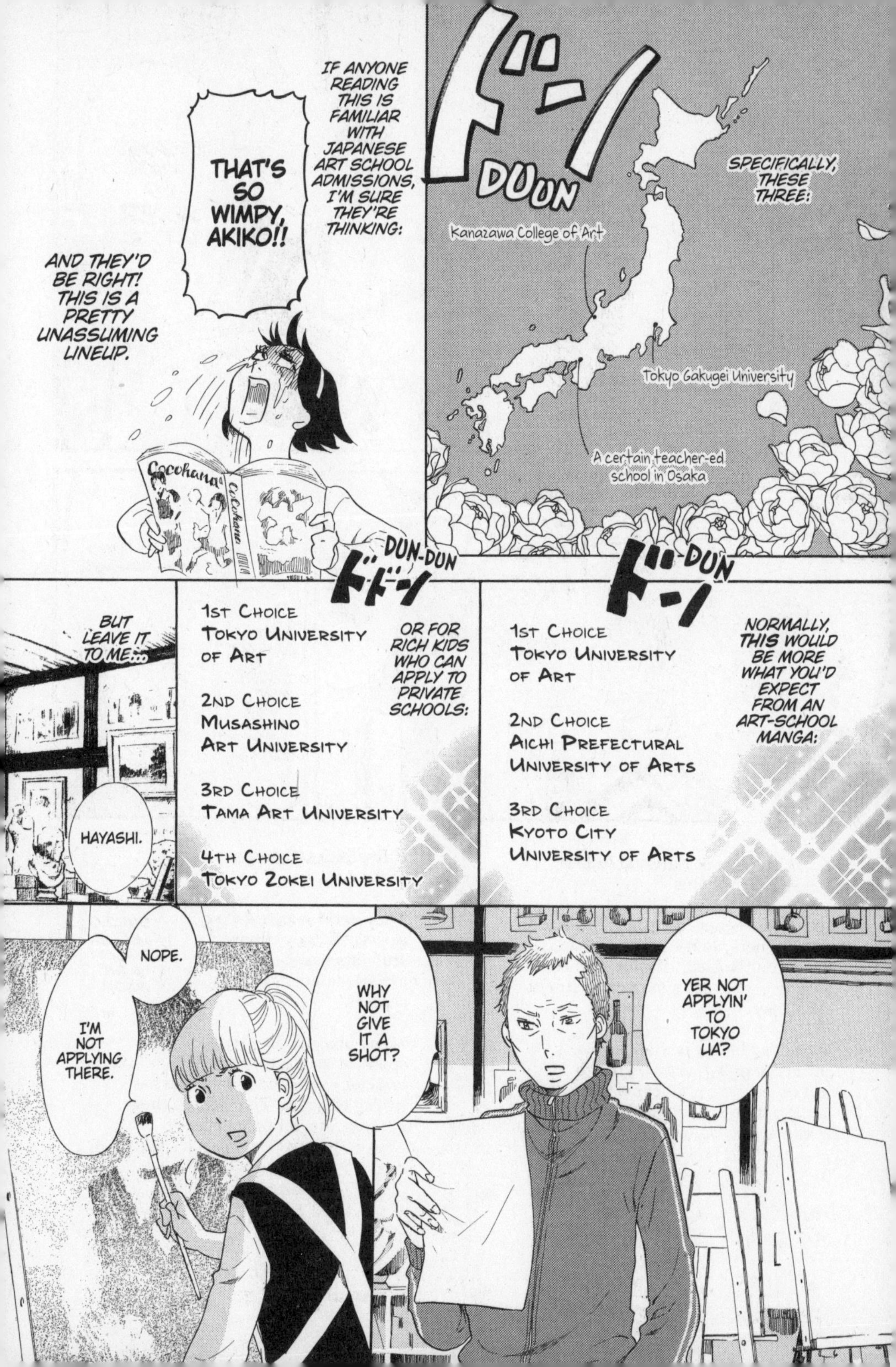
DUUN
SPECIFICALLY, THESE THREE:
Kanazawa College of Art
Tokyo Gakugei University
A certain teacher-ed school in Osaka
IF ANYONE READING THIS IS FAMILIAR WITH JAPANESE ART SCHOOL ADMISSIONS, I'M SURE THEY'RE THINKING:
THAT'S SO WIMPY, AKIKO!!
AND THEY'D BE RIGHT! THIS IS A PRETTY UNASSUMING LINEUP.
DUN-DUN
NORMALLY, THIS WOULD BE MORE WHAT YOU'D EXPECT FROM AN ART-SCHOOL MANGA:
1st Choice Tokyo University of Art
2nd Choice Aichi Prefectural University of Arts
3rd Choice Kyoto City University of Arts
DUN-DUN
OR FOR RICH KIDS WHO CAN APPLY TO PRIVATE SCHOOLS:
1st Choice Tokyo University of Art
2nd Choice Musashino Art University
3rd Choice Tama Art University
4th Choice Tokyo Zokei University
BUT LEAVE IT TO ME...
HAYASHI.
YER NOT APPLYIN' TO TOKYO UA?
NOPE.
I'M NOT APPLYING THERE.
WHY NOT GIVE IT A SHOT?

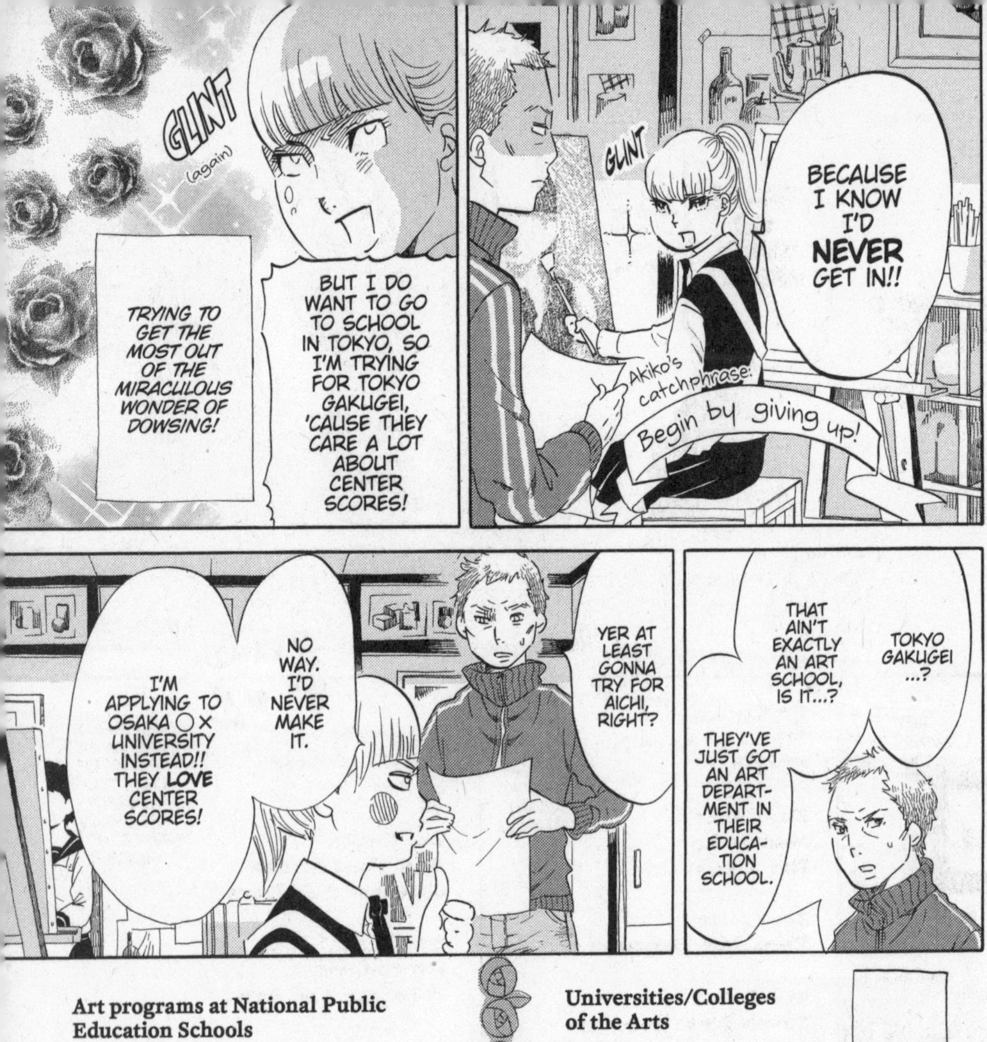

GLINT
BECAUSE I KNOW I'D NEVER GET IN!!
Akiko's catchphrase: Begin by giving up!
GLINT
(again)
BUT I DO WANT TO GO TO SCHOOL IN TOKYO, SO I'M TRYING FOR TOKYO GAKUGEI, 'CAUSE THEY CARE A LOT ABOUT CENTER SCORES!
TRYING TO GET THE MOST OUT OF THE MIRACULOUS WONDER OF DOWSING!
TOKYO GAKUGEI ...?
THAT AIN'T EXACTLY AN ART SCHOOL, IS IT...?
THEY'VE JUST GOT AN ART DEPARTMENT IN THEIR EDUCATION SCHOOL.
YER AT LEAST GONNA TRY FOR AICHI, RIGHT?
NO WAY. I'D NEVER MAKE IT.
I'M APPLYING TO OSAKA ○× UNIVERSITY INSTEAD!! THEY LOVE CENTER SCORES!

SORRY. LET ME EXPLAIN A BIT MORE.

Art programs at National Public Education Schools

These are generally meant for future art teachers, so it's easier for kids to get in on the basis of good grades. Center scores are a massive factor at play here.

An added bonus is that not many students spend years trying to get in, so most applicants are still in high school and only have art training from school or the occasional extracurricular class.

↓

Half-decent artists can still get in!

※ THIS IS JUST MY PERSONAL INTERPRETATION!!

Universities/Colleges of the Arts

They excel at cultivating artists, so they choose students based more on artistic talent than Center scores.

Many prospective students spend at least a year or two--or even four or five years!--trying to get in. That means there are tons of applicants who're extremely good artists (veterans who've spent years studying at prep schools meant for getting into art uni/colleges).

↓

Only people with incredibly strong art skills get in!

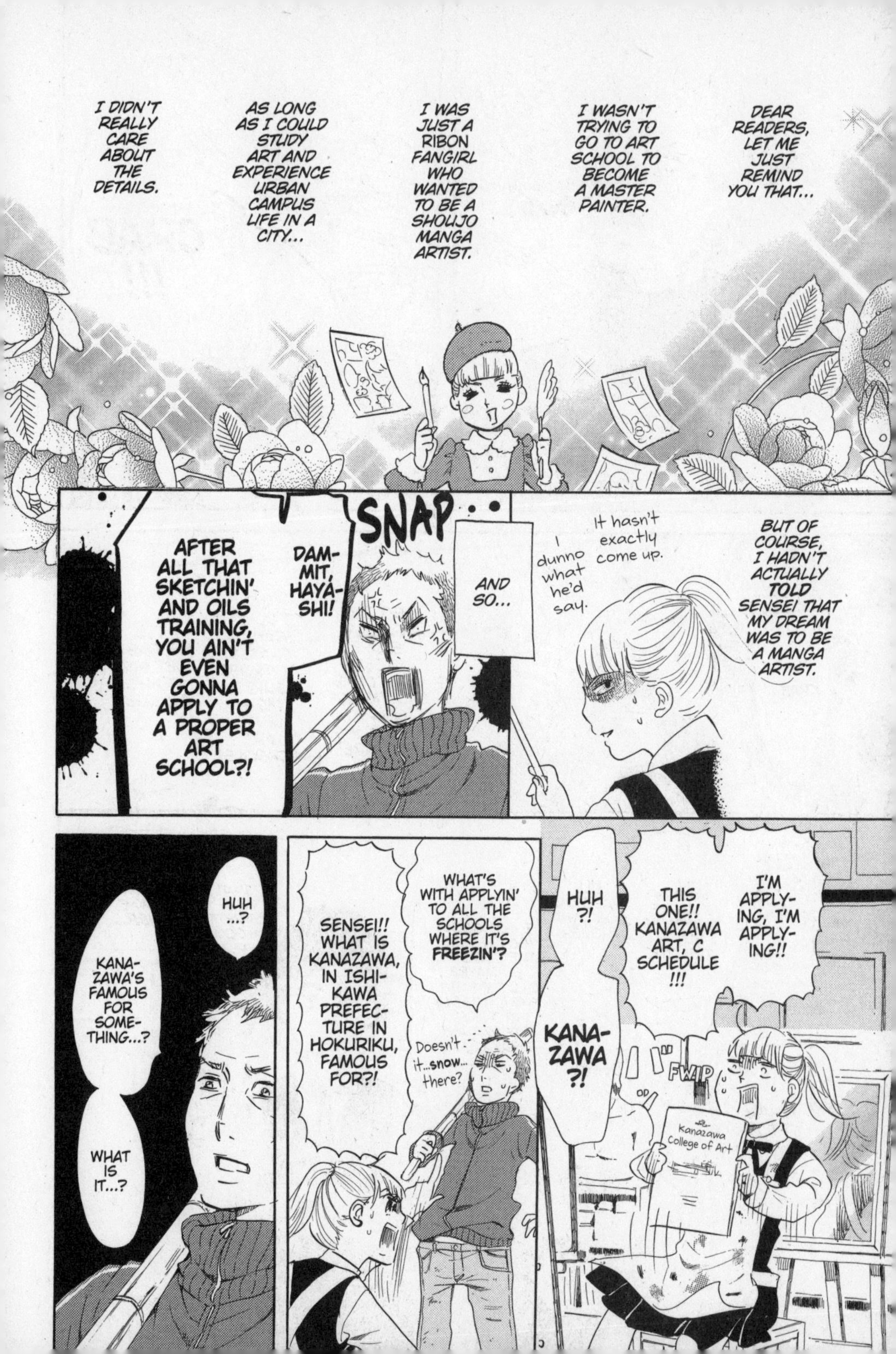
DEAR READERS, LET ME JUST REMIND YOU THAT...
I WASN'T TRYING TO GO TO ART SCHOOL TO BECOME A MASTER PAINTER.
I WAS JUST A RIBON FANGIRL WHO WANTED TO BE A SHOUJO MANGA ARTIST.
AS LONG AS I COULD STUDY ART AND EXPERIENCE URBAN CAMPUS LIFE IN A CITY...
I DIDN'T REALLY CARE ABOUT THE DETAILS.
BUT OF COURSE, I HADN'T ACTUALLY TOLD SENSEI THAT MY DREAM WAS TO BE A MANGA ARTIST.
It hasn't exactly come up.
I dunno what he'd say.
AND SO...
SNAP
DAMMIT, HAYASHI!
AFTER ALL THAT SKETCHIN' AND OILS TRAINING, YOU AIN'T EVEN GONNA APPLY TO A PROPER ART SCHOOL?!
I'M APPLYING, I'M APPLYING!!
THIS ONE!! KANAZAWA ART, C SCHEDULE!!!
HUH?!
KANAZAWA?!
FWIP
Kanazawa College of Art
WHAT'S WITH APPLYIN' TO ALL THE SCHOOLS WHERE IT'S FREEZIN'?
SENSEI!! WHAT IS KANAZAWA, IN ISHIKAWA PREFECTURE IN HOKURIKU, FAMOUS FOR?!
Doesn't it...snow... there?
HUH...?
KANAZAWA'S FAMOUS FOR SOMETHING...?
WHAT IS IT...?

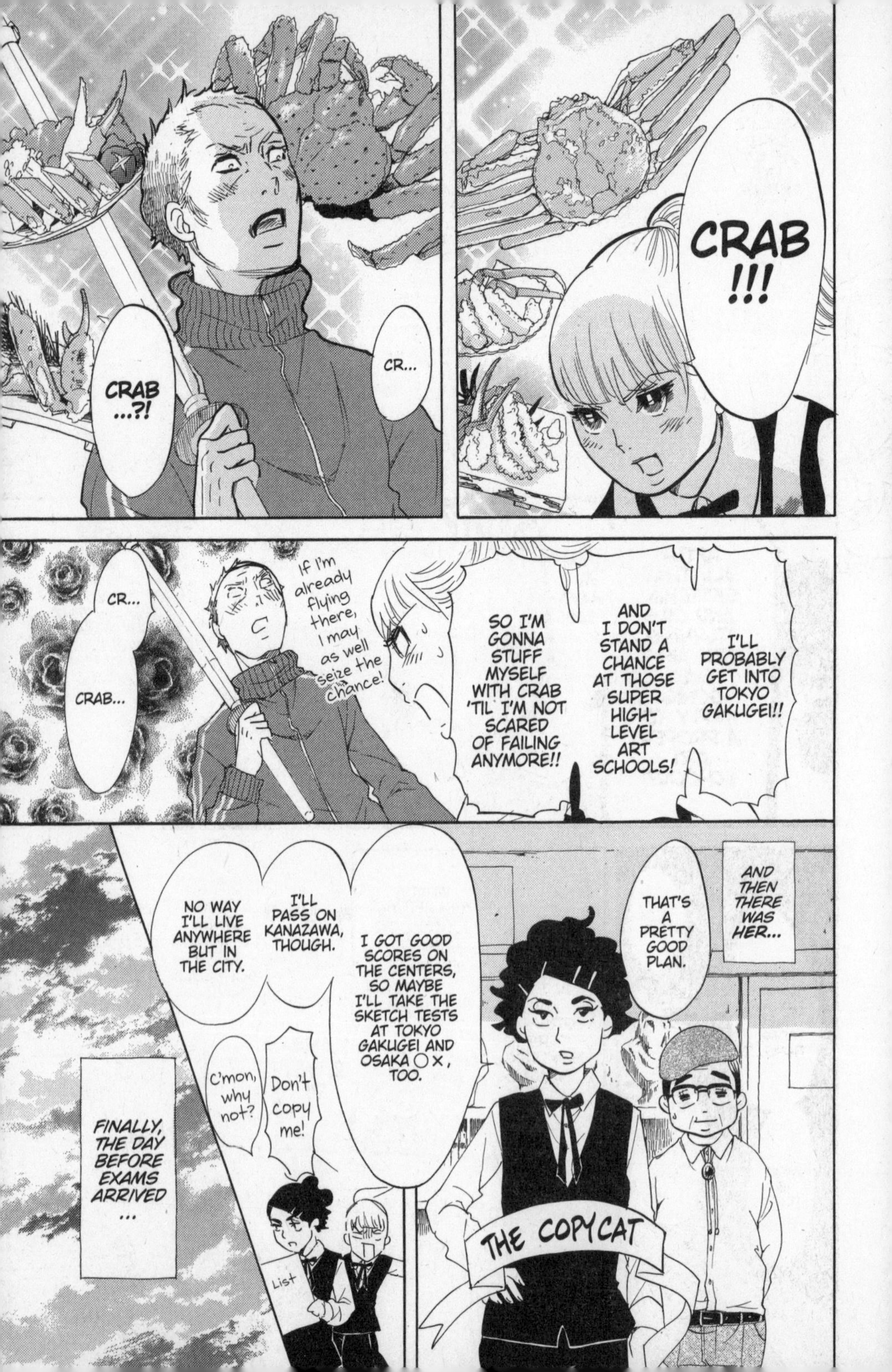
CRAB !!!
CR...
CRAB ...?!
I'LL PROBABLY GET INTO TOKYO GAKUGEI!!
AND I DON'T STAND A CHANCE AT THOSE SUPER HIGH-LEVEL ART SCHOOLS!
SO I'M GONNA STUFF MYSELF WITH CRAB 'TIL I'M NOT SCARED OF FAILING ANYMORE!!
If I'm already flying there, I may as well seize the chance!
CR...
CRAB...
AND THEN THERE WAS HER...
THAT'S A PRETTY GOOD PLAN.
I GOT GOOD SCORES ON THE CENTERS, SO MAYBE I'LL TAKE THE SKETCH TESTS AT TOKYO GAKUGEI AND OSAKA ○×, TOO.
I'LL PASS ON KANAZAWA, THOUGH.
NO WAY I'LL LIVE ANYWHERE BUT IN THE CITY.
Don't copy me!
C'mon, why not?
THE COPYCAT
List
FINALLY, THE DAY BEFORE EXAMS ARRIVED ...

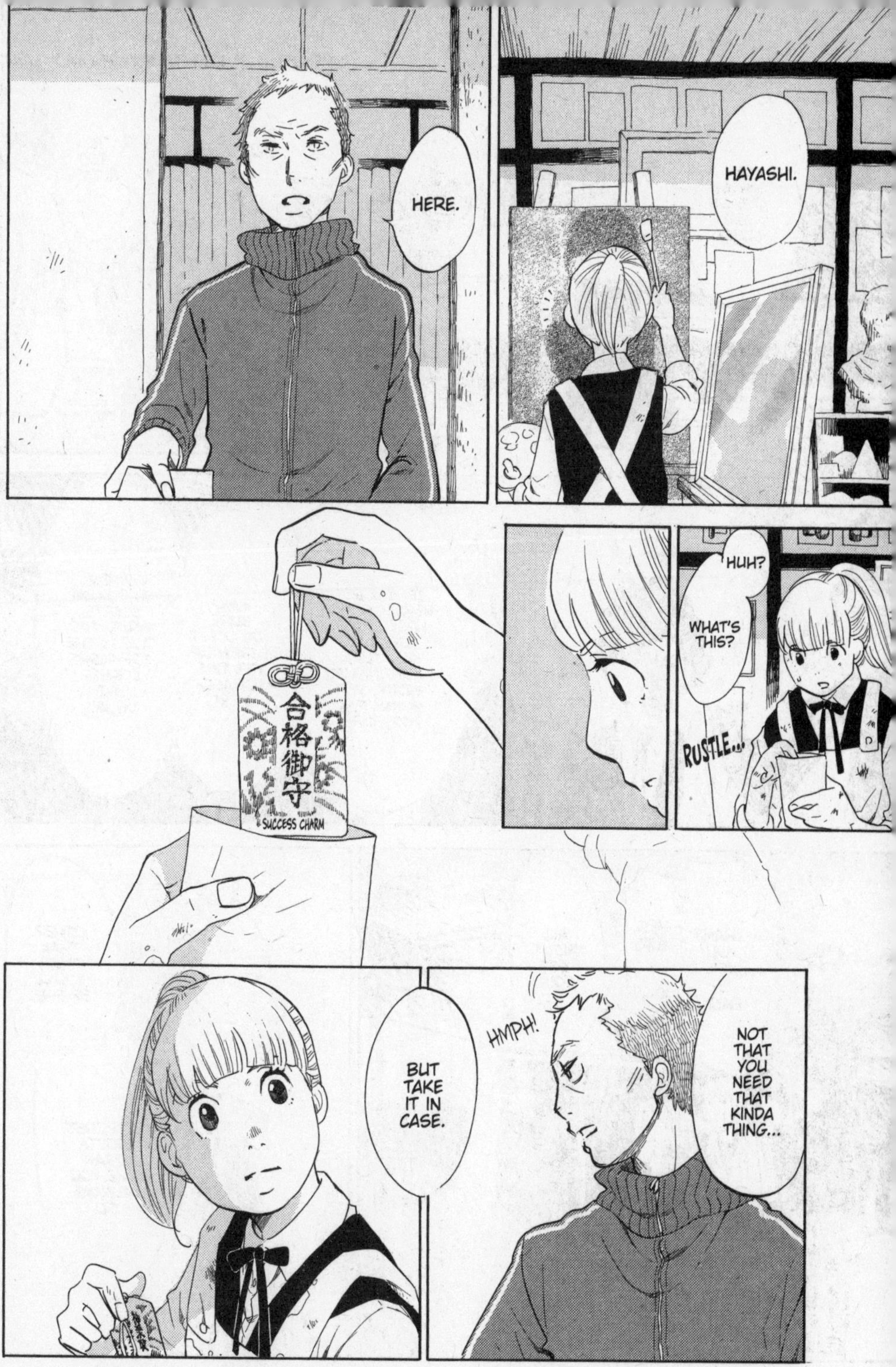
HAYASHI.
HERE.
HUH?
WHAT'S THIS?
RUSTLE...
合格御守
SUCCESS CHARM
NOT THAT YOU NEED THAT KINDA THING...
HMPH!
BUT TAKE IT IN CASE.

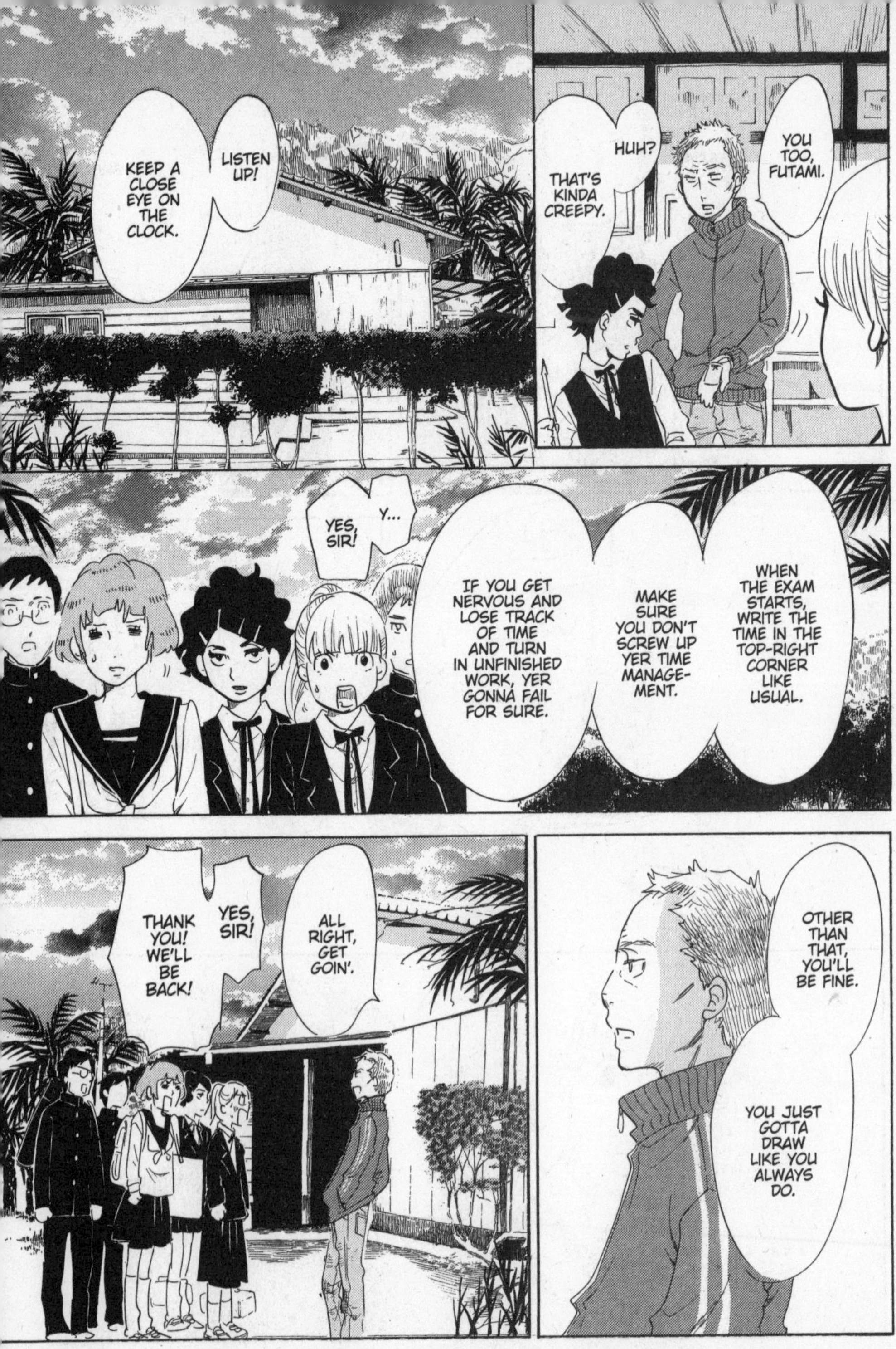
YOU TOO, FUTAMI.
HUH?
THAT'S KINDA CREEPY.
LISTEN UP!
KEEP A CLOSE EYE ON THE CLOCK.
WHEN THE EXAM STARTS, WRITE THE TIME IN THE TOP-RIGHT CORNER LIKE USUAL.
MAKE SURE YOU DON'T SCREW UP YER TIME MANAGE-MENT.
IF YOU GET NERVOUS AND LOSE TRACK OF TIME AND TURN IN UNFINISHED WORK, YER GONNA FAIL FOR SURE.
Y...
YES, SIR!
OTHER THAN THAT, YOU'LL BE FINE.
YOU JUST GOTTA DRAW LIKE YOU ALWAYS DO.
ALL RIGHT, GET GOIN'.
YES, SIR!
THANK YOU! WE'LL BE BACK!

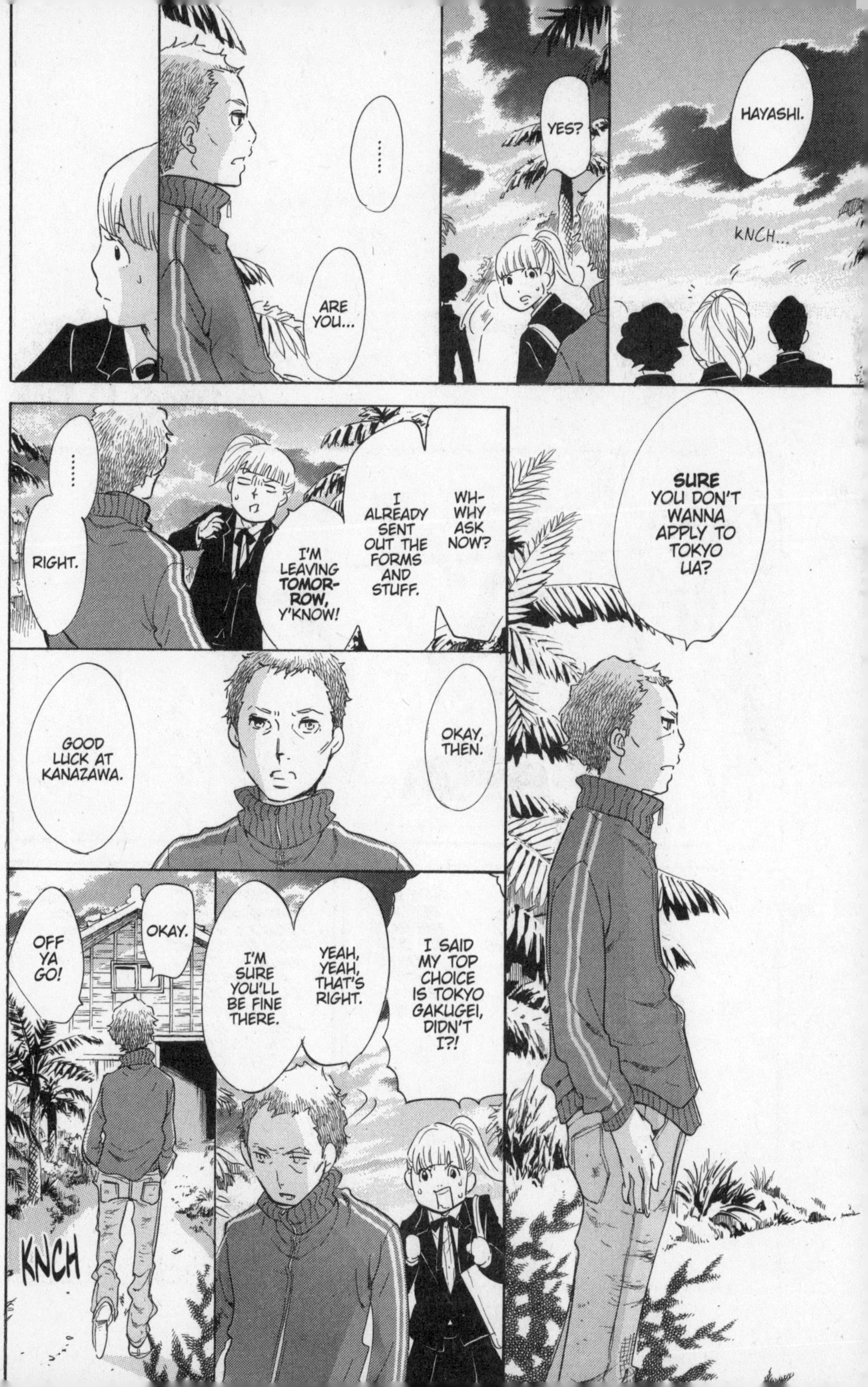
HAYASHI.
KNCH...
YES?
......
ARE YOU...
SURE YOU DON'T WANNA APPLY TO TOKYO UA?
WH-WHY ASK NOW?
I ALREADY SENT OUT THE FORMS AND STUFF.
I'M LEAVING TOMORROW, Y'KNOW!
......
RIGHT.
OKAY, THEN.
GOOD LUCK AT KANAZAWA.
I SAID MY TOP CHOICE IS TOKYO GAKUGEI, DIDN'T I?!
YEAH, YEAH, THAT'S RIGHT.
I'M SURE YOU'LL BE FINE THERE.
OKAY.
OFF YA GO!
KNCH

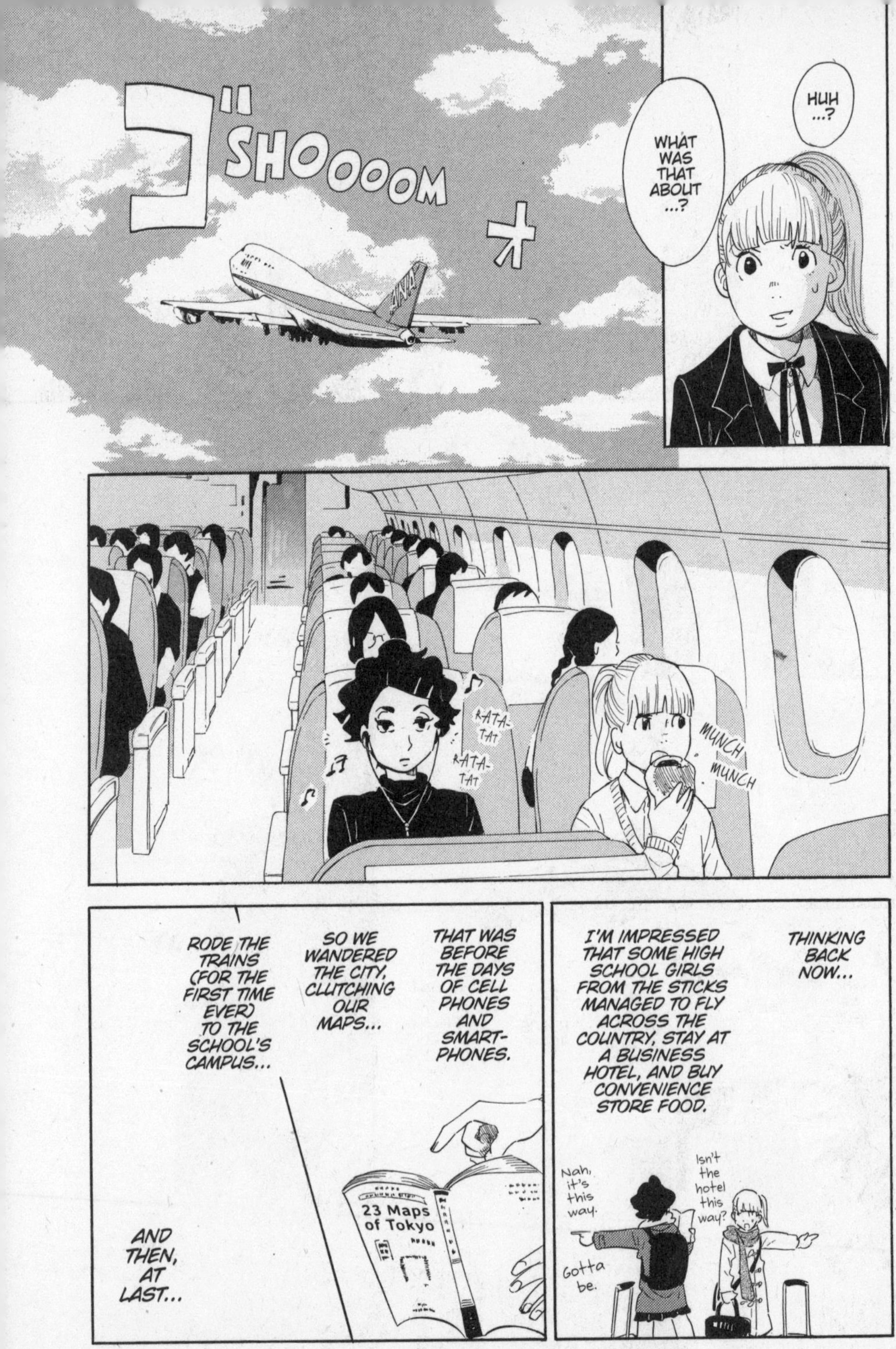
HUH ...?
WHAT WAS THAT ABOUT ...?
ゴ SHOOOOM ォ
RATA-TAT
RATA-TAT
MUNCH MUNCH
THINKING BACK NOW...
I'M IMPRESSED THAT SOME HIGH SCHOOL GIRLS FROM THE STICKS MANAGED TO FLY ACROSS THE COUNTRY, STAY AT A BUSINESS HOTEL, AND BUY CONVENIENCE STORE FOOD.
Isn't the hotel this way?
Nah, it's this way.
Gotta be.
THAT WAS BEFORE THE DAYS OF CELL PHONES AND SMART-PHONES.
SO WE WANDERED THE CITY, CLUTCHING OUR MAPS...
RODE THE TRAINS (FOR THE FIRST TIME EVER) TO THE SCHOOL'S CAMPUS...
23 Maps of Tokyo
AND THEN, AT LAST...

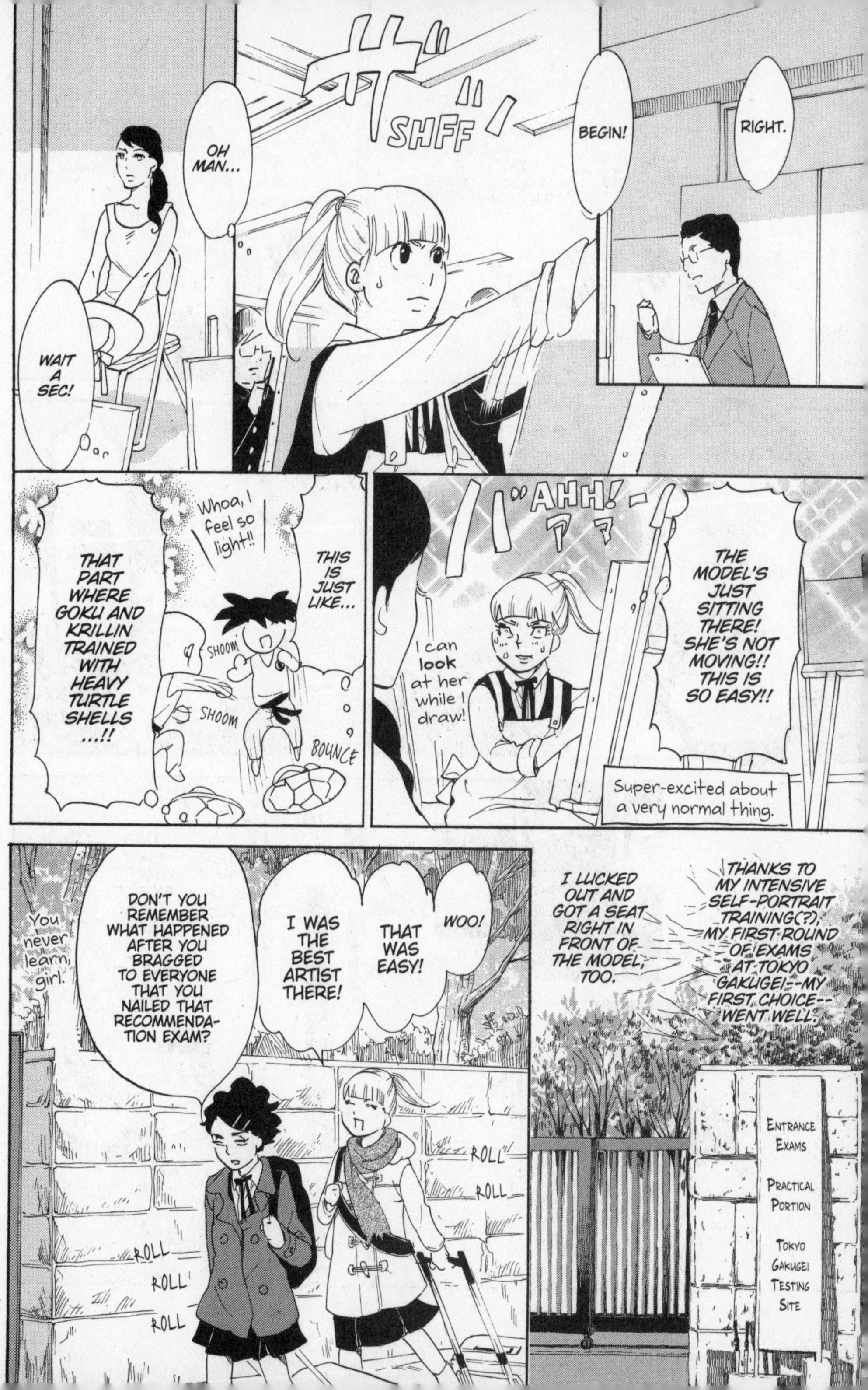

RIGHT.
BEGIN!
SHFF
OH MAN...
WAIT A SEC!
AHH!
THE MODEL'S JUST SITTING THERE! SHE'S NOT MOVING!! THIS IS SO EASY!!
I can look at her while I draw!
Super-excited about a very normal thing.
THIS IS JUST LIKE...
Whoa, I feel so light!!
THAT PART WHERE GOKU AND KRILLIN TRAINED WITH HEAVY TURTLE SHELLS...!!
SHOOM
SHOOM
BOUNCE
THANKS TO MY INTENSIVE SELF-PORTRAIT TRAINING(?), MY FIRST ROUND OF EXAMS AT TOKYO GAKUGEI--MY FIRST CHOICE--WENT WELL.
I LUCKED OUT AND GOT A SEAT RIGHT IN FRONT OF THE MODEL, TOO.
Entrance Exams
Practical Portion
Tokyo Gakugei Testing Site
WOO!
THAT WAS EASY!
I WAS THE BEST ARTIST THERE!
DON'T YOU REMEMBER WHAT HAPPENED AFTER YOU BRAGGED TO EVERYONE THAT YOU NAILED THAT RECOMMENDATION EXAM?
You never learn, girl.
ROLL
ROLL
ROLL
ROLL
ROLL

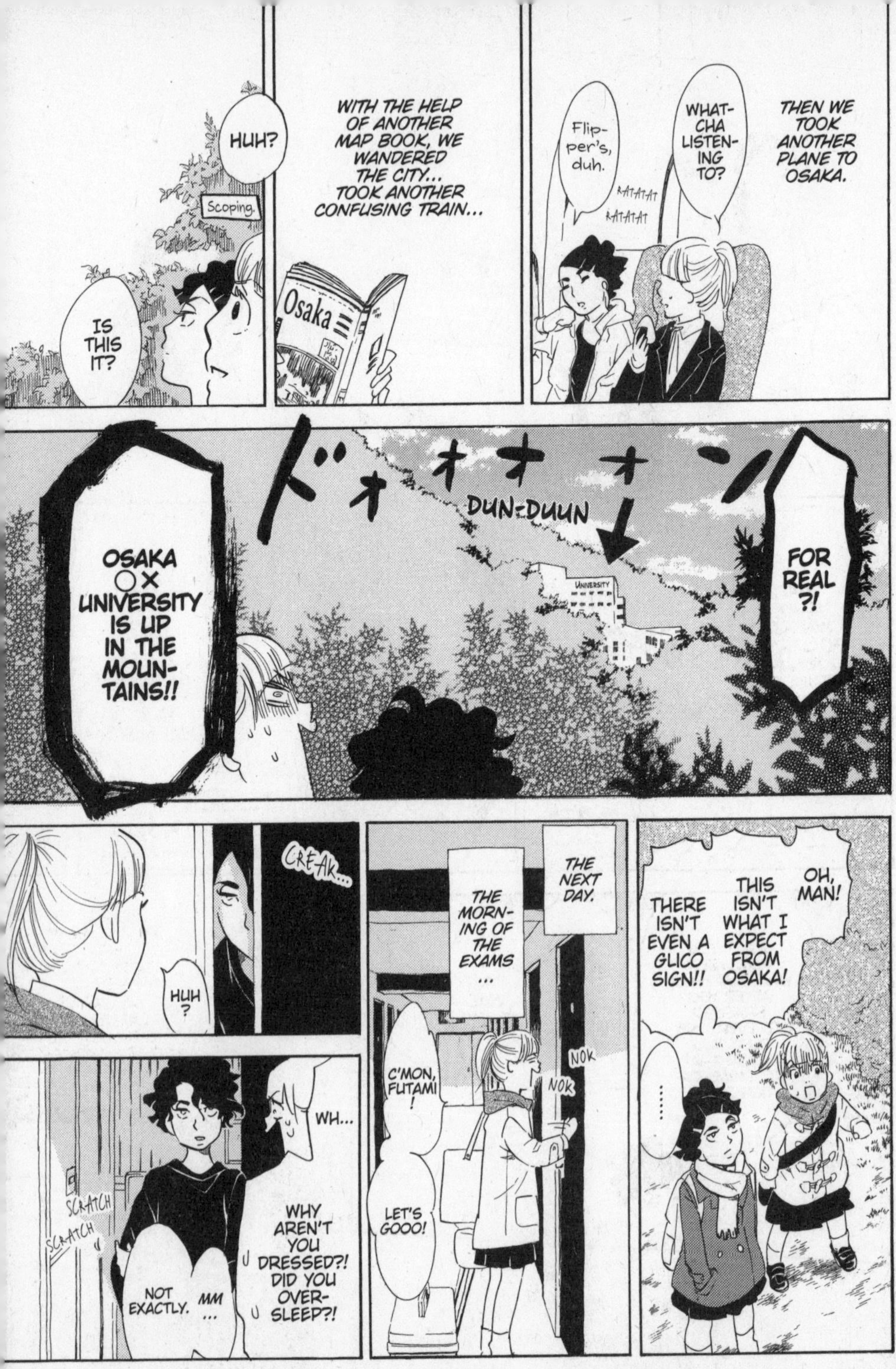
THEN WE TOOK ANOTHER PLANE TO OSAKA.
WHATCHA LISTENING TO?
Flipper's, duh.
RATATAT
RATATAT
WITH THE HELP OF ANOTHER MAP BOOK, WE WANDERED THE CITY... TOOK ANOTHER CONFUSING TRAIN...
Osaka
HUH?
Scoping.
IS THIS IT?
FOR REAL?!
ドォオオーン
DUN-DUUN
UNIVERSITY
OSAKA ◯× UNIVERSITY IS UP IN THE MOUNTAINS!!
OH, MAN!
THIS ISN'T WHAT I EXPECT FROM OSAKA!
THERE ISN'T EVEN A GLICO SIGN!!
......
THE NEXT DAY.
THE MORNING OF THE EXAMS...
NOK
NOK
C'MON, FUTAMI!
LET'S GOOO!
CREAK...
HUH?
WH...
WHY AREN'T YOU DRESSED?! DID YOU OVERSLEEP?!
MM...
NOT EXACTLY.
SCRATCH
SCRATCH

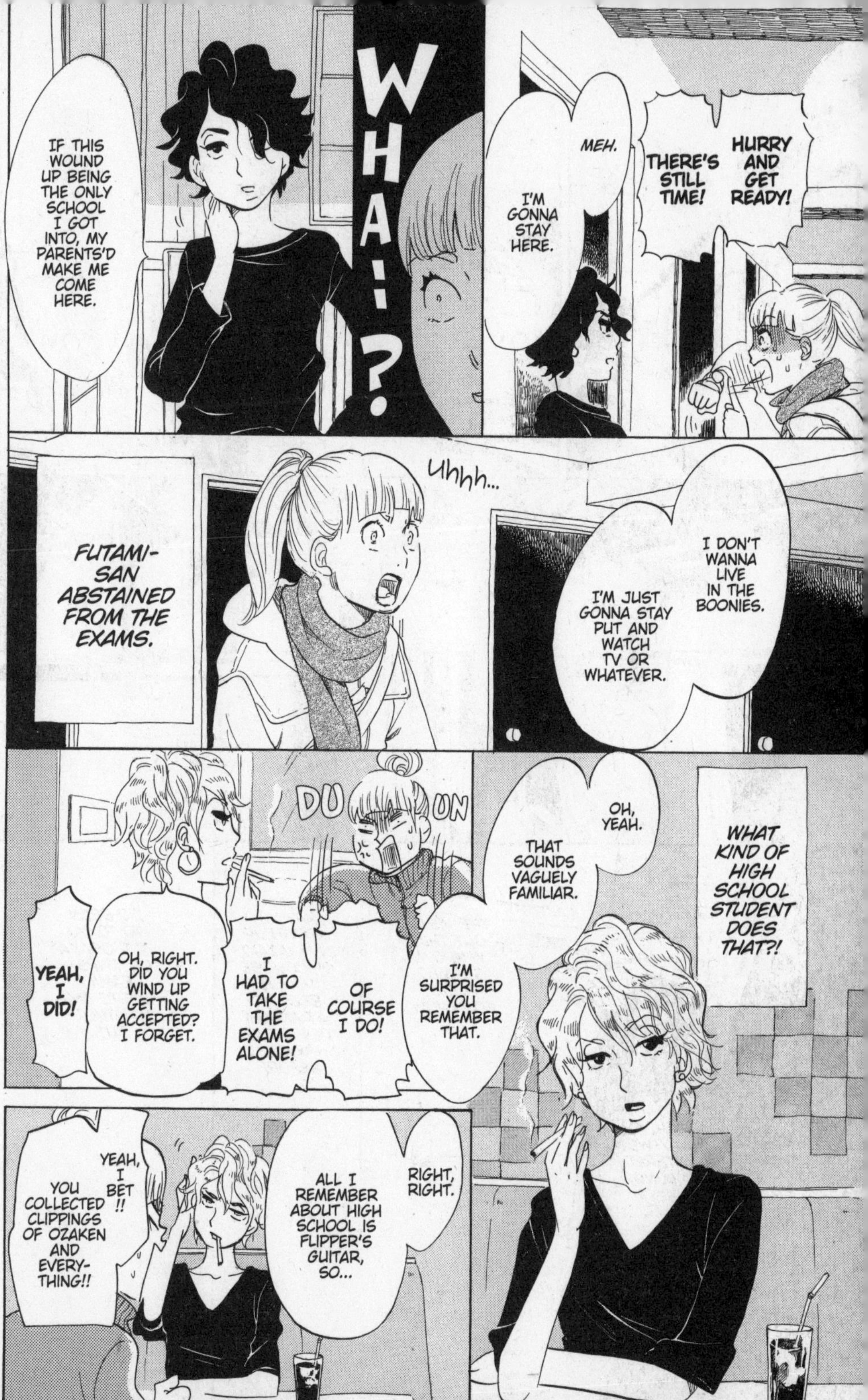

HURRY AND GET READY!
THERE'S STILL TIME!
MEH.
I'M GONNA STAY HERE.
WHA!?
IF THIS WOUND UP BEING THE ONLY SCHOOL I GOT INTO, MY PARENTS'D MAKE ME COME HERE.
I DON'T WANNA LIVE IN THE BOONIES.
I'M JUST GONNA STAY PUT AND WATCH TV OR WHATEVER.
Uhhh...
FUTAMI-SAN ABSTAINED FROM THE EXAMS.
WHAT KIND OF HIGH SCHOOL STUDENT DOES THAT?!
OH, YEAH.
THAT SOUNDS VAGUELY FAMILIAR.
I'M SURPRISED YOU REMEMBER THAT.
OF COURSE I DO!
I HAD TO TAKE THE EXAMS ALONE!
DU UN
OH, RIGHT. DID YOU WIND UP GETTING ACCEPTED? I FORGET.
YEAH, I DID!
RIGHT, RIGHT.
ALL I REMEMBER ABOUT HIGH SCHOOL IS FLIPPER'S GUITAR, SO...
YEAH, I BET!!
YOU COLLECTED CLIPPINGS OF OZAKEN AND EVERYTHING!!

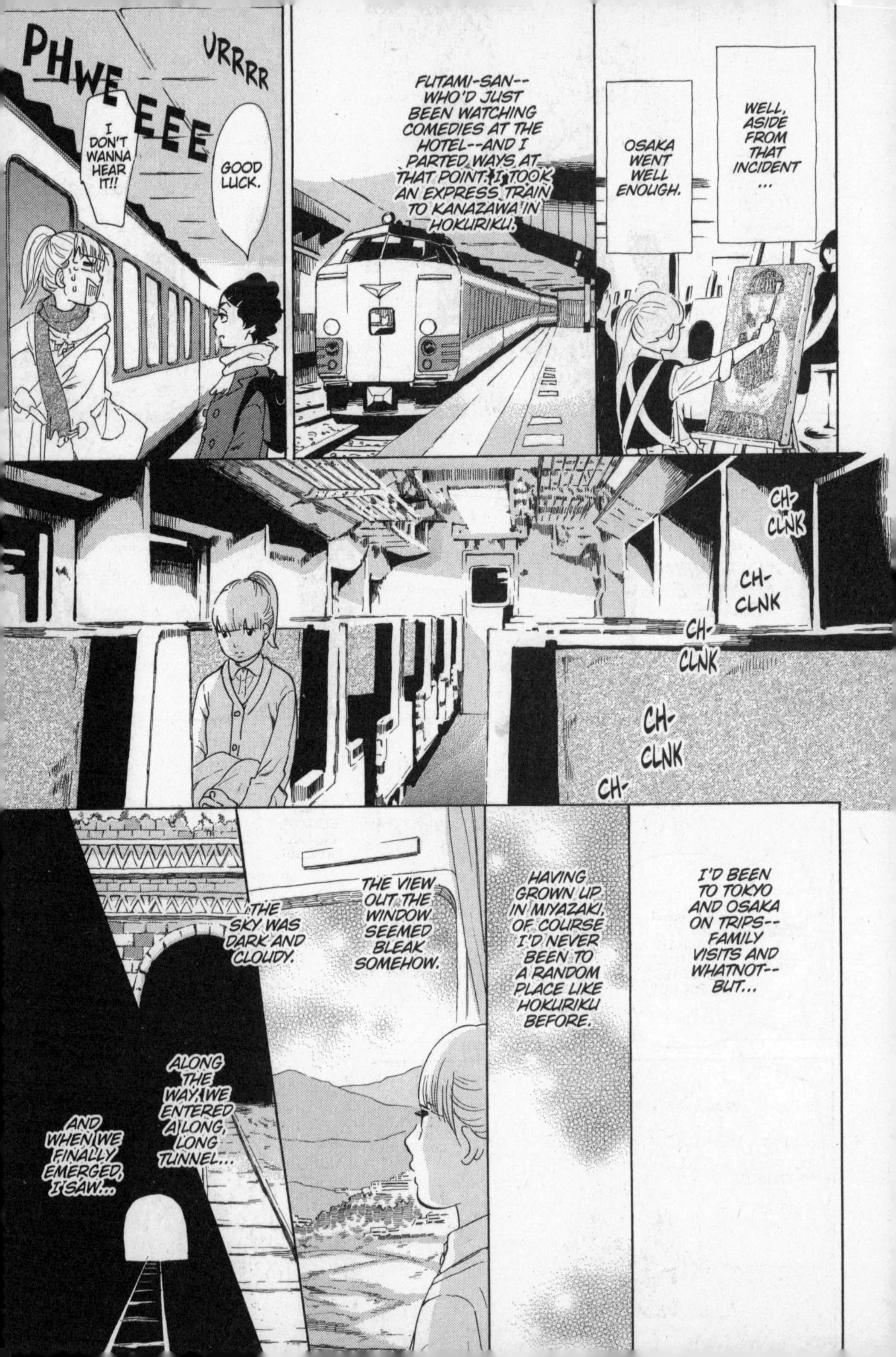
WELL, ASIDE FROM THAT INCIDENT...
OSAKA WENT WELL ENOUGH.
FUTAMI-SAN--WHO'D JUST BEEN WATCHING COMEDIES AT THE HOTEL--AND I PARTED WAYS AT THAT POINT. I TOOK AN EXPRESS TRAIN TO KANAZAWA IN HOKURIKU.
URRRR
PHWEEEE
GOOD LUCK.
I DON'T WANNA HEAR IT!!
CH-CLNK
CH-CLNK
CH-CLNK
CH-CLNK
CH-
I'D BEEN TO TOKYO AND OSAKA ON TRIPS--FAMILY VISITS AND WHATNOT--BUT...
HAVING GROWN UP IN MIYAZAKI, OF COURSE I'D NEVER BEEN TO A RANDOM PLACE LIKE HOKURIKU BEFORE.
THE VIEW OUT THE WINDOW SEEMED BLEAK SOMEHOW.
THE SKY WAS DARK AND CLOUDY.
ALONG THE WAY, WE ENTERED A LONG, LONG TUNNEL...
AND WHEN WE FINALLY EMERGED, I SAW...

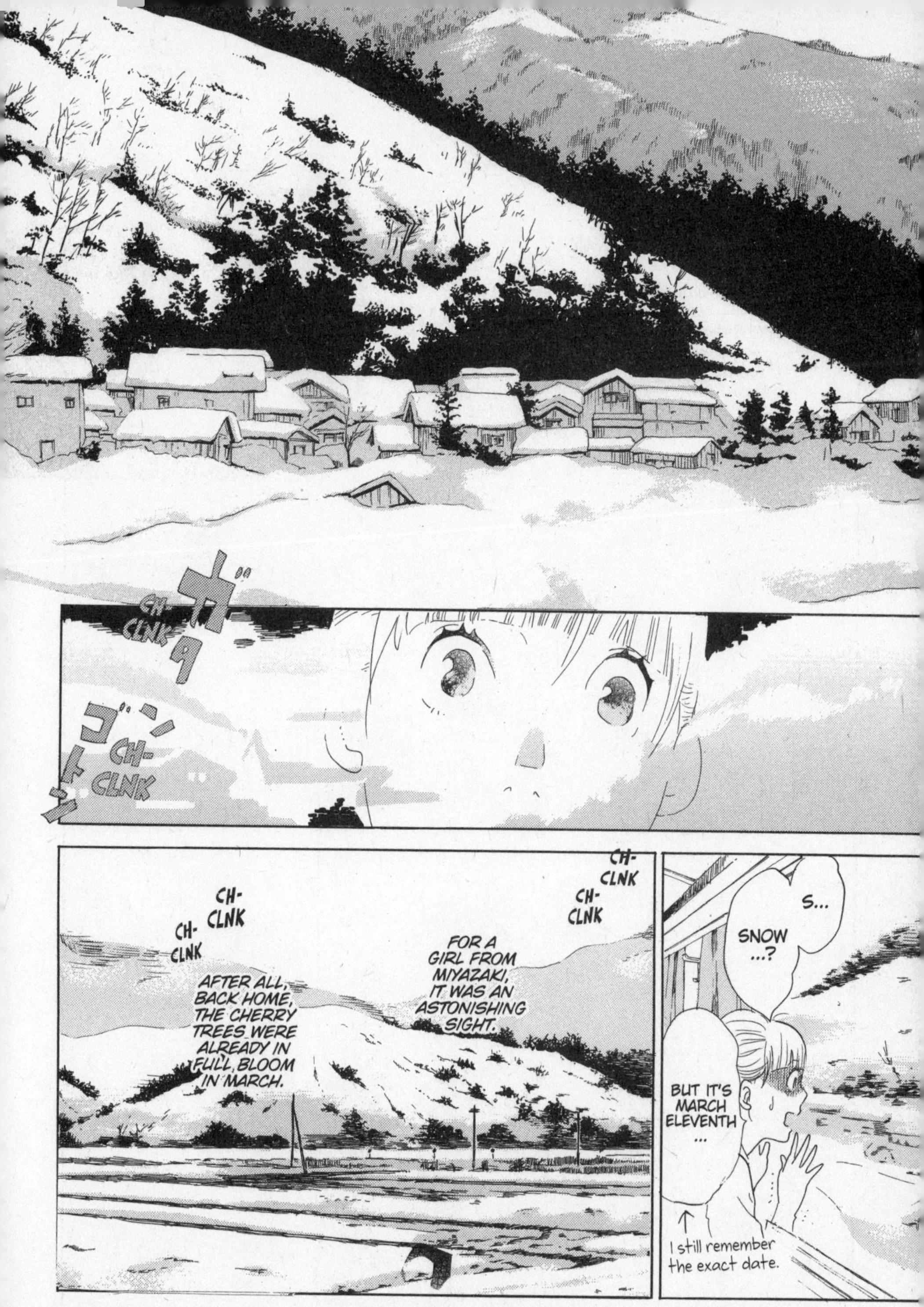
CH-CLNK
CH-CLNK
S...
SNOW ...?
BUT IT'S MARCH ELEVENTH ...
I still remember the exact date.
CH-CLNK
CH-CLNK
FOR A GIRL FROM MIYAZAKI, IT WAS AN ASTONISHING SIGHT.
CH-CLNK
CH-CLNK
AFTER ALL, BACK HOME, THE CHERRY TREES WERE ALREADY IN FULL BLOOM IN MARCH.

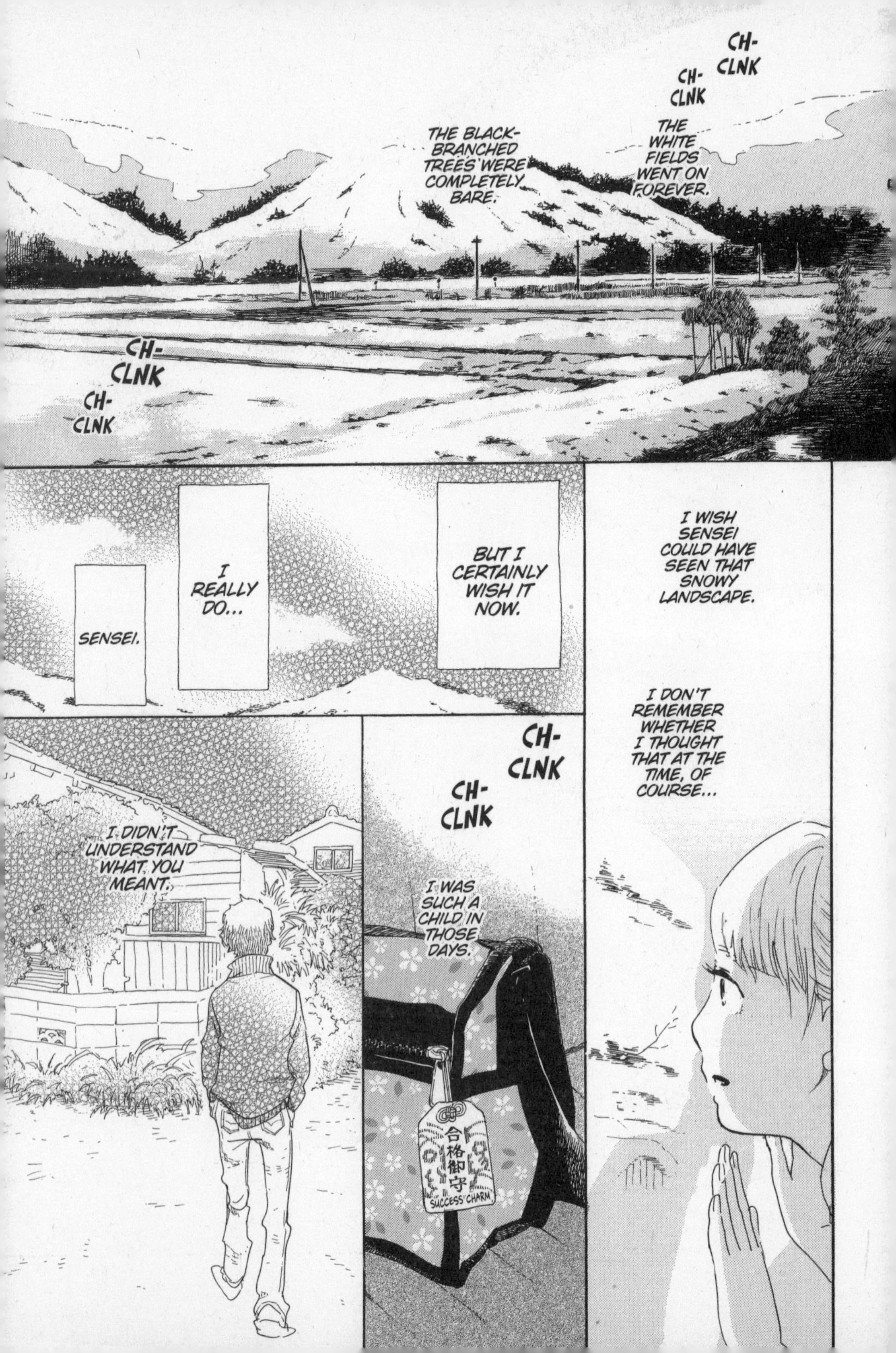
CH-CLNK
CH-CLNK
THE WHITE FIELDS WENT ON FOREVER.
THE BLACK-BRANCHED TREES WERE COMPLETELY BARE.
CH-CLNK
CH-CLNK
I WISH SENSEI COULD HAVE SEEN THAT SNOWY LANDSCAPE.
I DON'T REMEMBER WHETHER I THOUGHT THAT AT THE TIME, OF COURSE...
BUT I CERTAINLY WISH IT NOW.
I REALLY DO...
SENSEI.
CH-CLNK
CH-CLNK
I WAS SUCH A CHILD IN THOSE DAYS.
合格御守
SUCCESS CHARM
I DIDN'T UNDERSTAND WHAT YOU MEANT.

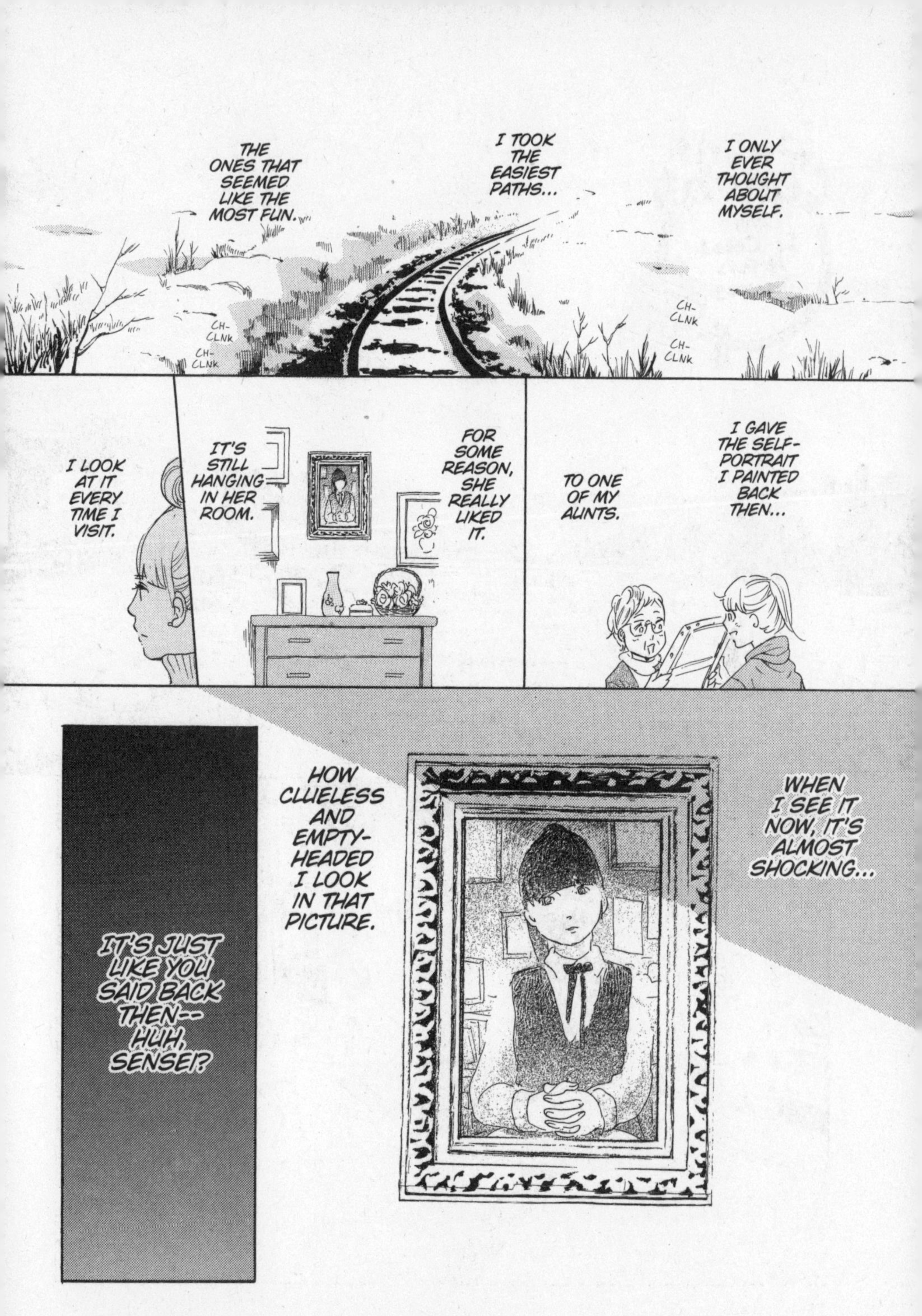
I ONLY EVER THOUGHT ABOUT MYSELF.
I TOOK THE EASIEST PATHS...
THE ONES THAT SEEMED LIKE THE MOST FUN.
CH-CLNK
CH-CLNK
CH-CLNK
CH-CLNK
I GAVE THE SELF-PORTRAIT I PAINTED BACK THEN...
TO ONE OF MY AUNTS.
FOR SOME REASON, SHE REALLY LIKED IT.
IT'S STILL HANGING IN HER ROOM.
I LOOK AT IT EVERY TIME I VISIT.
WHEN I SEE IT NOW, IT'S ALMOST SHOCKING...
HOW CLUELESS AND EMPTY-HEADED I LOOK IN THAT PICTURE.
IT'S JUST LIKE YOU SAID BACK THEN--HUH, SENSEI?

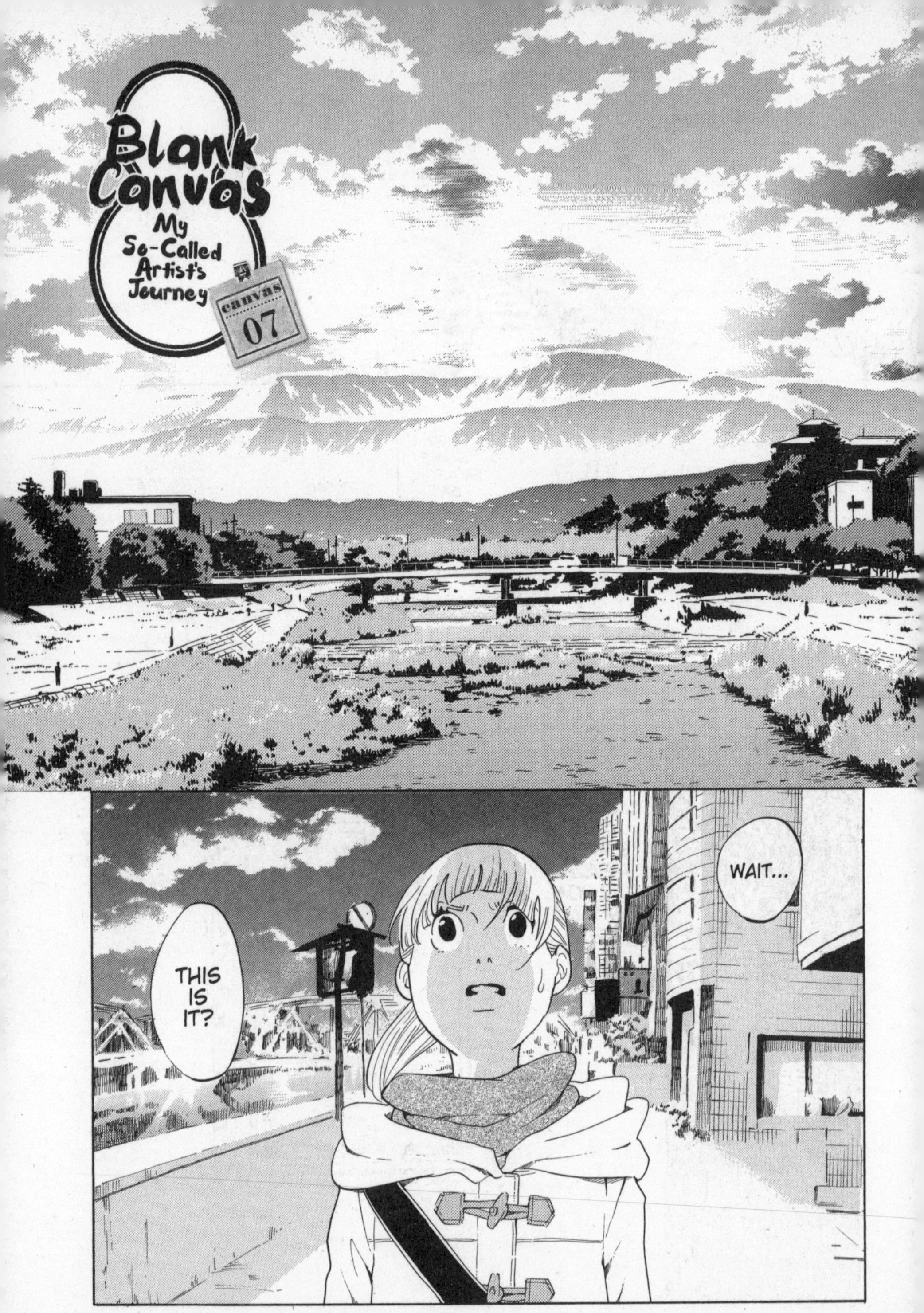
Blank Canvas
My So-Called Artist's Journey
canvas
07
WAIT...
THIS IS IT?

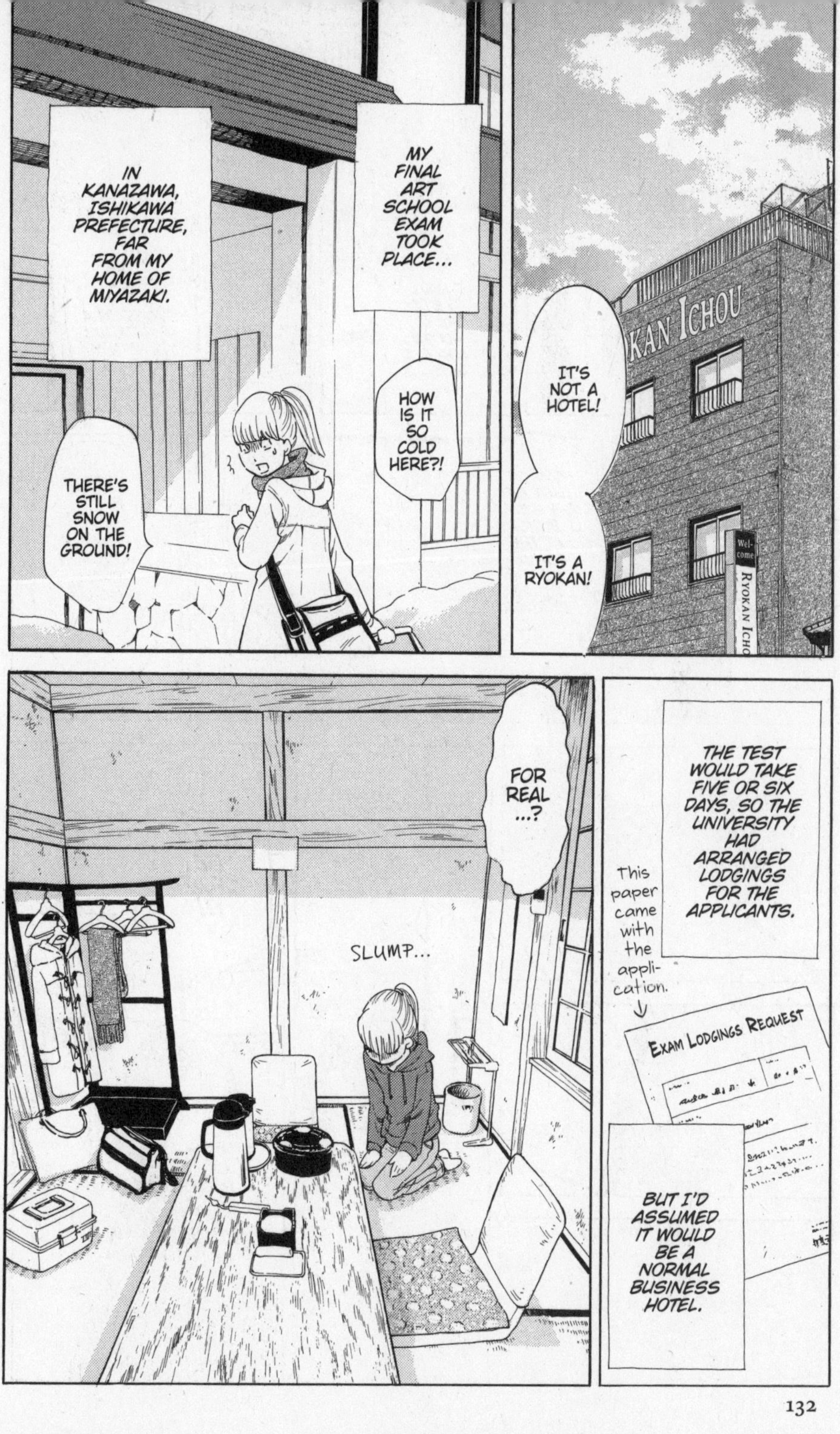

IT'S NOT A HOTEL!
IT'S A RYOKAN!
MY FINAL ART SCHOOL EXAM TOOK PLACE...
IN KANAZAWA, ISHIKAWA PREFECTURE, FAR FROM MY HOME OF MIYAZAKI.
HOW IS IT SO COLD HERE?!
THERE'S STILL SNOW ON THE GROUND!
THE TEST WOULD TAKE FIVE OR SIX DAYS, SO THE UNIVERSITY HAD ARRANGED LODGINGS FOR THE APPLICANTS.
This paper came with the application.
EXAM LODGINGS REQUEST
BUT I'D ASSUMED IT WOULD BE A NORMAL BUSINESS HOTEL.
FOR REAL ...?
SLUMP...

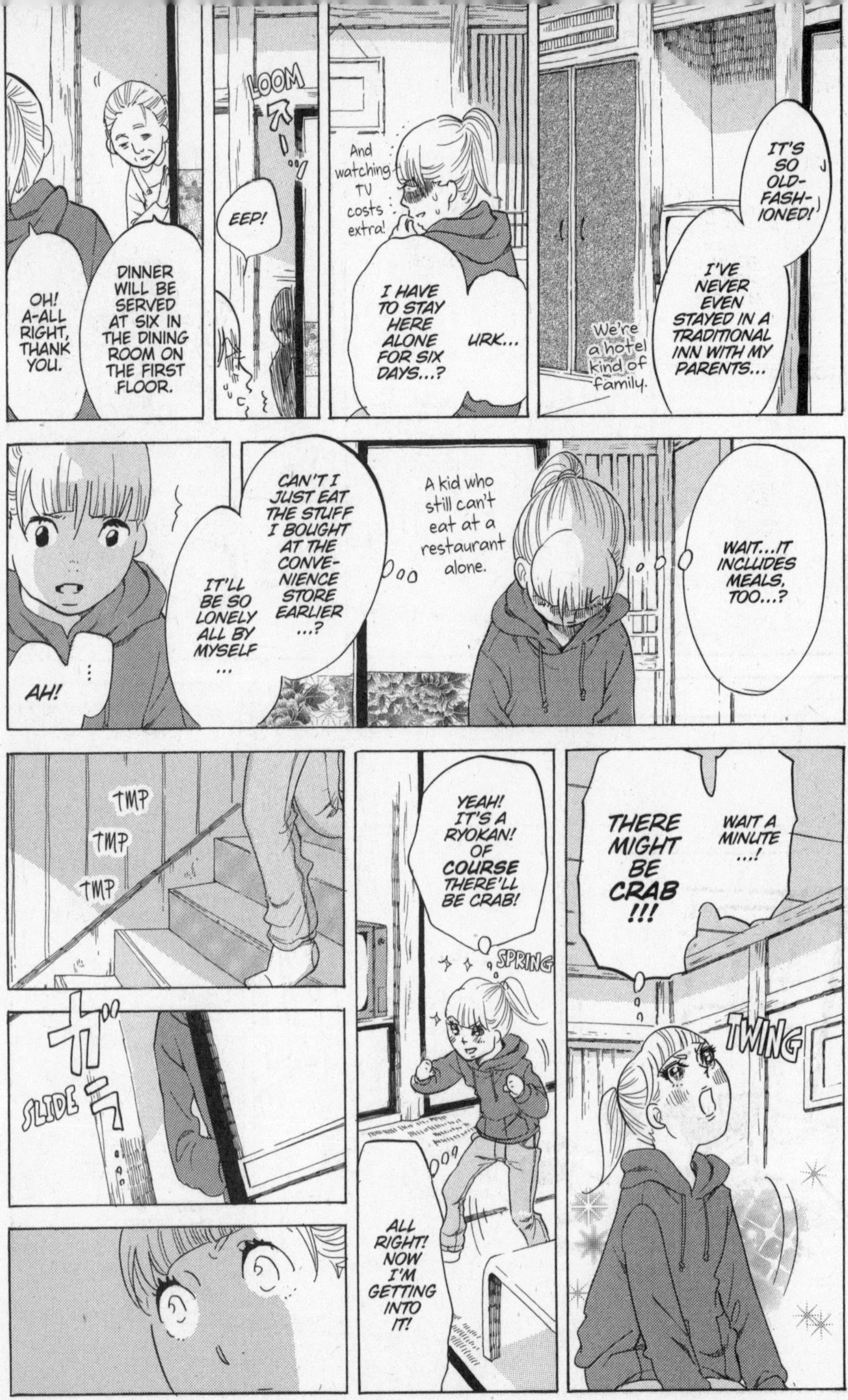
IT'S SO OLD-FASHIONED!
I'VE NEVER EVEN STAYED IN A TRADITIONAL INN WITH MY PARENTS...
We're a hotel kind of family.
And watching TV costs extra!
I HAVE TO STAY HERE ALONE FOR SIX DAYS...?
URK...
LOOM
EEP!
DINNER WILL BE SERVED AT SIX IN THE DINING ROOM ON THE FIRST FLOOR.
OH! A-ALL RIGHT, THANK YOU.
WAIT...IT INCLUDES MEALS, TOO...?
A kid who still can't eat at a restaurant alone.
CAN'T I JUST EAT THE STUFF I BOUGHT AT THE CONVENIENCE STORE EARLIER...?
IT'LL BE SO LONELY ALL BY MYSELF...
AH!
WAIT A MINUTE...!
THERE MIGHT BE CRAB!!!
TWING
YEAH! IT'S A RYOKAN! OF COURSE THERE'LL BE CRAB!
SPRING
ALL RIGHT! NOW I'M GETTING INTO IT!
TMP
TMP
TMP
SLIDE

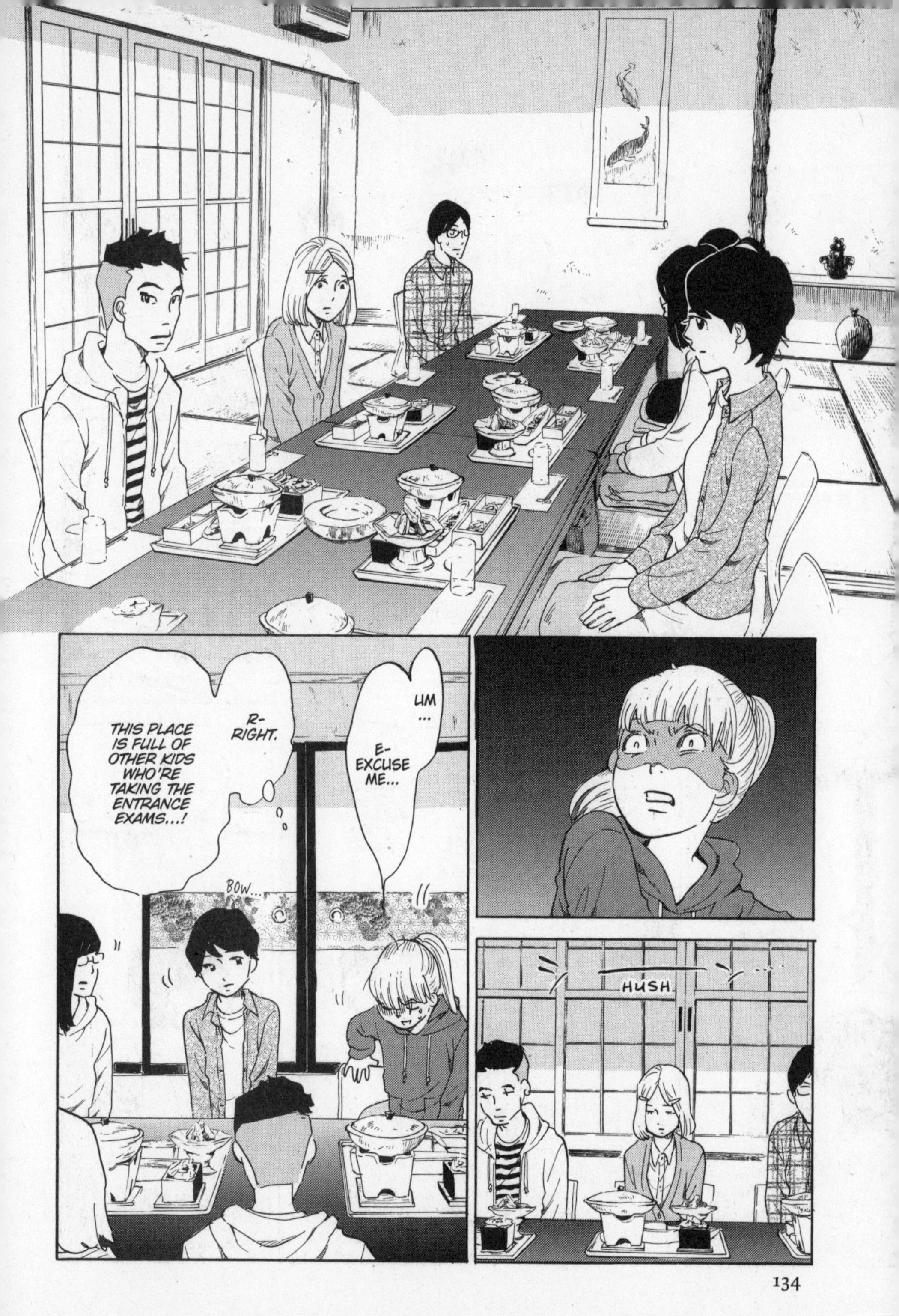
HUSH
UM...
E-EXCUSE ME...
R-RIGHT.
THIS PLACE IS FULL OF OTHER KIDS WHO'RE TAKING THE ENTRANCE EXAMS...!
BOW...

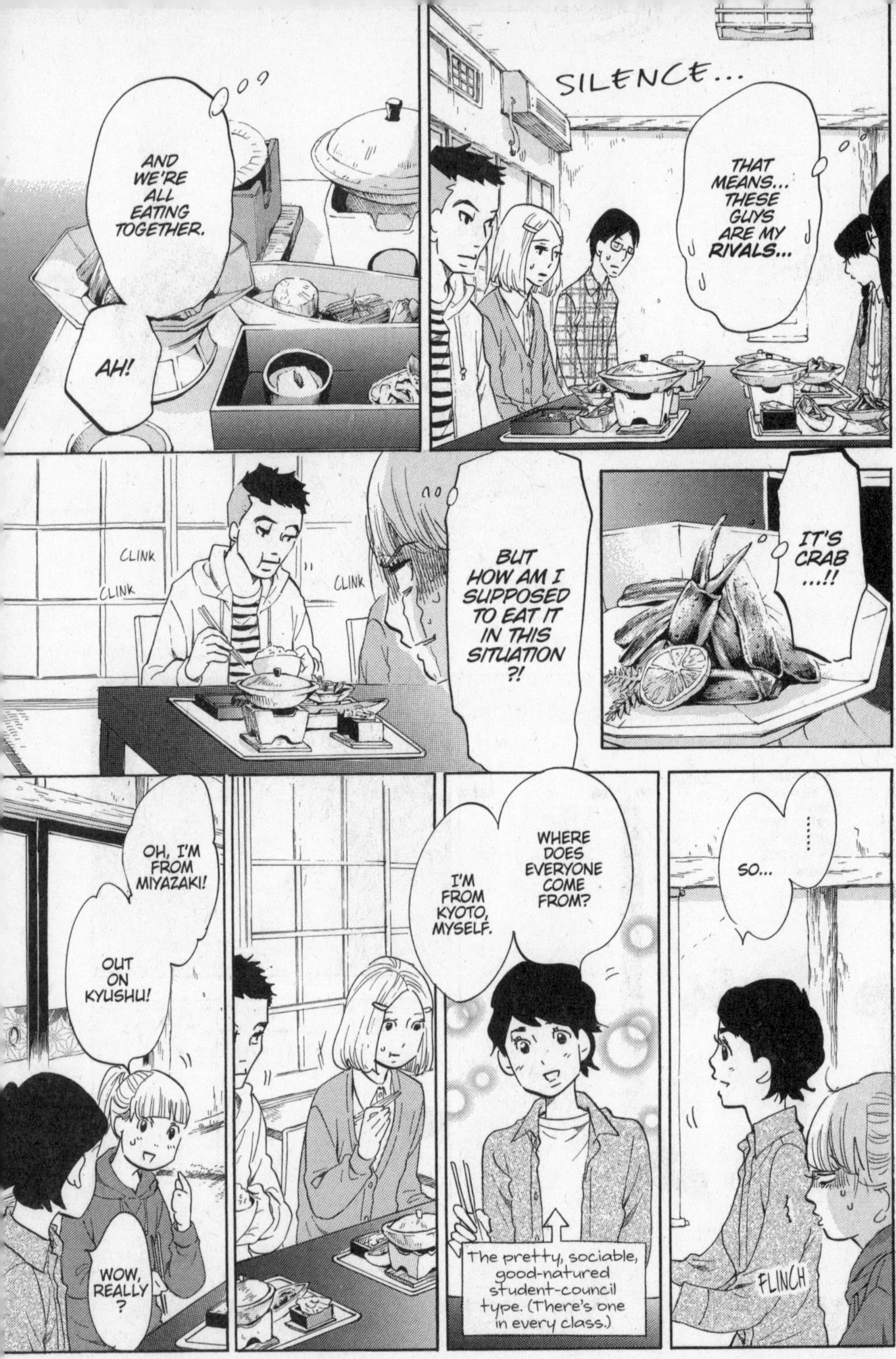
SILENCE...
THAT MEANS... THESE GUYS ARE MY RIVALS...
AND WE'RE ALL EATING TOGETHER.
AH!
IT'S CRAB...!!
BUT HOW AM I SUPPOSED TO EAT IT IN THIS SITUATION?!
CLINK
CLINK
CLINK
......
SO...
FLINCH
WHERE DOES EVERYONE COME FROM?
I'M FROM KYOTO, MYSELF.
The pretty, sociable, good-natured student-council type. (There's one in every class.)
OH, I'M FROM MIYAZAKI!
OUT ON KYUSHU!
WOW, REALLY?

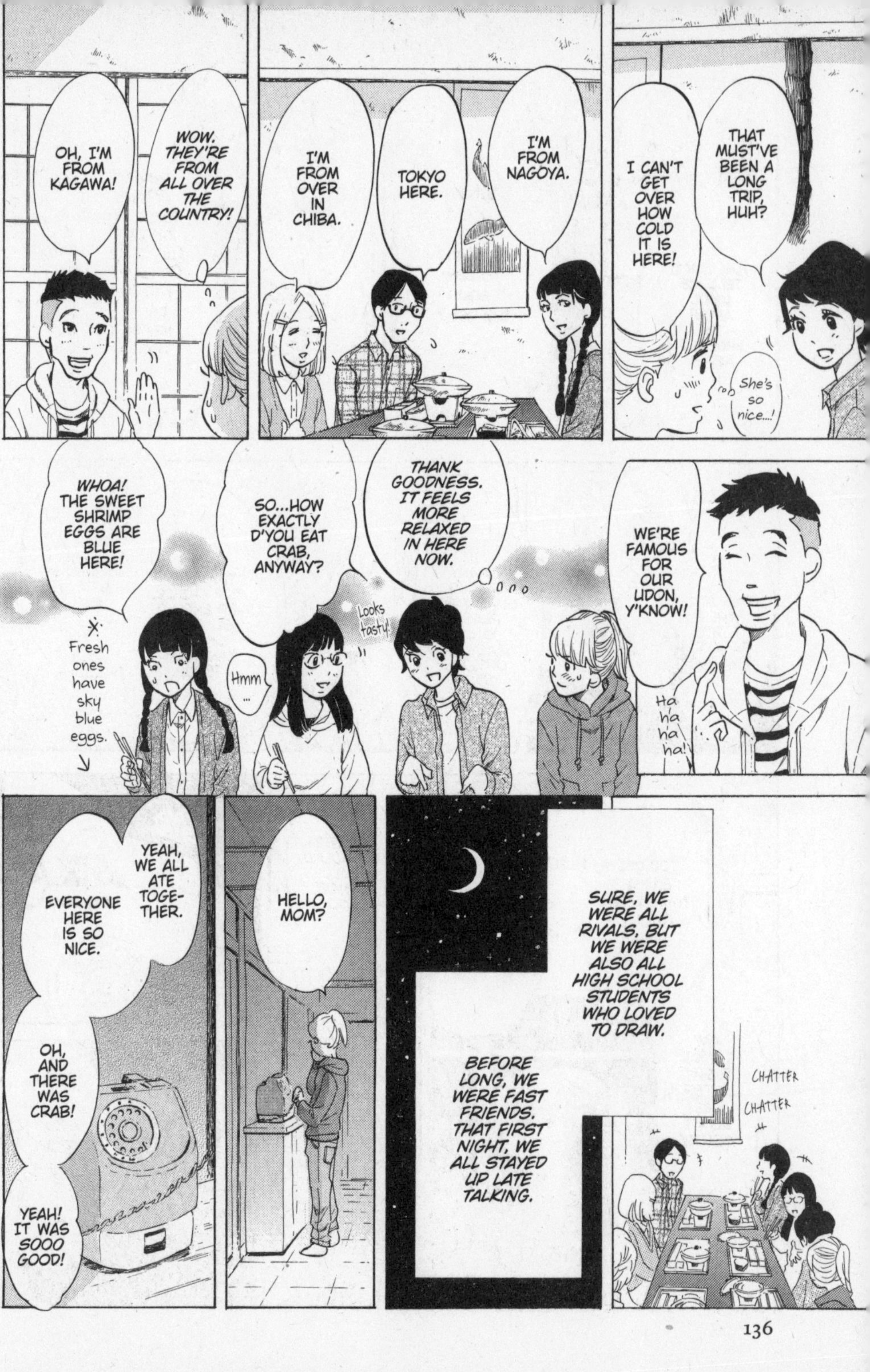
THAT MUST'VE BEEN A LONG TRIP, HUH?
I CAN'T GET OVER HOW COLD IT IS HERE!
She's so nice...!
I'M FROM NAGOYA.
TOKYO HERE.
I'M FROM OVER IN CHIBA.
WOW. THEY'RE FROM ALL OVER THE COUNTRY!
OH, I'M FROM KAGAWA!
WE'RE FAMOUS FOR OUR UDON, Y'KNOW!
Ha ha ha ha!
THANK GOODNESS. IT FEELS MORE RELAXED IN HERE NOW.
SO...HOW EXACTLY D'YOU EAT CRAB, ANYWAY?
Looks tasty!
Hmm...
WHOA! THE SWEET SHRIMP EGGS ARE BLUE HERE!
* Fresh ones have sky blue eggs.
SURE, WE WERE ALL RIVALS, BUT WE WERE ALSO ALL HIGH SCHOOL STUDENTS WHO LOVED TO DRAW.
CHATTER
CHATTER
BEFORE LONG, WE WERE FAST FRIENDS. THAT FIRST NIGHT, WE ALL STAYED UP LATE TALKING.
HELLO, MOM?
YEAH, WE ALL ATE TOGE-THER.
EVERYONE HERE IS SO NICE.
OH, AND THERE WAS CRAB!
YEAH! IT WAS SOOO GOOD!

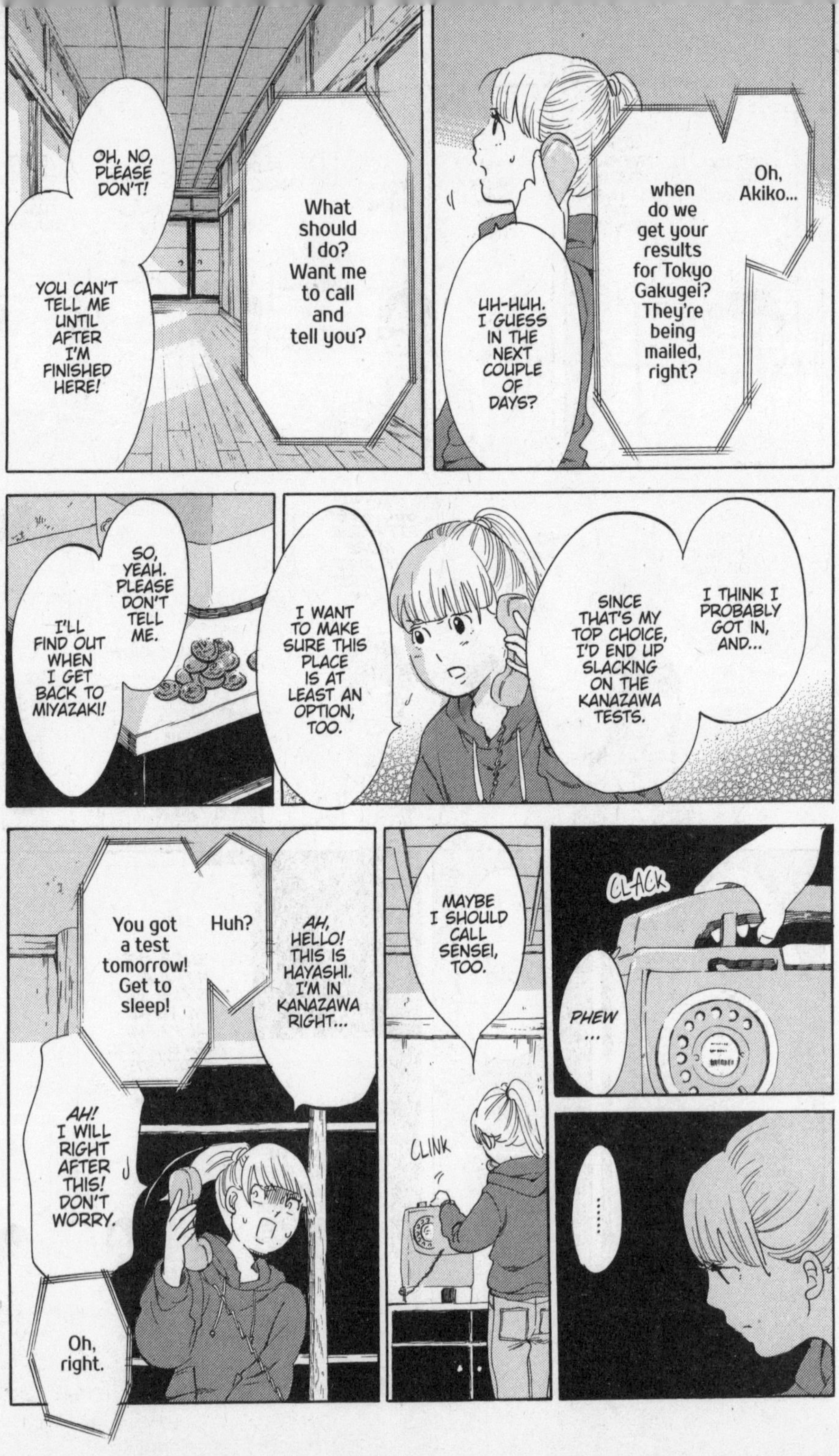
Oh, Akiko...
when do we get your results for Tokyo Gakugei? They're being mailed, right?
UH-HUH. I GUESS IN THE NEXT COUPLE OF DAYS?
What should I do? Want me to call and tell you?
OH, NO, PLEASE DON'T!
YOU CAN'T TELL ME UNTIL AFTER I'M FINISHED HERE!
I THINK I PROBABLY GOT IN, AND...
SINCE THAT'S MY TOP CHOICE, I'D END UP SLACKING ON THE KANAZAWA TESTS.
I WANT TO MAKE SURE THIS PLACE IS AT LEAST AN OPTION, TOO.
SO, YEAH. PLEASE DON'T TELL ME.
I'LL FIND OUT WHEN I GET BACK TO MIYAZAKI!
CLACK
PHEW...
......
MAYBE I SHOULD CALL SENSEI, TOO.
CLINK
AH, HELLO! THIS IS HAYASHI. I'M IN KANAZAWA RIGHT...
Huh?
You got a test tomorrow! Get to sleep!
AH! I WILL RIGHT AFTER THIS! DON'T WORRY.
Oh, right.

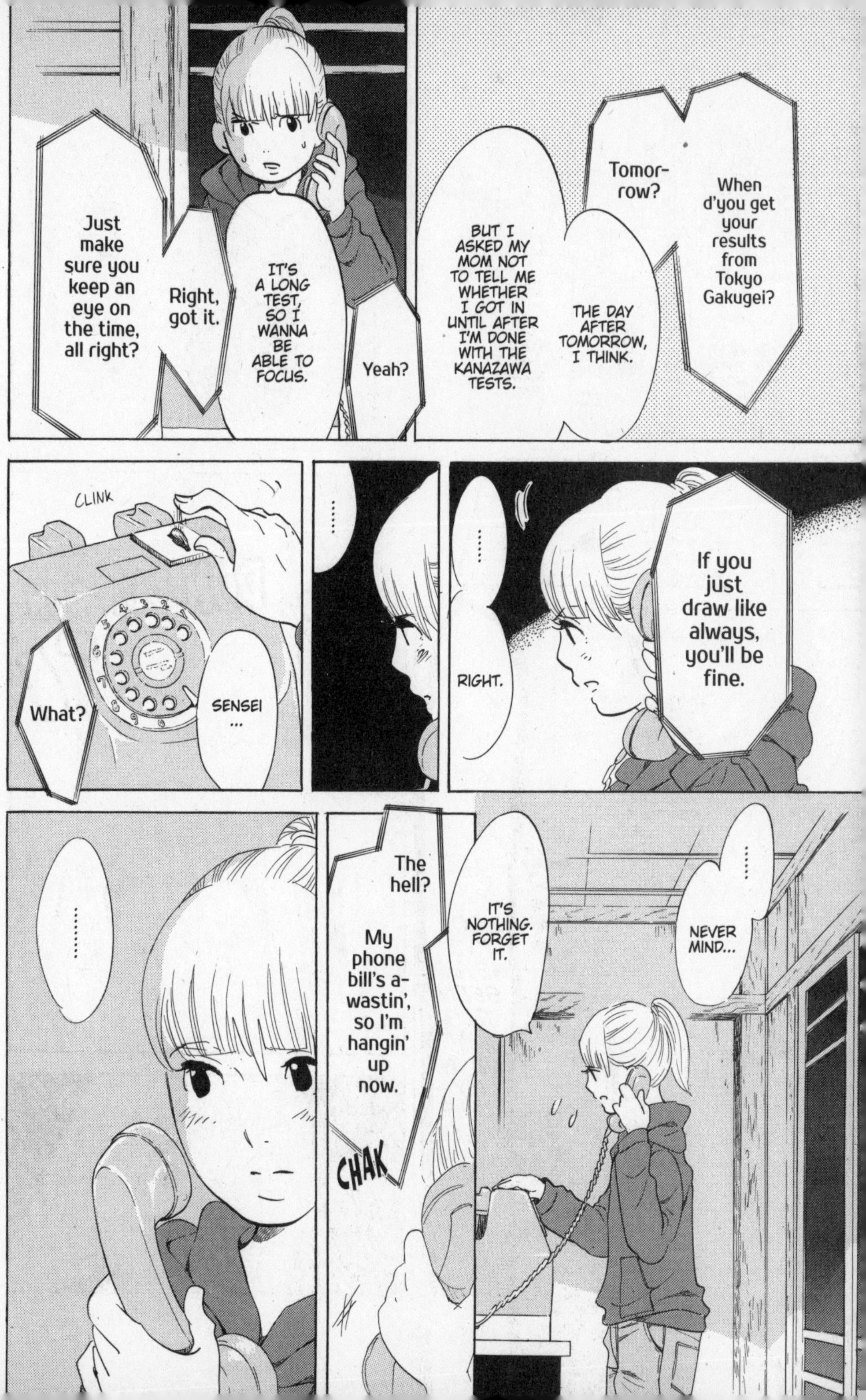
When d'you get your results from Tokyo Gakugei?
Tomorrow?
THE DAY AFTER TOMORROW, I THINK.
BUT I ASKED MY MOM NOT TO TELL ME WHETHER I GOT IN UNTIL AFTER I'M DONE WITH THE KANAZAWA TESTS.
Yeah?
IT'S A LONG TEST, SO I WANNA BE ABLE TO FOCUS.
Right, got it.
Just make sure you keep an eye on the time, all right?
If you just draw like always, you'll be fine.
......
RIGHT.
......
SENSEI ...
What?
CLINK
......
NEVER MIND...
IT'S NOTHING. FORGET IT.
The hell?
My phone bill's a-wastin', so I'm hangin' up now.
CHAK
......

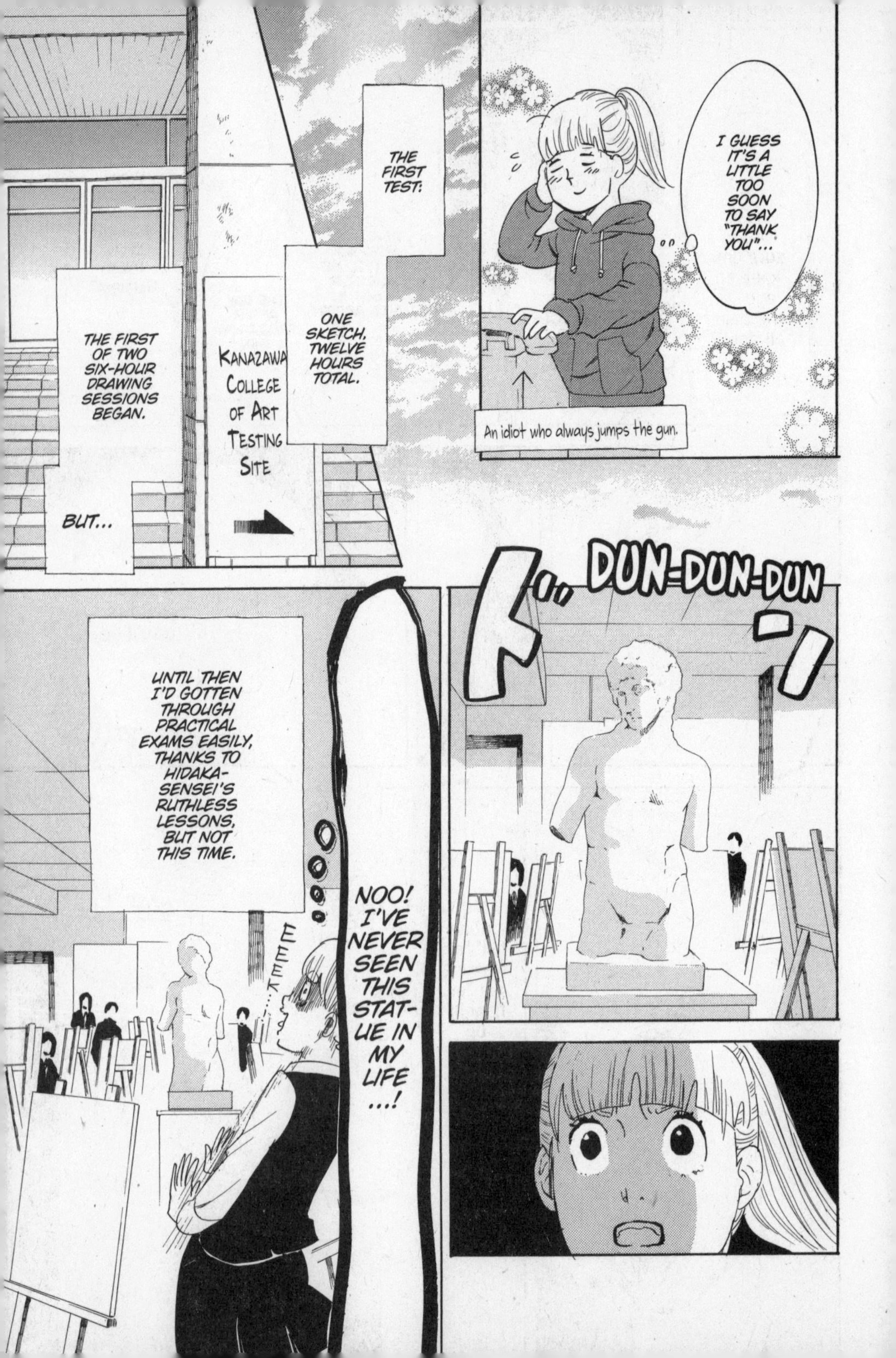

I GUESS IT'S A LITTLE TOO SOON TO SAY "THANK YOU"...
An idiot who always jumps the gun.
THE FIRST TEST:
ONE SKETCH, TWELVE HOURS TOTAL.
KANAZAWA COLLEGE OF ART TESTING SITE
THE FIRST OF TWO SIX-HOUR DRAWING SESSIONS BEGAN.
BUT...
DUN-DUN-DUN
UNTIL THEN I'D GOTTEN THROUGH PRACTICAL EXAMS EASILY, THANKS TO HIDAKA-SENSEI'S RUTHLESS LESSONS, BUT NOT THIS TIME.
NOO! I'VE NEVER SEEN THIS STAT-UE IN MY LIFE ...!
EEEEK...

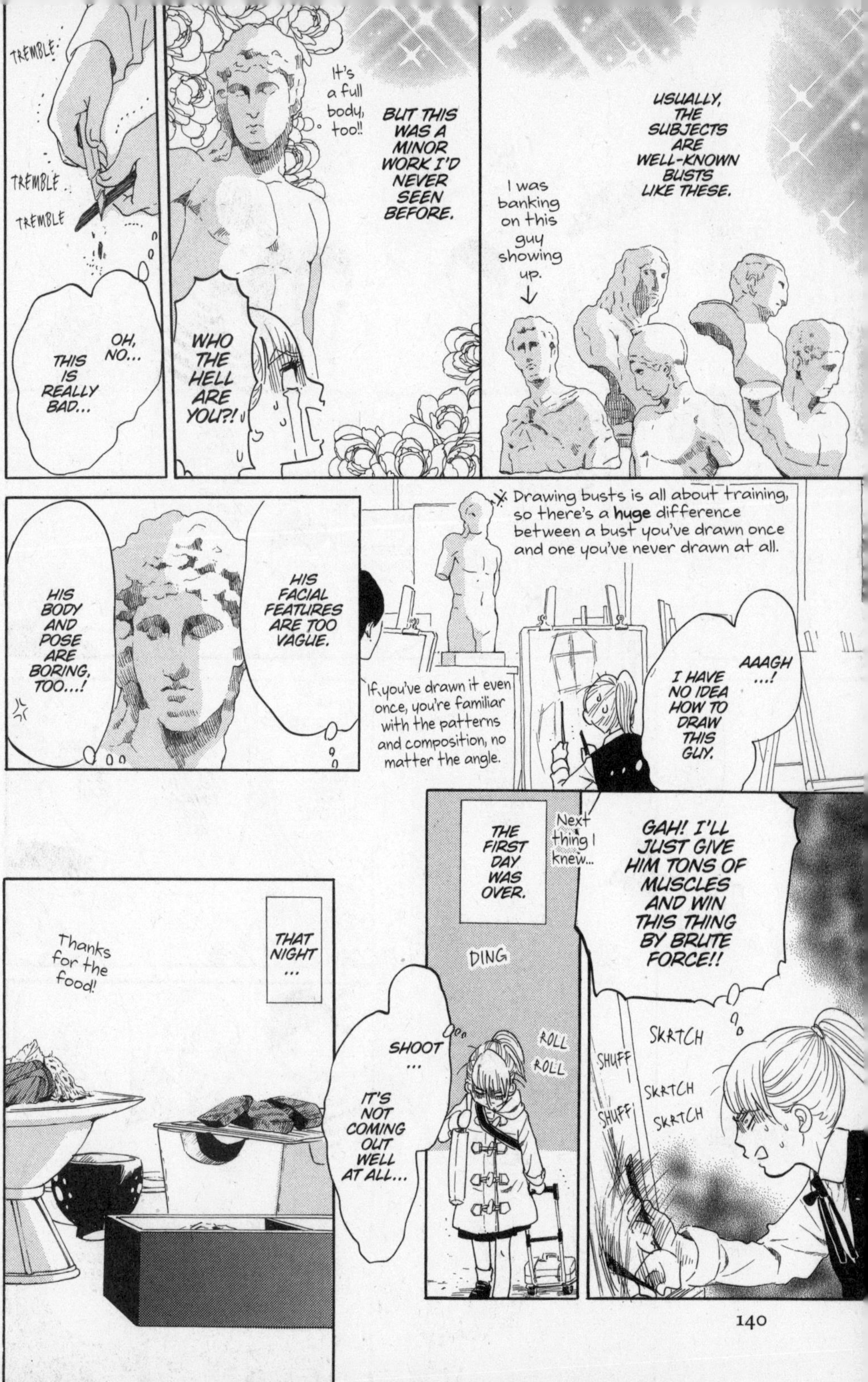
USUALLY, THE SUBJECTS ARE WELL-KNOWN BUSTS LIKE THESE.
I was banking on this guy showing up.
BUT THIS WAS A MINOR WORK I'D NEVER SEEN BEFORE.
It's a full body, too!!
WHO THE HELL ARE YOU?!
TREMBLE
TREMBLE
TREMBLE
OH, NO... THIS IS REALLY BAD...
※ Drawing busts is all about training, so there's a **huge** difference between a bust you've drawn once and one you've never drawn at all.
AAAGH...!
I HAVE NO IDEA HOW TO DRAW THIS GUY.
If you've drawn it even once, you're familiar with the patterns and composition, no matter the angle.
HIS FACIAL FEATURES ARE TOO VAGUE.
HIS BODY AND POSE ARE BORING, TOO...!
GAH! I'LL JUST GIVE HIM TONS OF MUSCLES AND WIN THIS THING BY BRUTE FORCE!!
SKRTCH
SHUFF
SKRTCH
SHUFF
SKRTCH
Next thing I knew...
THE FIRST DAY WAS OVER.
DING
ROLL
ROLL
SHOOT...
IT'S NOT COMING OUT WELL AT ALL...
THAT NIGHT...
Thanks for the food!

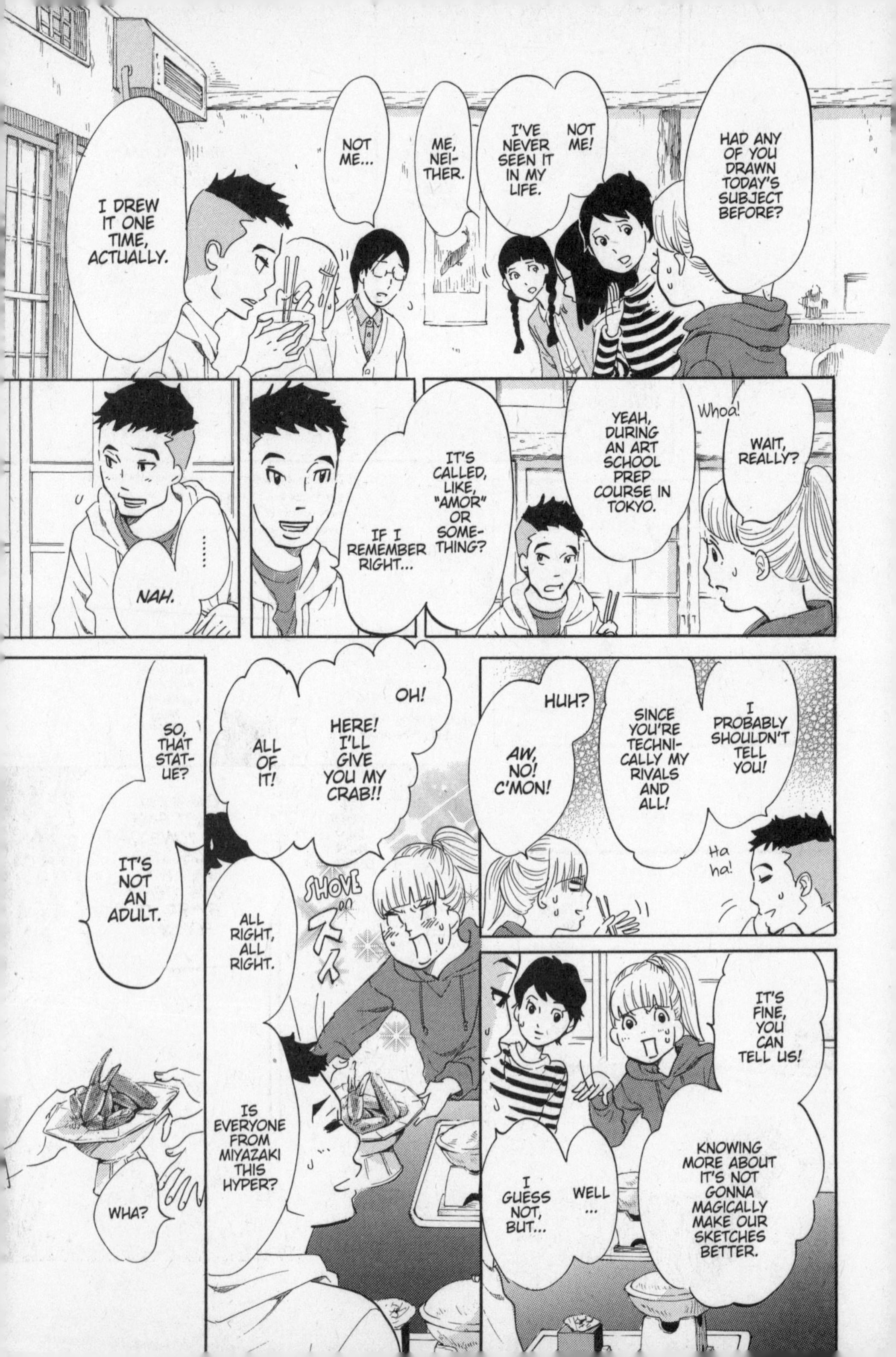
HAD ANY OF YOU DRAWN TODAY'S SUBJECT BEFORE?
NOT ME!
I'VE NEVER SEEN IT IN MY LIFE.
ME, NEITHER.
NOT ME...
I DREW IT ONE TIME, ACTUALLY.
Whoa!
WAIT, REALLY?
YEAH, DURING AN ART SCHOOL PREP COURSE IN TOKYO.
IT'S CALLED, LIKE, "AMOR" OR SOMETHING?
IF I REMEMBER RIGHT...
......
NAH.
I PROBABLY SHOULDN'T TELL YOU!
SINCE YOU'RE TECHNICALLY MY RIVALS AND ALL!
Ha ha!
HUH?
AW, NO! C'MON!
IT'S FINE, YOU CAN TELL US!
KNOWING MORE ABOUT IT'S NOT GONNA MAGICALLY MAKE OUR SKETCHES BETTER.
WELL...
I GUESS NOT, BUT...
OH!
HERE! I'LL GIVE YOU MY CRAB!!
ALL OF IT!
SHOVE
ALL RIGHT, ALL RIGHT.
IS EVERYONE FROM MIYAZAKI THIS HYPER?
SO, THAT STATUE?
IT'S NOT AN ADULT.
WHA?

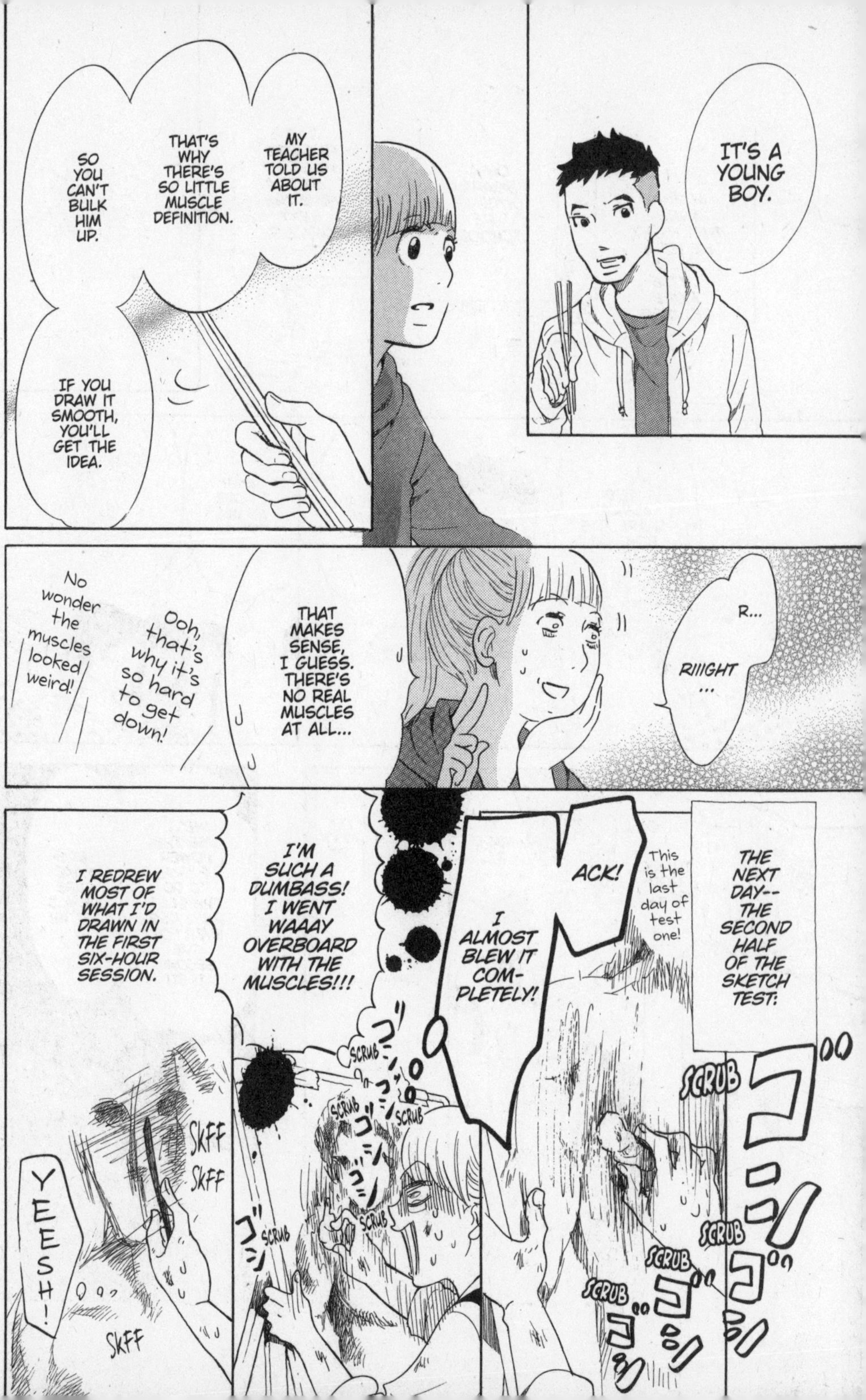
IT'S A YOUNG BOY.
MY TEACHER TOLD US ABOUT IT.
THAT'S WHY THERE'S SO LITTLE MUSCLE DEFINITION.
SO YOU CAN'T BULK HIM UP.
IF YOU DRAW IT SMOOTH, YOU'LL GET THE IDEA.
R...
RIIIGHT...
THAT MAKES SENSE, I GUESS. THERE'S NO REAL MUSCLES AT ALL...
Ooh, that's why it's so hard to get down!
No wonder the muscles looked weird!
THE NEXT DAY-- THE SECOND HALF OF THE SKETCH TEST:
This is the last day of test one!
ACK!
I ALMOST BLEW IT COM-PLETELY!
SCRUB
SCRUB
SCRUB
SCRUB
I'M SUCH A DUMBASS! I WENT WAAAY OVERBOARD WITH THE MUSCLES!!!
SCRUB
SCRUB
SCRUB
SCRUB
SCRUB
I REDREW MOST OF WHAT I'D DRAWN IN THE FIRST SIX-HOUR SESSION.
SKFF
SKFF
YEESH!
SKFF

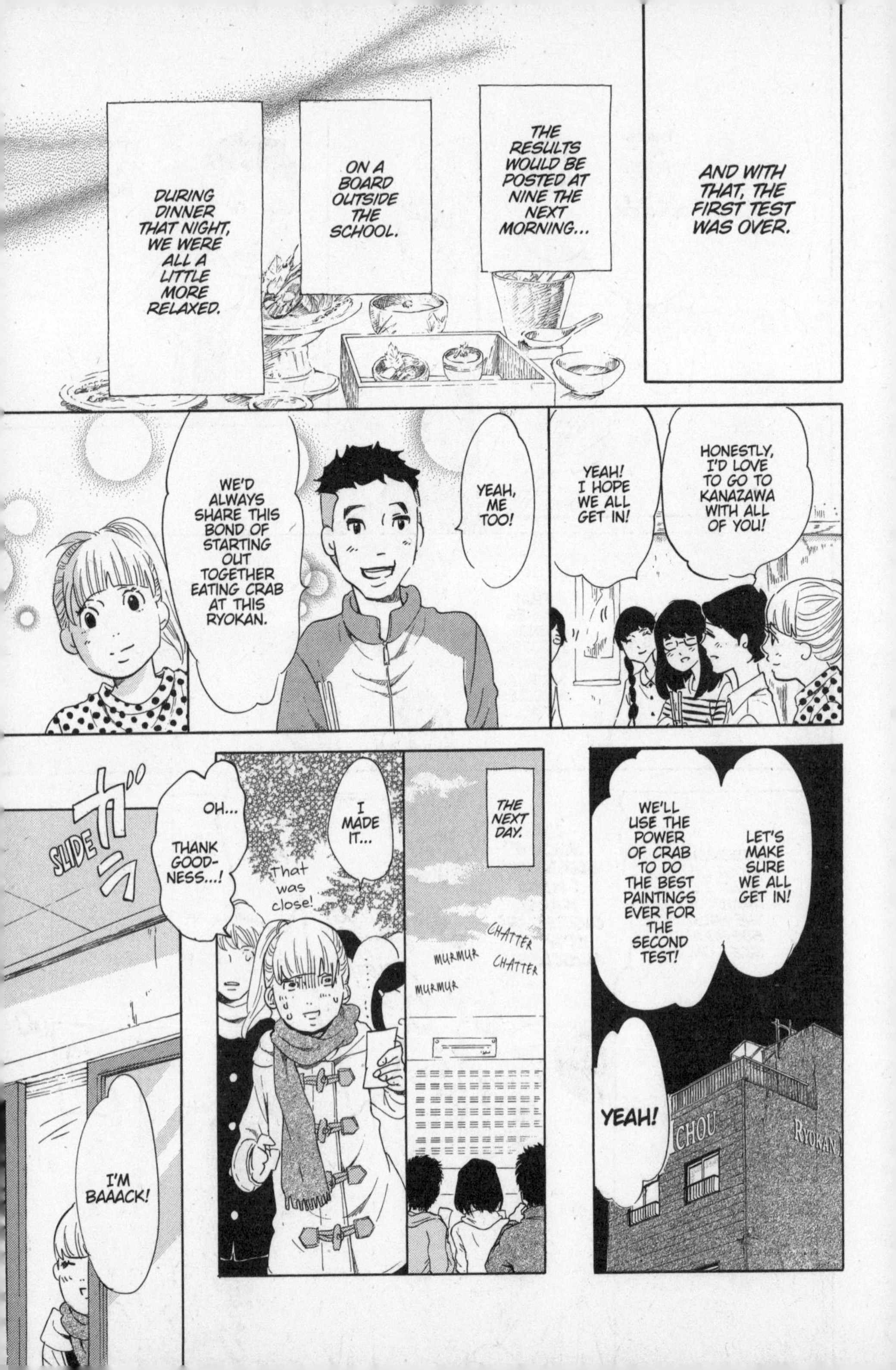
AND WITH THAT, THE FIRST TEST WAS OVER.
THE RESULTS WOULD BE POSTED AT NINE THE NEXT MORNING...
ON A BOARD OUTSIDE THE SCHOOL.
DURING DINNER THAT NIGHT, WE WERE ALL A LITTLE MORE RELAXED.
HONESTLY, I'D LOVE TO GO TO KANAZAWA WITH ALL OF YOU!
YEAH! I HOPE WE ALL GET IN!
YEAH, ME TOO!
WE'D ALWAYS SHARE THIS BOND OF STARTING OUT TOGETHER EATING CRAB AT THIS RYOKAN.
LET'S MAKE SURE WE ALL GET IN!
WE'LL USE THE POWER OF CRAB TO DO THE BEST PAINTINGS EVER FOR THE SECOND TEST!
YEAH!
CHOU
RYOKAN
THE NEXT DAY.
CHATTER
CHATTER
MURMUR
MURMUR
I MADE IT...
That was close!
OH...
THANK GOODNESS...!
SLIDE
I'M BAAACK!

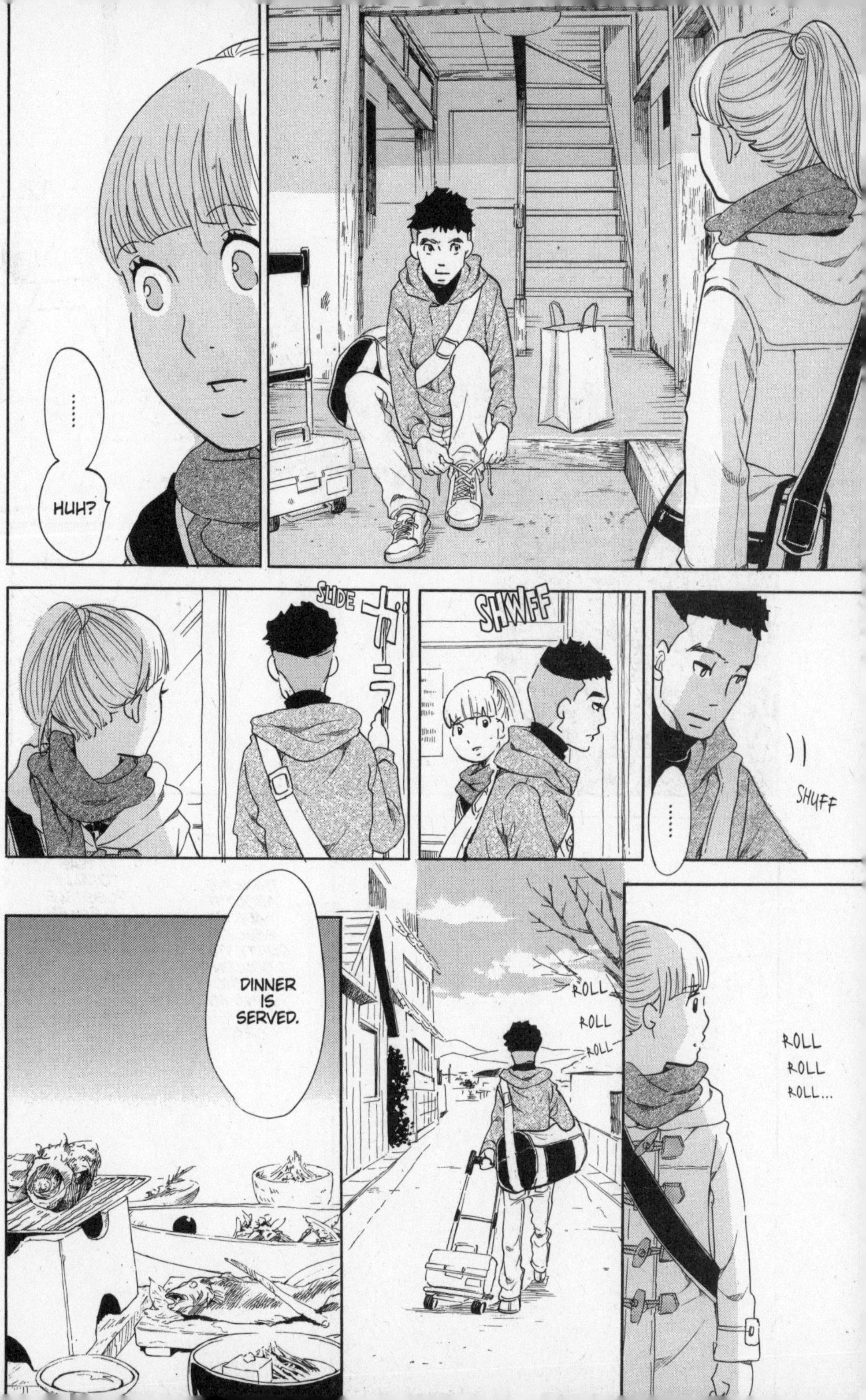
……
HUH?
……
SHUFF
SHWFF
SLIDE
ガラ
ROLL
ROLL
ROLL...
ROLL
ROLL
ROLL
DINNER IS SERVED.

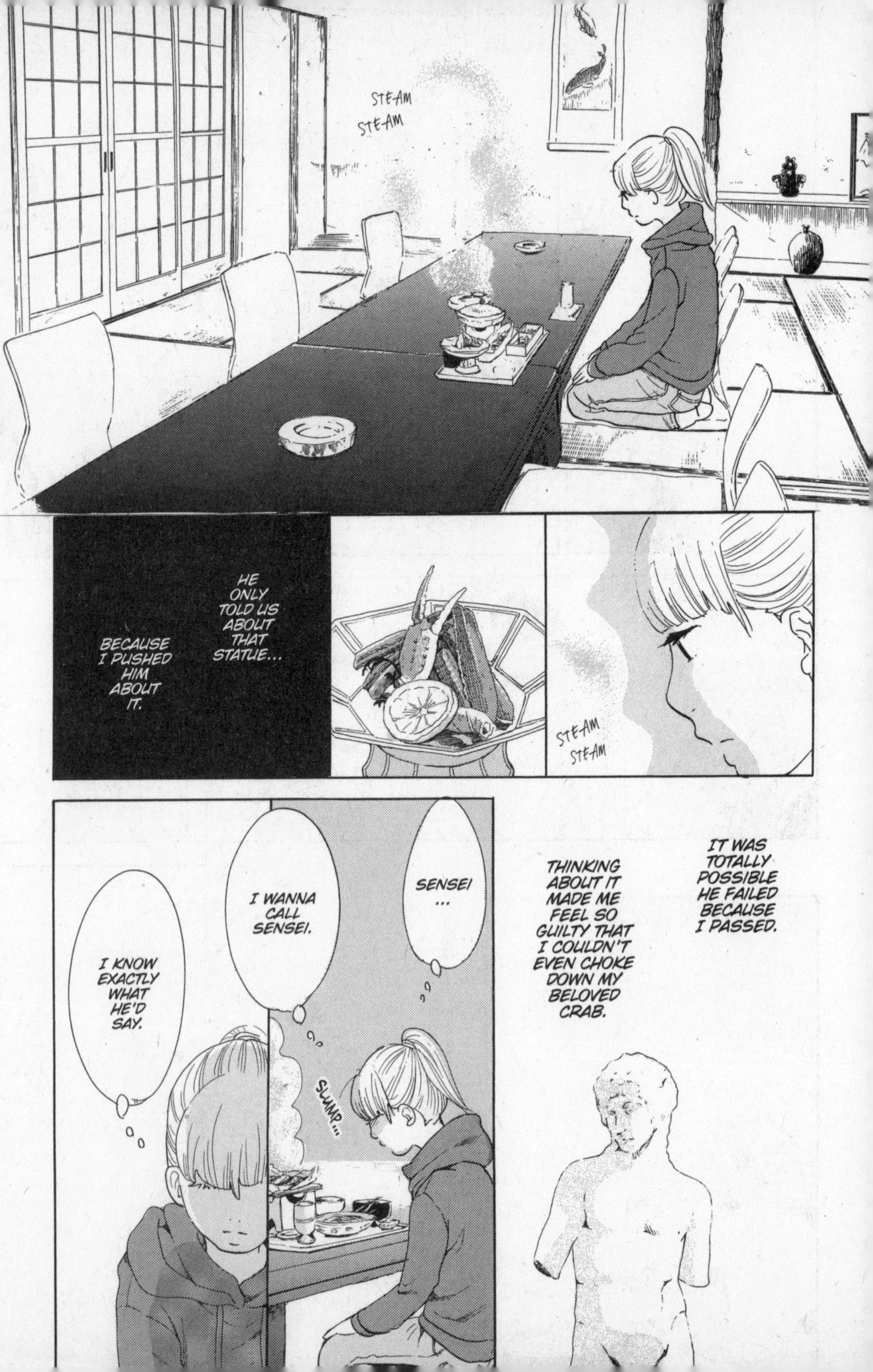
STEAM
STEAM
STEAM
STEAM
HE ONLY TOLD US ABOUT THAT STATUE...
BECAUSE I PUSHED HIM ABOUT IT.
IT WAS TOTALLY POSSIBLE HE FAILED BECAUSE I PASSED.
THINKING ABOUT IT MADE ME FEEL SO GUILTY THAT I COULDN'T EVEN CHOKE DOWN MY BELOVED CRAB.
SENSEI ...
I WANNA CALL SENSEI.
SLUMP...
I KNOW EXACTLY WHAT HE'D SAY.

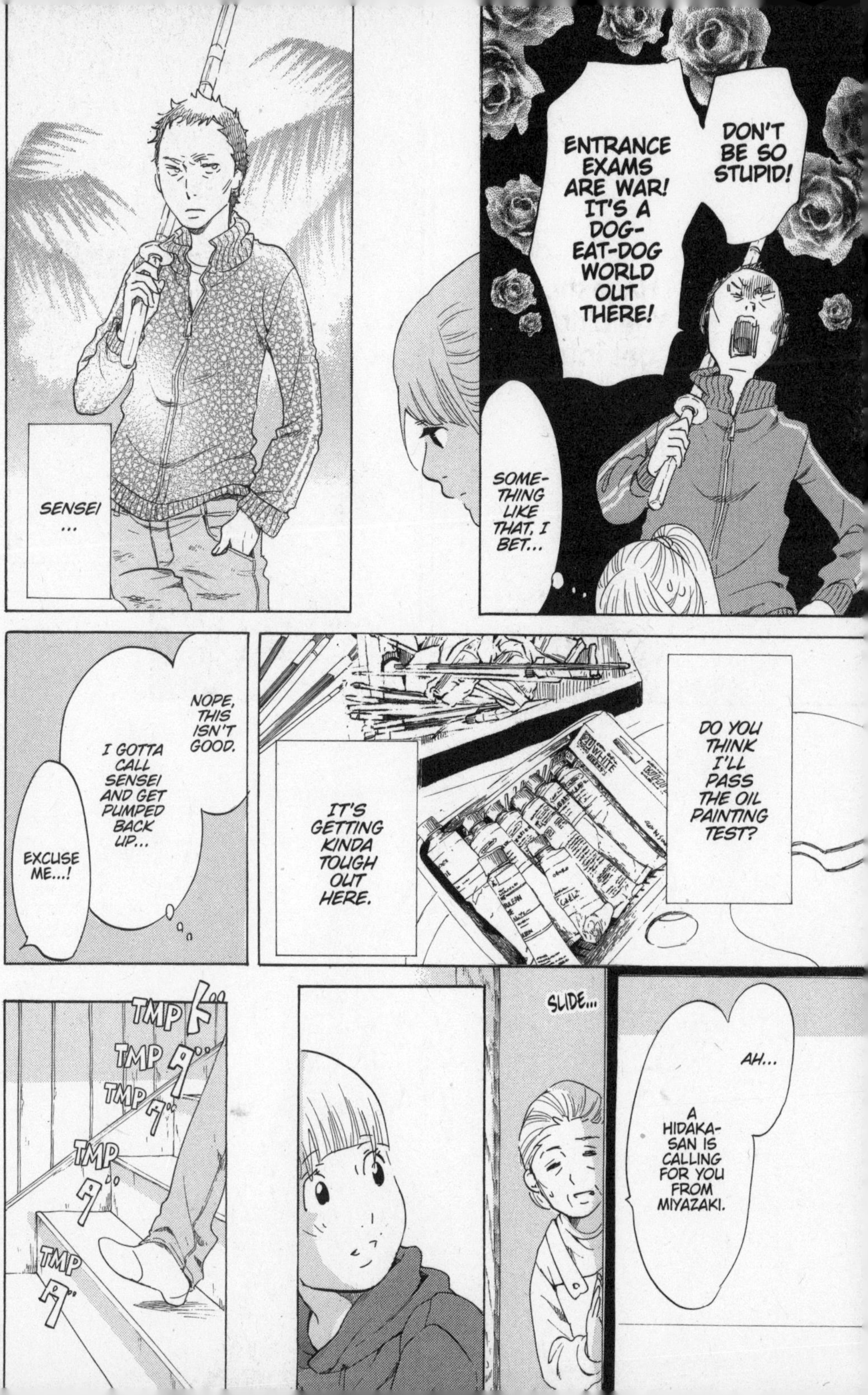
DON'T BE SO STUPID!
ENTRANCE EXAMS ARE WAR! IT'S A DOG-EAT-DOG WORLD OUT THERE!
SOME-THING LIKE THAT, I BET...
SENSEI ...
DO YOU THINK I'LL PASS THE OIL PAINTING TEST?
IT'S GETTING KINDA TOUGH OUT HERE.
NOPE, THIS ISN'T GOOD.
I GOTTA CALL SENSEI AND GET PUMPED BACK UP...
EXCUSE ME...!
AH...
A HIDAKA-SAN IS CALLING FOR YOU FROM MIYAZAKI.
SLIDE...
TMP
TMP
TMP
TMP
TMP

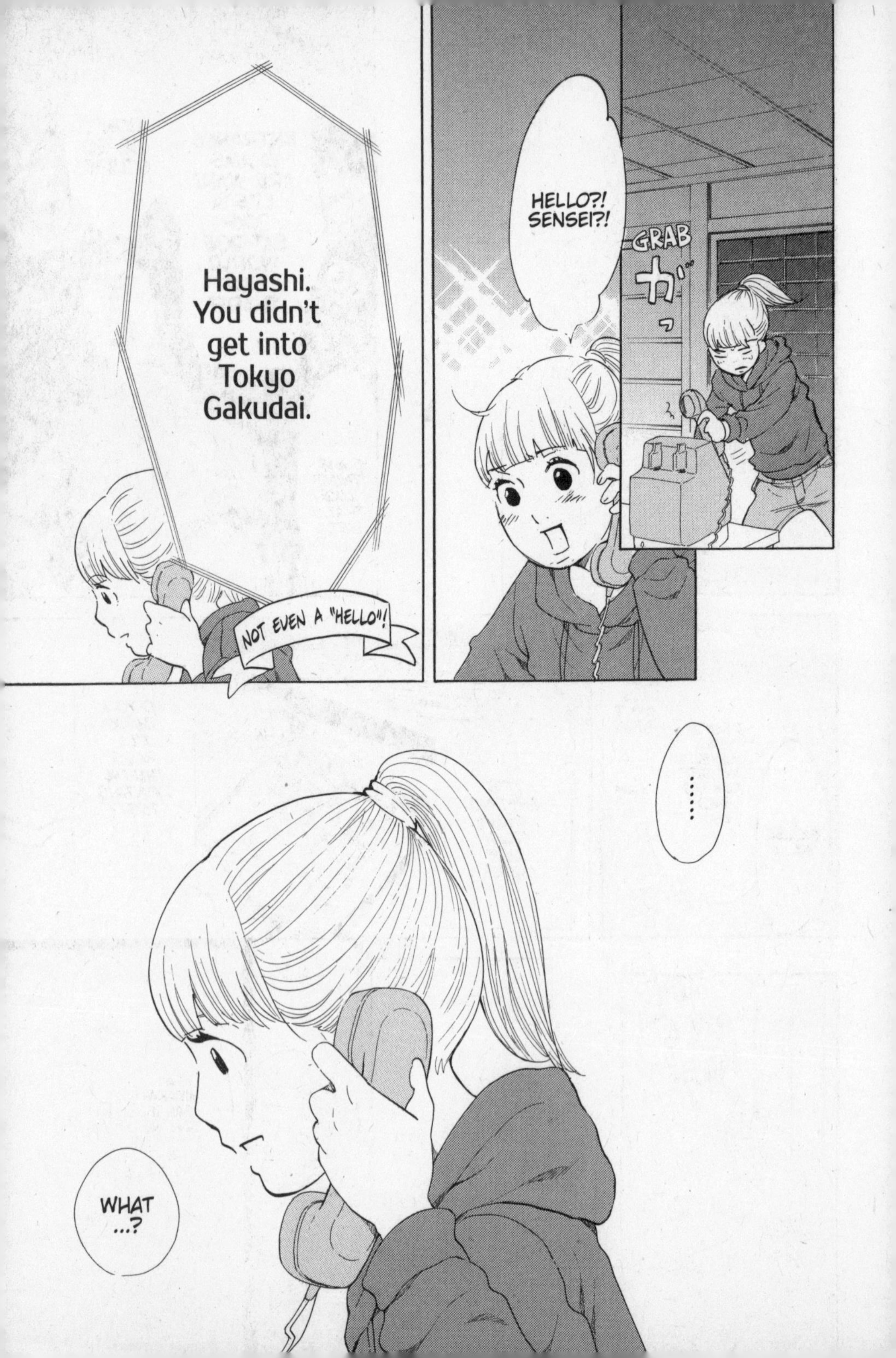
GRAB
ガッ
HELLO?! SENSEI?!
Hayashi. You didn't get into Tokyo Gakudai.
NOT EVEN A "HELLO"!
......
WHAT ...?

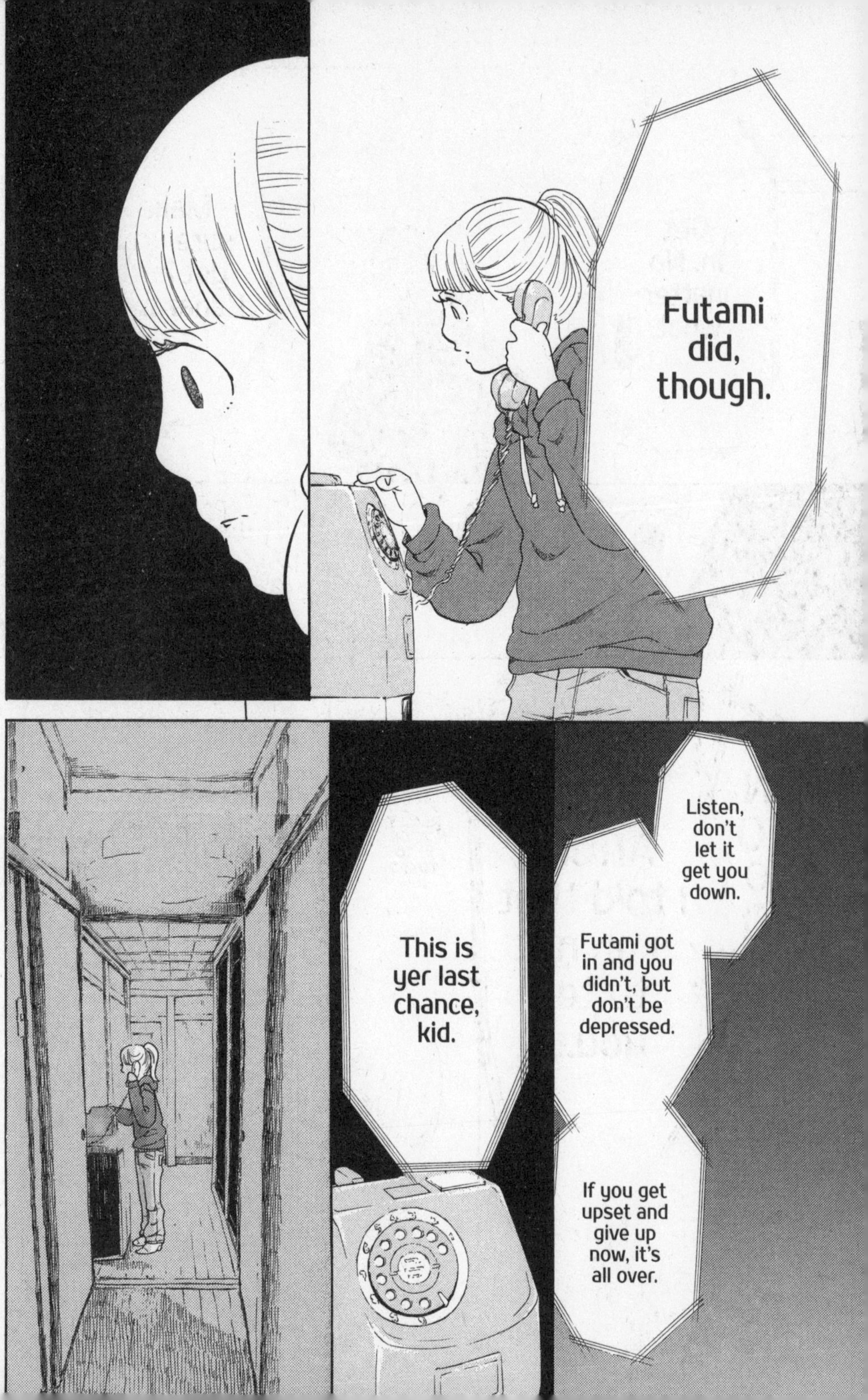
Futami did, though.
Listen, don't let it get you down.
Futami got in and you didn't, but don't be depressed.
If you get upset and give up now, it's all over.
This is yer last chance, kid.

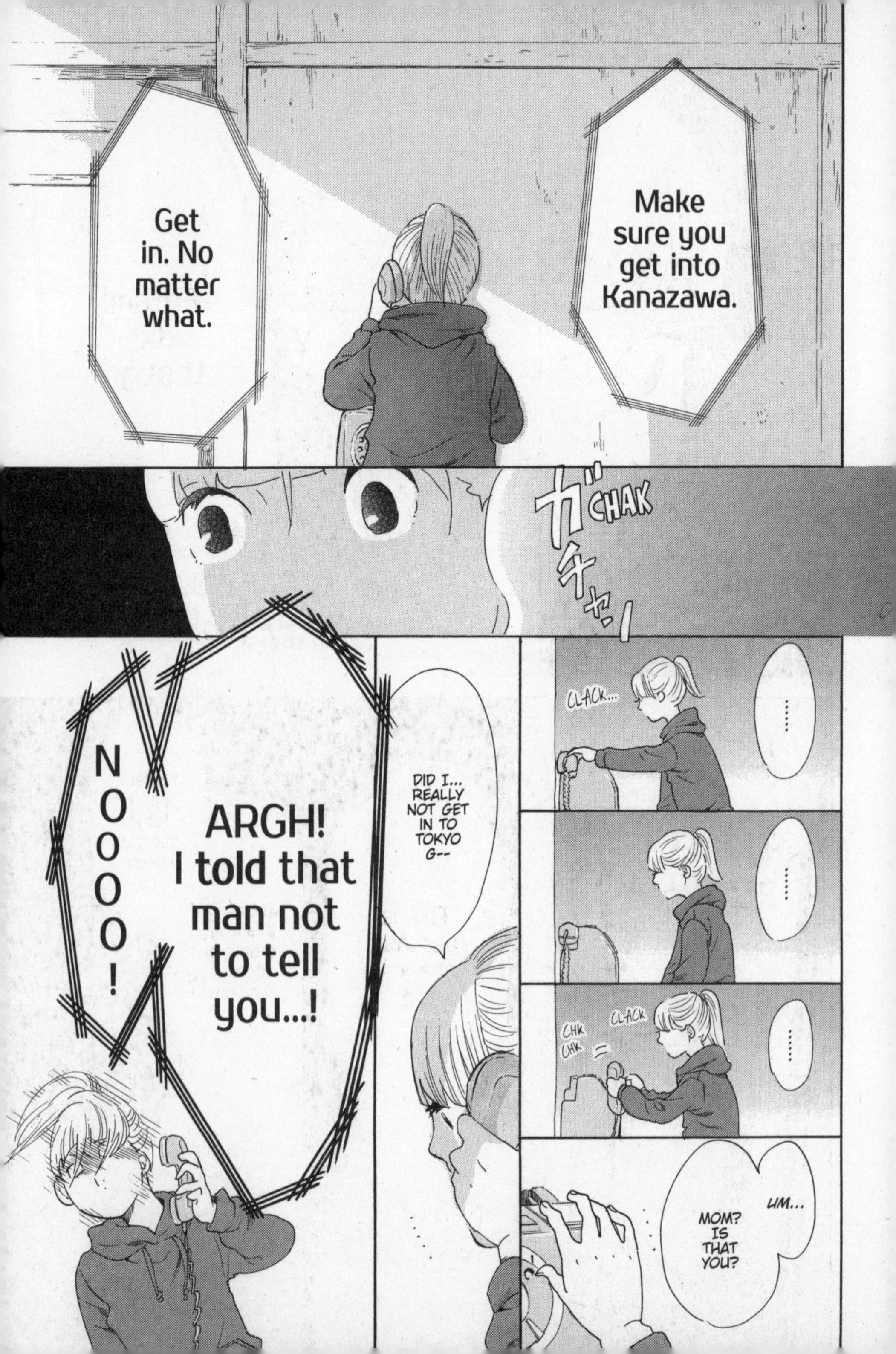
Make sure you get into Kanazawa.
Get in. No matter what.
CHAK
......
CLACK...
......
......
CLACK
CHK CHK
UM...
MOM? IS THAT YOU?
DID I... REALLY NOT GET IN TO TOKYO G--
NOOOOO!
ARGH! I told that man not to tell you...!

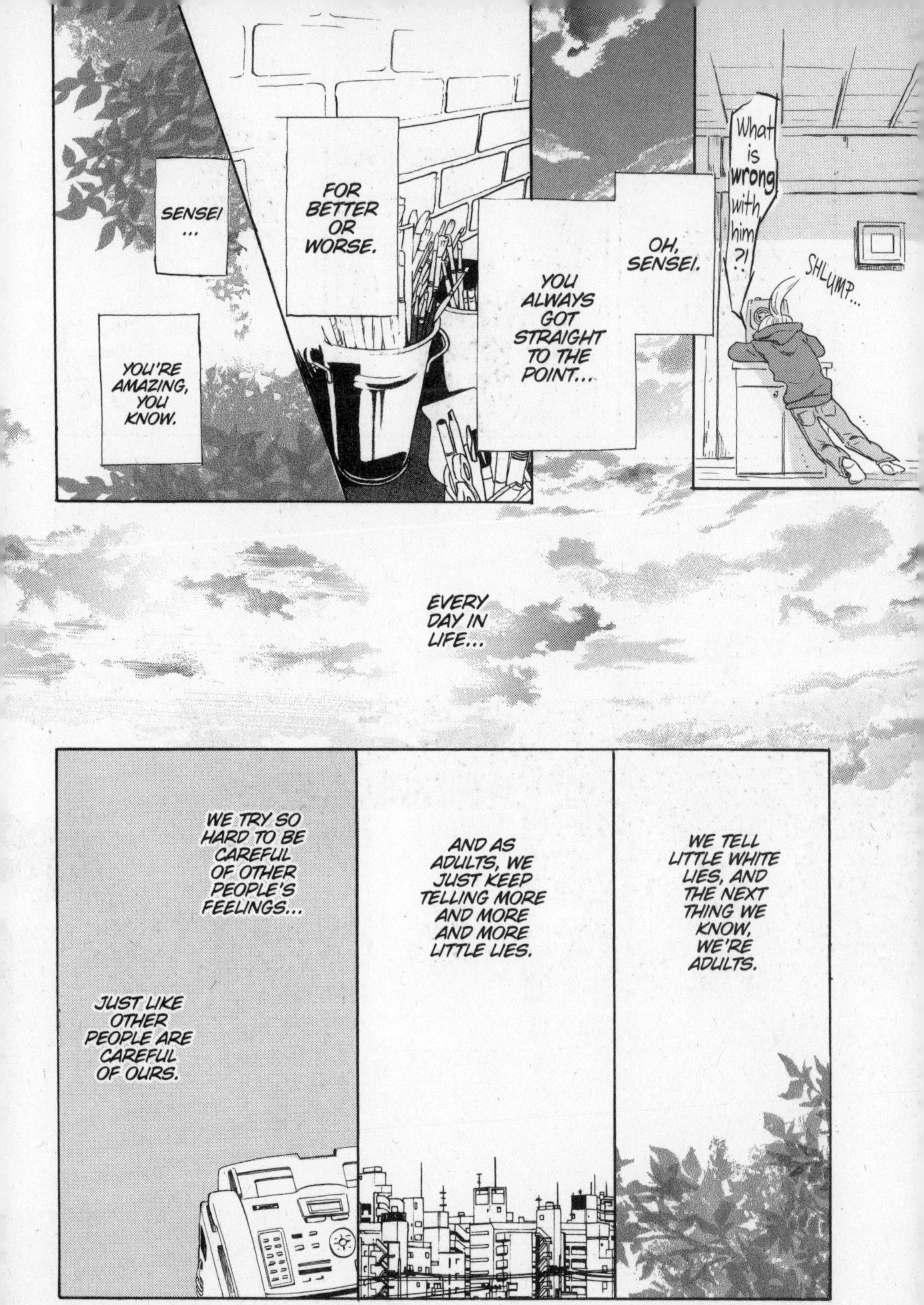
What is wrong with him?!
SHL'UMP...
OH, SENSEI.
YOU ALWAYS GOT STRAIGHT TO THE POINT...
FOR BETTER OR WORSE.
SENSEI...
YOU'RE AMAZING, YOU KNOW.
EVERY DAY IN LIFE...
WE TELL LITTLE WHITE LIES, AND THE NEXT THING WE KNOW, WE'RE ADULTS.
AND AS ADULTS, WE JUST KEEP TELLING MORE AND MORE AND MORE LITTLE LIES.
WE TRY SO HARD TO BE CAREFUL OF OTHER PEOPLE'S FEELINGS...
JUST LIKE OTHER PEOPLE ARE CAREFUL OF OURS.

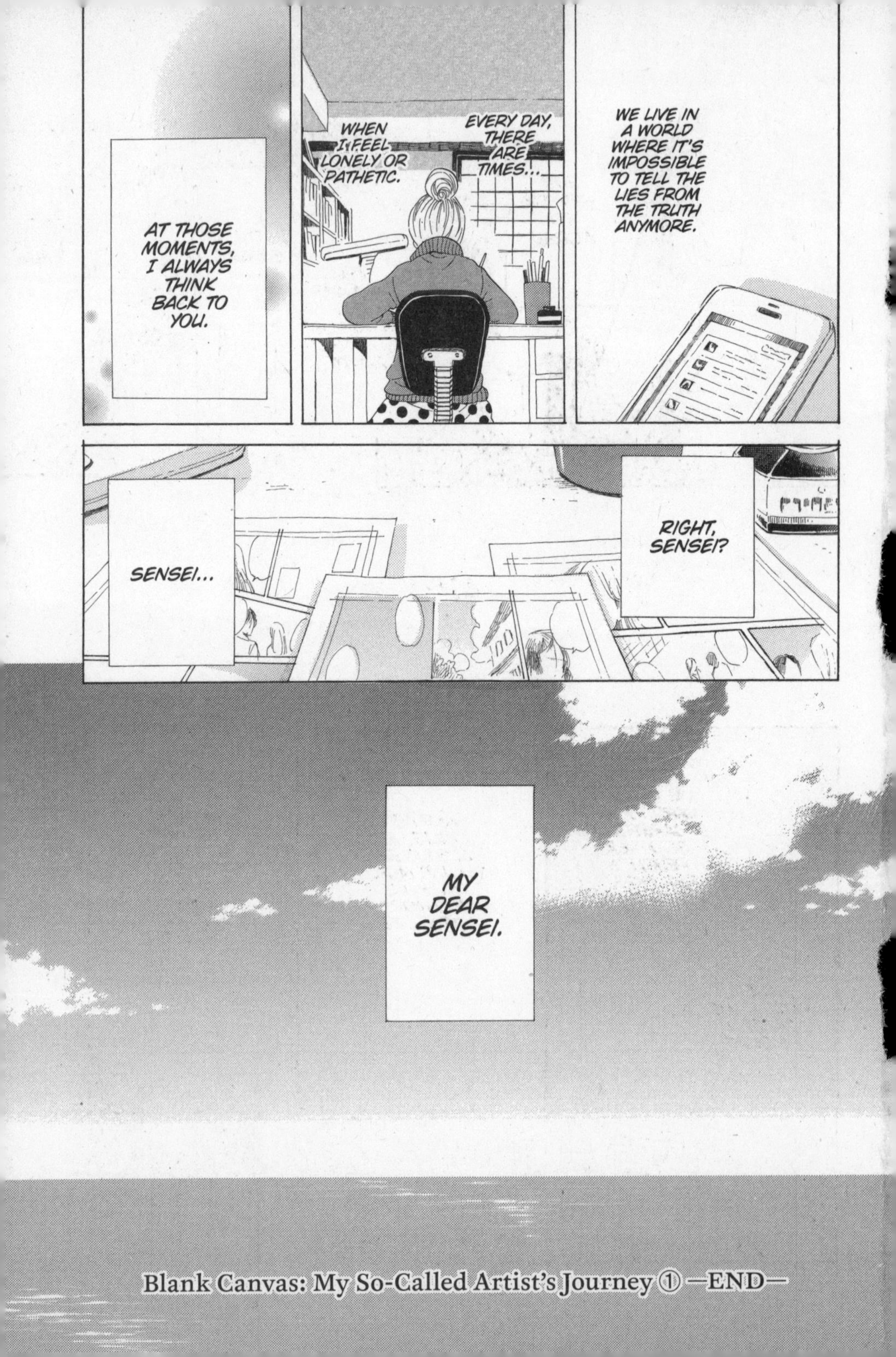
WE LIVE IN A WORLD WHERE IT'S IMPOSSIBLE TO TELL THE LIES FROM THE TRUTH ANYMORE.
EVERY DAY, THERE ARE TIMES...
WHEN I FEEL LONELY OR PATHETIC.
AT THOSE MOMENTS, I ALWAYS THINK BACK TO YOU.
RIGHT, SENSEI?
SENSEI...
MY DEAR SENSEI.

Blank Canvas: My So-Called Artist's Journey ① —END—

SEVEN SEAS ENTERTAINMENT PRESENTS

Blank Canvas
My So-Called Artist's Journey

story and art by **AKIKO HIGASHIMURA**   **VOLUME 1**

TRANSLATION
Jenny McKeon

ADAPTATION
Ysabet MacFarlane

LETTERING AND LAYOUT
Lys Blakeslee

COVER DESIGN
KC Fabellon

PROOFREADER
Kurestin Armada
Danielle King

EDITOR
Jenn Grunigen

PRODUCTION MANAGER
Lissa Pattillo

MANAGING EDITOR
Julie Davis

EDITOR-IN-CHIEF
Adam Arnold

PUBLISHER
Jason DeAngelis

KAKUKAKU SHIKAJIKA © 2011 by Akiko Higashimura
All rights reserved.
First published in Japan in 2011 by SHUEISHA Inc., Tokyo.
English translation rights arranged by SHUEISHA Inc.
through TOHAN CORPORATION, Tokyo.

Seven Seas press and purchase enquiries can be sent to Marketing Manager
Lianne Sentar at press@gomanga.com. Information regarding the distribution
and purchase of digital editions is available from Digital Manager CK Russell
at digital@gomanga.com.

Seven Seas and the Seven Seas logo are trademarks of
Seven Seas Entertainment. All rights reserved.

ISBN: 978-1-642750-69-0

Printed in Canada

First Printing: May 2019

10 9 8 7 6 5 4 3 2 1

FOLLOW US ONLINE: *www.sevenseasentertainment.com*

READING DIRECTIONS

This book reads from **right to left**, Japanese style.
If this is your first time reading manga, you start
reading from the top right panel on each page and
take it from there. If you get lost, just follow the
numbered diagram here. It may seem backwards at
first, but you'll get the hang of it! Have fun!!

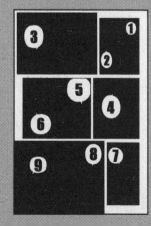

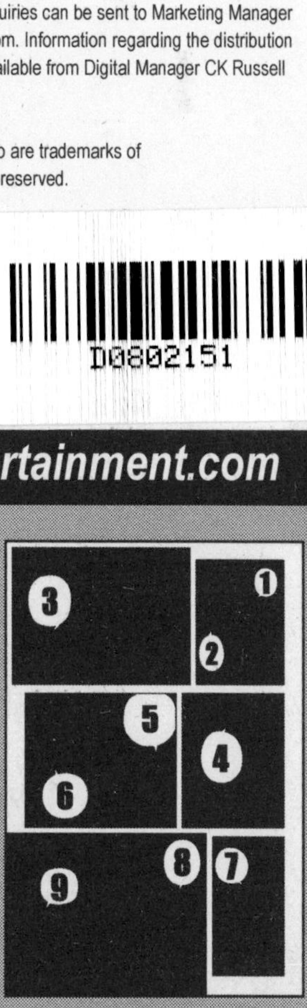